The BIG BOOK of NEAR-DEATH EXPERIENCES

Also by P.M.H. Atwater

Beyond the Indigo Children (2005)
We Live Forever (2004)
The New Children and Near-Death Experiences (2003)
Coming Back to Life (2001)
The Complete Idiot's Guide to Near-Death Experiences (1999)
Children of the New Millennium (1999)
Future Memory (1999)
Goddess Runes (1996)
Beyond the Light (1994)

The BIG BOOK of NEAR-DEATH EXPERIENCES

The ULTIMATE GUIDE to What Happens When We Die

p.m.h. atwater

HAMPTON ROADS
PUBLISHING COMPANY, INC.

Cover design by Frame25 Productions
Cover images by Dragan Trifunoric (doorway), Thierry Maffeis (man silhouette),
Gilles Cohen c/o Shutterstock (fish and bowl), Guillermo Lobo c/o iStock (dead man).

Hampton Roads Publishing Company, Inc.
1125 Stoney Ridge Road
Charlottesville, VA 22902
434-296-2772
fax: 434-296-5096
e-mail: hrpc@hrpub.com
www.hrpub.com

If you are unable to order this book from your local
bookseller, you may order directly from the publisher.
Call 1-800-766-8009, toll-free.

Library of Congress Cataloging-in-Publication Data

Atwater, P. M. H.
The big book of near-death experiences : the ultimate guide to what happens when we die / P.M.H. Atwater.
p. cm.
Summary: "Near-Death Experiences encompasses every aspect of the near-death phenomenon: the experience, aftereffects, and implications. Atwater investigates and reports on the power of changed lives, the reality of deceased who come back, visitors at death's edge, out-of-body travel, the expansion of normal faculties, the awesome presence of Deity, and the importance of spirituality"--Provided by publisher.
Includes bibliographical references and index.
ISBN-13: 978-1-57174-547-7 (alk. paper)
1. Near-death experiences. I. Title.
BF1045.N4A875 2007
133.901'3--dc22

2007025698

ISBN 978-1-57174-547-7
10 9 8 7 6 5 4 3
Printed on acid-free paper in Canada

Contents

Book Reviews

"If you've ever had any questions about the near-death experience, but, quite literally, weren't 'dying' to find out the answers, this book is a 'must' for you to read. The author will stretch your belief systems horizontally, vertically, and inside out. I guarantee that there is no other book available that even vaguely compares to this one in terms of its comprehensive, detailed, and authoritative approach. Every point of view, from the enthusiastic, life-affirming accounts of NDE experiencers to the scathing criticisms of skeptics is covered. No other writer comes close to possessing the impressive credentials that P.M.H. Atwater has earned in this challenging field—both through her own personal experiences as a three-time near-death survivor, and through her intensive and extensive interviews with thousands of other NDE experiencers.

"This book's clarity of writing style and amazing collection of mind-bending accounts of extraordinary experiences makes for riveting reading."

—Robert L. Van de Castle, PhD, Professor Emeritus,
Health Center, University of Virginia, clinical psychologist, and
author of *Our Dreaming Mind*

"Excellent reading for parents, educators, anyone who works with children, anyone who is involved with children of any age and anyone who was a child. Well-documented research into the physical aspects of brain development, spiritual development, and case studies of children and adults who have experienced near-death, the aftereffects, and how those involved with someone who has had a near-death experience can assist in recovery and coping with growing up with the knowledge acquired from the near-death experience. With the developments in technology, our society will see more and more resuscitations of clinical death and those having near-death experiences might not be strangers anymore."

—T. Orlando, New York City

"I am ever so grateful to have recently discovered this book. Yes, yes, yes! Having had a profound NDE-like mystical experience, I could relate directly to everything you have written. I feel you have given an enormous gift to our earthly community with your books and website. Your courage, your open heart and sharpened intellect, and your own experiences must have helped pave a path for many to integrate these profound experiences in a meaningful and balanced way. It means so much for me personally to know that I am not alone in having this experience, and that others are also facing similar challenges 'returning to Earth.'"

—Phillip Laird, Perth, Australia

"This book contains a wealth of information about many aspects of near-death studies and some related areas, presented vividly, concretely, and simply, all of which will keep the naive reader turning pages despite the volume's otherwise daunting length. It is very useful for its intended purpose of introducing the field and orienting the newcomer. Researchers and other seasoned readers will also find much that is helpful here, particularly in the abundant case studies, many from Atwater's own files."

—Gracia Fay Ellwood, PhD, author of
The Uttermost Deep: The Challenge of Near-Death Experiences

"P.M.H. Atwater is a well-respected long time researcher and prolific writer on the subject of near-death experiences (NDEs). Her fascination for the subject originated with her own multiple NDEs. She presents an excellent and thorough discussion of all aspects of the characteristics and many possible aftereffects of the NDE. This book also addresses a multiplicity of other subjects such as prebirth memories, reincarnation, future memory, a review of the author's classification of four type of NDEs, and even the sense of feeling alien, to name but a few. There is something fascinating for every reader of every background. This is a mind-stretching work!"

—Barbara R. Rommer, MD, author of
Blessing in Disguise: Another Side of the Near-Death Experience

"I'm sure you've heard this before, but I just had to tell you how much I loved this book. I'm not an experiencer myself, but I find the subject fascinating and I was completely blown away by all the accounts. It's always nice to hear a new perspective on things."

—Jennifer Crawford, seventeen

"Just a very short note to say, Magnificent, with respect to this book. It is the most exhaustive/informative compilation that I've ever had the pleasure to read on the subject. I thank you for the effort you put into the work."

—Ken Bennett

"The Ultimate NDE Guide: Whether you've had a near-death experience or just wanted to gain a better understanding of what NDEs are all about, you'll be fascinated by this book. Author P.M.H. Atwater is fully qualified to examine this phenomenon, since she experienced three near-death episodes in 1977 and has been seriously studying the phenomenon since 1978.

"I love the way she organized this book into sections that help clarify the NDE. Different types of near-death experiences are described in detail, along with the differences between adult and child experiences. Common aftereffects such as enhanced psychic abilities, transformations of consciousness, and altered views of reality are also described in detail.

"This book is fun to read, because almost every page contains an interesting tidbit of information pertaining to near-death experiences. I am intrigued that the vast majority (80 to 90 percent) of near-death experiencers report looking and acting younger, feeling substantially more energetic, becoming increasingly sensitive to sound and light, feeling much less boredom, regarding things as new even when they're not, and healing wounds much more quickly.

"This is a great reference book because it is easy to understand, contains numerous near-death experience stories, and summarizes current research in the field clearly and succinctly."

—Cynthia Sue Larson, author of *Aura Advantage*
and the e-newsletter *Reality Shifters*

"Atwater's book, readable for sure, goes beyond the expected. She has presented a survey of what the religions of the world have to say about NDE and the afterlife. She also gives helpful advice on how to deal with your own NDE or that of a loved one or friend. She confronts the stereotypes about NDEs, such as the presumption that they are all alike; for example, not everyone experiences going through a tunnel. She talks about the controversies surrounding the research on NDE and presents arguments on both sides of the fence regarding various interpretations of the meaning of NDE. She reveals the less discussed aspect of NDE, namely that they are not always positive and some people are worse off for having had them. She even discusses the intellectually challenging ideas from philosophy of science about objective versus subjective reality."

—Henry Reed, PhD, author of *The Intuitive Heart*

"This book by P.M.H. Atwater is to me the definitive work on near-death experiences, and stands somewhere between being a Bible for the field and an encyclopedia of it. It is a tremendous achievement—and it's warm, compulsively readable, engaging, provocative, and fun as well. Were I a hat wearer, I would doff mine to the ground to Atwater in admiration of her monumental contribution to our understanding of near-death experiences."

—Kenneth Ring, PhD, author of many books including
Lessons from the Light

Dedication

There is no hesitation on my part as to who this book should be dedicated to.

It is Kenneth Ring, PhD, author of *Heading Toward Omega, Lessons from the Light,* and many other provocative works of exceptional research and remarkable insight. It was Ken who validated Raymond Moody's efforts, and, in so doing, established near-death research as the field of study it is today. What he has accomplished, though, as important as it is, is not why I salute him. True, he discovered me. He was snooping around a bookstore in Hartford, Connecticut, when he purchased a copy of my first attempt to write about near-death experiences called *I Died Three Times in 1977* (clever title, huh?). Well, that's what he thought, so he bought a copy. He later tracked me down via telephone and then came to our house for a visit, staying overnight, and learned much to his surprise that I, too, was a researcher. It was Ken who invited me to join the larger community of those interested in the topic, and it was Ken who sat me down years later and said, "You're ready now to write a book." The result was *Coming Back to Life.* But my work differed somewhat from his, conceptually. Perhaps that's because he sought to test the "Moody Model" with his research, while I had instinctively done things differently. Over the years that followed, he became my worst nemesis and my most ardent supporter—both at the same time. We fought, argued, and shunned each other, until, finally, we discovered how we were both saying the same thing and always had been. To say I am indebted to Kenneth Ring is hardly sufficient. He has proved to be an incredible friend and I feel privileged to know him.

Special Thank-Yous

Long ago and far away this book originally existed as *The Complete Idiot's Guide to Near-Death Experiences* (Alpha Books, 2000). Randy Ladenheim-Gil was my editor then and David Morgan my assistant. Both were invaluable helpmates in assisting me in creating this, the very first "encyclopedia" about near-death experiences, their aftereffects and implications. My thanks to them is everlasting. The version you have before you now, though, is larger, more thorough than the previous, and a lot more fun and informative—an update of classical proportions. A "cast" of thousands made this book possible—perhaps millions, as it contains the results of more than thirty years of concerted effort in researching near-death states. To everyone involved and especially the experiencers themselves, I offer this sincere thank-you. You are the heroes here; I, but your humble servant—an experiencer turned researcher. Half of every royalty check on sales for this book will go to the International Association for Near-Death Studies. At the end of five years, they will inherit full ownership and I will bow out. This book is not mine. I am clear about that. It belongs to the people it speaks to.

Terry Atwater, my patient husband, gave unwavering encouragement throughout this project. Bruce Greyson was ever-ready to answer endless questions. Kevin Williams fact-checked websites and articles, and my webmaster Steff Wiltse proved to be worth her weight in gold for all she did with myriad extra tasks. To each and all, thank you—a million times over!

Foreword

In the 1950s, when I began researching and writing about the world of the unexplained, those remarkable cases in which people appeared for a time to die and then return to life with inspirational accounts of visitations to the Other Side were called "pseudo-death experiences." For the serious psychical researcher, the most important aspect of these "false deaths" was that they appeared to demonstrate that we had a spirit or soul that could exist apart from the physical body, and that when we died we might reasonably expect our soul to enter a spiritual realm and continue to exist. If you are at all curious—and perhaps a bit confused—about the many claims made for the phenomenon commonly known today as the near-death experience (NDE), you could find no better guide to a more complete understanding of the mystery than Dr. P.M.H. Atwater. Dr. Atwater is among the most knowledgeable researchers in the field of near-death studies, and she has the added advantage of being an "experiencer," having survived three NDEs. After suffering a miscarriage that led to severe complications, she "died" three times from January to March 1977. On each occasion her NDE was different, although one did seem to lead into another as if they were progressive facets of one larger experience. After she had recovered, she was left with the deep conviction that her mission in life was to investigate the near-death experience and to evaluate the enigma for as large an audience as possible. In addition to drawing upon her own vivid memories of a visit to a spiritual realm, she was aided in her research by the skills in investigative techniques that she had learned from her police officer father. Combining these mental and spiritual attributes, Dr. Atwater has now investigated accounts of more than 3,000 adult and 277 child experiencers and written such landmark books in the field as *Coming Back to Life, Beyond the Light, Future Memory,* and *Children of the New Millennium* (republished as *The New Children and Near-Death Experiences*).

In this book, Dr. Atwater has assembled the most complete look at the mystery of the near-death experience and its aftereffects ever to be published. In twenty-six compelling chapters, she examines the entire gamut of reactions to the near-death experience—the positive and the negative, the joys and the fears, the illuminations and the confusions, the epiphanies and the exaggerations. Many never-before published research findings and stories provide the reader with insightful analyses of NDEs as well as actual drawings of otherworldly spiritual encounters by experiencers of all ages. Unafraid of the doubters, Dr. Atwater answers the various debunkers of the phenomenon, deals with those orthodox believers who have religious objections to certain experiencer claims, and examines carefully the eternal question of what we might expect when we make our final transition to the other side. The research of other experts in the field is also included to make this book the most complete reference and resource book ever compiled on the subject of near-death experiences. I highly recommend this magnificent magnum opus by Dr. P.M.H. Atwater, one of the world's most highly regarded researchers in the field of near-death studies.

—Brad Steiger

Mr. Steiger is the author of more than 100 books, including *One with the Light* and *Returning from the Light.*

Introduction

The purpose of this book is to provide you with the most complete, 360-degree look at the entire near-death phenomenon in all its positive and negative aspects. I've created it for the widest possible audience—a book that can fascinate gentle readers like yourself and, at the same time, prove to be a major source of information for teachers and students alike, medical personnel, fellow researchers, and the religious community.

The book is divided into five parts:

Part 1: The Experience/The Experiencer sets the stage by covering what we know of the early history of the subject, while bringing us up to date with some enormous changes that are now happening in the field of near-death studies. The early model of what constitutes a near-death experience has not proved to be useful in the medical world, so a new standard of criteria is being developed. In this section, we look at the four different types of episodes people generally have, along with variations reported by both adult and child experiencers.

Part 2: Afterward goes much deeper into the phenomenon and its pattern of physiological and psychological aftereffects—a pattern that affects child and adult experiencers alike. How this challenges individuals is both encouraging and alarming, especially with children who can have a more difficult time than adults dealing with the experience, and who are six times more likely to repress what happened to them than are their elders.

Part 3: Time Out for Questions opens the door to skepticism and some questions that really need to be asked. For instance, are the dead really dead? How is death determined? Is there another explanation? We jump right into the fray here by giving the debunkers a fair hearing, then debunking them as we admit that near-death researchers—as good a job as they have done—still have a long way to go with investigations of the phenomenon.

Part 4: Taking a Leap Beyond stretches our minds as we consider different ways of interpreting experiencer storylines. We also tackle the entire subject of transformations of consciousness—the traditions and aftermath of unusually striking changes people undergo who are consumed in a sudden burst of light that brings with it new knowledge of a higher order to life—and the spiritual dimensions of the soul. The three types of inner light people experience are also discussed.

Part 5: Back Down to Earth returns us to the regular world of everyday people who must grapple with the challenge of making sense out of what can be learned from near-death experiences, and to what extent they can use that knowledge in their lives. This includes the experiencer, too, for he or she is faced with integrating what happened—the incident and its aftereffects—into daily life. Emerging from this challenge are messages for the twenty-first century that can make a dramatic difference not only in your life, but for society as well.

And if all this isn't enough for you, I've included five appendices, each one chock-full of information that will enable you to have a hands-on opportunity to explore even more.

One more thing—you'll find short bits of information appearing in side boxes scattered throughout the text. These kernels highlight extra material and meaningful new words in a style that is quick and easy to grasp, and should prove most helpful as you read along. All of this was done to make your journey through the puzzling yet awe-inspiring world of near-death experiences as enjoyable as possible. Have a great read!

Part 1

The Experience/The Experiencer

Although the term "near-death experience" was coined as recently as the 1970s, these episodes have occurred, and been written about, for thousands of years. Plato wrote of a near-death experience in the *Republic*. And in the Old Testament, there are repeated cautions to the Hebrew people against following the practices of their neighbors, who believed that the dead lived on and could be communicated with—calling such beliefs and activities "an abomination unto the Lord."

It's understandable that death fascinates us; it's so much a part of life. In these chapters we'll take a moment to wander briefly back in time for a look at our all-too-human interest in this very meaningful and personal facet of our lives. Then we'll return to the present to examine what this "near-death experience" is: To whom does it occur? What do experiencers experience? And what does it tell us about life?

Aren't the answers to those questions the reason you picked up this book? There's much to learn, so let's get started on our quest for knowledge!

1

The Resurrected

To die will be an awfully big adventure.

—Sir J. M. Barrie, *Peter Pan*

Medical students have traditionally been taught that death is a failure, an error. The thrust of their training is to save lives, and at any cost. (In some societies, the doctor is paid only if the patient gets well!) Historically, though, humankind has thought otherwise. Excavations of burial sites the world over—including the well-known explorations of Egyptian tombs—have shown that ancient peoples believed that death was one of life's many passages, the deceased being buried with artifacts necessary for successfully completing the passage.

While most tribal and some societal religions supported these practices, others spoke out vehemently against them. But whatever the official or popular position, the one agreed-upon fact was that whatever death was, there were only two ways we could know about it for sure: by dying and finding out for ourselves, or by communing with the dead. The living, in other words, could not themselves know about death or what, if anything, lay beyond it. In the late nineteenth century, and decidedly more so in the last quarter of the twentieth century, that viewpoint has radically changed.

A Brief History

Since the beginning of time, humans have been fascinated with birth and death—the beginning point and seeming ending point of life. But is death really the ending point of life? Has history not shrouded it in mystery like the mystery of birth? In the next sections, we'll take a look at how this

New Word

The belief in **metempsychosis** is the belief that at death, the soul passes into another body.

attitude is changing, thanks to research on the near-death experience.

Old Testament Views

In the Old Testament, the implication appears to be that humans originally had the means to live forever. In the Garden of Eden was a tree of life whose fruit was forbidden to Adam and Eve. It was only after they disobeyed God by eating the fruit of the forbidden tree that they were denied access to the tree of life. Death was now a punishment. We now-turned-mortal human beings were thereafter fated to work for our livelihoods, after which we would "return to the ground; for out of it wast thou taken; for dust thou art, and unto dust that shalt return." Or, as the wise woman of Tekoa tells King David, we are to die, and then there is nothing more: "We are as water spilt on the ground, which cannot be gathered up again."

Neighbors of the Israelites, though, believed that not only did the dead live on, they could be communicated with for counsel. But for the Israelites, such beliefs and practices were considered "an abomination unto the Lord." Only God was to be sought out for advice. Nonetheless, in a lengthy and exceptional biblical scene in the Book of Samuel I, we're told that Saul consulted with a medium prior to going into battle at Endor in order to contact the deceased Samuel and obtain his advice regarding how to conduct himself.

Despite injunctions against such practices, they apparently continued among the people. As late as the time of the writing of the Book of Ecclesiastes—estimated to be written between 300 and 200 BCE—the people were still being warned, "For the living know that they shall die, but the dead know not anything; neither have they any more a reward; for the memory of them is forgotten." These words would not have seemed necessary if many did not continue to believe that not only was there life after death, but that the dead lived on in some type of communicative state.

Among the Greeks

During Hellenic times, immortality and life after death gained intellectual acceptance. One of the greatest Hellenic thinkers, Plato (c. 427–347 BCE), in order to explain much of human thought and consciousness, draws heavily on there not only being life after death, but on there being such a thing as *metempsychosis.*

Even more interestingly, toward the close of his book *The Republic,* Plato relates the story of Er, a soldier slain in battle who, ten days after being killed, revives on his funeral pyre and to the amazement of all, tells of having left his body and journeyed toward "a straight light like a pillar, most nearly resembling a rainbow, but brighter and purer." On his journey, Er, in the company with others who had died, arrives at a mysterious region where there are two openings in the earth, side by side, along with two more openings heavenward above and over the first two. Judges are sitting between the openings. After judging each person, they tell the righteous to wear a token of what was decreed and go to the right and upward to heaven. The unjust are told to go to the left and downward, they, too, wearing signs of all that had befallen them. When Er's turn comes to face the judges, they tell him that he must return to life and become a messenger to mankind, spreading the news about this other world and what determines an individual's fate.

Hieronymous Bosch's sixteenth century painting *The Ascent into the Empyrean*

In the Arts

Several painters have depicted scenes of dying that strikingly predate current reports by near-death experiencers. In Hieronymous Bosch's sixteenth-century painting *The Ascent into the Empyrean,* for example, souls are shown being taken to heaven by angels—they're passing through a tunnel toward a bright light! And poet and painter William Blake (1757–1827) is well known for having painted many scenes of the afterlife, the details of which he maintained were revealed to him by spirits. In his watercolor *Jacob's Dream,* angels ascending a winding stairway are leading souls toward heaven, which appears at the end of the staircase as a bright light.

Coming Up to Modern Times

Though not actual near-death experiences, so-called "deathbed visions" were widely reported in the nineteenth century. At the time, most people died at home in the company of family members, who often reported that the dying person would speak of "otherworldly" scenes before dying.

William Blake's nineteenth-century painting *Jacob's Dream*

A Child of Long Ago

In 1864, at the age of ten, Daisy Dryden died in San Jose, California. On her deathbed, she told of visions of Jesus, angels, and her deceased brother. She also told those family members and friends at her bedside that at the same time she was seeing them, she also saw spirit beings.

Last Words

As reported by those present, the last words of inventor Thomas Edison were "It is very beautiful over there."

Earlier Than That

Other publications in the 1800s that describe and explore what we now call a "near-death experience" are:

Schoolcraft	1825
Barrow	1848
Colby and Rich	1851
Winslow	1868
Livingstone	1872
Cozzins	1873
Clarke	1878
Little	1881
Munck	1881
Cobbe	1882

Only recently discovered are publications earlier than the 1800s. (Thanks to Bruce Greyson, MD.)

Though these individuals were in fact still alive at the time, their "sightings" of death and the afterlife are very much in keeping with those reported by near-death experiencers.

According to leading researcher Bruce Greyson, MD, the near-death phenomenon as such—though it wasn't referred to by that name—wasn't given serious clinical attention until 1892. In that year, Albert von st. Gallen Heim published a collection of accounts by mountain climbers who had fallen in the Alps (as he himself had done), soldiers wounded in war, workers who had fallen from scaffolds, and individuals who had nearly died in accidents or near-drownings. All reported experiencing "life after death." Heim's article, "Remarks on Fatal Falls" (see appendix C), was translated into English in 1972 and is a precursor to the investigations of modern times. The first article by a medical professional to acknowledge the phenomenon was A. S. Wiltse's "A case of typhoid fever with subnormal temperature and pulse." It appeared in the *Saint Louis Medical and Surgical Journal* in 1889. (Thanks to researchers Janice Minor Holden, EdD, and Rozan Christian, PhD.)

We Learn to Talk about Death

Shortly before the English translation of Heim's work, psychiatrist Elisabeth Kübler-Ross published *On Death and Dying*, a landmark book that broke the long-established silence—and taboo—about speaking about death. Listening to the stories of her dying patients, she heard account after account of mystical experiences suggesting that there may be life after death. Without any background to understand what her patients were saying to her, she was uncertain of what to make of these accounts but could not ignore the consistency of their content.

After hearing hundreds of such reportings, Dr. Kübler-Ross came to conclude that no one ever dies alone, that someone—be it a spirit being, an angel, deceased relative, or guardian made of light—comes to comfort and receive those who are about to die. She also discovered that those who didn't die, who were resuscitated and recovered, had almost identical stories to tell. Intrigued and profoundly moved by what she was hearing, she subsequently wrote *On Life After Death,* a work geared toward families whose members are dying, as well as to those who fear death.

New Word

The **near-death experience** (NDE) is an intense awareness, sense, or experience of "otherworldliness," whether pleasant or unpleasant, that happens to people who are at the edge of death. It is of such magnitude that most experiencers are deeply affected—many to the point of making significant changes in their lives afterward because of what they went through.

Before Moody Met Him

Spiritual Frontiers Fellowship popularized George Ritchie and his near-death account long before Raymond Moody ever met him. The organization, chartered in 1956 to explore and interpret the growing interest in psychic phenomenon and mystical experience within the Church as it relates to effective prayer, spiritual healing, and personal survival, is credited with bringing together several early researchers in the field of near-death studies and actively supporting their work.

The Moody Miracle and the Beginning of Scientific Inquiry

In 1943, having contracted double pneumonia, twenty-year-old U.S. Army private George Ritchie was pronounced dead, and his corpse was taken to the morgue. An orderly, however, thought he saw a movement from Ritchie's body. Ritchie's death was reconfirmed by the medical personnel, but the orderly insisted that he'd seen Ritchie's hand move. On the basis and conviction of the orderly's claim, adrenaline was injected into Ritchie, his vital signs returned, and he came back to life. Afterward, Ritchie became a psychiatrist, often speaking of the extraordinary experiences he'd had while clinically considered dead.

In 1965, an undergraduate philosophy student at the University of Virginia—Raymond Moody Jr.—overheard Ritchie telling his story and became fascinated by it. But he didn't pursue it. Over the years, however, he heard other similar stories, the contents of which were nearly identical to that first account he'd heard as an undergraduate student. In 1972, Moody decided to enter medical school. By this time, he had acquired a sizeable number of

A True Best-Seller

As of 2006, 13 million copies of *Life After Life* by Raymond A. Moody, Jr., MD, PhD, have sold. The book has been translated into 26 languages.

To date, the IANDS website gets over 400,000 page hits per month (www.iands.org). Several other popular websites about the near-death experience report an average of 2.5 million hits per month (www.near-death.com and www.nderf.org).

accounts about people pronounced dead who had revived and returned to life with stories of an afterlife. Dr. Moody was encouraged to give public talks about what he called *near-death experiences*. In 1975, and now a medical doctor, he published an account of 150 stories he'd gathered, in a landmark book titled *Life After Life*.

The furor Moody's book elicited would never have continued to pack the wallop it did, even decades later, were it not for Kenneth Ring, PhD. He was so moved by the implications inherent in the near-death experience that he launched the first scientific study of the phenomenon. Five years later, Ring was able to verify Moody's work in *Life At Death*, and in so doing opened wide the floodgates to serious inquiry—which established that the near-death experience is no dream, vision, fairy tale, hallucination, or the product of anyone's imagination. It is a real event that happens to real people, regardless of age, culture, education, or belief.

Because of all the sensationalism surrounding his book and the term "near-death experience," Dr. Moody in 1977 invited over a dozen professionals to a meeting in Charlottesville, Virginia, to discuss how best to handle the situation. From that meeting emerged the Association for the Scientific Study of Near-Death Phenomena. Three years later, after Dr. Ring verified Dr. Moody's findings, the peer-reviewed journal *Anabiosis* was established.

This initial effort led to the creation in 1981 of what exists today as the International Association for Near-Death Studies (IANDS). A nonprofit organization, IANDS serves as a clearinghouse to impart information about near-death experiences and their implications, encourage and support research on the experience and related phenomena, and aid in the formation of local groups to explore the subject. Called Friends of IANDS, these groups are located throughout the United States and Canada, and stretch from Europe to South Africa. Among their many publications are the scholarly *Journal of Near-Death Studies*; a general-interest newsletter, *Vital Signs*; and an "NDE Online Continuing Education Class" for health-care professionals. Membership is open to anyone. Personal near-death experiences are solicited on an ongoing basis for the archives.

What Is the Near-Death Experience?

Near-death states can occur when an individual brushes death, almost dies, or is pronounced clinically dead, yet later revives or is resuscitated. Typically, near-death experiencers register neither pulse nor breath for an average of five to fifteen minutes. It's not uncommon to hear of those who were dead for more than an hour. Regardless of how long the experiences last, though, near-death episodes are significant in that they remain lucid and coherent in the experiencer's mind over time.

These experiences happen to anyone at any age, including newborns and infants. A 1982 Gallup poll estimated that 5 percent of the general population in the United States had undergone a near-death experience. That was around eight million people then; now 5 percent is closer to fifteen million. This computes as roughly 12–20 percent of those who are at death's door. No subsequent polls are counted as they lack scientific credibility. But the 1982 survey, and all the others ever done, only addressed adult experiencers. In his groundbreaking study of child experiencers done in the late 1980s, Melvin Morse, MD, author of *Closer to the Light* (see appendix C), estimates that among children close to death, more than 70 percent have had a near-death experience.

Near-death experiences can range in content from an out-of-body experience (OBE) to being in the presence of God. They imply that there may be life after death because of the imagery encountered and the accuracy of details verified by a third party that often could not have been known by the experiencer in advance.

The most striking feature of a near-death experience is that while a human's brain can be seriously, even permanently, damaged in three to five minutes without sufficient oxygen, no matter how long a person is dead, there's usually little or no brain damage. On the contrary, there's brain *enhancement* once the person revives. As we'll talk more about in chapters 7 and 8, this condition is one of the ways to know that what happened was indeed a genuine near-death experience.

Where's My Body?

For some experiencers, locating their bodies when it's time to return can be quite challenging—especially if, as happened to George Ritchie, their bodies are in a morgue. Ritchie claims that if it wasn't for his left hand hanging below the morgue sheet with his class ring on one finger, he might have never figured out which body was his!

I Know Nothing

It's easy to jump to the conclusion, and many do, that near-death episodes are self-fulfilling experiences of those who are already predisposed to believe in them. Cardiologist Michael Sabom of the United States and psychologist Margot Grey of Britain, however, discovered that those who know about near-death states are rarely among the people most likely to have them.

Why Aunt Sarah and Not Me?

Nobody is certain why one person experiences a near-death episode and another doesn't. Still, researchers have discovered a few conditions that seem to have a bearing on who may undergo such an episode:

> **New Word**
>
> A **scenario** is the content of the near-death experience: imagery, feeling-tones, sensations, landscapes, events, sounds, colors, beings, messages, light, or darkness.

- The closer you are to physical death (as opposed to being in a coma, unconscious, or simply scared out of your wits), the more likely you are to have a near-death experience, especially if you have surrendered to the prospect of dying.

- The fewer drugs in your system, the better, as drugs actually impede the phenomenon and can lead to hallucinations that are a far cry from the lucidity and clarity of the real thing.

- If you are at a critical juncture in your life, or have paid little heed to spiritual matters, you are a prime candidate, since those who lead balanced, happy lives centered around worship and service to others do not report as many episodes.

Common Elements in Near-Death Scenarios

Thousands of near-death scenarios have now been studied worldwide, revealing common elements and patterning, even though the actual way the various elements are experienced and described may vary widely.

Some people report finding themselves in a garden, walking along a road, or skipping through a pasture. Others describe great cities that sparkle like jewels or what it's like to hop aboard a light ray for a trip through the universe. Many speak of entering huge libraries or halls of judgment, while a large number wind up in a familiar terrain talking with deceased loved ones or playing with former pets that act just like they did while they were alive. Religious figures such as Jesus or Buddha, angels of various persuasions, beings of light, and spiritual guardians of every sort are reported so often they have become the mainstay of near-death literature.

Moody's original work identified fifteen elements overall:

- Ineffability, beyond the limits of any language to describe
- Hearing yourself pronounced dead
- Feelings of peace and quiet
- Hearing unusual noises
- Seeing a dark tunnel
- Finding yourself outside your body
- Meeting "spiritual beings"
- A very bright light experienced as a "being of light"
- A panoramic life review
- Sensing a border or limit to where you can go
- Coming back into your body
- Frustrating attempts to tell others about what happened to you

- Subtle "broadening and deepening" of your life afterward
- Elimination of the fear of death
- Corroboration of events witnessed while out of your body

Two years later, after hundreds more interviews, Moody added four more elements to his list of common components to what experiencers claim to have encountered:

- A realm where all knowledge exists
- Cities of light
- A realm of bewildered spirits
- Supernatural rescues

Let's focus on this last element for a moment. Many near-death experiencers report experiencing what have come to be called supernatural rescues. These are occurrences in which the person benefits physically from "heavenly" intervention, as in having tumors disappear or a "physical," detached hand that suddenly appears from out of nowhere to pull the person to safety.

As more research was done, other professionals noted that near-death states could also include features besides the mystical, such as *depersonal* elements and *hyperalertness*.

A Closer Look at Some Near-Death Scenario Features

Although near-death experiences have been popularized in newspapers and movies, it's important that we take a closer look at some of the commonly reported features as well as some illustrative, verified accounts.

New Words

Depersonal occurrences are when individuals experience a separation from their bodies and the emotions associated with them. **Hyperalertness** is when their sensory faculties become sharper and awareness more vivid than what is considered "normal."

Look Ma, No Body!

Out-of-body experiences can happen to anyone—children as well as adults—at any time, anywhere. People can even be taught how to have them through the use of certain relaxation and visualization techniques. But while out-of-body-experiences are not unique to a near-death experience, the out-of-body component to near-death states is said to be much more intense, vivid, and detailed than those that occur naturally or because of a learned skill.

Bye-Bye Body

During an out-of-body episode, you have the sensation of suddenly separating or floating away from your physical body and being able to view it from a place apart. The experience is "teachable," that is to say, some people can be taught how. Success seems to depend on your willingness to do it and the belief that you can, coupled with lots of practice and on-site verifications.

Feeling Foreign

Finding yourself back in your physical body after experiencing a near-death state is seldom pleasant. There is usually a need to "shrink" or somehow squeeze back in, as if you were larger outside your body than inside. There can be anger, even tears, at the realization that you are no longer on "the other side." Some feel as if they were kicked out of heaven.

In my book *The New Children and Near-Death Experiences* (formerly titled *Children of the New Millennium*—see appendix C), I discuss the childhood case of Carl Allen Pierson of Hinton, West Virginia, who, at the age of eight or nine, was struck by lightning. Since what happened to him typifies the out-of-body component to near-death states, I'll use his story as an example and in his own words:

"During a thunderstorm, with a metal washtub over my head, I went to untie the cow from the tree for my uncle. When I got approximately fifteen feet from the tree, lightning hit it and bounced to the tub. I was barefoot, standing on wet grass. Lightning took all galvanizing off the tub, and knocked me and the tub away from the tree. Turned the tub black. I was hovering above as my family encircled my body lying on the grass. It was communicated that I was dead. I was trying to tell them I was not dead, but made no sounds. Soft light, warm glowing feeling. Something or someone told me that everything would be okay, then blackness.

"Next I was lying in a dark house on a couch but could not hear or see, yet I was aware of what was going on. I could not move anything, like my body muscles were locked up. Great pain. Blackness. Then I was in a hospital or doctor's office on a gurney. I had a vision and saw myself hovering over my body again, but this time no one was present. My body was larger (adult size). I remember hearing the news on the radio, something about a boy who had been killed by lightning. There was mention of it in the local paper, too. Both turned out to be false reports, as you can readily see."

Tripping through the Tunnel

Some experiencers mention traveling through a tunnel as part of their near-death scenario. Some refer to this tunnel as long and dark and that they were alone in it throughout the journey. Others say there were bright lights that flashed along its walls, or that it was colored or even transparent, and that other people were there. Almost everyone states that they swooshed through its length at great speed. Some said they heard and felt the sensation of wind rushing by them. Just as many people say the tunnel went up as down, or straightaway.

In most cases, a light appears at the end of the tunnel, and experiencers note that is where they are headed—a light described as brighter than the sun but that doesn't hurt their eyes if they look at it. This light is invariably experienced as loving, intelligent, accepting, forgiving, and ever so wonderful.

Ishtan Natarajan of Charlottesville, Virginia, recalls that one day, when he was just a youngster, he started to sit down when something happened to him. He has no memory of exactly what, except the aching sensation that he may have been attacked. Since his earliest years were filled with beatings and abuse, his suspicion may be right. About four hours later, when he regained consciousness, his mind filled with the awareness of a wonderful tunnel he had just been in. He began to paint that tunnel and continued to do so throughout his childhood and into his adult years. He often retreated there when young, as it became a place of safety and love. Still today, he regards the tunnel with deep affection. (I'll tell you more about Ishtan's experiences in chapter 17.)

A Joke

The idea of passing through a tunnel into the light has become the butt of many jokes and cartoons. One of the jokes goes like this: "ATTENTION, ALL PERSONNEL. Due to budget cuts, the light at the end of the tunnel has been turned off until further notice."

But What's Typical?

To give you an opportunity to gain a sense of what the typical experiencer might go through, here's the story of what happened to Elli Covelli of Dallas, Texas, when she was thirty-six years old. She was unsure about her relationship with her boyfriend at the time and felt keenly that something important was missing in her life. As she and her boyfriend debated whether or not they had a future together, she began to experience a severe pain in her lower back and on the right side. She was rushed to the hospital, where doctors discovered she had a large kidney stone that needed to come out. Here's Elli's story, as she tells it:

"Well, the next day, the doctors decided to manipulate the stone out of me, so I was taken to surgery. As I was laying on what I call a meat wagon, this really cute guy comes over to me. Turns out he was my nurse. After positioning me just right on the table, once we got to the operating room, he says he needs to place these electrodes on me. I tell him to give them to me and I'll do it. After all, I was butt-naked under those covers and I wasn't about to give this guy a free show and touch session. I was giving him a hard time when all of a sudden I got this horrible pain in my heart. He asked what was wrong. The anesthesiologist heard us talking and he came over to see what was going on.

Drawing of tunnel by Ishtan Natarajan. Although an admittedly simple depiction, this is a perfect example of how compelling the tunnel experience can be.

"Everything happened real fast after that. He started yelling for people to get my temperature and white blood cell count. Someone came and packed me with ice under my head and on my feet. I remember thinking what could be going on. Then the pain got even worse. It felt like someone was pouring hot molten liquid into my heart. I started to feel real cold. Someone called a code blue and put lots of blankets over me. Then I started going through a tunnel. I can't draw my tunnel but I can describe it. The sensation was like going up to a drive-in bank and feeling yourself being placed into the cartridge and then finding yourself in that tube that sucks the cartridge into the bank. It sort of reminded me of *Star Trek*. Beam me up, Scotty. The tunnel was to me like a wormhole to another world, and in order to get there you have to leave your physical body behind.

"Feelings of love and peace followed, like nothing I've ever experienced before. Drugs and alcohol don't even compare to this kind of high. As I drifted it came to me that I was exiting off planet Earth. All my life I've had this feeling that someday I was going to leave the planet, and this was it. I became all-knowing in an instant and found myself in the presence of a white light that seemed to accept me just as I was. There were no words spoken, but I was given my life review. I judged myself against what I had been taught down on planet Earth versus what I had newly learned. It seemed like a lot of things were just the opposite of what they should be. I mean I knew something was wrong with the way people believed as opposed to how things really are. But what I learned was overwhelming. I had wanted answers, but this was too much. I don't know how much time passed. The light was very patient letting me be in awe. Boy, was I humbled.

"I knew it was time to make a choice. I could stay there if I wanted to, because life down on planet Earth would be even more difficult for me than it had been if I returned. With that, I was sucked back down into my body but didn't come to until much later. When I did wake up, I was in a room hooked up to a bunch of machines. My parents came in and said they had been in the waiting room when the doctor announced that he had almost lost me. He had asked them why they didn't tell him about my heart problems. My parents answered saying they had no clue I ever had heart problems. It seems that my kidney stone was so big it blocked something up, causing an infection to get into my blood that interfered with the valves in my heart. The result was a cardiac arrest. Two days later they did get my stone, without causing any complications. When I got back into the swing of things later on, it hit me. All of a sudden I didn't want to be doing the things I had done before. Everything that I had thought was so important seemed to mean nothing to me anymore. I was different, and I knew I would never be the same again."

The Birth of a Controversy

As I mentioned, it's important to take a closer look at some of the near-death scenarios, and now I'll explain why.

The truth is that despite popular

views and dramatizations, seldom will any near-death experiencer's scenario contain all the elements that have been noted so far and commonly cited as "typical." Indeed, the average experience will only consist of about half of them, ofttimes less.

The famed "tunnel" component, for example, is present in less than one-third of the actual experiences. In the first-ever national poll taken on near-death states by Gallup in 1982, only 9 percent claimed to have passed through a tunnel. Because the image is so captivating and has been widely popularized, experiencers have been known to make up a tunnel component to their episode or call any form of darkness they encounter a tunnel, just so they can convince themselves and others that what happened to them was genuine.

In short, the now-popular notion that all experiencers leave their bodies, go through a tunnel into the light, meet deceased relatives in heaven, and are then told to come back, is fanciful at best and confusing at worst—misleading not only to the general public but to experiencers as well.

Different Experiences

Don't doubt the authenticity of your experience if you have a near-death episode that doesn't contain all the scenario elements now considered "typical." The number-one complaint expressed the world over at chapter meetings of the International Association for Near-Death Studies continues to be, "My experience doesn't match the universal model."

Excluded almost entirely from public view are unpleasant and hellish scenes, feelings of distress, threatening beings, flashes of light and dark, complicated and lengthy involvement with otherworldly teachers, experiments with matter and creation, short trips that seem to have little meaning, disembodied voices, historical backgrounds, and so forth. These are as much a part of many individuals' near-death states as the more familiar elements.

Questions

Despite several decades of research, as of this writing, there is still no consensus as to how near-death states can best be defined and recognized—even though the near-death experience is the most researched subjective state in all history!

The Controversy Continues

The "alarm bell" regarding the confusion about what constituted a "true" near-death experience and what didn't was ultimately sounded by the health-care community, which was trying to train medical personnel on how to recognize if a patient might be in the process of having or might just have had a near-death experience. What they had to go on was "the universal model" that, as we've seen, wasn't proving to be very helpful. As a result, the standards the health-care community was hoping to find proved not to exist.

A Promising Solution

Bruce Greyson, MD, in an effort to achieve consensus, contacted all the top researchers of near-death states by letter and said, in essence, that the time has come when we must have a common criteria the health-care community can use, and, for that matter, anyone else.

In establishing the *context* in which the experience occurs, he offered two modes or conditions most often present:

A) Symptoms or signs suggestive of death, or of serious medical illness, injury, or physiological crisis/accident of some kind, or

B) Experiencer's expectation or sense of imminent death

Considering *content,* his suggestions and those of others are summed up as follows:

Content is always an intense awareness, sense, or experience of "otherworldliness," whether pleasant or unpleasant, strange or ecstatic. The episode can be brief and consist of only one or two elements, or can be lengthy and consist of multiple elements.

Elements commonly experienced are:

- Visualizing or experiencing being apart from the physical body, perhaps with the ability to change locations

- Greatly enhanced cognition (thoughts clear, rapid, and hyperlucid)

- A darkness or light that is perceived as alive and intelligent and powerful

- Sense of a presence

- Sensations of movement (one's own or things around oneself)

- Hyperalert faculties (heightened sense of smell, taste, touch, sight, and sound)

- Sudden overwhelming floods of emotion or feelings

- Encounter with an identified deceased person or animal or seemingly nonphysical entity

- Life review (like a movie or in segments, or a reliving)
- Life previews possible (futuristic)
- Information can be imparted, perhaps dialogue

Today, Dr. Greyson defines the near-death experience as a set of "profound psychological events with transcendental and mystical elements, typically occurring to individuals close to death or in situations of intense physical or emotional danger."

IANDS defines the near-death experience as a lucid experience associated with perceived consciousness apart from the body, occurring at the time of actual or threatened imminent death.

Contemporary medical procedures sometimes make it possible to survive clinical death. Those who have done so have come back to tell us tales that we still don't quite understand, but that inspire us and, as we'll see in subsequent chapters, challenge our understanding of life as well as death.

2

Types of Experiences

Life is a great surprise. I do not see why death should not be an even greater one.

—Vladimir Nabokov, *Pale Fire*

It's easy to forget, when speaking of near-death experiences, that more is involved than just "a neat story." Trauma and the specter of death can exact a heavy toll on a person's life. After experiencing three near-death episodes myself in 1977, I knew first-hand just how profound the experience could be. So in 1978, healed from the aftermath of my own experiences, I began researching what had become for me a baffling yet life-changing experience. I wanted to find out what was real and what wasn't real.

Through a meeting with famed medical doctor, psychiatrist, and author Elisabeth Kübler-Ross, I acquired a name for what I had undergone. She referred to it as a "near-death experience." Her description was my only reference to that term. I'd not yet heard of Raymond Moody nor his best-selling book.

I began an investigation process consisting of interviews with other near-death experiencers, detailed observations, and some questionnaires, plus sessions held with the experiencers' "significant others." This investigation spanned three decades and involved both adult and child experiencers. I checked and cross-checked my findings three to four times with different people in different parts of the country, at different times. I did not want my research to be simply anecdotal. You might say I was obsessive-compulsive about this.

I discovered, among other things, that having just one way of regarding this experience misleadingly suggests that we're talking about a single, uniformly experienced event.

Cautions from Moody

During a lecture Raymond Moody gave in Houston, Texas, in 2006, he focused on what has long been known in the research field: No one experience contains all of the elements of a near-death experience; no two are identical; the sequence of what happens is not universal; and each case is unique.

New Words

Signature features are those components of a near-death scenario that show up in the majority of cases. They include out-of-body experiences, a light that shines brighter than the sun, a "voice-less" voice that speaks telepathically, calming feelings of total acceptance and unconditional love, a sudden knowingness, and feeling the need or being told to return. (As you'll recall from chapter 1, tunnels are not signature features.)

Nothing could be further from the truth. As you'll soon see, there are clearly four distinct types.

To Each His Own

Near-death states can be ever so brief, or they can be quite lengthy and involved. They can consist of *signature features,* those characteristics widely found, or a diversity of elements that occur less often.

Even though there are certain shared signature features in a majority of cases, there's no uniform set of characteristics that everyone's near-death episode has. Sometimes an individual hears only a voice and nothing more. But that disembodied voice can prove to be a life-changer in the person's life! Sometimes an individual is transported by an extraordinary means to distant universes, or "hovers" around the death scene.

Even researchers don't agree on what properly constitutes a description of a near-death experience. Some label an episode that is brief a mere fragment of the "real thing"; others consider anything unpleasant to be nothing more than an inverted near-death state and not a true experience.

A Loving Flight

One woman I interviewed was involved in a serious car accident. In the midst of the twisted steel she saw and felt herself rise up from her body and enter a gorgeous blue ball. In the ball she felt protected and loved, and totally without pain or concern for what had happened to her.

The ball floated in and around the accident scene, giving her an opportunity to view everything from both close up and far away. She saw emergency vans rushing to the site and noticed that her husband, who worked for the hospital rescue squad, was in one of them. She discovered that she could move the blue ball with her thoughts, so she guided it to where her husband was as he fought his way through the wreckage. The moment he recognized his own wife's body, she watched as he fell apart with grief. His grief so touched her that she decided to return to her body so she could console him. That desire instantly brought her back.

Nothing More Than a Corpse

In 1975, Ricky Bradshaw, of Staunton, Virginia, had his torso literally ground in half when he became trapped between two automobiles backing into each other at a grocery store parking lot. He had been knocked to his knees by the force of the blow while attempting to put grocery bags in the trunk of a car. Only his spine and a few cords around it were left intact before the drivers realized what had taken place and let up on the gas.

Ricky was pronounced dead at the hospital and his body heaped onto a gurney in a corner. A group of medical students noticed the cadaver and requested that they be allowed to experiment with it (the hospital was a teaching facility). After an hour of "high jinks," the heart monitor they'd hooked up to the body began to register beeps. Thinking the machine was malfunctioning, the students sought out a physician. Suddenly, what began as a chance to experiment with a fresh corpse turned into a serious emergency.

Two years and twenty-four surgeries later, Ricky's survival made medical history. His case is termed "unexplained" by the medical community. You and I would call his survival a miracle. And you guessed it, he had a "humdinger" of a near-death experience, one that featured an out-of-body experience, brilliant light, loving voices, and being able to view all of history from beginning to end.

Animals, Too

The appearance of animals is frequently reported in near-death scenarios. Usually, they are pets who had previously died. Occasionally, they are unknown to the individual, yet lovingly endear themselves as a guide, messenger, or comforter. Sometimes they "speak" telepathically. There are a few child experiencers who tell of having to visit an animal heaven before they can go to the heaven where people are.

In a television interview with Diane Sawyer on *Primetime* (December 20, 2004), Roy, of the famed Las Vegas entertainers Siegfried and Roy, claimed that his tigers were present in his near-death experience. One had nearly killed him in an attack while they were on stage. "No doubt, when it is my time," said Roy, "my cats should greet me—they are my family."

Medical High Jinks

Although no one can be certain how or why Ricky Bradshaw survived, he believes some of the credit goes to those medical students who were "playing around." By tugging here and stretching there, they wound up reconnecting vital parts in a manner necessary for reconstructive surgery. Ricky is grateful they "happened by" after he was pronounced dead.

> **Stay or Go**
>
> In some cases, the experiencer chooses to return; in others, the person is sent back, usually with the admonition that he or she has a job yet to perform or a mission to do. There are a number of reports where the experiencer chose to stay but was sent back anyway.

A Startling Incident

One time, early in my research, I was giving a public talk on near-death states at a senior-citizen center. At the close of my talk, I invited any experiencers in the audience to come up and share their story. A clean-cut man in his late twenties shyly came forward and started talking. His episode was so uplifting and wonder-filled, it brought tears to the eyes of everyone there. Then he made this shocking statement: "This experience is the worst thing that ever happened to me. It has ruined my life and filled me with pain."

Immediately, a woman in the crowd, of about the same age, stood up. Her episode was starkly different from his. At the moment of her death, she spoke of finding herself trapped in a raging whirlpool that was sucking her down into its bowels. She had to fight back against the current to free herself and then fight some more, struggle with all her might, to reach shore. The sky was blackened by a huge storm. Strong winds tore at her while thunder roared. She, too, shocked the crowd with her next words: "This is without a doubt the most wonderful experience in my life. It taught me that there is always a second chance, that we are never lost, no matter what happens to us. We have the power to change anything."

I was aghast. Yet I found myself hearing more and more of these surprising responses: What you and I might call a heavenly experience, someone else might term horrible, and vice versa.

Problems in Communication

As I continued my research, I came to realize that it wasn't the experience per se that made the biggest difference, but rather, how the individual felt and talked about it. And talking about—communicating—the experience was in itself often part of the problem in trying to understand not only the meaning but also the nature of a near-death experience.

The Language Barrier

Near-death experiences are fundamentally ineffable—beyond the limits of language to be adequately described. Adults struggle for the right words to use, and never quite seem to find any combination that really works to help them get their point across. So you can imagine, therefore, that if adult experiencers find the constraints of language a barrier, child experiencers struggle even more to find the "right" words. Tough stuff!

I have come to believe this problem of finding the "right" words to describe one's experience is the major reason why so many experiencers fall back on simply painting the kind of word picture they feel they can most easily convey to others. Remember, after all, the experience itself is startlingly unique, and many discount it. There's safety in numbers: You're not as apt to be labeled "a nut" if you describe your experience in language typical to that of your family, religion, or society.

Dental Drugs

Kenneth Ring, in a paper for the *Journal of Near-Death Studies,* suggested that the encounter with a "meaningless void" or "alternating circles that spin or click" occur most often to people while they are sedated with nitrous oxide during dental work or childbirth. Women seem to be especially vulnerable to the drug and are often terrified by the "apparitions" they experience while sedated. Men, however, usually report only pleasant sensations from the drug.

Embarrassed into Secrecy

Seldom do experiencers return with their lifelong beliefs intact. Invariably, the beliefs are challenged or stretched beyond what was once normal or typical for the person. This can be both good and not so good, depending on the individual involved. One woman, who was a minister's wife, told me that after her near-death experience she could no longer attend church and listen to her husband's sermons. "What he's telling the congregation is wrong. I know better, I was there, and God doesn't ask that of us," she said.

Just as with everyday life, in near-death states, if what you experience runs counter to—or even completely contradicts—your previous beliefs or upbringing, it won't necessarily be the language problem that keeps you from sharing your experience. It could be embarrassment or suddenly feeling "out of sync" with the world around you. Additionally, out of shame, or for a million other reasons, an experiencer may not want to admit to others that his or her experience was hellish instead of heavenly.

Attitude Makes a Difference

As I continued my research, I was fascinated by the fact that how a person really feels about himself or herself and life in general can also influence and further complicate attempts to describe near-death episodes in a meaningful way. Some of us, for instance, see an obstacle as an exciting challenge, while others see the identical obstacle as another of life's many setbacks. In a similar way, two near-death experiencers can encounter the exact same episodic elements, yet may describe and interpret them differently, depending entirely on their attitude and any deeply held beliefs they may have or cultural expectations.

The following table shows how, in near-death scenarios containing elements that are exactly the same (such as beings, environment, voices, feelings, and sensations), individuals can nonetheless perceive and describe their experiences in radically different ways.

Contrasts with Interpretation

Element	**Considered Heaven-Like**	**Considered Hell-Like**
Beings	Friendly and supportive	Lifeless or threatening
Environment	Beautiful and lovely	Barren or ugly
Voices	Conversations and dialogue	Threats, screams, indifferent
Feelings	Total acceptance and love	Discomfort, danger, or dread
Sensations	Warmth, and a sense of having found one's true home	Cold (or of temperature extremes), and a sense of loneliness, separation

Is Hell Common?

Maurice Rawlings, a cardiologist, indicated in his book *Beyond Death's Door* that patients tend to repress anything negative. Of those he interviewed right after resuscitation, nearly half described hellish features in their near-death episodes; later on, the same people usually recalled only positive, uplifting imagery. Rawlings's research, however, has yet to be replicated, even by fellow cardiologists interviewing patients under the same conditions.

Nancy Evans Bush, MA, a pastoral care counselor and near-death researcher, estimates that 17 percent of near-death states are distressing to experiencers. She cautions that there is no single episode common to all; rather, at least three general types have been identified (inverted, void, hell-like), with a possible fourth (guilt-laden life review). Her work and the percentage she discovered is similar to mine.

The Stigma of Deviation

There are many near-death experiencers who truly feel they journeyed to hell, not heaven. These people are usually silent about the whole affair, fearing scorn from others. And rightly so, for there are experiencers and researchers alike who are quick to declare that only murderers, liars, and cheats undergo unpleasantness in death or wind up in hell. Others think that only "Bible Belters" (Christian fundamentalists) are "condemned" to hellish experiences, because only dogmatic people like them believe in eternal hell and damnation. Wrong on both counts!

There is no evidence whatsoever that links frightening or hellish experiences with "bad" people or those who hold more fundamentalist religious views. Quite the contrary, such states are encountered most often by ordinary people, many who were family-oriented and active in their communities and business.

A Common Range of Patterns

From the beginning of my research, I noticed four distinctive types of near-death experiences and, interestingly, subtle personality predispositions that seemed to correlate with each. This discovery has held up for three decades with more than 3,000 adult experiences and 277 child experiences (the distinct types are discussed further in my book *Beyond the Light;* see appendix C). This classification of the four basic types of experiences includes consideration of common as well as uncommon elements plus differences in interpretative styles. It provides an overall model of near-death states that has remained consistent, regardless of the experiencer's age, social background, beliefs, educational level, or country of origin.

The Book of Life

About 30 percent of adult experiencers report having seen "The Book of Life" during their episode. Seldom do children claim this. Of those who do encounter such a phenomenon, some say it is an actual book, a large one—perhaps in a library of them—that has a record of each moment of a person's life contained in its pages. Others say "The Book" is really a hologram or a television-like showing. Most, however, never mention a book or a library filled with them. Rather, they speak of histories recorded upon "the skeins of time," as if such memories were held at certain frequencies accessible when we are in that energy field.

Some Examples of Each Type

I believe that the best way to present the four scenario types is to provide examples of each. Let's take a look at some examples from cases in my files, including accounts from child and adult experiencers. This will help you recognize the patterns yourself and notice how experiential components typical to each type can vary from person to person.

Initial Experience

John Raymond Liona, Brooklyn, New York; birth complications:

"I was strangled by my umbilical cord during birth. Once born, I was given a tracheotomy to get me breathing—[I had] black eyes, swollen face, cuts from forceps. My mother didn't see me until the third day. I relive the event in my dreams from time to time, vividly. I remember being bent over or kneeling down fighting with these knots. I was very upset and angry. Just when I was thinking I was getting in control of these things, I get hit in the face (the doc with the forceps). I start struggling even more.

"All of a sudden I become very peaceful. Everything I was feeling before just poured out of me and I was so calm. I remember looking at my hands but the details are not clear. I think I was floating because I was trying to move forward but could not. I was trying to reach this woman in the distance. The material of her gown was glowing with little specks of light trailing off. There was a buzzing or humming sound. She floated away toward

The Four Types of Near-Death Experiences

1. *Initial Experience—sometimes referred to as the "nonexperience" (an awakening).* Usually involves only one—maybe two or three—element such as a loving nothingness, the living dark, a friendly voice, a brief out-of-body-experience, or a manifestation of some type. Usually experienced by those who seem to need the least amount of evidence for proof of survival, or who need the least amount of shakeup in their lives at that point in time. Often, this becomes a "seed" experience or an introduction to other ways of perceiving and recognizing reality. Rarely is any other element present.

Incident rate: 76 percent with child experiencers, 20 percent with adult experiencers

2. *Unpleasant and/or Hell-Like Experience—sometimes referred to as "distressing" (inner cleansing and self-confrontational).* Encounter with a threatening void, stark limbo, or hellish purgatory, or scenes of a startling and unexpected indifference (like being shunned), even "hauntings" from one's own past. Scenarios usually experienced by those who seem to have deeply suppressed or repressed guilt, fear, and anger, and/or those who expect some kind of punishment or discomfort after death. Life reviews common. Some have previews.

Incident rate: 3 percent with child experiencers, 15 percent with adult experiencers

3. *Pleasant and/or Heaven-Like Experience—sometimes referred to as "radiant" (reassurance and self-validation).* Heaven-like scenarios of loving family reunions with those who have died previously, reassuring religious figures or light beings, validation that life counts, affirmative and inspiring dialogue. Scenarios usually experienced by those who most need to know how loved they are and how important life is and how every effort has a purpose in the overall scheme of things. Life reviews common. Some have previews.

Incident rate: 19 percent with child experiencers, 47 percent with adult experiencers

4. *Transcendent Experience—sometimes referred to as "collective universality" (expansive revelations, alternate realities).* Exposure to otherworldly dimensions and scenes beyond the individual's frame of reference; sometimes includes revelations of greater truths. Seldom personal in content. Scenarios usually experienced by those who are ready for a "mind stretching" challenge and/or individuals who are more apt to use (to whatever degree) the truths that are revealed to them. Life reviews rare. Collective previews common (such as the world's future, evolutionary changes).

Incident rate: 2 percent with child experiencers, 18 percent with adult experiencers

the left. I was calling to her, yelling, but the light, it was all around. It was coming from the right, and was so bright. She could not hear me. I was so upset as I wanted to go with her."

Tannis Prouten, Vancouver, B.C., Canada; twenty years old, severe anxiety attacks:

"As a young adult, stepping out into the working world without the necessary

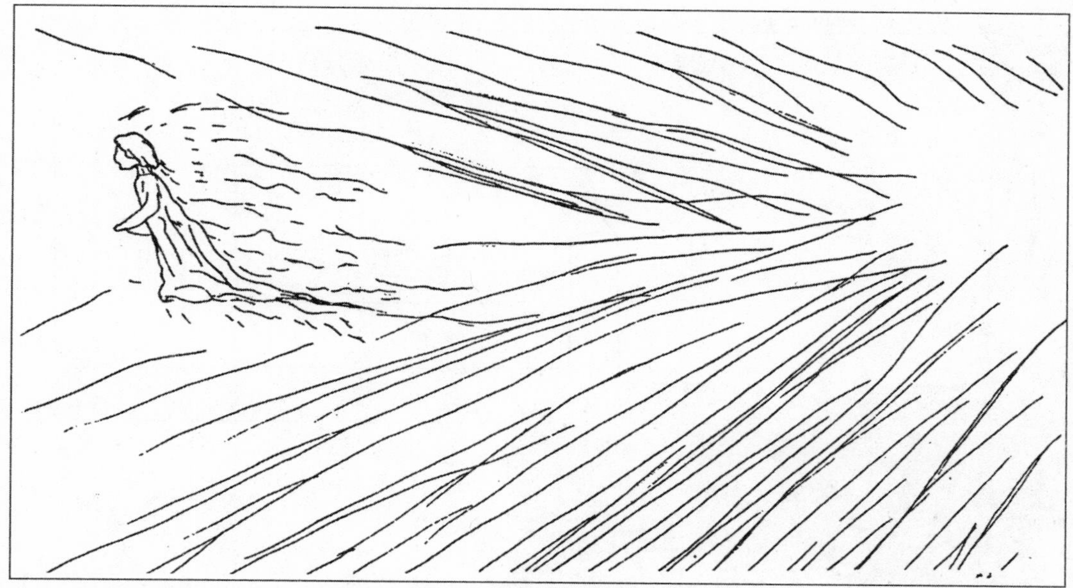

This drawing by John Raymond Liona illustrates his experience in his mother's womb.

coping skills, years of stress and worry escalated. I would throw up my food after each meal. I could not even retain water in my stomach. I had become emaciated with a weight of approximately eighty-six pounds. I was so thin a size-three dress hung on me. I had bruises up my spine because I had no padding on my bones; my hipbones looked like a saddle. My father would sit with me at the breakfast table coaching me to eat, but I could not hold it down. I entered a period of depression where I felt my soul had died though my body still existed. I could see myself suspended in darkness—the Valley of the Shadow of Death.

"One evening I could not sleep. I was lying on the living room sofa and my father was sitting in a chair across the room from me. I called out in a whisper, 'God, what is wrong with me?' Instantly, I felt myself move down within, then up and outward. Rather like a U-turn, I felt the most wonderful, gentle, loving, warm wave start at my toes and move up my whole body. I felt love, and on the screen of my inner mind a message was imprinted by God in very large, black, capital letters: 'LOVE.' I left my body through my head and suddenly moved rapidly toward the corner of the ceiling. I did not look back or see my body on the sofa. I was on my way!

"I felt like ducking as the ceiling was only an inch from me, then I was outside, moving through very dark, very vast space. As I moved, I became distracted by something to my left. Looking there, I saw small, round, glowing spheres of light. They seemed like people or spiritual presences. I felt they were lost, sad, and I wanted to help them, but I was not allowed to be sidetracked. I was aware of a presence at my right side keeping me on purpose. I was a point of pure consciousness, racing toward an unknown destination. I felt no fear. I did not miss anyone or anything I left behind.

"Gradually a light started to appear ahead of me. Very rapidly I was

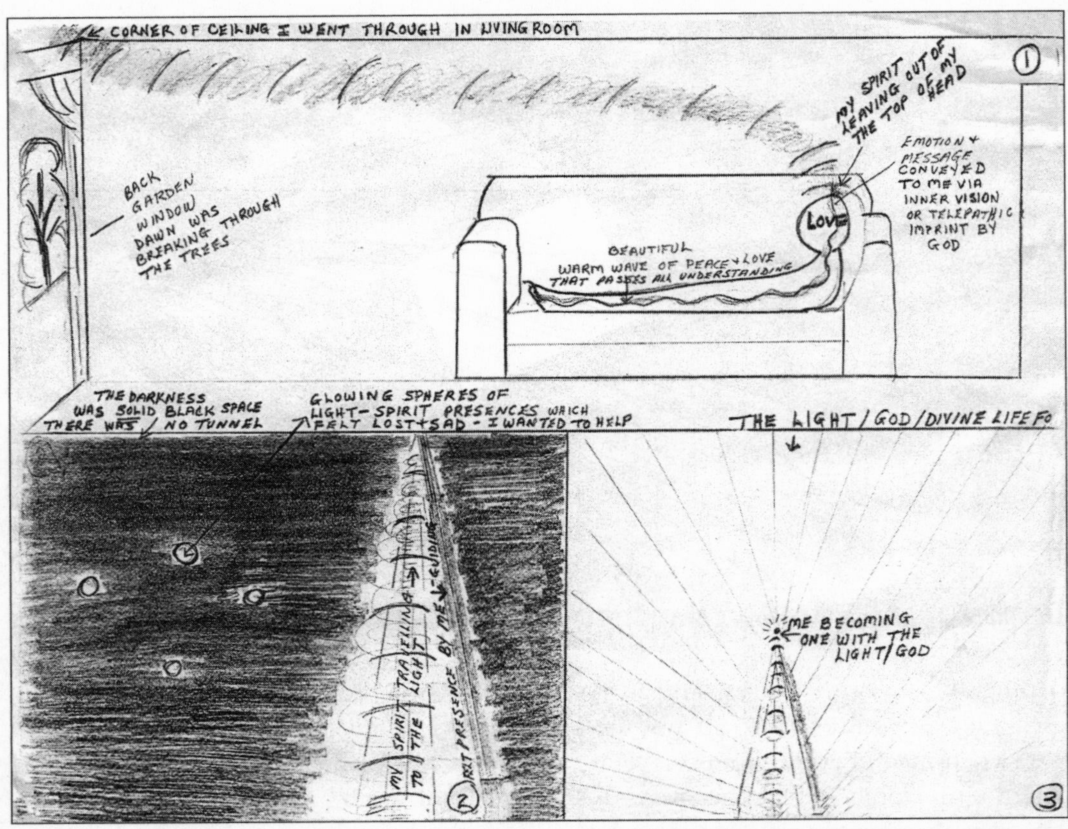

Drawing by Tannis Prouten illustrating her position on the sofa when she left her body. A glowing consciousness without form, she rushed along a passageway of love to become one with God. The circles in the darkness to the left represent souls who were sad and had lost their way.

enveloped within this most divine, living, golden-white light, my HOME. The joy, bliss, humility, awe were beyond human capability to bear. The LIGHT was an infinite, loving, accepting BEING without form. IT had personality. IT communicated with me telepathically. IT was pure TRUTH.

"I was the LIGHT and the LIGHT was me. I was still a unique, separate, point of consciousness with the same sense of humor and awareness that I had always had, but the paradox is that I was MORE. I had become homogeneous with the LIGHT. I was all love, wisdom, truth, peace, joy, for all eternity. Human words fail to express this experience. Not only was the message of my true nature conveyed to me telepathically, but I experienced the SPIRIT of the message—I felt IT with every speck of my being. There was absolutely no possibility of hiding, distorting information, or lying in communicating with the LIGHT. I fell madly in love with the SPIRIT OF TRUTH! There was no concept of space or time in the GREATER REALITY. All takes place or exists in the ETERNAL NOW. That is my last conscious memory of the experience."

Unpleasant and/or Hell-Like Experience

This case comes from Richard Bonenfant, a fellow researcher in Clifton Park, New York (now a resident of Florida where he continues his research in and through various medical centers there). It concerns a boy named Scott who was hit by a car when he was six years old. Richard interviewed both parents as well as Scott. During their session together, Scott's mother handed him notes she had made two years after the accident. From those notes:

"It was supposed to be a small after-dinner treat for our family. We went across the street to get ice cream from the Mr. Ding-a-Ling truck. It was a fun thing for all of us. Scott was excited about crossing the street with me and his older brother Graham, who was nine at the time. I cautioned him to stick with me and was a little frustrated with his distractedness and lack of focus. As I paid for the ice cream, and was thanking the vendor, I became conscious of Scott's movement away from me to my left, while at the same time I became aware of a car coming toward us from the right. I turned toward Scott and yelled, 'Scott! Wait! No! A car!'

"I don't know the precise moment when I knew the car wasn't going to stop. I just know that I dropped the ice cream and started to run. I tasted my terror. It was a physical thing. I lunged after Scott, missing him by about two feet. I saw him look, far too late, to his right, saw the moment of terror flash across his face, saw him try to run faster. I heard the car slam into him, heard the deceleration of the engine and the squeal of its brakes as the driver stopped. There was nothing but silence as I watched the upper half of Scott's body arc away from the car hood, launching him into three complete somersaults in the air as he catapulted away from the car and about twenty-five feet up the street. He settled onto the pavement as if someone were laying him there."

During Richard's interview with Scott, the boy remembered trying to beat the car as he ran to the opposite side. He closed his eyes just before being "punched" by the oncoming vehicle. He recalls that he briefly remembered being inside his body but also watching the accident from the vantage point of a nearby tree until his consciousness shifted to outside his body. "One of the events that seemed strange to him," Richard noted, "was that nobody heard him when he spoke. And when he attempted to hug his father, the father passed right through him. He also recalls shouting to his brother Graham to play with him. His older brother remembered hearing Scott's voice and told his parents that he did at the time of the accident."

> **Devils and Demons**
>
> Occasionally, experiencers describe devils or demonic-type beings who were part of their near-death episodes. Some report torture chambers, moans and screams, and say they were attacked. Of the 18 percent in my research base (if you count child experiencers) who had unpleasant experiences, only a third of them were truly hellish.

Richard continued, "Scott next remembered being in a dark place. That place was peaceful and quiet. Then he felt himself being propelled through a dark tunnel. He described his motion through the tunnel as a combination of floating and being pushed along. It was like a 'wind tunnel,' with the sides whirling around. While going through this dark tunnel Scott encountered the Devil. The Devil accused him of being bad and severely frightened the boy. Scott referred to him as an evil force that was trying to suck him away from God. This entity was described in terms of being male but not conforming to the usual depictions of a black demon with horns and a tail. To Scott, the Devil appeared as a large glob of rotting flesh. He not only was angry and evil, the boy described this Devil as acting sick and crazy at the same time. He shouted to Scott that he was bad and would not be allowed to leave. Scott was extremely frightened at the prospect of being trapped with this creature but had the faith that God would take care of him.

"He next described crossing a room and seeing his uncle, who had died two years earlier. The uncle was covered by the same sheet or blanket that Scott had seen when the uncle was dying of cancer. The man recognized Scott and told him that he would be all right. They conversed in a kind of telepathic way. Following his encounter with his deceased uncle, Scott became aware that he was being 'escorted' through a dark open place toward a distant light. He described the light as being brighter than the sun but it didn't hurt his eyes. He felt that this light was God, and he felt safe in its presence. The light communicated to him somehow that he would be okay. There were other presences in the light, like the angels on a Christmas tree. Scott could not find words to describe them. The best he could do was to state that they did not have wings, or halos, or play 'horns' (trumpets). He said they were clear and bright but had no gender.

"He was next taken to what he calls a dungeon. 'Not the kind in the movies with stone and hay,' but a large dark room without windows or doors where he would be safe from the Devil. Scott feels that he was not alone in this room, but sensed that good beings where there also. The next thing he remembers was waking up in the hospital several hours later. His parents confirmed that he had been kept in an induced coma while being treated for a number of injuries. Scott told his parents about what happened to him the day following recovery. He was plagued with nightmares about the horrific encounter with the Devil for several months after the accident. During the interview, Scott reported that the greatest change in his life resulting from his near-death experience was that he has tried to become closer to God because he doesn't want to ever meet the Devil again. Scott also said that he was often unkind toward others before his near-death experience, but that the episode has made him more sensitive to the feelings of others."

Gracia Fay Ellwood, another researcher, told me about and helped me locate Gloria Hipple of Blakeslee, Pennsylvania, who experienced a hellish episode during setbacks after a miscarriage. "I had been taken to Middlesex Hospital in New Brunswick, New Jersey," Gloria began. "Placed in a ward because I was a military dependent, the doctor who was to care for me never came. I was placed at a forty-five-degree angle due to bleeding and was left that way for almost eight days. No one heard my pleas. By the eighth day, I could not hear anyone, my eyes could not see, and I was later told that my body temperature registered 87.6 degrees. I should have been dead.

Drawing of the Devil done by Scott right after the accident. Tops of the side portions represent skeletal claws and were originally colored green like slime. The body and head were red as a way to show scabs and rotting flesh. The "dd" letters signify the Devil's raspy voice.

"I recall being pulled down into a spinning vortex," continued Gloria. "At first, I did not know what was happening. Then I realized my body was being drawn downward, head first. I panicked and fought, trying to grab at the sides of the vortex. All I could think of was my two children. No one would care for them. I pleaded, 'Please, not now,' but I kept moving downward.

When he was eleven years old, five years after the accident, Scott again attempted to draw what he had seen. Notice the more human-appearing face and the emphasis on "Your bad."

"I tried to see something, but all there was to see was this cyclonic void that tapered into a funnel. I kept grabbing at the sides, but my fingers had nothing to grasp. Terror set in, true terror. I saw a black spot, darker than the funnel and like a black curtain, falling in front of me. Then there was a white dot, like a bright light at the end of the funnel. But as I grew closer, it was a small white skull. It became larger, grinning at me with bare sockets and gaping mouth, and traveling straight toward me like a baseball. Not only was I terrified, I was really livid, too. I struggled to grab hold of anything to keep me from falling, but the skull loomed larger. 'My kids, my baby is so little. My little boy, he's only two years old. No!' My words rang in my head and ears.

Hell's Positive Effect

As is often true with hellish cases, the experience can have a positive effect on the person afterward. Because of her battle with the skull, Gloria Hipple was transformed from someone dependent on the will of others and on the material goods she possessed, to a confident, take-charge individual determined to change her life. The courage she gained from her experience is quite remarkable.

With a bellowing yell, I screamed, 'No! damn it, no! Let me go. My babies need me! No! No! No! No!'

"The skull shattered into fragments and I slowed in movement. A white light, the brightest light I have ever known or will ever see again, was in place of the skull. It was so bright, yet it did not blind me. It was a welcome, calming light. The black spot or curtain was gone. I felt absolute peace of mind and sensed myself floating upward, and I was back. I heard my husband calling me, off in the distance. I opened my eyes but could not see him. Two doctors were at the foot of my bed—both were angry and compassionate at the same time. I was taken to the operating room, given several pints of blood, and was released one week later.

"No one would believe my handshake with the grim reaper. Scoffers almost put me in tears. Everyone laughed at me, including my husband, so I never told my story again until you came along. It was the most horrendous, yet the most gratifying experience I've ever had in my life. I was given a second chance at life. I am blessed and cannot ask for more."

Pleasant and/or Heaven-Like Experience

Gracie L. Sprouse, Keene, Virginia; age eleven, drowning:

"I was swimming with my sisters when suddenly I found myself unable to reach the top of the water for air. I felt like I had just stepped into nothingness. I went down twice and was coming up for the third time when I managed to yell for help. Before I was pulled from the water, I saw a filmstrip of my life. It was just like being in a theater, as I sat cross-legged and watched the things I'd done wrong to my sisters. I was not judged by the angel who showed me this, I judged and convicted myself. The angel hovered in midair, to the upper left of the screen. I remember thinking that I was leaving my family and sisters and started to feel sorrow. The sorrow left immediately and I felt as if I'd been assured they would be fine.

"Then, there was such a feeling of bliss that it's indescribable. Since then, I have had a lifetime of unexplained happenings. My entire outlook is different from the norm. I see with my heart and I know things."

Arthur E. Yensen, Parma, Idaho; age thirty-four, single-car rollover:

A university science graduate and nationally syndicated cartoonist, Art decided to take some time off in 1932 to research his weekly cartoon strip, "Adventurous Willie Wispo." Since his main character was a homeless hobo, he became one for a while, bumming

In this drawing by Gracie L. Sprouse, she depicts the scene where an angel showed her how she had hurt others. This life review was like a filmstrip flashed on a large theater screen.

rides cross-country. A young man in a convertible coupe picked him up on the way to Winnipeg. Driving too fast for road conditions, the man hit a ridge of oiled gravel and flipped the car into a series of violent somersaults. Both men were catapulted through the cloth top of the car before it smashed into a ditch. The driver escaped harm, but Art was seriously injured, losing consciousness as two female spectators rushed to his aid.

"Gradually, the Earth scene faded away," Art recalled, "and through it loomed a bright, new, beautiful world, beyond imagination! For half a minute I could see both worlds at once. Finally, when the Earth was gone, I stood in a glory that could only be heaven.

"In the background were two beautiful, round-topped mountains. The tops were snowcapped, and the slopes were adorned with foliage of indescribable beauty. The mountains appeared to be about fifteen miles away, yet I could see individual flowers growing on their slopes. I estimated my vision to be about one hundred times better than on Earth. To the left was a shimmering lake containing a different kind of water: clear, golden, radiant, and alluring. It seemed to be alive. The whole landscape was carpeted with grass so vivid, clear, and green that it defies description. To the right was a grove of large, luxuriant trees, composed of the same clear material that seemed to make up everything.

"I saw twenty people beyond the first trees, playing a game. They were having a hilarious time. As soon as they saw me, four of the players left the game and joyfully skipped over to greet me. They appeared young, their bodies almost weightless with a grace and

Holy Ones

Religious figures like Jesus, Buddha, Mohammed, or Lord Yama are occasionally seen by near-death experiencers in their episode, but not all that often. The majority are more apt to be greeted by a deceased relative or close friend. There are numerous reports, however, of experiencers encountering beings made entirely of light that seem somehow holy or special. Usually genderless, these holy ones can be regarded by adults as angels or light beings; by children as "bright ones" or "the people." Child experiencers are more likely than adults to see them as winged.

Drawing by Arthur E. Yensen, excerpted with permission from his self-published book, *I Saw Heaven.*

beauty of movement fascinating to watch. Both sexes had long hair entwined with flowers, which hung down in glossy masses to their waists. Their magnificence not only thrilled me, but filled me with awe.

"The oldest, largest, and strongest-looking man announced, 'You are in the land of the dead. We lived on Earth, just like you, til we came here.' He invited me to look at my arm. I looked, and it was translucent; that is, I could dimly see through it. Next they had me look at the grass and trees. They were also translucent. Then I noticed that the landscape was gradually becoming familiar. It seemed as if I had been here before. I remembered what was on the other side of the mountains. Then with a sudden burst of joy, I realized that this was my real home! Back on Earth I had been a visitor, a misfit, and a homesick stranger. With a sigh of relief, I said to myself, 'Thank God I'm back again. This time I'll stay!'

"The oldest man, who looked like a Greek god, continued to explain. 'Everything over here is pure. The elements don't mix or break down as they do on Earth. Everything is kept in place by an all pervading Master-Vibration, which prevents aging. That's why things don't get dirty, or wear out, and why everything looks so bright and new.' Then I understood how heaven could be eternal."

Art did not want to ever leave, but after a lengthy dialogue with the spirit beings, he was told, "You have more important work to do on Earth, and you must go back and do it! There will come a time of great confusion and the people will need your stabilizing influence. When your work on Earth is done, then you can come back here and stay."

Art died in his nineties, after fulfilling what had been asked of him and becoming the quiet benefactor of thousands. His self-published book, *I Saw Heaven* (see appendix C), is still available through his son, Eric Yensen.

Transcendent Experience

Transcendent episodes—those lengthy and complex experiences that involve such things as touring the universe, attending a heavenly university, or seeing all of history from beginning to end—are rare with child experiencers under the age of puberty. Child experiencers of transcendent states tend to be exceptionally protective of what was revealed to them. Adults are a little more open about this, although they can be protective, too. Keep in mind that these scenarios are so powerful they are usually regarded as "sacred." If shared, they tend to challenge all who hear them, not just the ones who experienced them.

Ray Kinman gives us an example of experiences both before and after puberty. Notice that once he is older, his scenario becomes more involved and deeper.

The first one occurred at the age of ten. "I went to Catholic school and was horsing around with a friend after school on the playground. He was showing me a new Judo move that he had learned in his martial arts class. He was going to flip me over his shoulder onto the ground. Something went wrong and I landed directly on my head. I picked myself up from the ground with intense pain in my head and my spine and was going to run to the bathroom, but I fell flat on my face on the concrete. Blacked out completely.

"It felt as if my body had just 'come apart' and my vision went spiraling out of control. Swirling colors seemed to disappear to a point somewhere—like a funnel or something. No, not a tunnel—a funnel. I was really scared. Somehow I knew that I had to just let go of my fear and roll with the funnel of swirling light. My body was gone—it felt like a blender had just ripped it apart. I still had a 'body,' but it was entirely different. I could see in three dimensions as if I had no body at all, but was just a 'floating eyeball.' There were no directions or dimensions as we think of them. I was greeted by a being of Light and Love. It seemed to be just a brilliant glow that absorbed me inside of itself. Love is far too weak a word to describe this experience. I became Love—my entire being, every strand of my spirit spreading throughout the Universe had become Love times a million billion. I found myself in front of some giant golden gates. There was some kind of fog that obscured any sense of direction, but my pet dog Skippy was there. Skippy had died some years earlier and was the only 'person' that I had any real family connection with that was dead. I was overwhelmed with Joy and Love and embraced my dog with my spirit. At this point I was told that I must go back, that it was not my time. If it is possible to describe the 'funnel' experience in reverse, this is what it felt like coming back: It felt like my spirit was being stuffed into a jar that was far too small and painful to hold it. I heard the paramedics. I didn't want to come back but I had to."

The second one happened when Ray was sixteen. "I will skip the details of the death part, as it is far too embarrassing to admit that I had an accidental overdose. When I left my body it was similar to the first time, but much scarier. I thought that I was going crazy, that I must be losing my mind. I started up the same 'funnel' that I saw many years before. It had a much more intense, fragmented feeling and a

Almighty God

Most child experiencers of near-death states describe God as a loving father or grandfather type—always male, never female. The younger the child, the more this is true. Teenagers and adults, however, are more likely to experience God as a sphere of brilliant, all-knowing, all-loving light. If challenged by the experiencer to reveal himself, the figure regarded as God invariably dissolves into a burst of brilliance "brighter than a million suns" and "more powerful than all the bombs on Earth combined into a single blast." This figure is said to be beyond human comprehension and cannot be compared to any other image or presence.

certain 'wrongness' as my ego disintegrated into Spirit. I was frightened and totally out of control. Again I realized that I might as well let go and hang on for the ride, no matter what. The swirling funnel sucked my Spirit out of this world and my body. The intense Love and Peace and pleasure began to overcome me and I was no longer Ray. My ego dissolved, but I had the same sense of humor and the same hangups. I was once again escorted by a Being of immense Light and Love and Holiness, but this time the Being was taking me on a trip.

"Now, this is very difficult to describe. Time ceased to exist. Past and future were completely nonexistent. I was traveling in an intense, burning 'now.' 'Now' was everything. I ceased to be a noun (person, place, or thing) and became a verb (an action). I was Ray-ing instead of Ray. I was given a huge message. The Being told me, 'This is Who You Really Are,' as the Universe opened up to me. I could not tell the difference between myself and the infinite galaxies. I became all-powerful and all-knowing—yet I was still Ray. Then the Being introduced me to another Being of the most Incredible Beauty and Love that anyone could comprehend. It was a Greater Being of intense Light. It was God. The first Being guided me to this Light and let it enfold and swallow me up. I became one with Love times a million, billion, trillion forever and ever. We were made of the same stuff! Every Being that had ever existed in all of Creation was now part of this Greater Whole Being called God. I was one with all of them, and yet I was still Ray—all powerful, little old me!

"'This is Who You Really Are,' thundered the Light. It looked like a galaxy except the points of light were not stars, they were Beings. Every Being there was singing this incredibly beautiful music and praising God. After some indefinite length of Now-ness, I was told that I must go back. I was given another message that was very important. I was told I may return anytime I wished to. Coming back to my body felt like I was stuffed into a vessel of pain and exhaustion."

Mellen-Thomas Benedict, California; thirty-three years old, inoperable brain tumor:

During my interview session with him, Mellen-Thomas told me he had once been an accomplished lighting/cameraman for feature films and had racked up a lifetime of major events before he was thirty. Retiring from the frenzied world of filmdom, he moved to Fayetteville, North Carolina, to be near his parents and operate a stained-glass studio. That's when the diagnosis was made: cancer. His condition worsened rapidly. One morning he awakened knowing he would die that day, and he did. As the typical heaven-like scenario began to unfold, Mellen-Thomas recognized what was happening *as it was happening!*

Just as he reached the light at the end of the tunnel, he shouted, "Stop a minute. This is my death and I want to think about this." By consciously intervening, he willfully changed his near-death scenario into an exploration of realms beyond imagining, and a complete overview of history from the Big Bang to four hundred years into the future.

Then, he was pulled through the light away from the tunnel, far away from Earth, past stars and galaxies, past imagery and physical realities, to a multi-angled overview of all worlds and all Creation, and past even that to a second light at the edge of existence where vibrations cease. He saw all wars from their beginnings, race as personality clusters, species operating like cells in a greater whole. By merging into the matrix of his soul, he confronted the "NO THING" from which all things emerge. Mellen-Thomas saw planetary energy systems in detail and how human thoughts influence these systems in a simultaneous interplay between past, present, and future. He learned that Earth is a great cosmic being. He was aware of "falling" back into his body after deciding to return from his journey; as near as his hospice caretaker could determine, his experience took about ninety minutes. His doctor's assessment, though, was the most shocking—the cancer he had once had completely *vanished.*

"Because this happened to me my fear is gone, and my perspective has changed. You know, we are a very young species. The violence that formed the earth is in us, too. As the earth is mellowing, so are we as a people. Once pollution slows, we will reach a period of sustained consciousness. We have evolved as life forms from single-celled organisms to complex structures, and finally to a global brain. Employment levels will never again be as they once were, which will force a redefinition of human rights. We will adopt a more nurturing type of consciousness, freeing the mind for exceptional achievement. I now know that all the answers to the world's problems are just beneath the surface in US ALL. Nothing is unsolvable."

Since his experience, Mellen-Thomas Benedict has been flooded with ideas for inventions and the marketing plans necessary to promote them. He has been granted a number of U.S. patents and is actively engaged in advanced DNA research on the frontiers of science.

3

Near-Death Look-Alikes

> What's in a name? That which we call a rose, by any other name would smell as sweet.
>
> —William Shakespeare, *Romeo and Juliet*

The International Association for Near-Death Studies sent out a questionnaire in 1992 inquiring about those who considered themselves to be near-death experiencers. How close had they been to physical death when their episode occurred? Of the 229 who replied, 23 percent experienced the phenomenon during actual clinical death, 40 percent at a time of serious illness or trauma, and 37 percent had theirs in a setting unrelated to anything that could be construed as life-threatening.

The 37-percenters claimed to have had experiences every bit as real, involved, and life-changing as those that happened to people during death or close-brush-with-death crises; and their reports duplicate or parallel the same spread of scenario types and a pattern of psychological and physiological aftereffects.

The questionnaire legitimized the large contingent of near-death-like experiences that have consistently been reported over the years, and the growing realization that the physical body's possible demise is not tantamount to undergoing such a state. What we now know is that you can have a near-death look-alike under just about any condition imaginable, as it's truly a random and unpredictable event.

Near-Death-Like Experiences

The *near-death-like experience* has been made an official category in near-death studies. These states can be heavenly or hellish, pleasant or distressing, or brief or lengthy, just as with those of

> **New Words**
>
> It's possible to experience the near-death phenomenon without being physically challenged by the onset of death. An individual may be terrified by what seems to be imminent death, only to be rescued or saved before the worst happens. Or experiencers can be engaged in everyday life routines when such an episode suddenly occurs. These episodes are considered **near-death-like experiences.**

the near-death phenomenon. And, as is true of the latter, value and meaning are determined by the aftermath as well as the changes that experiencers undergo.

What triggers a near-death-like experience? There's some research in the field to indicate that *perception* might be a deciding factor. In other words, a near-death-like experience can be prompted by the perception an individual has that death is imminent, whether true or not.

A Close Call

To explore the idea that the state of our mind might be more important than the state of our body, let's consider the case of Julian A. Milkes, whose near-death-like experience was devoid of body illness or injury.

I met Julian on a bumpy train ride to Long Island Sound, where I was slated to speak at a near-death study group meeting in Syosset, New York. He is a retired teacher and was returning that day from buying concert tickets in Times Square. Here is what he told me. "My mother and I were driving out to the lake one afternoon. My dad was to follow later when he finished work. We were having company for dinner, and, as we rode along, my mother spotted some wildflowers at the side of the road. She asked if I wouldn't stop the car and pick them as they would look nice on the dinner table."

Julian continued: "I pulled over to the right side of the road (it was not a major highway), parked the car, and went down a small incline to get off the road to pick the flowers. While I was picking the flowers, a car came whizzing by and suddenly headed straight for me.

"As I looked up and saw what I presumed would be an inevitable death, I separated from my body and viewed what was happening from another perspective. My whole life flashed in front of me, from that moment backward, to segments of my life. The review was not like a judgment. It was passive, more like an interesting novelty.

"I can't tell you how many times I think of that near-death experience. It seems as though it happened only yesterday." Julian was not hurt. The speeding car veered off just as suddenly as it had appeared, and sped away. His perception of what seemed to be his fate apparently initiated or was somehow important in jump-starting what I identified in the previous chapter as an initial type of near-death scenario—complete with life-changing effects.

A Horrible Encounter

Unlike Julian, a woman, who asked to remain anonymous, had an unpleasant, more hellish type of experience, not because she thought she was going to die, but because she was frightened out of her wits when she sensed a malevolent, unseen "presence" that seemed threatening to her.

The woman was attending a psychic development class at a spiritualist church when she suddenly bolted out the door after sensing a negative energy that horrified her. Later, when she was alone and preparing for bed, she was overwhelmed by a dark tunnel that had formed in midair. She was fully conscious and wide awake, yet the power of the spinning vortex sucked her in. The tunnel was real and large, and she was beside herself with fear. Inside it there was no light, just suffocating darkness. The woman fought back, hitting the tunnel sides, demanding that it release her and leave her alone. After what seemed to be a fight for her life, the tunnel disappeared as quickly as it had come.

She became convinced later on that the event must have been a negative near-death experience. The fact that she was in perfect physical health and not in the throes of a real-life, potentially fatal condition when her experience took place was inconsequential to her in arriving at this conclusion. It was that the tunnel matched everything she had ever read or heard about hellish, near-death episodes. It's possible that the negative energy she first encountered in the church may have manifested as the dark tunnel or somehow influenced the tunnel's formation. In other words, she could have brought it home with her. This cannot be determined for certain, however.

New Word

I have observed this unique mental state with countless others. The terror of imminent death—the type of fear that sees no hope, no other outcome but death itself—is sometimes enough to push people into a near-death-like episode, with the same pattern of aftereffects as a near-death state. Today, researchers refer to this as a **fear-death experience**.

A Key Determinant

Research has been ongoing to try and understand accounts such as the previous two. Glen O. Gabbard, MD, of the C. F. Menninger Memorial Hospital in Topeka, Kansas, and Stuart W. Twemlow, MD, of the University of Kansas School of Medicine in Wichita, have spent more than a decade investigating out-of-body experiences and the near-death phenomenon. They coauthored an article that asked "Do 'Near-Death Experiences' Occur Only Near Death?" that was published in the *Journal of Near-Death Studies* (see appendix C).

They confirmed their original supposition that: "The perception of being near-death, independent of the actual reality of the situation, is the key determinant of the classical [near-death experience]." They went on to establish that with such episodes the state of a person's mind is more important than the state of his or her body.

www.sacredcowsonline.com www.cafepress.com/sacredcows

The Unpredictability of Near-Death-Like Episodes

What about cases where ordinary people are doing ordinary things, with nary a thought about anything more important than their next cup of coffee, when—pow!—the very air in the room parts and out pops a near-death scenario, or something akin to it? How do you explain that? Perception is not a determinant in such episodes. So what is?

Consider this example: A woman in Waynesboro, Virginia, stepped out on her front porch one Sunday morning and bent over to pick up the newspaper. As she stood, she glanced at the rising sun and was immediately enveloped by a light bigger and brighter than anything she had seen before. She left her body and traveled out into space, viewing Earth and its history from a point apart, unifying, as she did, with all Creation. (To put it another way, she became one with every molecule and cell, as if she and Creation were one and the same.) She experienced a reliving of her years since birth, knew and understood what she was here for, then returned to consciousness so overcome by what had happened that she withdrew from "regular" living and sought out a contemplative lifestyle.

Or consider the following.

An Adult's Walk to Heaven

The late Haisley Long of Montreal, Quebec, Canada, had a near-death-like experience under conditions as simple and routine as what happened to the woman in Virginia. He was watching television, got up, walked across his living room floor to open the window, turned, and walked back to his chair, when the room lit up and he found himself "on the outskirts of heaven."

The experience was the most beautiful, brilliant thing that had ever happened to him. As he walked into this light-filled world, he was overcome by the power he encountered. He claimed that it was millions of times more potent than humans can imagine, a power that welcomes you into it. Waves of unselfish love and unlimited knowledge nearly "blew him away."

As Haisley explained: "I wondered how I was able to withstand this. It was like standing in front of a huge star, and being amazed at the power a star can pump out, then having the star go supernova and the power jump incredibly, but you're not fried. It was total ecstasy. More and more waves came. You just cry and cry and cry, while waves wash you and clean you and remove what little pieces of humanity are left stuck to you, so that when you go into heaven you are as perfect as the environment you are in.

"I became aware that there was someone standing next to me: Jesus. When I looked at Jesus, I saw myself. How can this be more me than I am myself? It was like looking at a big mirror. So I reached out to try and touch Jesus, and I did. The word that exploded in my mind was expansion, and I started to use, to blend and become part of the Awareness of Consciousness Himself, Jesus. I absorbed all the information, all at once.

"It was not necessary to ask a lot of questions while I was there. The answers to all my questions were given to me and locked into my head."

But here's what may be the most intriguing and thought-provoking aspect of his encounter: "Before this experience," Haisley said, "I had no interest, and paid no attention to biblical matters whatsoever. For myself, it took a trip to heaven, and to come into contact with Life directly, going through the gates of heaven, traveling at the speed of thought through Life's presence, and coming into contact with God in His natural state, before I turned to biblical matters."

Haisley returned from his experience radically transformed; friends hardly recognized him. Zealously, he began sharing what he learned during his experience, and expounding on "the real substance" of biblical scripture. What he had to say amazed a number of theologians who heard him, especially since he had never read the Bible before his near-death-like experience.

Haisley died quite suddenly a few years ago, after he had inspired a host of people to reexamine and rediscover the Christian Bible.

Intensity—the Difference

Some researchers state that the entire span of a near-death experience is merely differing aspects of the out-of-body phenomenon. For those who have experienced both an OBE and NDE, there is no question that the latter are far more intense, powerful, and life-changing than the perception or sensed reality of leaving one's body as if a consciousness apart. This conviction is also maintained by near-death-like experiencers, whose episode matched or came close to the NDE model—even if the prospect of dying was not a factor. OBE states are commonly an aspect of the larger genre, but do not define it.

A Child's Nighttime Surprise

Margaret Evans of Roscoe, Illinois, experienced a near-death-like episode when she was six. She and her twin sister were sound asleep in the same room when, for no apparent reason, Margaret sat bolt upright. That is to say, half of her did, the half that projected out of her body.

Exploring Consciousness Itself

"In my view, the only possible empirical approach to evaluate theories about consciousness is research on NDE, because in studying the several universal elements that are reported during NDE, we get an opportunity to verify all the existing theories about consciousness that have been discussed until now. Consciousness presents temporal as well as everlasting experiences. Is there a start or an end to consciousness?"

—Pim van Lommel, MD, from "Brain Death and Disorders of Consciousness" (see appendix C)

"I looked straight at this being of light, just a little off to my left, but in my line of vision," Margaret said. "The being generated the white-gold light I was bathed in—a very soothing, accepting, loving light. It was very bright but not hard on my eyes. The angel was neither male nor female and had no distinct features, just the sense of them. Communication between us was telepathic. My first thought was a remembrance that this moment had been prearranged between us before my birth. It was an opportunity for me to leave this life if I so desired, and the angel was there to offer me that choice.

"To my right, coming out of the light, were my dead grandparents. They were kinda like on the other side of a doorway. I knew they were there, but I couldn't see them. I wanted to go to them so badly. I was happy about the reunion waiting for us, but then I turned and somehow saw my sister and myself still asleep in bed. I thought of my parents in the other room and how I would miss them if I left. They would be very hurt. I decided to stay."

Margaret claims that as soon as she made the decision, the angel told her she would live a long life, and then disappeared, along with her grandparents and the light. Never once did she ever regret her decision to stay, as "the angel and my deceased grandmother have protected me throughout the years since."

Indirect Near-Death-Like Events

We've had an opportunity to see just how unpredictable near-death-like experiences can be. Even though near-death episodes center around or are offshoots of the death of the physical body, near-death-like events are much more random in their occurrence. And nobody knows why or what causes them.

I've noticed, though, that there are certain conditions common to the majority of cases. These conditions revolve around the reality of death (the possibility of yours or the reality of someone else's), an incidence of unusually strong emotions or high stress, or a sudden but powerful upwelling of spiritual inspiration, specifically:

- The perception of probable death
- Being in close proximity to another's death
- While attending or taking part in a funeral

- An immediate and overwhelming fear
- Unusually difficult bouts of stress
- An intense unitive experience
- Vivid visualizations that register as real

New Words

Unitive experiences are those in which an individual suddenly and unexpectedly becomes "one with all things." They are hyperstates of a radiant, luminous consciousness that unify or bring together in "oneness" the Creator with the Created. Ego boundaries and physical borders vanish; the sense of "separateness" is replaced by an identification with spiritual totality. Religious writings are filled with such accounts.

At the Deathbed

A near-death-like experience that was the result of being in close proximity to another's death is what happened to Julia Clasby of Surrey, England, when her husband George died. As Julia tells it: "I truly feel that 'God' saw that I needed a giant kick in the pants to get me 'moving'—so he kick-started me with George's death. I was ignoring the signposts, markers, and 'hints' he'd been placing in my life, and I needed an awakening. When God plays reveille, you listen! This is the sense in which I feel I had a near-death experience by proxy. George did the dying, but I got the salutary lesson."

Julia, in her communications with me, described the days leading up to George's death. But it wasn't until afterward, when she was allowed into the hospital room to be alone with his corpse, that a most unusual thing happened. "Up until the moment I knew George had died, I never thought much about life after death and what it all 'means.' In fact, I quite arrogantly used to show how 'sensible' I was by saying, 'Once you're gone, you're gone—that's it, finished.'

"I arrived an hour after George was pronounced dead. A nurse escorted me into the room and then left me shortly afterward. I started talking to him [George]. I sensed he was still around, though, more definitely, not in his body, and in a bad temper. I felt he was angry and frustrated at being dead and was holding me responsible for his misfortune. As I was having a one-sided conversation with him, I was addressing the corner of the room near the ceiling. His 'Georgeness' was disembodied and I couldn't touch him. Touching his physical body offered me no comfort because I knew he wasn't inhabiting it anymore. I kept speaking to the top corner of the room."

Shortly before his death, George talked about "visits" he had been having with deceased friends. Julia accepted this, but the medical staff was not so understanding. "The nurse later told me that he didn't know where he was at the end. I don't believe that. I believe that he was having a pre-death vision and was conversing with his dead Hungarian friends, one who had recently died," said Julia.

"George hasn't been back to 'haunt me' or manifest in any way, but I have been 'different' ever since I spoke to

Watch Out for Corners

In those scenarios in which the near-death or near-death-like experiencer had an out-of-body episode, those I spoke with said they first viewed their body either from a point directly above or from a top corner of the room. Many claimed that after vacating their body, they "floated" elsewhere in a bodiless state. Initially, though, the main "staging area" was the left side of the room, especially the upper left corner. A few spoke of being drawn to the right side, almost always to a ceiling corner.

him in the hospital room," she continued. "Since his funeral, I notice that I 'become one with' my environment very easily now, have more inner strength, no longer need the approval of others, somehow attract and calm animals, am able to 'read' what people want, can feel energy, have become quite sensitive to energy fields, am more intuitive and creative, more knowing."

Julia Clasby has remarried. Yet she closely identifies with near-death experiencers in the sense that she, too, exhibits many of the aftereffects typical of near-death states—traits such as she described here, plus a heightened sensitivity to light and sound (these are detailed in chapter 7).

While Saying Good-bye

A dream that wasn't a dream happened to a young man named Mark in Provo, Utah. "Two days after my twelfth birthday," recalled Mark, "my parents were involved in a terrible accident that took both of their lives. It was a Sunday, and I was down at the baseball field at the time, about three blocks from home. We heard the crash, and were puzzled because our first impression was that of a car backfiring. Some friends of my parents picked me up. My oldest brother flew in from Iowa, and advised me not to go to the funeral. I didn't.

"The next Sunday, my older brother ordained me a deacon in the LDS (Mormon) Church. Many people came to the ordination. That evening as I lay in bed, I was very sad that my parents were not there. I wept silently and prayed that I would be able to see my parents 'just one more time.' I kept repeating this, until I felt satisfied of the communication with God and fell asleep.

"I found myself in a place distant from Earth, although I could see Earth below me. I had the most intense feeling of peace, glory, and joy, which continued with me all during the experience. I thought I was dead, but immediately felt no worries, no cares about that. This place gave me such a good feeling that I wanted to stay there forever. I was allowed to see selected things, and became aware that I was in a 'dressing room.' A married couple there dressed me in a beautiful white robe. They were not my parents.

"I then left the room by a door at one end. I saw my father standing about fifteen yards away. I ran to meet him, but he motioned me to stay back. He was a spirit, a just man, and did not want to confuse or deceive me, because his form was not the material element that I knew before. My father was dressed in typical clothes, a short-sleeved shirt and dark-colored slacks. Then my mother walked in from my father's left side. They stood close together and were talking, but I couldn't hear them. I could determine what they were saying by watching the expressions on their faces.

"Mother was worried about what would become of me. My father told her not to worry, that everything had been taken care of. This visit with my parents lasted less than two minutes perhaps, but the comfort I received by knowing of the wonderful and beautiful place where they are has comforted me all my life. When I was led away from them, a guide explained things. I did not see him but felt his presence. While seeing the Earth below again, I realized that if I had died during this experience, my aunt would be very sorrowful. After all, she had just lost my parents that week. It was then that the vision ended and I woke up in bed."

Mark emphasized that his "trip" was not like any dream he had ever had before or since, and that it changed him utterly. "My experience was that of visiting my parents for real in the spirit world." The aftereffects he has had since this event closely match those of the near-death phenomenon. Again, like Julia and the others, changes can be extensive and include such characteristics as unusually heightened sensitivities and sensations, as well as many other psychological and physiological differences.

During a Brutal Murder

Barbara Ivanova witnessed a man kill a woman with a knife on a street in Moscow, Russia. She ran over to help the woman but fell down a few feet from the body. Half-conscious, she began to whisper "Help me, help me," as if speaking for the dying woman. She then began to see images in her mind of a time as a child when she was wearing a dress strange to her and playing with large toys. Her solar plexus hurt, as if life was being extracted from her. She kept pleading for help until the ambulance arrived, then lost consciousness and was carried home by a stranger.

"This was no dream," said Barbara. "It was very real. I seemed to be experiencing her life review, as the inner pictures I was receiving were not mine." The pain in her solar plexus continued for days—at the exact spot where the woman had been stabbed. Barbara is convinced that she unwittingly became the woman's *surrogate*!

I hope by now you have a sense of how broad-ranging near-death-like experiences can be. What all of the cases presented so far have in common is an unusual intensity of effect, rather than any particular condition or scenario imagery. This confounds the research community. Yet there may be a plausible explanation if you're willing to consider a radical thought: Maybe near-death states are not a singular, separate phenomenon, but part of a larger one—transformations of consciousness. We'll explore this idea in part 4.

> **New Words**
>
> A **surrogate** is a substitute, a stand-in, one who acts in place of another.

A Startling Revelation

It is estimated that seventy million people from all walks of life have experienced the extraordinary when mourning. Melvin Morse, MD, suggested that a majority of widows and parents who have lost children have visions of the departed within a year of death (Morse and Perry, 1994).

Andrew Greeley (1987) and the University of Chicago's National Opinion Research Council found that 42 percent of the U.S. population answered in the affirmative to the question, "Have you ever felt you have been in contact with someone who died?" He went on to write an article about this entitled, "Mysticism Goes Mainstream," which was published in the Jan/Feb 1987 issue of *American Health Magazine*.

Widows and widowers commonly report evidence that suggests their counterparts have survived (Gallup and Proctor, 1982).

Shared Journeys

The ability to co-participate in another's death usually happens in one of three ways: by accident, by being open and receptive to the opportunity, or on purpose, with the individual willfully projecting his or her awareness into the situation. For those who choose to, guided visualizations (see the next section) help to set the stage; what seems to work best is a visualization experience patterned after a near-death scenario.

In the meantime, let's discuss accounts that relate to the "deathbed" experience and the effect this can have on the living. Although technically not near-death-like states, these episodes can be perceived in that manner, especially since they occasionally engender life-changing effects afterward that are on a par with those of near-death states.

Empathic Experiences

An increasing number of people present at the deathbed are admitting that they consciously share in the moment of death as it happens. Researchers like myself are receiving more and more reports concerning these "empathic" experiences, in which one individual "becomes one with," "takes on," or "witnesses fully" the death experience of another individual. These events are not superficial, nor do they consist of fanciful imaginings, but are occurrences that involve all the senses and are accepted as absolutely real.

For instance, one woman told me that as she sat next to the bed where her brother lay dying, she began to hear soft melodious music. She looked around to see if a radio was on, and, as she did, a brilliant light filled the room. She turned just in time to see her comatose brother open his eyes, smile, and raise his arms upward. Then, "As real as anything I've ever seen, a being of light reached out and took my brother by his wrists and pulled. My brother's spirit popped right out of his physical body—snap—just like that. I was so surprised, I jumped." With eyes wide open, she witnessed the being of light and her brother, now in spirit, float out of the hospital room through a mist-like archway that had formed in a nearby ceiling corner. There was a scent of roses around where the discarded body shell lay.

The woman was awestruck for months afterward, unfazed by the fact that she was the only other person in the room. "No matter," she told me. "What I saw was sacred and holy, and I was privileged to be there. I don't care who believes me and who doesn't." To say this event transformed her life would be an understatement.

There are increasingly numerous stories like hers—coming from people unafraid to speak up about the subject of death and what it's like to be there in love and support when someone dies. The ability to view a soul's departure appears to be on the increase, judging by the numbers who admit they have done it.

What Happened in Russia

A 2005 television documentary produced by BBC and HBO focused on the children who survived the Chechen terrorist takeover of their school in Beslan followed by fights with Russian Specnaz forces. One girl, who had lost her mother and many friends during the siege, said that her friend and schoolmate (a boy) had come to her several times in her dreams and later in a classroom in her new school. The boy told her, "I did not die. I still live. Can you see me? I am sitting with my friend in one desk."

Near-Death Scenarios as Guided Visualizations

Empathic experiences are shared experiences, where two or more join together in consciousness and feeling. These episodes are heartfelt and can be quite involved and detailed. In situations where someone is about to die, empathic events can be so intense that those who remain on this side of death's curtain usually undergo a major life change following the event.

Here are some suggestions for dealing with empathic experiences, considering the three ways they usually occur:

1. *Accidentally.* As with the woman and her dying brother, the actual moment of death is unpredictable. If you're not alert, you could miss it. What might prepare you is to know the common precursor "signals," such as the suddenness of soft music, a pleasant smell, light that brightens, a glow around the dying person, changes in his or her behavior that indicate a heightening of awareness, and a sense or feeling of an unseen presence. Should any of these things occur, immediately look at the dying individual and allow your vision to diffuse (as if you were looking past him or her). Relax. Wait. You may sense more than you see.

2. *By invitation.* This involves knowing about the "signals" just mentioned, clues that alert you to what may be about to occur, and the willingness to relax, wait patiently, and be open and receptive. More important, though, intention is involved. Your desire to be

> ### Holding the Door Open
>
> According to Bruce Horacek, PhD, professor at University of Nebraska at Omaha, empathic experiences enable a person to share the emotions and imagery of the dying process with the one about to die. This act inspires and uplifts all who participate, and "holds open the door" to glimpses of eternity. Many times, the individual who remains is forever changed by the experience, to the point of displaying later on some of the aftereffects of near-death states.

an active participant needs to be admitted and prearranged, either with the dying individual, if that person is capable of communicating, or with the family. Once the appropriateness of your being there has been established, I recommend that you:

- Consider your role as being that of a helper
- Telepathically "tell" the dying individual this, if he or she cannot respond
- Hold his or her hand, if possible
- Reassure the individual that it's okay to "leave"
- Be in touch with your own feelings and inner promptings
- "See" yourself "walking" him or her into the light, if it feels right to do so
- Allow subjective imagery to arrange itself by itself
- Withhold any tendency to force or control the situation, or go farther than the initial entry into the light
- Offer a prayer or some form of positive upliftment
- Share on whatever level feels right, then let go, and release

3. *Pre-planned and guided.* The next step with empathic experiences, if agreed upon by all parties, is to prepare in advance for the death event with the one about to die. You must be comfortable with your role in this preparatory exercise—relaxed, respectful, and in a spiritual frame of mind. Prayer or some form of positive upliftment is helpful to begin, then do a guided visualization using the basic elements of near-death states as a pattern:

- Pace your breathing with that of the dying individual. Should his or her breathing be erratic, calm things down with your own steady breaths.

- Talk softly, saying that the individual is now leaving his or her body and floating upward. Speak of how easy and effortless this is, how good to leave the heaviness and the pain of the physical body behind.

- Acknowledge the gathering of simple shapes and forms in the air, dark or light, as if something were coming together. The body may still be seen down below, but the fascination now is with what seems to be forming midair.

- Affirm the presence of a special light that is slowly growing brighter and brighter, but does not hurt the eyes to see.

- Mention that any sudden sense of

speed is okay, that it's all right to go faster and faster, and feel a wind brushing your face.

- Prepare the individual for an abrupt stop and an increase in light, and for the presence of strangely familiar but melodious music and sweet smells.
- Greet those who might appear, be they a loved one, angel, light being, religious figure, or pet or other type of animal.
- Encourage engagement, dialogue, talking, or a question-and-answer session, and to whatever degree feels right.
- Remain for a while, then return as you came, back to Earth, back to the individual's body.
- Linger with the feeling of being back, continuing to talk softly to the individual in a reassuring manner until he or she opens both eyes or when you sense that sleep has come.

Should you use a guided visualization such as this, or something like it, remember to involve all the senses. The more you get into it, the more feelings and sensations you can describe and invite, the more successful you will be. Once may be enough, or several times may be necessary. Eyes open or closed really makes no difference if the intensity is there and if the imagery is vivid, nor does it matter if the dying individual is conscious, asleep, or comatose. The brain can still register what is being said, in most cases.

Empathic experiences, like many other near-death-like states, can be life-changers for all involved. The depth of intimacy and core spirituality that can be reached through them is quite extraordinary. Whether done as part of a religious ritual or a simple sharing of love and support, they can and often do mimic or duplicate the near-death phenomenon.

4

The Innocents

> Suffer the little children to come unto me, and forbid them not: for such is the kingdom of God.
>
> —Mark 10:14

As we've already seen, children, too, have near-death episodes—experiences that occur, as you would expect, after toddlerhood, or, most intriguingly, prior to or even during birth. Moreover, 50 percent of those people I interviewed could remember the circumstances of their births! These memories were verified as accurate by the mothers I was able to contact. Often, how they describe what it was like for them while still in the womb is delightfully and utterly funny. One little boy lamented, "I couldn't stand up in there."

Another complained about intestinal noise when his mother ate food that did not agree with her. One child shrugged off any desire for more freedom of movement while cramped in the fetal position by simply saying, "I just sucked my thumb and waited to get out."

Most, though, describe the process of birth as scary, "with a lot of heaviness and force pushing me around." Some say it hurt, others say it wasn't so bad. Remembering their births is but one of

Through Eyes of Children

Child experiencers of near-death states are studied by adults who use adult models for research comparisons, bypassing, for the most part, how the children regard themselves and what happened to them. My book *The New Children and Near-Death Experiences* (see appendix C) is the first large research project to focus on seeing through children's own eyes what they do and feel.

Shorter for Kids

Children's scenarios are usually brief, generally consisting of one to three elements. Of the four types of near-death states I identified in chapter 2, 76 percent of the child experiencers I interviewed had the initial kind. The majority journeyed out of their bodies as part of their scenario and returned with details impossible for them to have known otherwise—details that were later verified.

the unique characteristics of child near-death experiencers. There are other occurrences that are unique to their episodes that are not shared by adults. For the most part, though, scenario elements and types are virtually identical for both.

Child Experiences: A Breakthrough in Understanding

The original scientific study of children's near-death experiences was published by Melvin Morse, a pediatrician, in the late 1980s. He was intrigued by one of his young patients, a child by the name of Katie, who, though rescued from certain death in a watery grave, lingered at death's door for three days. When she finally revived, she surprised the doctor with a tale of a strange and wonderful spiritual journey she had taken while everyone else thought she was dying. Katie was the first of the children too young to have absorbed adult attitudes about death that Dr. Morse studied, who described experiences consistent with what Raymond Moody had discovered (see chapter 1). Thanks to an open-ended grant from the National Cancer Institute, Dr. Morse went to work. He wanted to know if he could detect any medical explanation for children's stories like Katie's, or if somehow these kids were tapping into another reality, perhaps life beyond death. What he found became the subject of his best-selling book, *Closer to the Light* (refer to appendix C).

Other health-care professionals have since come to the fore—atheist docs and disbelieving nurses who made a complete U-turn in their religious and spiritual beliefs after encountering children who had near-death experiences. Today, the fear of being ostracized by their peers has lessened greatly, giving way to a friendlier climate for discussing what they, too, have found. Many books have followed; most of them are collections of child near-death accounts that inspired this book's author.

I've encountered hundreds of child experiencers, and I've come to find that the heavy emphasis others place on what kids say is sometimes problematic. Since kids are highly susceptible to the influence of parents, teachers, and other authority figures, they can—and sometimes do—alter their reports in order to please. Because of this, I learned early on to be very cautious when interviewing the young.

Also, as near-death studies are primarily adult-centered, children's scenarios are often characterized as simply miniature versions of adult accounts.

That's not always so. For example, children's reports have, for the most part, a special purity and boldness that adult cases seldom have. Kids get right to the point—if no one interferes with their storytelling or shames them for what they have to say. For this reason, their stories can be very surprising—even startling.

Needing to Be with Her Daddy

The following news item (dated February 1996, Richmond, Virginia) was sent to me by Pat Kennedy, a friend of the family involved:

> A mother with two small daughters lost control of her car and flipped it over in a ditch. The oldest nearly lost a leg, and three-year-old Victoria died. Refusing the grim verdict, a police officer began CPR (cardiopulmonary resuscitation) on Victoria's lifeless body. Five minutes later the little girl breathed. Her first words were: "I saw Jesus. But he told me it wasn't my time and I need to go back and be with my daddy." The child's grandfather, a man who drank heavily and "messed around," was so overcome by Victoria's message that he quit drinking and started to read the Bible.

Not Wanting to Cause Sorrow

Celeste Weitz, of Yuma, Arizona, recalls:

> At just a few months old, while sleeping in my father's arms as he sat on the porch, he

Kids' Books

Denise Mendenhall, with the help of her father, Doug, wrote *In His Arms* about her near-death scenario and its aftermath. This is the first book known to be written by a child experiencer—*while still a child.*

Although written thirty years after the fact, the book *A Journey with the Angel of Light,* by Aafke H. Holm-Oosterhof, remains today one of the most vivid accounts of a child's near-death experience written by a child experiencer once grown. Artwork by Aafke was painted as remembered.

Kathy Forti, who had her near-death experience as a young teen, used what happened to her to write *The Door to the Secret City*—as a way to help other children. She has gone on to write other children's books. (She was shown that she would do this in her episode; her case is detailed in my book *Future Memory.*)

Carol McCormick wrote *A Bridge for Grandma,* basing her storybook for the very young on what she learned about children's near-death episodes.

Linda A. Jacquin, a child experiencer of a near-death state, was the consultant for the grade-school book *Near-Death Experiences,* written by Michael Martin. This book is part of a series through Capstone Press that features *The Unexplained.* Recommended for students from third to sixth grade.

(Refer to appendix C for a complete listing of each book.)

realized I had 'died,' apparently without cause (sudden infant death syndrome?). My mother rushed to call the fire department. By the time she came back, she says my father got me breathing again. She does not know how. What I remember is coming back (from where I don't remember), and hovering above and somewhat behind my father's right shoulder. There were 'others' with me. I didn't see them, but have a strong sense that they were there. These beings seemed to have no physical shape; they, like I, consisted of light. My father was extremely distressed and was yelling something that started with a 'B.' Seeing no reason for his distress I was confused—everything was great as far as I was concerned. Upon realizing his distress was due to my not being in the body, I became somewhat upset that I was responsible for the state he was in. This is the point I believe I chose to go back to the body.

Celeste Weitz drew this scene from the perspective of hovering above and to the right of her father, as he held her body—a scene still fresh in her memory to this day.

Being Both Loved and Disbelieved

Tonecia Maxine McMillan, of Oxon Hill, Maryland, talks about an incident that happened to her when she was eleven. "I was on an inner tube in the water off a beach in Delaware. I had ventured out too far. My grandmother (who raised me, as I never lived with my siblings) motioned for me to come back to shore. I misjudged the depth. I stepped out of the inner tube and began to drown. I left my body. I could see myself in the water. I saw my grandmother trying to come and get me, and I saw my brother cut his left foot.

"Then I was in a very beautiful, peaceful, picturesque place like a meadow. I felt very loved. The colors were brilliant; they were nothing like I have ever seen before. There is simply no comparison—the yellows, greens—so very beautiful, so peaceful. During the time of my drowning, I was on a 'black beach,' so to speak. Delaware still was practicing segregation. I was told that two white men were on the beach at the time. These two men saved my life by pulling me to shore, *then they simply disappeared.*

On the way to the hospital, when I asked my brother how his cut foot was doing, I was met with stony silence. He couldn't deal with the fact that I saw his accident while I was out of my body."

A Guide at Death's Door

Children who experience near-death states, like adults, often describe a "greeter." It seems to be the greeter's job to welcome or warn, depending on the circumstances, and to guide the individual deeper into the experience. Typical greeters are:

- *Deceased relatives and friends*—always authentic as to whom (even if not previously known), but seldom historically correct as to age and appearance when last seen. These people are usually experienced as younger, brighter, healthier, and happier than when the experiencer knew them.

- *Animals and deceased pets*—appearing as "friends" or "guides"; on occasion they speak telepathically. Physical sensations of being licked, rubbed, pawed, or nosed by the animal are felt and enjoyed. Usually only smaller animals appear (besides pets). The most common are birds and bunnies.

- *A religious figure*—experienced as an "extra-special being of love," yet is referred to in terms consistent with the experiencer's exposure to religious training and social traditions, which can be rather strict. For instance, in Thailand, religious greeters in children's scenarios are referred to as Yamatoots, servants of the Lord Yama (God of the Underworld). Seldom are Yamatoots seen as friendly.

- *Spirit beings*—run the gamut from heavenly angels to threatening demons. Usually talkative or instructive, they can also convey a "mountain of messages" simply by their presence or with a single look.

Previews for Kids

"Children often see the effect their death will cause for those left behind," says Cherie Sutherland, PhD, an Australian researcher of near-death states. She notes that many are also given their purpose for being alive, or told what their "mission" is that they need to accomplish once grown.

Skin Tones

Even though child experiencers in my research identified religious greeters in terms typical to their upbringing, they were consistent about racial skin color. Jesus and Mohammed, for instance, had brown skin, Buddha, yellowish—irrespective of historical record, or of the child's own race or exposure to other races. Future studies are needed with child experiencers, to further explore this and other findings about the greeters they describe.

Heavenly Criticism

A variation of the critical parent greeter may be the life review reported by so many teenage and adult experiencers, in which individuals are given an opportunity to witness and relive how their actions affected others. Some report a tribunal "hearing" (judges actually judging them for past indiscretions, errors, and mistakes); most claim that it was "me judging me." Regarding life judgments, children seem mostly to be given "instruction" or "lectures" about their lives; tweens, teens, and adults are "shown" their life in a review or preview. A parental type of being usually leads the kids through this instruction process; older experiencers are most often left to make their own discoveries and instigate behavioral changes by themselves.

- *Deity*—for the young, always described as a male, most often a kindly father or grandfather type; for teenagers and adults, predominantly encountered is a huge sphere of all-knowing, all-loving light that is brighter than a million suns.

Lectures and Judgment

It's not unusual for child experiencers to be met on the other side of death's door by a being whose role is that of a critical or loving "parent." This parental figure can give orders, judge the child for past misdeeds, or threaten punishment; he or she can also heap praise and encouragement upon the child and offer comfort, reassurance, and aid. Often, this particular type of greeter seems to serve a greater purpose—to prepare the youngster for his or her destiny, and conduct advance instruction in behavior. Many times, foreknowledge of events yet to come is conferred as a special gift.

Images of a critical or loving parent-type are found most often in near-death cases from Asia and indigenous cultures, especially Native Americans. Yet child experiencers in the industrialized nations describe similar "lecture" episodes, as well.

Living Greeters

Sometimes, though it is rare, "greeters" in children's accounts can be real people from their immediate lives. Dr. Melvin Morse came across this in his research, as did I. These living individuals are usually a playmate or a favorite teacher if the child was of school age. With those I've interviewed, this particular type of greeter remained visible only long enough to calm the child and ease him or her into other aspects of the episode. Once this was done, the person disappeared, replaced by beings more commonly associated with near-death states. It was as if the only purpose this individual had in the child's scenario was to provide a touch of the familiar.

Unborn Siblings

Occasionally, as part of the near-death scenario, child experiencers are met by unborn siblings. These are brothers and/or sisters previously miscarried or aborted, or siblings yet to be conceived. One young girl, who choked to death but later revived, described her "little brother" as standing around with a smile on his face, assuring her that she would be fine. The mother was puzzled when told of this, as her daughter was the youngest in the family and there was no prospect this fact might change. Several years later, a miracle occurred—the mother, told she could never have another child, delivered a baby boy, the same one her daughter had seen during her near-death episode. (I detail one very similar to this in *The New Children and Near-Death Experiences*—formerly *Children of the New Millennium*—complete with a drawing of the event showing the unborn sibling.)

I've also come across several accounts where the child experiencer was a first-born and met all of his or her future siblings in the same scenario, each calling the other by name as if they somehow knew each other from "before."

Any Age

I want to emphasize again that anyone at any age can have a near-death experience. That includes tiny ones still in the womb, babes being born, infants, and toddlers. Once they are verbal, our smallest experiencers do their best to convey what happened to them—through speech, drawings, words on paper, or actions. The way their attempts to share their story are received determines, to a large extent, whether or not their episode has a positive influence on their life or is tucked aside, ignored, or repressed. Although the pattern of aftereffects cannot be denied, the experience can be.

New Words

A **prebirth experience (PBE)** is memories of existence before birth—memories that in most cases are later verified by the mother or a relative. Forerunners in this new field of study are Sarah Hinze *(Coming From the Light)*, Craig Lundahl and Harold Widdison *(The Eternal Journey)*, and Elisabeth Hallett *(Soul Trek)*. See appendix C for more details.

Womb with a View

Fascinatingly, one-third of the 277 child experiencers in my research base had clear, coherent memories of happenings that occurred with their parents or in their parent's affairs before they were born. Theirs was a *prebirth* experience.

Her Father's Abuse

Two weeks before the birth of Carroll Gray, of Atlanta, Georgia, the doctor informed Carroll's mother that there was no heartbeat and the baby was dead. At the moment of this particular memory, Carroll recalls seeing her father, screaming and enraged that his wife had "killed his son" (he had expected her to deliver a boy). He grabbed his wife and threw her across

Oops

It's scary what some children can remember from their prebirth existence in the womb. Things like parental debates and arguments, conditions in the home, even how their mother felt about her own life—and her thoughts!—are subject to recall. Emotionally charged issues are remembered more readily, especially if the child's welfare is threatened.

the room into the corner of a large table, rupturing her uterus. The mother was rushed to the hospital where a dead baby girl was delivered via an emergency cesarean section. Then, to everyone's astonishment, the child began to breathe.

Two and a half years later, in front of both of her parents and several relatives, Carroll Gray repeated to her father every word he had said when he threw his pregnant wife into the table. She also accurately described the setting of the room, including furniture placement. Her parents were dumbfounded, as no one had known the full story of what had actually occurred, nor had the family ever discussed that day among themselves.

Later, Carroll described how she had been cared for during the lengthy stay she had in the hospital, and what she had looked like at birth—details that were abnormal because of the unusual condition of her birth and the medical interventions used. All of this was confirmed by her mother.

Stories with the accuracy of Carroll Gray's are so numerous, they challenge the notion that unborn babies are oblivious to anything outside their mother's womb.

Threats of Abortion

I am continually amazed at reports of child experiencers who several years later confronted their mothers with questions like, "Why did you try to kill me when I was in your tummy?" (My amazement comes not so much from what the child says, for I have ceased to be surprised at the comments from any of our littlest experiencers, but from the mother's reply. Those who I interviewed admitted the child's claim.)

Whether the mother had only considered an abortion or whether she physically tried to have one at a clinic or self-induced one but failed, the child would be aware of this as part of the near-death scenario, or suddenly "know." Sometimes the child would just "remember," and that memory, most of the time, would trace back to around six to eight weeks in utero (the older the fetus, the clearer the memory).

The mother's admission that she had, indeed, considered or arranged to have an abortion and the unborn child's subsequent revelation of knowing this implies that the fetus might be a rational, thinking being from its very beginnings, capable of responding to its environment, which includes the thoughts and feelings of its mother. There is nothing in medical science to support this supposition, nor can accounts be explained by what is now known about the development of the human brain. Within the field of med-

New Word

An **anomaly** is that which deviates from consensual reality. Someone or something that is odd, peculiar, strange, weird, or out of place is considered an anomaly—until accepted by society or proven to be true.

ical science, a fetus being this sentient would be considered an inexplicable *anomaly*. The fact is, however, that such reports are becoming increasingly more common—and confirmed by the parent.

Womb with a Soul

Medical research has confirmed that twenty-six-week-old fetuses can feel and respond to pain, a discovery that strikingly coincides with the accounts of the majority of child experiencers in my near-death research who report the beginning of memory "as a soul resident within a human body" at that same time. I found that strong emotions, trauma, or upset on the part of the parents can also be a deciding factor in triggering such memories, although not always. Sometimes, I could not isolate any event that could have made a difference.

The Missing-Twin Phenomenon

There is ample material in medical journals that confirm a high mortality rate in pregnancies initially diagnosed as twins: Only one child ultimately is born, not two. Not surprisingly, I suppose, near-death experiencers have pulled me aside throughout the years

When the Soul Enters

The age-old assumption that the soul doesn't enter our bodies until we're born and take our first breath is now subject to serious challenge, thanks to the recent medical discovery about pain awareness for the fetus in utero and my findings about prebirth memories reported by child experiencers of near-death states. Both indicate that entry may occur before birth.

The "Other" One

Although the medical community maintains that the occurrence of an unborn twin is not that unusual, mothers feel just the opposite and so do most surviving twins, many of whom go on to develop relationships via spirits with their other half. Elvis Presley was such a one. He communicated with his "bodiless" brother, Jesse, all his life.

and whispered things like, "I'm not all here. There's another one of me. I have a twin, but my twin doesn't have a body." This "missing twin" occasionally made itself known to these experiencers as a "co-participant" during prebirth awareness states, or in a near-death scenario that occurred at birth. With most of these cases, the "other one" disappeared or died shortly thereafter. Sometimes, individuals didn't discover they ever had a twin until they were older and had a near-death episode, during

The Public Wants to Know

Two major national debates have brought the issue of "missing twins" to the forefront: the abortion conflict, and a growing concern, even among the mainstream populace and accredited researchers, about alien abduction claims. There are therapists who now specialize in the field. Raymond W. Brandt, PhD, publishes Twin World magazine for twins in general, and a Twinless Twin newsletter for singles who are attempting to deal with the grief of losing their twin and the driving need they feel to find him or her so they can be whole again (see appendix E for ordering information). Near-death research is finally addressing such accounts, as more and more of them are showing up in experiencer reports.

which the twin visited them. Hardly anyone, however, will speak openly about any of this as it seems too far-fetched.

All the obstetricians I interviewed on the subject felt that the incidence of twin loss was "no big deal." In cases where twins were diagnosed but only a single child was born, most doctors tossed off the vanished "other" to nature's efficient "waste disposal system." Their thinking is that fetuses that may have been damaged, malformed, or incomplete are either absorbed by the healthy twin or reabsorbed by the mother.

An example of meeting an unborn twin during a near-death experience is the story of Robin H. Johnson of Plymouth, New Hampshire. Robin had three near-death episodes, the first at age two from drowning, the second during a health-care crisis when she was twenty-three, and the third at age thirty while undergoing surgery. The first one made the greatest impact on her. Yet, because of being shamed or ignored whenever she tried to speak of it, she repressed it. Robin then fell into a habit of denying her inner truth, a self-betrayal that undermined her ability to form trusting relationships with other people. This situation changed after her third episode, by which time she'd given birth to a son after "losing" his twin. In this third episode, Robin met the missing twin. "It wasn't until I met my nonphysical daughter, Sarah," Robin says, "that I learned that her purpose for being in my life was to teach me to have unequivocal trust in my intuition, my knowing." It wasn't the surviving twin who formed a relationship with the vanished "other," in Robin's case. It was she, the mother, who in discovering Sarah, was able to reclaim her self-confidence that she had lost at the age of two and heal herself.

Choosing Genes and Physical Characteristics

As if this weren't enough, there is additional news from the near-death front that may startle you. Either as a prebirth memory or as part of the individual's near-death scenario, a number of experiencers claim to have been shown their conception and their participation in the choice of what genes they received.

Deciding on Who You Want to Be

Berkley Carter Mills of Lynchburg, Virginia, is one such case. Although an adult experiencer, during his scenario he relived being a tiny spark of light traveling to Earth and entering his mother's womb as soon as egg and sperm met. In mere seconds, he said he had to choose hair color and eyes out of the genetic material available to him, and any genes that might give him the body he would need in this life. He bypassed the gene for clubfootedness, then watched from a soul's perspective as cells subdivided. He could hear his parents whenever they spoke, and feel their emotions, but any knowledge of his past lives dissolved.

The idea that afflictions could ever be "chosen," as implied in Berkley's account, has been noted in the work of other near-death researchers, among them Arvin S. Gibson in his paper, "Near-Death Experience Patterns from Research in the Salt Lake City Region," published in the *Journal of Near-Death Studies.* In his paper, he wrote about a young man by the name of DeLynn who was told during his experience that he, as a soul, had chosen to be born with a debilitating disease. DeLynn states: "The specific choice of cystic fibrosis was to help me learn dignity in suffering. My understanding in the eternal sense was complete—I knew that I was a powerful, spiritual being that chose to have a short, but marvelous, mortal existence."

Handicaps

Some experiencers I interviewed who remembered having chosen their affliction said the choice was made from the soul level—their "higher self"—and was done with the idea of what would help them advance spiritually. Others, however, said the affliction was given to them, indicating that, in their case, choice was not a factor.

Choosing Your Parents

Many experiencers remembered in the midst of their scenario or were shown that they had a choice in selecting the parents they would come to have.

Alice Morrison-Mays of Quincy, Illinois, because of vivid prebirth memories as well as several near-death episodes, recalled deciding when she was still a soul which parents to choose before incarnating. A good candidate that "resonated" with her was a musically gifted couple who were eager to have another child after having lost a baby son soon after his birth three years earlier. Feeling especially welcomed by them, she made the choice to be their child and basked in joy and anticipation for most of the nine months in utero. "About the time of my birth, my peaceful and happy gestational existence was shattered. I found myself being 'hit' with and immersed in terrible shadow and dark mist-like clouds. I seemed to be swimming in agony. I didn't want to go on with the birth but I couldn't return to where I had come from."

New Word

The principle of life that animates human form, yet exists apart from the physical body or at a different energy frequency—as a distinct entity—is called the **soul**. Most religions maintain that the soul survives death and is eternal. Some traditions teach that everything has a soul. Others state that only humankind has a direct connection with God through the soul.

The Electrical Soul

Thomas Edison (1847–1931), another great scientist who believed in life after death, claimed that the soul was made of "life units." These microscopic particles could rearrange into any form and retain full memory and personality, and were indestructible. He was working on a machine that would detect these life units in the environment and allow living individuals to communicate with the dead, but died before it could be finished. Now, research has found that in almost every ghost haunting and poltergeist there are certain electrical elements at work. Using electromagnetic field (EMF) detectors, ghost hunters can monitor these electrical forces because when ghosts are present, the readings are higher than the EMF produced by an electrical appliance. (From Patti Dolezal, *The Artwork of Alfred A. Dolezal,* Shangri La Studios; see appendix E.)

The unexpected death of Alice's maternal grandfather and her mother's shock at her adored father's passing turned out to be what threatened the pregnancy. Thrown into turmoil because of her mother suppressing her grief and the doctor administering a drug to delay delivery, Alice received a "double whammy" that she believes gifted her with an unusual emotional sensitivity that helped in her career as a symphony cellist and predisposed her to a rare and severe form of emphysema that was genetic and slowly crippled, then later killed her.

The supposed ability to choose parents apparently carries with it no guarantees. Some have regretted their choice. But regardless of the pleasure or displeasure of being born into a certain family, the consistent message is that there is, before birth, the existence of a self called the *soul.*

Typical Behavior after the Experience

After their near-death experience, children often begin to "speak" in the language of otherworldly realities, which is based not on words, but on feelings, tones, and images. It's as if they become "creative intuitives": The invisible becomes visible to them. This enables them to giggle with angels, play with ghosts, and see the future matter-of-factly. Certainly, most children are like this anyway, but with the child experiencer this behavior is even more prevalent. Parents generally find such responses cause for panic. Either the kid's imagination has run wild, they say, or the little darling needs a therapist.

The explanation for this may be relatively simple, as near-death states are known to expand our normal faculties. Since it's known scientifically that the average person is aware of only one-sixtieth of what goes on around him or her, such an expansion could open experiencers up to incredible new vistas of experience, perhaps even more of the electromagnetic spectrum. Drugs, pulsed sound currents, electrical probes, and meditation are other ways a person's level of awareness can be altered and shifted around, yet none of these can compare with the sudden, unexpected "punch" that the power of near-death states can have on an individual's life. And with children, this expansion of sensitivity is even more pronounced.

The Red Man

One of the things I discovered with children who are unusually sensitive is the common report of seeing a "Red Man" just before they are about to come down with a fever. Here is an example, as told by Vienna M. Collins, Santa Barbara, California:

"When I was two years old, I had a serious case of scarlet fever which may have accounted for my shift in sensitivities, or it could have possibly been when I fell off a two-story building. I remember both incidents happening, but I am not sure if I actually crossed over.

"When you talk about children seeing a 'Red Man' when they become ill and have a fever, I vividly remember seeing him on several occasions when I was little. He used to terrify me because of the strange way he moved around and leered at me. He looked like he was made of red fire and moved around like a flame. I kept wishing he would go away and never return because he scared me so badly, and because I always got sick after he visited. He finally left when I was around four years old. I don't remember seeing him after that."

Prayer Power

While teenage and adult experiencers occasionally say that they were able to "see" the power of prayer during their episode, children, on the other hand, are excitedly outspoken about this phenomenon.

The youngsters I interviewed often said that once they left their bodies and "could see better," they saw prayers turned into beams of radiant, golden, or rainbow light that would arc over from the one saying the prayer, no matter how many miles away, to where the children, themselves, were "hovering" near death. Once the prayer beam "hit" them, they described it as being akin to feeling a "splash" of love or an incredible "warming." One little boy said prayer beams tickled when they touched him.

Because so many child experiencers have seen and felt the effectiveness of prayer, they afterward consider prayer the natural way to talk with God and share God's healing love with others. These children are far more likely to emphasize the reality of paranormal, spirit worlds and the importance of

Lively Children's Scenarios

The paranormal takes on an unusual intensity when youngsters describe their near-death states. Their stories are rich with poignant imagery: choirs of angels singing beautiful music, elf-like beings atop cribs, bright hands that pop out of the sky, birds that speak, visits from relatives dead long before the child's birth, Jesus driving a school bus, demons scolding them for misbehavior, the devil wagging a finger.

Visitations

Child experiencers typically have "visitations" and slip into other realms of reality after their episodes—the "other worlds" they know exist. This is very real to them, and perfectly acceptable. Accusing them of having an overactive imagination can cause many problems and create a wedge between adult and child.

worship in the celebration of church than are others their age who have never experienced near-death or near-death-like states.

Angels and Ghosts

Dr. Melvin Morse stated that 70 percent of the children who had near-death states in his study encountered angels during their experience. I discovered the same thing.

I also noticed that the younger the child, the more likely the angel was described as having wings. Once of school age, children used the term "winged" less and less. Kids of any age spoke of black-colored angels as well as white ones, and angels colored "like real people are" with varying flesh tones. Angels were also seen as being so bright with light that it was difficult to distinguish features—except to note a sphere or cylinder shape to them, maybe a form similar to humans. In other cultures, the angelic ones have very different names and looks, like the Yamatoots from the Lord Yama in Thailand. Still, whoever the bright ones, they are unique and impressive. In those cases in which children challenged the bright ones, or, as they often called them, "the people," the angels immediately "exploded" or went "poof" and became a mass of light energy. All form then dissolved. Angels, regardless of how they appeared, commonly continued to be a part of the child's life after the episode was over. This friendly companionship sometimes extended into the individual's adult life.

Along with angel friends, child experiencers can take on relationships with spirit beings and ghosts. Children are usually explicit as to the lineage of their otherworldly companions, stating that angels are from the heavenly realms, while ghosts and other such folks are connected to Earth.

Lynn, for example, experienced a lengthy and detailed near-death scenario at the age of thirteen, which included watching her soul as it exited her body during a surgical crisis when doctors were not certain they could save her. She described what it was like to be resuscitated afterward and then wake up hours later looking up at myriad tubes. Unable to speak, she recalls being fascinated by shadows moving among the medical staff, shadows that she came to realize were people who had died in the hospital. Lynn began conversing with these deceased spirits, causing her doctor to release her after a month because he was afraid that all the time she spent talking to dead or misplaced souls was a sign she was going crazy. What alarmed the physician became an ordinary aspect of her everyday life.

Ghostly Doings

Although there is no scientific proof that ghosts exist, they have been seen throughout the ages. Sightings are common when there was a violent history or a sudden death. Many ghosts don't believe they are dead and often feel the need to communicate something. Unexplained noises such as knocking, footsteps or muffled voices, electrical appliances turning on and off by themselves, and other mysterious happenings can be signs of an active ghost. Most ghosts look like a ball of light or a misty vapor. The best times to see them are during a new or full moon or solar storms. (From Patti Dolezal, *The Art of Alfred A. Dolezal,* Shangri La Studios; refer to appendix E.)

The following two photographs were sent to me from an adult experiencer named Chris Lovelidge, an amateur photographer who lives in Halfmoon Bay, British Columbia, Canada. The photos illustrate how very dynamic and real the ability is to see beyond the normal viewing range, especially for children, and lend more support to what the youngsters tell us.

Chris was sitting at a small table in a bar at the time. The chair on the other side was empty. He aimed his camera in the direction of the empty chair and just started taking pictures, adjusting the focus when it "felt" right to do so. He explains, "I took several frames in this particular bar because I had reason to

No one is sitting where this white figure appears. (Photo taken by Chris Lovelidge)

When Chris Lovelidge focused his camera setting, this detailed image emerged—not to his eyes, but on the developed film.

believe that energy beings of this type frequent the locations where they had been happiest during their earthly life, i.e., drinking at a bar. I have no doubt a few will accuse me of altering the pictures, but the truth is I wouldn't know how." The two photographs, says Chris, "were taken on Kodak fast infrared black-and-white film. The setting was 1/60 at f5.6 with a strobe flash and 2S red 1 filter." (Chris has since gone on to specialize in photographing subtle energies. Refer to appendix E.)

The above photograph shows what happened when Chris altered his camera focus.

Who Cares

Child experiencers seldom recognize their body once they leave it. For most, their vacated body has no meaning and is quickly ignored, or it is thought to belong to someone else. Just the opposite is true with adults. They tend to linger for a while, studying their body—amazed that it occupies one place while they exist in another.

Recognizing Child Experiencers

A child doesn't necessarily have to be near death to experience a near-death or near-death-like state. Just as with adult experiencers, they can be in the throes of a high fever, get knocked in the head, fall down stairs, or simply be frightened out of their wits, and still have one. Several researchers, especially Kenneth Ring, PhD, have established that the closer an individual is to actual physical death, the more apt they are to experience such a state; but that does not preclude less dangerous situations or a seeming threat to survival that never transpires. The truth is no one knows what really causes these states. We just know that most of them happen during life or death crises and are powerful in their effects.

Because children have such a struggle verbalizing what happens to them under the best of circumstances, their efforts at talking about their near-death experiences are usually quite bewildering and seemingly fanciful. Here are some of the more common characteristics that might help you identify if a child has undergone a near-death experience. Notice the exceptional emphasis child experiencers generally place on "home," as if they were trying to recreate their heavenly home within their earthly one:

- A powerful need to have a "home," even if it's only their own bedroom.

- An equally important desire to have an "altar" of some kind in their "home."

- Anything on the altar is holy to them.

- An intense curiosity about God, worship, and prayer. Many insist that their parents take them to a house of worship afterward—any one is fine.

- An unusual sensitivity to whatever is hurtful or to lies, especially as reflected in world events, the media, and in the "white lies" parents and siblings occasionally tell.

- Loss of boundaries, as if they have "no skin."

- An ability to merge into or become one with animals, plants, or whatever is focused on. Borders on self-identification in multiples (having more than one existence at the same time). Can ease back to normal self-image with age and increased socialization.

- Heightened otherworldly activity and psychic displays. Drawn to mysticism and the paranormal.

- A change in sleep patterns. May forgo naps entirely in favor of increased flow states (floating or relaxing into a "zone" of absolute nothingness, a state of "flow," in which the individual is not only refreshed, but he or she "wakes up" more creative and knowing than before).

- An awareness of "the life continuum" and anything "future," including the ability to "pre-live" the future—as if rehearsing how to manage what is about to happen.

- A shift toward becoming fast talkers and fast thinkers, with a driving need to create, invent, read, learn.

- Behavioral changes in school. May become disruptive and withdrawn. This can carry over into family life, with

Don't Be Fooled

Altered behavior in child experiencers, including the presence of hyperactivity, may be misdiagnosed as attention deficit disorder (ADD). In this case, parents should explore alternatives first before considering drugs.

Imprinting to Other Worlds

Newborns, infants, and toddlers who have near-death experiences often show signs as they age that they may have imprinted to the otherworldly realms they encountered on the "Other Side" of death, rather than to their family and their earthly home. It is not unusual for these tiniest of the tiny to think of themselves later on as somehow "foreign," or "the odd-one-out," or "alien." Some go as far as to claim they are extraterrestrial, and came to this planet from another one.

"authority figures" merely tolerated. Usually the child has to relearn social courtesies, common rules, and regulations.

Children who have experienced a near-death episode may be, because of their subsequent behavior, looked upon as "weird." Indeed, we've seen that in some of the accounts included in this chapter. Diane K. Corcoran, RN, PhD, is a former army nurse and leading proponent of educating medical professionals about the near-death experience and its aftereffects, especially as it pertains to kids. She cautions: "Children may not realize that what they are feeling are common aftereffects. They may be able to see things others don't, or they may at special times know things that are going to happen but nobody believes them. We need to listen to children. And we need to let them know they're okay."

5

Suicide Enigmas

It's not that I'm afraid to die. I just don't want to be there when it happens.

—Woody Allen

Societal and religious traditions vary sharply on the subject of suicide. The kamikaze pilots of World War II, for instance, fearlessly dove their planes straight into their targets, choosing to die "gloriously" in the service of their ruler. Christian crusaders sometimes killed themselves to magnify their cause; the soldiers of Islam have a long history of doing the same, as did the ancient Aztecs. Even today, there are those who set themselves ablaze or refuse food to make a "statement," or retain their family's "honor" by killing themselves rather than face troubling problems.

What about near-death experiences? Do those who attempt suicide have near-death states? If they do, what are they like? Since most experiencers describe their episodes as ones of heavenly bliss and unconditional love, how does that apply to suicides? If those who try to kill

An Unusual Book on Suicide

Pamela Rae Heath, MD, PsyD, and Jon Klimo, PhD, teamed up to write *Suicide: What Really Happens in the Afterlife?* Their groundbreaking work explores suicide from every aspect, including channeled conversations with the dead, after-death and deathbed communications, near-death experiences, murder, fighting over religion, self-sacrifice and martyrdom, grief, terrorism, preteen and teenage rage, and Internet sites that glorify death.

themselves experience beauty and love, where's the punishment for bad deeds and selfish behavior, where's the justice? Although research is sparse on the subject, we have made a few discoveries, and what we've found may surprise you.

A Picture Too Pretty

During the early to mid 1980s, there was tremendous fear that individuals, upon hearing all the wondrous tales of near-death experiencers, would commit suicide in large numbers. The fear was fed by a "plague" of incidents in which teenagers were killing themselves for reasons few could understand. Since suicide can be "contagious," in that a family member or best friend of someone who commits suicide can decide to copy that person and take his or her own life, the fear seemed justified.

The major concern was that experiencers, almost to a person, were saying heaven was so much better than Earth that they could hardly wait until they finally died and stayed dead so they could go back. The problem this caused emergency medical teams was gut-wrenching in that they didn't know whether they should resuscitate a dying patient. What if the individual was having a near-death experience and they were the ones responsible for pulling him or her away from such ecstasy?

Bruce Greyson, MD, one of the best researchers in the field, answered this concern by publicizing twelve reasons why near-death states and stories about them should actually make people less suicidal. These are listed as follows, with additional comments from Drs. Pamela Rae Heath and Jon Klimo:

1. The near-death experience induces a feeling of cosmic unity (a sense that the individual is now part of something larger than self).

2. The near-death experience gives one a transpersonal perspective on life that helps one to understand failures and losses (what was once important is less so afterward).

3. The near-death experience makes life seem more meaningful or valuable (more precious).

4. The near-death experience makes one feel more alive (and life itself more real).

5. The near-death experience makes one feel better about oneself (enhances self-esteem).

6. The near-death experience makes one feel closer to other people (promotes a greater sense of bonding).

7. The near-death experience convinces one that escape by means of suicide is not possible (a sense that the suicide was not meant to be).

8. The near-death experience helps one to reevaluate his or her life and place it in a different perspective (especially if a life review is part of the scenario).

9. The near-death experience leads to improvements in one's problems, or makes it easier to get help for problems (a sense that personal situations are enhanced afterward).

10. The near-death experience leads to a strong moral conviction that suicide is wrong (ethically wrong).

11. The near-death experience sacrifices unwanted parts of the ego (so the remainder can go on).

12. The near-death experience is too terrible to risk repeating, for those who had hellish scenarios (can instill a fear of going through the experience again).

> **Wake-up Call**
>
> Dr. Greyson's list did make a difference in lessening the fear the general public had that near-death states were so wonderful people would even commit suicide to have them. But, with experiencers, it became a wake-up call for them to be more careful about what they said while being interviewed by reporters. Their claims were beginning to sound irresponsible, almost as if they were "anti-life."

According to Dr. Greyson: "The six *most* commonly offered reasons for not being suicidal after an NDE relate to transcendental matters, while the six *least* often mentioned reasons tend to be 'reality-oriented.' In other words, NDErs attribute their decreased suicidal thinking to a focus on transcendental issues."

What Those Who Attempt Suicide Say

Early in his research, Kenneth Ring, PhD, did a study to examine the differences, if any, between episodes that sprang from illness, accidents, and suicide. He discovered that suicide survivors tended to have brief accounts, usually peaceful, but lacking in the complexity and depth of those that resulted from other forms of death. Dr. Ring's study was duplicated by other researchers, all finding basically the same thing—except of late (which we'll discuss in a moment).

Early Stories

Like other experiencers, suicide survivors were seen as returning with a better outlook on life and a renewed

It Still Takes Time

I found a number of near-death experiencers who had their episodes in conjunction with attempted suicides and reported complex and richly detailed scenarios. Many of their reports were spellbinding. But I did notice that, no matter how healing their experiences were, it still took these people an inordinate amount of time to believe they actually deserved the help they had received from their episode.

sense of self-worth. But, while providing renewed meaning to their lives, their episodes were not a cure-all. Most experiencers were inspired by their scenario to realize that it was up to them to straighten out their lives.

A typical case was a young man who intentionally overdosed on drugs and ascended to a level of peaceful, warm light during his near-death experience. He felt loved and forgiven for what he had done, and was infused with the awareness and energy afterward to make significant changes in his life. He became evangelical in his desire to share his story so others would not be tempted to make the mistake he had. He commented: "Since then, suicide has never crossed my mind as a way out. It's a cop-out to me and not the way to heaven. I hope my experience will help stop someone from taking his own life. It is a terrible waste."

Later Stories

As more near-death suicide survivors began telling their stories, their accounts have called for a reexamination of former conclusions. Newer work has uncovered a much broader view of suicide reports, with the scenarios ranging from horrific hellish encounters replete with such imagery as dungeons and grotesque half-animal/half-human tormentors, to heavenly scenes, life reviews, and angelic guides who comfort as well as instruct. Perhaps the reason for this deviation from past reports is that more people who have attempted suicide are coming forward to share their stories, so we're learning more about them.

Whatever the case, we can now say that scenarios arising from suicide attempts can cover the same gamut of content as any other near-death experience and have the same impact: Some respond favorably to what happened to them while others do not.

One of the newer accounts that contradicts early research is the case of Stephanie Johnston of Richmond, Virginia. "At that time, my life was a mess," she told me. "My relationship with my fiance ended dramatically and unexpectedly. I was hospitalized for thirty days due to the fact that my blood pressure had skyrocketed to 210 over 180—borderline for a stroke or heart attack. I was released right back to the same stressful situation that had put me there. I finally decided that I wanted the pain to end, so I took two bottles of pills plus a fifth of booze. I lived for the next three days on heart monitors, as there was no counteractive drug they could give me.

"I experienced leaving my physical body in the ambulance. I could hear the conversation my friend [who accompanied her] was having with those who attended me as well as what they reported to the hospital, from a position outside and above the ambulance. I could see inside and outside the vehicle at the same time, and I could see surrounding houses as we went by.

"The next thing that happened was I found myself in a different place. The best way I can explain this place is it was a different dimension from what we know as the physical. Things were not concrete and fixed, but somehow 'fluid' yet not liquid. I conversed with a group of people there. They did not have physical bodies but were more of an energy that was iridescent. I had no fear. There was a sense of peace, almost as if I was dreaming, but I wasn't dreaming. It didn't feel strange; it felt normal. There was no pain, nothing physical, just me setting there talking to these people. They were telling me things, yet it wasn't verbal communication, more of mind-to-mind.

"I was given a life review. But I was not only shown what my life had been, but what it would mean, from this day forth, if I were not there. Not only did I see this, but I experienced what it would feel like for others—for people I knew and loved, and for people I had not met yet. I was told that I had a choice: I could stay or I could return and complete my life. The choice was up to me. I felt no pressure. I felt that whatever my choice, it would be all right. There was no sense of judgment of myself or others. It was the most overwhelming feeling of unconditional love, so totally accepting. And there was such a sense of freedom.

"All of this seemed to take a long time and yet there was no time at all. If this sounds contradictory, I agree, but that was what I experienced. This experience was not of this world, so to explain it in regard to this world cannot be done. The next thing I recall was being in the emergency room with the doctor. He was reciting my daughter's name. I credit this doctor with being very attuned, for if there was anything that could have swayed my decision, it would have been my daughter.

"I can't say that I woke up spiritually enlightened. I woke up to the life I wanted to leave. I was angry I didn't die and stayed that way for quite some time. I was still rather self-destructive. After about two years of horrendous anger, I found myself on my knees praying, 'Okay, God, you're not going to let me die, so teach me how to live.' I then started dealing with myself and my life. I began to seek professional help, as well as God's."

Depression and Suicidal Tendencies Afterward

Most near-death experiencers go through a period of depression after their episodes. Either they believe they're crazy and have no way to understand what happened to them, or they have problems integrating their experience into their restored physical lives, or they may feel somehow "lost."

Some go through feelings of shame from believing they were "kicked out" of

Whoops

Some near-death scenarios that result from suicide attempts are so negative, they can upset the individual more than the original problem. This kind of devastation can be transforming if used as a catalyst to help the person make the changes that comprise long-term solutions. These changes can come from an inner awakening, or from the fear that what was experienced may indeed herald the individual's ultimate fate if something is not done to turn things around.

heaven, sensing they weren't worthy to be there in the first place, or feeling that they hadn't become "perfect enough" after they got back. Depressed states for the majority are short-lived, but sometimes these states can recur over time. For others, though, depressions can be so severe they overwhelm the individual and he or she becomes suicidal.

Too Hard

In my research base of 3,000 adult experiencers, a little less than 4 percent admitted they had attempted suicide after their episode. Some tried it right away, others within five to twelve years. When I asked why, all of them said Earth life was just too tough. They knew the other side was better than this one, so they resolved to go back.

Still, there is another aspect to the issue of suicide we have yet to tackle. And it's a subject almost no one will admit, let alone discuss.

Dying to Return—How Adults Respond

Just because an individual has had a near-death experience does not prevent him or her from considering and perhaps attempting suicide at a later date. I'm aware most researchers claim the opposite to be true, but I cannot substantiate their claim. Of the experiencers who did attempt suicide, none I spoke with had any sense that they had committed a sin by taking such action, only that they were trying to go back to where they believe they belonged. The near-death experience, especially if uplifting, can be a suicide deterrent, but not always. We are not "saved" by having one, not even from ourselves.

One woman who contacted me spoke of being hospitalized twice for attempting suicide many years after her near-death episode. She had formerly experienced a scenario that was indeed soul-stirring and wonder-filled; but, with the passing of years and a life filled with tragedy and pain, the positive upliftment she had previously received seemed to fade. Memories of how glorious it was "over there" prompted her to try killing herself so she could return. She failed in both attempts and caused herself even more grief. When I last heard from her, she seemed reasonably back on her feet and more sensible, stating that she now realized there was no escape and she had better get busy and solve her problems herself.

Another woman who repeatedly brushed death and experienced a heavenly near-death episode each time seriously considered killing herself so she could return to the wonders of life on the other side of death. Although this woman did not follow through on her threats, neither did she obtain the counseling she needed. What has become of her I do not know.

Regardless of how meaningful a near-death state is, it will not necessarily protect or shield anyone from the realities of life. The experience is not magic. Surviving does not make you enlightened or superhuman. Life goes on. Your problems do not stop just because you momentarily did. They are still waiting when you get back. You may regain your health, but deep inside you can still be a mess.

A Secret Wish

Aftereffects from near-death states can be unsettling, or cause some experiencers to dissociate from normal living habits. Most episodes are a source of strength and guidance, but the impact from them can lessen somewhat over time. Psychiatrist and author Elisabeth Kübler-Ross claims that near-death experiencers harbor a secret wish that their final end hurries so they can return to where they once were. Even if actively involved in Earth life, she says their greatest joy and satisfaction seems to come from the memory they cherish of a time when they once had a "peek at heaven." It's almost as if they fully consume life so they can die again.

Dr. Kübler-Ross's observation is accurate. There are experiencers who believe that if they push the limits—if they do more—they can guarantee for themselves special dispensation from the spiritual realms. This way they can "leave" early (without killing themselves), and return to the heaven revealed during their near-death experience. Why, then, if the Other Side is so great, would the majority stay in this life and do so without the need to rush? "We stay because it makes sense to stay," one experiencer told me. "If it isn't your time, you will either cheat yourself out of what might have been had you remained, or you will not stay dead no matter what method you use to kill yourself."

The Challenge with Children

Children can be, and sometimes are, more confused and disoriented by their near-death episodes than from whatever life-threatening events that precipitated them. In their near-death state, the vast majority report feeling as though they'd found their "true home" and wanted to stay there, but couldn't.

It seems perfectly logical to a child that the way to rejoin the light beings met in death is to quit breathing and go back. This is not recognized by them as self-destructive. Yet, according to research, it is the children, not the adults, who are the most likely to leave the heaven of their near-death experience and return to life so their family won't be saddened by their death.

As we discussed in chapter 4, children don't process their near-death states in the same manner as adults, nor do they regard them in the same fashion.

Surprising Percentages

Of the 277 child experiencers I originally interviewed, 21 percent actually attempted suicide within twelve to fifteen years of their episode (substantially higher than with adults). One-third of those in my study turned to alcohol for solace within five to ten years (the incident rate with adult experiencers for alcoholism is about one in five); over half dealt with serious bouts of depression afterward (adults have a slightly higher incidence).

This teenager's story is a case in point: "I was very small when I had my near-death experience. When I could run and play like the other kids again, I'd go from room to room. I'd look under the beds, in the closets, behind the doors and furniture—from the top of the house to the bottom—other people's houses, too. I'd look and look but I never found them. They loved me. I know they did. They were warm and wonderful and bright with light. They came to me when I died and they left when I breathed again. I looked for years and years. Sometimes I'd curl up underneath my bed and cry. Why couldn't I find them? Where did they go? Why did they leave me in a place where no one cared and no one loved me? Was I that bad that they couldn't return?"

The girl who spoke these words was four years old when her heart stopped and beings made out of light came to get her. She recalls walking hand in hand with them into realms of music and joy and beauty, and so much love that she never ever wanted to leave. Then, suddenly, without choice or warning, she revived and found herself back in a body wracked with pain. Surrounded by strangers, she was forced to deal with the aftermath of major surgery alone and frightened. She has yet to recover from the shock and anger at feeling abandoned by the "bright ones" who loved her and then left her behind. She now sees a counselor and has requested anonymity.

Parent/child bonding is initially quite strong. These kids want to be with their Earth families. That bonding returns them to life, again and again. When I interviewed youngsters, their common response was, "I came back to help my Daddy" or "I came back so Mommy won't cry." The parent/child bond doesn't begin to stretch thin or break until after the child revives. That climate of welcome or threat with which they are greeted, as well as how their episode ended, directly impinges on everything that comes next, including the "cloud" of alcoholism and suicide that looms far too often over child experiencers.

The Importance of Endings

With the child experiencers I interviewed, how their episode ended, especially if abrupt, proved to be the deciding factor in their response—for good or ill. Children normally tend to personalize what goes on around them, and blame themselves if anything seems amiss or goes wrong. Those who experience near-death states are no exception.

What I noticed is, if a child is left with a sense of:

- Loss—it's their fault "everyone went away" and they feel guilty.
- Rejection—they're bad and they feel ashamed.
- Betrayal—they're unworthy and they feel abandoned.
- Acceptance—it's okay to leave their "real home" and they feel satisfied.
- Joy—they're trustworthy and they feel confident.
- Loved—they are extra special and they feel secure.

New Word

To **repress** is the act of rejecting something from consciousness that is too painful to remember, or is somehow either too disagreeable or too uncomfortable to acknowledge.

We tend to forget that a child's first response is geared toward feelings, not "thinking it through." Usually, they are straightforward about how they feel. If rebuffed or embarrassed by their elders, however, kids tend to retreat into silence, even to the point of *repressing* their experience.

The Different Way Kids Reason

As we try to understand why incident rates of alcoholism and suicide attempts are so high with child experiencers of near-death states, we need to admit that the kids have it tougher than adult experiencers. Adults can at least speak up for themselves or exercise a fair degree of choice. Should a child say anything, he or she may be either ignored or hushed. Although many youngsters are able to integrate their near-death episodes successfully, the reverse also occurs.

It truly takes a child experiencer to understand a child experiencer, and to understand why kids respond the unique way they do.

A young man, who prefers to call himself "A Child from Minnesota," was suffocated at the age of three and a half by an older brother. He has this to say about what it's like to experience the near-death phenomenon when a youngster: "Children react differently to near-death episodes than adults because the set of experiences they have to compare them with is smaller. To an adult, such a phenomenon is only one of many life occurrences. But to a child, a near-death experience is the world itself, or 'all there is.' A child has a more difficult time 'drawing the line' between what is eternal and what is earthly. Children are forced to rely on the experience more, simply because they lack what adults can draw from. This colors everything children think, say, and do."

He continues: "Speaking for myself, I have come to understand that the long-term effects of this phenomenon have been very large indeed. These effects include an ability to desensitize the self from physical sensations; an ability to communicate through nonverbal and nonauditory means; a partial loss of the ability to communicate verbally and auditorially; problems reintegrating the ethereal self back into the physical self; and challenges interacting socially.

"My experience of being out of

New Word

Dissociation was formerly used in the field of psychiatry as a label to describe individuals who "withdrew from" or "severed" any association with their body and/or environment. It was considered an unhealthy mental state. New research, however, indicates that dissociation may not be unhealthy or unusual after all.

body enabled me to learn very young how to perform the separation of body and spirit. My understanding of the process, however, was unconscious. I did not know what I was doing or how I was doing it until much later. This first experience arose as a result of intense pain; so, in the beginning, I used this skill simply to avoid pain. Since the skill itself was unconscious, it quickly became a knee-jerk reaction to discomfort of all sorts. Eventually, I came to remain in that state as much as possible. As I desensitized myself to my own feelings, I was equally unable to feel the pain or joy of others. And, as I explored this state, emotions, people, and all of social life grew ever more foreign to me—I grew ever more withdrawn. I have come to believe that body and spirit need to nourish each other, and cannot remain separate indefinitely."

To Be or Not to Be—That Is the Question

Almost every child experiencer becomes adept at *dissociation*, as did "A Child from Minnesota." For that matter, so do most adult experiencers.

Many mental health professionals are now recognizing that dissociation may actually be a natural by-product of consciousness as it develops along new lines of thought and creative imagination. Current thinking is that it is more a sign of adaptation than insanity. But, as "A Child from Minnesota" finally learned, even positive skills that enrich our lives can become "crutches."

Dissociation, the ability to turn the world on or off at will, is one of the typical aftereffects of near-death states. There are many others; some of them what you might expect, others rather peculiar, even unique. The phenomenon engenders far more than a simple change of attitude or a sudden appreciation of life's special moments. It's a complex dynamic that is not easily explained, nor understood.

Sooner or later, each experiencer is confronted by the question: Was it worth it to come back? Although the majority will give a hearty "yes" to that question, the issue still remains and the question still lingers to haunt quiet moments.

Trying to Cause a Near-Death Experience

Literally a form of suicide, people have chosen or been forced to risk the finality of death as a test to see if they were ready or able to become gifted healers and wise ones. Tribal traditions, going as far back in time as history can trace, tell of rituals people went through to either mimic death or actually cause it. If the individual survived the tests, and was able to transcend this world and in the process enter another one, they were then considered to be "initiated" and could advance in tribal favor and trust. The "extra" gifts and talents experiencers gained were said to come from the gods. So important was this tradition to the health and well-being of any tribal nation, that children were sometimes tested in the same manner to ensure that the line of "special" ones would remain unbroken.

Today, there are researchers who are trying to revive this practice, but not for the same reasons. Their goal is to entice volunteers to attempt suicide under controlled conditions so trial experiments can be conducted. The idea behind this "suicide project" is that, once clinically dead, the volunteer would witness what near-death experiencers encounter, while being tested to make certain conditions were genuine. Then, after the trials were completed, the volunteer would be revived by an attending physician and later quizzed as to what he or she experienced.

The suicide project is officially termed "The Near-Death Experiment" by its originator, Greg Kasarik, Australia (refer to appendix D). He plans to induce clinical death through the use of "hypothermic circulatory arrest," and is currently seeking further support for his project. Although his approach to near-death research is considered by most people to be repulsive, not to mention unethical, Kasarik is not deterred.

Even considering the willingness of any volunteer to die and come back in the name of science, there are no guarantees as to outcome or what might be experienced—if anything—nor were there for initiates long ago. Historical artifacts indicate that many died during these rituals. This fact should give anyone pause, especially near-death experiencers who believe suicide will guarantee them a quick return to the "Other Side." Just because you've been there before doesn't mean taking your own life will put you back where you once were.

Just for Kings

Egyptologists believe that the King's Chamber in the Great Pyramid was designed around a single sarcophagus, not for the purpose of burial, but as a way to cause near-death experiences. Once an individual was placed in the stone coffin and the lid attached, oxygen levels would quickly deplete. The lid would not be removed until a certain time had lapsed. Tradition has it that if the individual survived, he would be a good leader, possessed of special "gifts."

Part 2

Afterward

We've all seen true-life stories on television about close brushes with death, incredible last-minute returns to life, and near-death experiences that took place in between. But the real story begins where the media stories end. Like all pivotal moments in our lives—and believe me, having a near-death experience is most assuredly a pivotal moment—the real story begins when the moment ends and we look around us and ask, "How am I going to fit this experience into my life?"

In these chapters we'll continue our journey by looking at the aftereffects associated with a near-death experience. You'll see that it's here, in living with the aftereffects—not so much in the experience itself—that the meaning of life and death overlap.

6

Lives Turned Upside Down

Sometimes, I lie awake at night, and I ask, "Why me?" Then a voice answers, "Nothing personal —your name just happened to come up."
—Charlie Brown, in the cartoon strip *Peanuts* by Charles Schulz

Research tells us that people who undergo near-death experiences make significant changes in their lives afterward. Like the middle-aged police officer who died on the operating table and experienced a scenario. He's now a high school teacher. He couldn't go back to police work. A mobster "hit man" had a life review as death loomed large. He now ladles soup for the homeless and is determined to make amends for his previous behavior. A renewed sense of life? Certainly. But there's more to the aftereffects than this.

Among other things, despite what we saw in the previous chapter, near-death experiencers generally gain a stronger sense of self and become relaxed, kinder, and less anxiety-prone. But, though a renewed appreciation for life is wonderful, it hardly qualifies for the level of claims being made about the near-death experience.

So why are the range and depth of changes exhibited by near-death experiencers so consistently greater and more profound than those of people who survived similar incidences but did not experience a near-death state?

To answer this, to explore fully how unique, all-important, and life-changing a near-death experience and its aftereffects are, I've devoted the next several chapters to this topic so you can know the answer for yourself.

Feelings after Being Revived

Although the common notion is that the phenomenon is generally pleasurable—and usually it is—it's not always exactly a bed of roses.

A Total Turnover

"How does a guy go from a hopeless drug addict to managing a retirement residence, often sitting with and comforting the dying. From being nearly homeless and broke, to running one of *God's Homes*. . . I still cannot fathom the amazing transformative power of my NDE.

"I have not desired drugs or drink since. I do not desire to lie, cheat, or steal. I only desire to live a life of surrender and service to God. I once thought all things spiritual to be hogwash. I now spend countless hours reading the word, spiritual books, and meditating.

"I don't fully understand the implications of this event. I do know that my life is defined as—before and after my NDE. It is a mystery."

—Dan Williams (died in jail from heart failure)

A Peculiar Anger

The most common reaction experiencers report after a near-death episode is anger. And there are two types: anger at having to come back when they didn't want to, or anger that such an event has intruded upon their life to begin with, as they were perfectly happy with the way things were.

The most common positive reactions from experiencers are:

- *Ecstatic,* at the wonder and beauty and glory of it all
- *Thrilled,* because they feel so privileged to have experienced such a miracle
- *Grateful,* that anything so incredible could have happened to them
- *In awe,* possibly even beyond words or the ability to speak
- *Evangelistic,* and immediately desirous of telling others the good news about death and God and the power of love
- *Humbled,* by the magnitude of what happened

The most common negative reactions from experiencers are:

- *Anger,* for having been revived and forced to leave wherever they were
- *Guilt,* for not missing or even being concerned about loved ones
- *Disappointment,* at discovering they are once again encased in a physical body, with all the inconveniences that entails
- *Horror,* if their experience was frightening or hellish
- *Dumbfounded,* if they want to talk but can't or are afraid to
- *Depression,* at realizing they must now resume their former lives, that they couldn't stay where they were

Irrespective of the initial reaction—and there are others than the common ones I've listed—the next response is usually puzzlement. Why did it happen to me? What does it mean? What do I do next? Was it real? Will anyone believe me if I tell them about it?

For example, you've already read about Tannis Prouten's experience in chapter 2. But she has more to say: "It felt horrible to be squeezed and constricted back in a body that felt so heavy—like a cement cast. It made me feel extremely dull and limited in body and mind. I wanted to be free again, to fly, to travel the universe, to stay in the infinite love, acceptance, and warmth of the LIGHT, my TRUE HOME. I felt like an open wound afterward, hypersensitive to everything around me, particularly to lights, sounds, emotions. I seemed to come back with heightened psychic abilities. I didn't feel that I belonged here anymore, nor did I want to. The guilt, grief, bewilderment, and anxiety about the meaning of all this lasted for many years."

Tannis continues: "How was I to adapt to the world I found myself back in, and who could I tell my secret to? Not family or friends, and particularly not doctors! Any attempt would result in the people in my life getting all uptight and cutting off any further discussion. I was afraid they would think I was crazy and lock me up. I was like a homesick kid. I felt totally disoriented, like I had just landed on a foreign planet, like Mars. My whole concept of reality had shifted. I now knew there was a GREATER REALITY, one more colorful and alive than here. And I knew there is a loving, totally accepting GOD who is close to me always, with every breath I take."

A Cauldron of Conflict

To appreciate the psychological conflicts that can arise, imagine, if you will, that right this minute you are involved in a near-death episode while undergoing surgery. You are experiencing the most exciting, ecstatic event of your life, in a place of indescribable beauty, when suddenly you are jerked back into a confining body with an equally restricting lifestyle, both of which you thought were finished.

Now, be honest. Would you be pleased or angry?

Regardless of how you answer that question, how do you think telling about your experience would be received by those professionals working hard to save your life? Or by your worried and frightened family?

Instantly, all involved are at cross-purposes. Emotions and feelings collide. No one really hears or listens to the other, much less makes any attempt to understand what might really be happening. And it's what occurs in those first few moments, hours, or days after the experience that sets the tone for all that comes next.

> **No to Oxygen Deprivation**
>
> Lack of oxygen to the brain doesn't explain near-death episodes. Oxygen deprivation causes confusion, belligerence, and some frightening hallucinations, which are a far cry from the calm and meaningful clarity present with the near-death phenomenon.

Ain't Like No Dream I Ever Had

Near-death episodes are sometimes mistaken for dreams. Perhaps that's because scenarios seem to mimic

New Word

Otherworldly journey is a general phrase applied to those subjective experiences that seem to propel the experiencer to realms or places beyond that of the physical here and now. They usually feature a "storyline" in the sense that there is an orderly progression of imagery, actions, sounds, and perhaps odors that greatly impress the individual. Most storylines are oriented toward revelation or are somehow instructive.

dream states—until you take a second look. Neither dreams nor hallucinations transform the personality as do near-death episodes. Actually, there is no physical condition medical science has yet been able to identify that might explain the power and the complexity of near-death states.

There come a million questions and no answers, because none of us has the innate tools or skills with which to understand or evaluate our new awareness and how we feel. We struggle and stumble, sometimes alienating when we mean to inspire, confusing when we mean to clarify, threatening when we mean to soften, frightening when we mean to enlighten. The message we seek to deliver is sometimes lost in the translation.

The truth is that no one can help an experiencer for a while—except to just be there and listen. Often there are many tears.

It was a miracle. Or was it?

The Specter of Insanity

The average experiencer fears that his or her episode is a sure sign of mental incompetence. And the average medical staff and practically every family member usually agree. While this diagnosis is highly inaccurate, the terrible truth is that some near-death experiencers have in fact been, and still are being, involuntarily committed to psychiatric institutions—because they dared to share the story about their otherworldly journey and because they now act "different."

I know how serious this situation can be. After my own episodes in 1977, I, too, thought I was going crazy. That it took so long for me to heal was, I believe, because of this secret fear. Then when I began interviewing others like myself, I noticed that each person responded exactly as I had. At least at first. That's when I realized we weren't crazy, we were overwhelmed!

A New You

Most experiencers report shifts in personality, attitudes, and behavior that are along these lines:

- Loss of the fear of death
- Reduced anxiety levels
- Greater self-confidence
- Increased concern for others
- Increased belief in an afterlife
- Increased awareness and interest in the paranormal
- Reduced suicidal tendencies
- Reduced desire for materialistic gains
- Insatiable hunger for knowledge
- Greater appreciation of nature
- Greater transcendental feelings

Larger Than Life

The near-death experience appears to enhance and enlarge whatever characteristics, traits, or potentials existed within the individual at the time the incident occurred. Typically:

- The experiencer's energy accelerates
- A sense of newness permeates everyday routines
- Possessiveness fades
- Long-term gratification often replaces a need for short-term pleasure
- Simple joys outweigh the desire for quick "highs" or fantasy escapes

And along with this acceleration in energy and what happens because of it, inner-child issues (that is, unfinished business from childhood) come to the forefront. This means anything suppressed, repressed, ignored, or undeveloped surfaces and becomes larger than life, including latent talents and abilities, as well as problems and concerns. Sometimes exaggerated in content and form, this rush of "old stuff" can interfere with or distort the experiencer's insights and behavior. It's almost as if, in order to facilitate healing in others, the individual must first heal him or herself.

A Quest for Knowledge

Experiencers can go on learning binges afterward, craving knowledge like some people crave sweets. Physics and metaphysics are popular subjects, as well as the newest in quantum theories about light, luminosity, zero-point energy, and the fabric of space. Merely searching in a dictionary for a word can lead to hours of happy distraction.

Many enroll in schools and self-development classes, and take as many field trips as their budgets allow for hands-on learning. They often automatically gravitate to teaching and

> **You Can Even Look Different**
>
> It's not unusual for an experiencer's "before" and "after" photographs to differ somewhat. Occasionally, differences are so pronounced there is little resemblance in the individual's two appearances. Handwriting can change, too; body "clocks" often reverse—not to mention a whole host of other physiological and psychological changes that typically occur. (We'll look at these changes in more detail in chapter 7.)

> **The Big Scrubbing**
>
> The emergence of personal issues that seem unrelated to the phenomenon is commonplace. It's almost as if the near-death experience operates like a giant washing machine in the way it scrubs up and cleans out the individual's psyche, releasing anything locked in or held back. Because of this, along with the intensity of the episode itself, the phenomenon often takes years to integrate, which might account for the unusually high divorce rate experiencers have. Most researchers place that divorce rate at 75 to 78 percent.

IQ and Intelligence Soar

Intelligence and intuition are commonly heightened following a near-death experience. Before and after IQ tests can show unexplainable increases, especially with child experiencers. Almost everyone becomes more creative and innovative, as if they are now able to think "outside the box."

counseling roles, or to the areas of religion, spirituality, and healing.

The Strain on Relationships

As you have no doubt guessed from the high divorce rate among experiencers, relationships can become a major tussle. But not just spousal relationships. Experiencers' children and friends can also be confused by the aftermath of the phenomenon. These people deserve extra attention. They didn't have the experience and they don't know what's going on.

Tonia Hugus, formerly of New York City and now residing in Charlottesville, Virginia, tells the following story: "My mother's near-death experience and the subsequent decisions she made had both a profoundly negative and positive effect upon all her children while we were still quite young. On one hand, we all developed a sense of 'otherness.' My mother taught us that there was a very thin veil between this earthly existence and a 'heavenly existence,' and most importantly that all it took was a simple act of faith to plug into that Source and get help. I completely believed that, as surely as I have two eyes, a nose, and a mouth. This belief has gotten me through two almost fatal degenerative illnesses, from which I was able to come back healthier than before, and it has carried me through some very serious life crises.

"On the other hand, my mother chose to believe that God must be embodied in the orthodox Catholic tradition. She despised sexuality and made all of us feel ashamed. She stayed married to my father and went on to have six more children, even though our financial situation devolved into hopeless poverty. She also turned her head away from the serious abuse of myself and my two other sisters by our father.

"I would have to say that the good and bad were equally extreme because of my mother's near-death experience. In many ways, my brothers and sisters and myself are remarkable people. We are good parents, even though we were horrifically treated. But, also, thanks to mother, we learned to be impractical when it comes to earthly matters, the use of money, being on time to anything, feeling really 'here.'" Tonia spoke through many tears as she related being utterly fascinated by her mother, yet feeling absolutely abandoned by her. "She was too detached from the awful reality going on around her. She lived her life to get back to God; that determined her every action. She gave us a faith that could move mountains. But it was a mixed bag. I will probably be sorting it out for the rest of my life."

Tonia portrays her life with her mother as a "mixed bag," and that exactly describes the aftereffects and how experiencers respond to them. For those who are successful in integrating their experience—and the majority are—life becomes so wonderful and so joyful afterward that you honestly begin to wonder how you could have ever lived any other way.

Lifestyle Switcheroos

At the beginning of this chapter, I briefly mentioned instances in which people radically changed their lives after undergoing a near-death experience. Not everyone, though, completely changes his or her life. Many go back to "life as usual," although with a certain gleam in their eye and a lift to their step that is unmistakable. Some pretend nothing of significance happened to them, but either their behavior or their unusual attitudes give them away. Those who do alter their lifestyles—well, each one could easily qualify for the status of "miracle maker" in how they affect others.

There's a salesman who became a renowned opera star. A lawyer who discovered she had "healing hands." An athlete who suddenly "knew" physics and started writing equations of advanced quantum mechanics. You've already learned about Mellen-Thomas Benedict in chapter 2, who is now doing DNA research and exploring the effect of light as a medical tool. Then there is Olaf Swenson, who developed more than one hundred patents in molecular chemistry, all based on insights gained during his near-death episode at age fourteen.

And then, of course, there's Joseph McMoneagle, who, while stationed in Germany, suddenly fell victim to a serious heart ailment, died, revived, and soon discovered he had the ability to "view" people and places at a distance without ever going there. Described in *Readers Digest* as America's number-one remote viewer or "psychic spy," McMoneagle has quite a history of military assignments and CIA involvements, including spying on Russia and locating hostages via the "inner eye" of his mind. His track record is quite impressive. He wrote *Mind Trek* (see

Help for Family Members

Because near-death states can strain relationships, sometimes to the breaking point, the International Association for Near-Death Studies (IANDS) specifically addresses this issue at their annual conferences. Spouses, parents, and various family members are encouraged to attend special workshops geared toward the unique situation they find themselves in—trying to understand someone who has changed from the person they knew before.

New Word

A **remote viewer** is one who is trained through rigorous instruction to use his or her psychic ability to view certain people or places at a distance, and in detail.

The "found art" of Dan Rhema

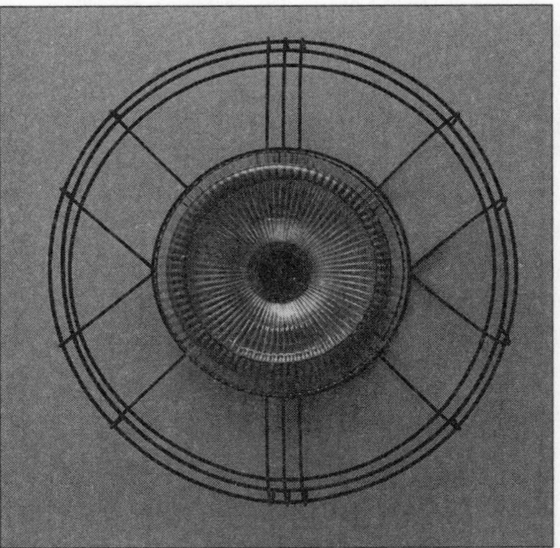

Dan Rhema's paintings, although simple of form, feature vivid colors and striking techniques.

appendix C) as a way to show how remote viewing is done and what can be accomplished using it.

Here are four more such stories, each a little longer than those already mentioned, to give you a better sense of the kind of switcheroos that can happen after a near-death experience.

Altered Visions

While serving as an intercultural training center director in Mexico in 1991, Dan Rhema contracted dengue fever (also known as breakbone fever) and spinal meningitis. Once he was taken back to the States, he was sent to the Centers for Disease Control in Atlanta, Georgia, for treatment. He died at the hospital but revived—reborn, he claims, because of the near-death episode he experienced. He calls what happened to him a spiritual journey or vision quest because of how it led him to express himself and his visions through "found art" (artwork that is created from scraps, discards, and the bits and pieces of everyday living that most people ignore).

"I was recuperating in Georgia," Dan recalls, "when I began to collect wild thorny vines. I twisted them into a piece that I called "Fever," which is still hanging in my gallery." Today, Dan creates masks, collages, sculptures, and paintings to match the surrealistic visions of his dreams. In theatrical productions, through his video *Altered Visions,* and because of the growing popularity of his art, the Dan Rhema story is touching the lives of countless people.

Sav-Baby

In 1982, Donna DeSoto was told during her near-death experience that if she wanted a second chance on Earth she must do something to help save God's children. Thinking adoption was what God meant, she and her husband first adopted Robert, then later Ben, a Hispanic-Indian, who had been abandoned at birth by his natural mother and tossed aside in a paper bag.

Then they heard of a newborn baby girl who had been found stuffed into a plastic bag and thrown onto someone's front yard like a piece of trash. This child, though, had died. Drawn to the funeral with her two boys, Donna noticed that a tear from Robert dropped right into the grave. "I could not get that image out of my mind," Donna remembers. "Seeing Robert's tear fall into that dead baby's grave pushed me closer still to the mission I had promised. I was just an everyday homemaker and housewife until that happened. The funeral of this little girl is why Sav-Baby was founded, a nonprofit agency to prevent the abandonment of newborns and to protect their legal rights. I installed a toll-free number out of my own money, hoping to reach girls before they got desperate enough to abandon their babies." The organization has since spread from her home state of Texas and, with the help of volunteers, has been able to find homes for many unwanted infants.

Help for Abandoned Babies

Sav-Baby, an alternative to baby abandonment, is a nonprofit organization dedicated to saving helpless infants. They also do whatever they can to assist desperate mothers in finding homes for unwanted babies. A volunteer is on duty twenty-four hours a day at the Texas hotline, 1-800-SAV-BABY. Until chapters of Sav-Baby are established in other states, out-of-staters can call the headquarters office at (210) 270-4600.

The CIA

In 1975, Dannion Brinkley was talking on the telephone during a thunderstorm when a bolt of lightning hit the phone line. Thousands of volts of electricity surged through him, tossing him into the air and stopping his heart. Twenty-eight minutes later, Dannion revived in the morgue, much to the shock of morgue personnel, and, when able to speak, had quite a story to tell. During those twenty-eight minutes, he underwent a long and detailed near-death episode recounted in his bestseller *Saved by the Light* (the book was the basis for a movie of the same name, starring Eric Roberts).

Dannion died again in 1989 when his damaged heart gave out during an attack of pneumonia, and once more a few years ago in another reversal of his health. He revived both times, each time having another near-death experience. Dannion's journey from a self-centered troublemaker to a generous benefactor of thousands as a result of what happened to him is admirable. Although a controversial figure, his stunning psychic abilities, along with the revelations he was given during his various episodes, still attract as many supporters as naysayers. No one can

Help for the Dying

The CIA believes that no one need die alone. They hold rigorous training sessions for people willing to work at the "deathbed," whenever needed or called. The organization depends entirely on donations; they charge no fee for their service. The public's grass-roots response to their call for volunteers and funding has been nothing short of miraculous. For more information, call their national office in Los Angeles at (323) 931-7315.

Walk-Ins

Ruth Montgomery first popularized the notion of "walk-ins" in her 1983 book, *Threshold to Tomorrow.* Through "guidance," she was directed to write that "advanced souls" can inhabit recently vacated bodies, for the purpose of taking a "shortcut" into Earth life to help humankind. Supposedly, "agreements" must exist between the two souls for this exchange to occur. Ruth identified Carol Parrish as one of these walk-ins, a claim Carol confirmed, because of all that occurred during her near-death episode. To say this notion caused a national stir at the time would be an understatement. It is still regarded as highly controversial and without substantiating evidence.

argue with the stand he has taken for hospice care, however, and the nonprofit organization he created and continues to lead called the CIA—Compassion In Action: The Twilight Brigade. The CIA (as their T-shirts proclaim) is now nationwide, operating as a credible nonprofit organization composed of volunteers whose goal it is to help the dying.

Sancta Sophia

During the birth of her child in 1958, Carol Parrish suffered an allergic reaction to the sodium pentothal she had been given and her lungs collapsed. The near-death state she experienced so totally changed her life that even today there is no denying the impact that moment had. In her book *Messengers of Hope,* she details her unusual story of how, at the moment of death, the soul residing within her body left and another soul, her current one, replaced it—a condition termed a "walk-in."

Whether or not you accept the walk-in theory, the "new" Carol "walked out" of the typical middle-American lifestyle that the "other Carol" had been living, became an ordained Christian minister, and went on to found Sparrow Hawk Village and its Light of Christ Community Church, located northeast of Tahlequah, Oklahoma. Her crowning achievement is Sancta Sophia Seminary, an accredited institution that awards degrees not only in religious ministry, but in the time-honored esoteric or mystical philosophies that are the basis of Christianity. The biblical "Gifts of the Spirit" are not only embraced there, but taught.

Deity Reigns

As a researcher, I can assure you that any type of near-death experience can be life-changing. But, as an experiencer, I can positively affirm that being bathed in The Light on the other side of death is more than life-changing. That light is the very essence, the heart and soul, the all-consuming consummation of ecstasy. It is a million suns of compressed love dissolving everything unto itself, annihilating thought and cell, vaporizing humanness and history, into the one great brilliance of all that is and all that ever was and all that ever will be.

You know it's God. No one has to tell you. You know. You no longer believe in God, for belief implies doubt. There is no more doubt. None. You now know God. And you know that you know. And you're never the same again. And you know who you are—a child of God, a cell in The Greater Body, an extension of The One Force, an expression from The One Mind. No more can you forget your identity, or deny or ignore or pretend it away. There is One, and you are of The One. One. The Light does that to you.

While not every experiencer speaks of God as I have here, the majority do. And almost to a person they gravitate toward a more spiritual viewpoint, preferring to recognize that which is sacred as an integral part of their everyday lives.

God Is No Fairy Tale

Although not all experiencers will agree, the vast majority return convinced that the testimonies about the existence of a deity are true—in the sense that a single intelligence permeates and enlivens all things. Most still use the term "God," while others prefer a more esoteric phrase like The One Mind or All That Is.

Knowing replaces believing as the majority come to embrace a direct, personal relationship with the deity. God for the average experiencer is no longer an abstract, or an illusion, or a fairy tale, or the product of wishful thinking. Rather, God is a very real, totally living and powerful Presence that, while defying description, is as vital as their next breath—and just as accessible. This vitality and the strength of their new vision concerning things spiritual is both wonderful and not so wonderful, for it can put them at odds with the prevailing views of their family and society.

The First Rule of Discipleship

There are churches that embrace "mystical revelation," as they call it, and encourage their congregants to share

> **Ways of Worship Alter**
>
> One-third of the experiencers in my research base remained in their same religious setting afterward. The other two-thirds either left their religious affiliation or weren't churchgoers to begin with. Alternatively, they pursued interests in metaphysical (New Thought) churches, Eastern religious traditions, shamanism, and varied esoteric orders. Most of those who left organized religion returned to some type of church setting within about ten years, especially if the church was of the open and tolerant variety.

> **New Words**
>
> **Spirituality** is most commonly defined as a personal relationship with God that can involve direct revelation, while recognizing and honoring the sacredness of all created things. **Religion** is a systemized approach to spiritual development based on set standards or dogmas that provide community support while establishing moral upliftment and behavior.

their special moments of truth—the dreams and visions that have made a profound difference in their lives. This practice enriches everyone present and strengthens church ties. But some religious groups are rather strident in their opposition to anyone who deviates, even one whit, from established creeds. Trying to blend back in to this type of institutional approach is where experiencers encounter situations that are sometimes quite painful.

Case in point: After delivering a speech in a large city in Texas, I met a youngster of about ten who was dying of a brain tumor. His mother was with him and spoke of how, after having a most amazing near-death episode, the boy had returned filled with love, and was still in communication with the angels who had greeted him on the other side of death. Instead of being supportive, the people in their church began making weekly visits to the family, condemning the boy and threatening that if he didn't quit telling such stories he would burn in hell.

Of his uncomfortable situation, the youngster said, "They don't know God like I do. I tried to tell them, but they won't listen." He then continued, "It bothers me what they're doing. It hurts my mother, and I don't want her to be hurt."

And lest you think this event occurred during the early days of near-death research, it didn't. It happened in October 1997. Church members had been harassing this family continuously since the summer of that year. I wish this were an isolated case. Unfortunately, it's not.

Most experiencers, at least initially, become like disciples in their zeal to spread "the good news" about God. Because of this, they would be wise to follow the First Rule of Discipleship. What is that rule? "Don't freak the natives."

Comments from Smiley-Jen

A near-death experiencer living in Australia, who prefers to call herself "Smiley-Jen," has this to say about what happened to her:

"If I came back with one thing, it is that there is nothing of importance but unconditional love and compassion. I had experienced a lot of tragedies in my life, quite a few sudden and violent deaths of dear friends including murder, which before the NDE I was very angry about. I was quite surprised to learn there is no 'judgment,' that as much as I'd ranted and raved about hating 'God' for letting these tragedies happen, he still loved me, and there was a better way to face such tragedies. During the NDE I learned so much about the essence of love and compassion. I 'know' my life here is to experience opportunities to show that it can still exist under difficult circumstances.

"My son, born by Caesarean, was paralyzed by a mistake made by the delivering doctor and died in my arms after twenty-eight days on a ventilator. While the doctor had the instinct to run from me, I was able to ease his fear and show him love and compassion. This had a remarkable effect on the doctors and nurses in the special care nursery, changing many of their lives.

"Two years ago this week, our beautiful fifteen-year-old daughter was hit by a car and killed while walking home. I was able to impart to her friends and authorities that the young driver was in need of understanding and compassion, and in doing so, averted the horrible path of 'blame' and anger that had been so destructive in my own life. If he hadn't learned by the consequences, then anger would not help him. It would only hurt those who loved her. Many people have come to tell me how watching me has altered their view of the world, and more important, how they interact with it and others.

"The only real trouble I got into with my NDE was mentioning during grief counseling how I envied my son, that death was so beautiful. Naturally, I was sent to see a psychiatrist who thought I was suicidal because I had no fear of death, in fact, a longing that he misinterpreted. I could only laugh at his ignorance (which probably didn't help my cause), since nothing could have been further from the truth. I knew it was not my time, that I had other things to do, but I was very, very homesick. I would go to sleep hoping that I would go back to the light, and wake disappointed. I didn't get on with this doctor. He was so pompous, yet ignorant, and I could not take him seriously. I think in his heart I threatened him, because I would not adhere to the textbook.

"I was transferred to another doctor who counseled and assessed me more fairly. He noted that I was 'a remarkably well-balanced woman who had endured an incredible amount of tragedy and was probably more sane than anyone he'd ever met.' He held no fear for my safety because I held life in all its glory as a sacred gift. Now I can say I'm sane and I have a psychiatrist's note to prove it!"

Consequences

The near-death phenomenon is experienced by most as a death-rebirth event; the old self dies while a new person is born. Center to the phenomenon's effects is a discovery of self-worth and an encounter with spiritual realities.

7

The Undeniable Aftereffects

> If you want the root from which all beauty exudes, remember this: The shell must be cracked open if what is inside is to come out. If you want the kernel, then you must break the shell.
>
> —Meister Eckhart, German Christian mystic, Dominican, university professor, and preacher

Most experiencers don't realize that what happened to them has aftereffects—a specific pattern of altered sensations and sensitivities—that themselves are quite incredible, aside from their connection to the near-death phenomenon. It's commonplace for years to pass before anyone makes the connection that maybe, just maybe, the "new you" is a result of the "old you" having undergone a major adjustment after surviving death's finality and being given a glimpse of the other side. Until one plus one begins to equal two, the individual tends to deny the whole thing: "What do you mean, I'm different now? Why, I'm the same as I've always been. It's you who have changed."

It's usually a spouse, child, best friend, or even a neighbor who finally "blows the whistle." In my case, it was my daughter Natalie. She sat me down one day and said, "You're friendlier now than you used to be, and you're easier to talk to. But you're not Mom, and I want Mom back." Well, we both spent years looking for that woman. Never did find her. Twelve years later I invited all three of my children to write down their impressions of "before" and "after." My oldest and youngest were glowing in their accounts of what they now saw in me. Natalie, the middle child, was rather critical, until the last paragraph. She then did a complete turn and announced: "You've done a lot of changing, Mom, and I'm proud of you. Now it's my turn."

Experiencers Don't See It

Of those who claimed that they had no discernible differences afterward, the significant others in their lives, at least the ones I was able to interview, disagreed. To a person, they insisted that just the opposite was true—that the individual who exists today is not the same person they once knew. Many laughed at their loved one's denial. One fellow said of his wife, "Don't listen to her. She doesn't see how she's changed. I do." An experiencer who was a lawyer flatly stated, "I am the same person I have always been." His partner winked at me and quipped, "No way."

Connecting the Dots

However inspiring or challenging the scenario, it is the aftereffects that confer value and meaning to the experience. Aftereffects can be positive or negative, depending on the individual's response. A 1994 compilation of my research data showed the following impact among experiencers:

- 21 percent claimed no discernible changes happened to them afterward
- 60 percent reported significantly noticeable changes
- 19 percent said changes were so radical they felt as if they had become another person

The following table shows the general pattern of aftereffects common to near-death states. I'll discuss some of these aftereffects in more detail in the sections that follow.

Not everyone exhibits all of these characteristic aftereffects, certainly, but the majority do. Whichever traits do appear can be brand new or expansions and enlargements of abilities already present within the experiencer (latent skills).

After a near-death experience, challenges come quickly. Confusions and misunderstandings stack up; changes are continuous. The whole drama may seem like "the luck of the draw" or simply "the way things are," until the experiencer begins to read research findings and talk to others who have had the same experience. Then "connecting the dots" starts to occur. It's always a surprise to realize just how much this particular phenomenon can alter you and the way you live your life—perhaps permanently.

Common Psychological Aftereffects

Aftereffects can be as varied among experiencers as the near-death scenarios themselves. The overall pattern is consistent, however. The most common psychological characteristics follow.

Love's Edge

Typically, near-death experiencers come to love and accept others without the usual attachments and preconditions society has come to expect. They see themselves as being equally loving and fully accepting of each person they meet. Their desire to be a conduit of love to others is more akin to the universal type of love historically referred

Major Characteristics Displayed by People Who Have Undergone Near-Death Experiences

Psychological

Most Common (80–90%): loss of the fear of death; become more spiritual/less religious; more generous and charitable; handle stress easier; philosophical; more open and accepting of the new and different; disregard for time and schedules; regard things as new even when they're not (boredom levels decrease); form expansive concepts of love while at the same time challenged to initiate and maintain satisfying relationships; become psychic/intuitive; know things (closer connection to Deity/God, prayerful); deal with bouts of depression; less competitive.

Quite Common (50–79%): displays of psychic phenomena; vivid dreams and visions; "inner child" issues exaggerate; convinced of life purpose/mission; rejection of previous limitations/norms; episodes of future knowing; more detached and objective (dissociation); "merge" easily (absorption); hunger for knowledge; difficulty communicating and with language; can go through deep periods of depression and feelings of alienation from others; synchronicity commonplace; more or less sexual; less desire for possessions and money; service oriented; healing ability; attract animals (good with plants); aware of invisible energy fields/auras; preference for open doors and open windows/shades; drawn to crystals; laugh more; adults younger afterward/children more mature (wiser) afterward.

Physiological

Most Common (80–95%): more sensitive to light, especially sunlight and to sound (tastes in music change); look younger/act younger/more playful (can be the opposite with children); substantial change in energy levels (can have energy surges); changes in thought processing (switch from sequential/selective thinking to clustered/abstracting, with an acceptance of ambiguity); insatiable curiosity; lower blood pressure; brighter skin and eyes; reversal of brain hemisphere dominance commonplace; heal quicker.

Quite Common (50–79%): reversal of body clock, electrical sensitivity, heightened intelligence, metabolic changes (doesn't take that long to process food, bowel movements can increase); assimilate substances into bloodstream quicker (takes less for full effect); loss of pharmaceutical tolerance (many turn to alternative/complementary healing measures—holistic); heightened response to taste/touch/texture/smell/pressure; more creative and inventive; synesthesia (multiple sensing); increased allergies; preference for more vegetables, less meat (adults)/more meat, less vegetables (children); latent talents surface; display indications of changes in brain structure and function (changes in nervous and digestive systems, skin sensitivity).

to as *agape* than to popular notions of a sexual attraction between people or possessiveness.

As experiencers begin to embrace broader and greater aspects of love, limiting behaviors and role playing are

New Word

Agape is the Greek word for "the love of God or Christ for mankind." The term was once used to describe the "brotherly" or spiritual love one Christian had for another, but eventually came to mean an unselfish, more detached or unconditional type of love—a love that is freely given and without expectations.

Sky High

In the mid-1980s, I spoke openly about my discovery that the divorce rate for adult experiencers of near-death states was 75 percent. Nancy Evans Bush, a fellow researcher, substantiated this in 1991 during research of her own; Dr. Bruce Greyson followed, confirming her observation. But it wasn't until September 2005 that Rozan Christian, PhD, LPC, set the record straight: "Prior to my study, no one had conducted a quantitative study specific to the issues of marital satisfaction and stability, and, therefore, the 75 percent number being used had not been supported through scientific research. I concluded that, based on my sample [and my study]—75 percent of NDE marriages ended in divorce, which corroborated what had been stated in previous writings."

cast aside. Their love becomes heart-centered rather than people-centered.

Poof! Go Stress Levels

Willoughby B. Britton, a doctoral student at the University of Arizona and coauthor of a study published April 2004 in *Psychological Science* (see appendix C), noted that near-death experiencers are far better at handling stress than anyone thought. "They aren't more likely to run away from stress." This surprises researchers, yet it is typical behavior for experiencers.

Lives change, careers switch, new values emerge. Fears they once had tend to disappear. Bruce Greyson, MD, a psychiatrist at the University of Virginia, explained further; "People who have NDEs tend to be a little healthier than others. They seem to have positive coping skills."

Confused family members and friends can tend to regard this sudden switch as oddly threatening, as if their friend or loved one has become aloof, unresponsive, or even uncaring and unloving. Some mistake this "unconditional" manner of expressing joy and affection as flirtatious misbehavior or disloyalty. Consequently, divorces are, unfortunately, numerous.

Fences Be Gone

One of the biggest reasons life seems so different afterward is that the experiencer now has a basis of comparison unknown before. Familiar codes of conduct can lose relevance or disappear altogether. Boundaries, rules, limits, "shoulds," and "have-tos" are often dropped in favor of inventive new ways of thinking and acting, even to the extent of the experiencer appearing to be almost childlike in how he or she responds.

With the fading of previous norms, basic cautions and discernment also fade. This can leave the individual a "sitting duck" for all manner of difficulties. Health-care professionals sometimes misconstrue these new behaviors as a sign of mental instability, and family and friends can express disgust or embarrassment at what seems to them a person indulging in an ego trip—when nothing of the kind is true.

A Dividing Line

Strangely, experiencers often refer to their episodes as if they were a divider, a "time-fence" so to speak, separating one life phase from another. Some even declare that what occurred before they "died" was their first life; what they have now is their second.

Revelations

Many near-death experiencers report that during their episode or soon afterward, they were given revelations about future events. Such revelatory claims are now so numerous, hardly an eyebrow is raised—even when they later prove to be accurate.

Poof! Go Clocks and Calendars

Once you have experienced timelessness, you are no longer governed by "the tyranny of time." And, in that regard, experiencers do indeed develop a sense of timelessness about them. Many go so far as to reject schedules and refuse to use clocks or wristwatches. They begin to "flow" with the natural shift of light and dark, and display a more heightened awareness of the present moment and the importance of being in the "now." Tom Coates, an experiencer of a near-death-like state, puts it this way, "Now is the address at which eternity resides."

As you can imagine, this habit of "seeing past time" can sometimes make an experiencer appear "spacey" and can irritate others to the point that they tend to ignore the individual.

Being Psychic—Gift or Curse?

Let's be straightforward about this situation and admit that experiencers who weren't psychic before become so after; those who were psychic before usually skyrocket in such abilities afterward. Out-of-body experiences can continue, the light beings met in death can become a daily part of life routines, the future is often known before it occurs, extrasensory perception becomes normal and ordinary.

That association with the future can take on several modes of awareness in the sense that experiencers claim they can see or hear what is to come, just know without any apparent reason for that knowing, or feel as if they are "physically" living a given segment of their future in advance of it happening. I call the latter an episode of *future memory*.

New Word

Based on experiencer accounts, I define **future memory** as the ability to fully live a given event or sequence of events subjectively before physically living the same incident. The experience is then usually, but not always, forgotten, to be remembered later when some "signal" triggers its memory. Sensory-rich, future memory is so detailed and thorough, it's indistinguishable from everyday reality while occurring.

Don't confuse future memory with déjà vu (a French term denoting that sense of "having been before to a place first visited"). Déjà vu concerns the past and what was done in the past. Future memory differs in that it covers incidents that cannot be linked to what is normally regarded as memory. Rather, the fact that such episodes could even occur suggests that we can access the future as if in some manner it preexists, or at least that time itself does not necessarily operate as we think it does. I discuss the importance of being able to access the future and what this ability might mean in chapter 22.

These new awarenesses—the paranormal, and all that is associated with it—become increasingly comfortable to experiencers. Some friends and loved ones ignore this, but others hurl all manner of charges, including devil worship or madness. The experiencers' previous religious beliefs do not alter or prevent the amplification of things psychic. What manifests as "gifts of the spirit" still fosters irrational fear in far too many people.

Don't Let Your Eyes Fool You

Gregory L. Little, EdD, an expert in brain processes and author of a popular college textbook, *Psychopharmacology,* reminds us that humans can only see 5 percent of what exists in the electromagnetic spectrum. The rods and cones in the human eye respond *only* to this 5 percent range. Beings normally not visible to us, worlds and realms beyond regular perception, seem to exist, in his opinion, in the ultraviolet and infrared ends of the spectrum. "Just because we can't see something," he advises, "doesn't mean it's not real."

Awakening to a New Reality

Although the physical world may seem petty afterward, the impression of having visited a more perfect place is so strong it tends to "fuel" the individual's determination to in some way make life better for others. Fears and worries tend to dissolve as life paradoxes begin to make sense.

Hard-driving achievers and materialists often transform into easygoing philosophers, while those more uncommitted or disinterested before can become "movers and shakers" afterward. Personality shifts such as these seem to depend more on what is "needed" to round out the experiencer's inner growth than on any uniform outcome.

Whatever change they undergo, experiencers tell me over and over again that it's as if they have awakened from a deep sleep and can at last recognize the difference between that which is true in life and that which only seems to be true.

A Shared Event

Significant others can utterly "lose" it in trying to relate to and understand the changes near-death experiencers often "grow" through. In some households, however, relatives can be so impressed by what they witness that they, too, change, making the episode a "shared" event. In other families, though, the response can be so negative, alienation results. Not all near-death survivors are "survivors."

Body Jackets

Saint Teresa of Avila, the great Spanish mystic and reformer, said, "After you die, you wear what you are." And the vast majority of experiencers confirm that what we are is a living soul, a child of God, and that the body is a "jacket" the soul wears on Earth but discards at death in preparation for its next journey—"elsewhere." Some experiencers put it this way: "We are currently encased in a carbon-based, electromagnetic lifeform more commonly referred to as a body."

After their near-death experiences, it may take a while before many are once again comfortable in physical form and accept the importance and specialness of their own bodies, but, eventually, they do.

Language on a Higher Plane

Once an individual experiences being one with the universe, little else is of much interest. What was once foreign becomes familiar; what was once familiar becomes foreign. Rationale tends to lose its logic. Some reorient themselves to Earth life with a certain enthusiasm fairly quickly, perhaps within a year's time, but the majority take much longer than that.

During this initial phase of "dealing with it," experiencers tend to think and talk abstractly and in grandiose terms rather than in the linear mode of sequential thinking. New ways of using language—even whole new vocabularies—often emerge. This can turn a simple conversation into a major production, missing the topic at hand altogether. Communications get jumbled, putting a further strain on relationships.

With time, the language and communications differences do diminish, relationships often mend, and routines can return. Yet the experiencer remains ever and always more in tune with a "sound current" few others can hear.

Common Physiological Aftereffects

Whoever conjured up the idea that near-death states merely bump an individual's appreciation of life up a notch or two on a scale of one to ten, didn't know much about the phenomenon. The physical brain and various body systems are affected, in addition to the

Ouch!

Sensitivity to light and sound is such a major issue that at near-death conferences sponsored by IANDS, video equipment is now restricted (television crews must do their filming in the halls outside the auditoriums), houselights are subdued, and sound systems are tuned to decibels lower than for a regular conference. If these precautions are not taken, the complaint is always the same: Pain!

mind. In 80 to 95 percent of the cases, experiencers report:

- Looking and acting younger, being more playful
- Brighter skin, eyes that sparkle
- Substantial alterations in energy levels
- Becoming more sensitive to light, especially sunlight
- Becoming more sensitive to sound and noise levels
- Regarding things as new even when they're not

Gimme Your Gold

Health-care practitioners who also practice acupuncture are now reporting a need to change needles when working on a near-death experiencer. They have discovered that switching to gold needles, rather than using stainless steel ones, gives a quicker, more thorough effect for deep healing. One practitioner said, "Using stainless steel needles on an experiencer is a waste of time."

- Boredom levels decrease or disappear
- Stress is easier to handle
- Wounds heal more quickly
- Changes in the way the brain functions

Additionally, in 50 to 79 percent of the cases, experiencers list:

- Metabolic changes, where the body seems to assimilate substances quicker than before, necessitating smaller doses of whatever might be needed in the way of supplementation or medication

- An increase in allergies, even to the point where pharmaceutical prescriptions successfully taken in the past can no longer be tolerated

- A greater sensitivity to household chemicals, fabric and wood coatings, food preservatives, sprays, and perfumes

- Breathing anomalies can occur—can cease suddenly for no apparent reason, then resume later on, without any apparent effect on consciousness and performance. The longest stoppage I am aware of was for eight minutes.

- Substantially lower blood pressure; pulse rate can also decrease

- A reduction in red meat consumption or a conversion to vegetarianism

- A preference for open doors, open windows, few if any shades, no locks—even closet doors left open

- An ability to "merge" with whatever is focused on and to exist in more than one dimension simultaneously

- The capacity to attract animals and birds, even in the wild, and often "hear" them speak. True also with plants. Small children also seek out experiencers as if attracted to their energy.

- A thirst for knowledge; latent talents surface; laugh more

- Cognitive abilities sometimes switch, as the thinking process continues to alter and change

- Reversal of body clocks (night people become day people and vice versa)

- Heightened sensations of taste-touch-texture-smell

- Develop healing gifts

- Many become more orgasmic

- Continue to "see" and "hear" beings met in death

- *Synchronicity* becomes commonplace

Sleep Patterns Change

It is common knowledge that sleep patterns change for experiencers after their near-death experience.

Research done in 2004 at the University of Arizona, separating near-death experiencers from nonexperiencers, found that 22 percent of the near-death experiencers exhibited a rare brain-wave pattern known as "synchronized brain

New Word

The Swiss psychiatrist Carl Jung coined the term **synchronicity** to describe the phenomenon of seemingly unrelated events occurring in unexpected relation to each other, not connected by cause and effect but by simultaneity and meaning. Simply defined as "meaningful coincidence," this phenomenon is unpredictable and seemingly random in occurrence, yet it happens more often than we might think.

It's 3:00 A.M. and All is Well

Experiencers often report waking up during the wee hours of morning—mostly around 3:00 A.M.—perhaps staying up for a while and then going back to sleep. A possible explanation for this might be because the majority of experiencers shift to natural circadian rhythms afterward.

Earth's magnetic field, pushed by solar winds, peaks around 3:00 A.M. each night, no matter where you are in the world. This "ambient" or surrounding circulation is considered *unstable* by scientists, yet artists consider it *creatively stimulating.*

Experiencers say they feel strangely energized by the air and by the sense of feeling they have at that time.

The Mysterious Limbic

The limbic system is located in a semicircle in the middle of the brain, capping off the topmost extension of the brain stem. Consisting of various sections, it's known to be the seat of our basic instincts for sex, hunger, sleep, and survival, and of fear. The limbic system is often referred to as our "gut" or third brain. In it originates the wide range of emotional perceptions and awareness that are elaborated on and refined in the brain's left and right hemispheres. It has a direct neural connection with the heart. Many professionals now believe that if the limbic system does not originate mind, it certainly is the gateway to mind.

activity" in the left temporal lobe. This simultaneous firing of neurons, previously existing only in people who suffered epileptic seizures, was a surprise. "This is the first study ever to find neurophysiologic differences in people who have had these [near-death] experiences," said Willoughby B. Britton, the UV researcher who led the study (published in *Psychological Science,* 2004—refer to appendix C).

The group of near-death experiencers in the study also exhibited other unusual sleep patterns, among them a longer length of time than normal to reach REM sleep (rapid eye movement/the dream stage of sleeping). "This may explain the change in temperament these people have," stated Britton. He pointed out that a long REM delay shows an emotional bias toward the positive, with less risk for depression.

Synesthesia and Electrical Sensitivity

I mentioned that among the aftereffects reported by experiencers are heightened sensibilities—found in 50 to 79 percent of the cases. Two of these heightened sensibilities in particular are quite fascinating and worth taking a closer look.

Multiple Sensing

"Synesthesia" is the scientific term for multiple sensing. People who have this condition experience an awareness of the world around them in multiple clusters that seem odd to the average person. For example: synesthetes (people who have synesthesia) can do things like "hear" paintings, "smell" sounds, "taste" vision, or "see" music. In other words, they receive stimuli of one type (for example, sight) that is also experienced as a sensory experience of another type (for example, smell). Clinical experiments identify synesthesia as a product of the limbic system in the brain.

The neurologist famous for his investigation of people who display synesthesia is Richard E. Cytowic, MD. He's written a number of books on the subject, including *The Man Who Tasted Shapes: A Bizarre Medical Mystery Offers Revolutionary Insights into Emotions, Reasoning, and Consciousness* (see appendix C). Dr. Cytowic states that the phenomenon is not something new but has always existed, and that sensing through a given faculty in multiple ways can be developed at will.

It's fascinating to me that the limbic system, as the seat of our survival urges, seems to be central to the entire near-death experience. And, after an episode, the experiencer begins to show signs of limbic system acceleration or enhancement, like synesthesia. Actually, there are many such signs, all of them suggestive of the same premise: Near-death states, if intense enough, may somehow trigger changes in brain structure, chemistry, and function.

Electromagnetic Fields

Electrical sensitivity is a term near-death researchers use to refer to those people whose energy, and the energy field around them, seems to affect or control electrical and/or electronic equipment. The interference caused by their energy can lead to malfunctions, breakage, or other unusual reactions that cannot be rationally explained.

It has been established that "electrical sensitives" often have many allergies, report a very high incidence of psychic phenomena, claim to have "healing gifts," are emotionally intense or unstable, and exhibit an abnormal sensitivity to light and sound. Of the experiencers I interviewed, 73 percent fit this profile and gave numerous reports of electrical snafus such as microphones that "fought" them, recorders that began to "smoke," computers that "crashed," television channels that "flipped," electronic memory systems that "wiped out," or streetlights that "popped" as they walked by. None could wear watches anymore without constantly repairing or replacing them. All of them reported a heightened awareness of *electromagnetic fields* in general.

> **New Words**
>
> **Electromagnetic fields (EMFs)** refer to the array of electrical currents and magnetic radiation that surround any given object or being. These field arrays are representative of the larger spectrum of electromagnetic waves, which includes radio waves, light, X rays, and gamma rays. Only a small fraction of the spectrum is visible to the average person.

> **Light to the Rescue**
>
> The problem with watches may have a solution. It seems that watches that run on light (solar power), rather than on batteries, can be safely tolerated and worn by most near-death experiencers—and without any difficulty.

Experiencers claim to have a new awareness of invisible energy fields and a sensitivity to electricity and geomagnetic fields. Many claim to "see" sparkles or balls of energy in the air, the aura (or energy) surrounding all things, and to develop a sensitivity to meteorological factors such as temperature, pressure, air movement, and humidity.

Short Circuits

Many are the tales of the different ways electrical sensitivity has manifested and the confusion or property loss that has resulted. Add one more: weather. I

The "Pauli Effect"

Swiss physicist and Nobel laureate Wolfgang Pauli noted that experimental equipment was widely known to fail in his presence. Dr. Pauli delighted in this phenomenon, which became known as the "Pauli effect." All kinds of breakdowns occurred in technical equipment, experimental apparatus, and machines. Otto Stern is said to have forbidden Wolfgang Pauli to enter his institute, in order to prevent such malfunctions. As one friend of Dr. Pauli noted about him shortly after one such incident: "He senses the mischief already before as a disagreeable tension, and when the anticipated misfortune then actually hits—another one!—he feels strangely liberated and lightened." (From Charles P. Enz's book *No Time to be Brief: A Scientific Biography of Wolfgang Pauli,* refer to appendix C. Submitted by Cynthia Sue Larson, a bioenergetic-field researcher, see appendix E.)

have noticed that during weather extremes when there is a lot of electricity in the air, near-death experiencers can be affected, sometimes significantly. Allow me to share what happened to me on April 8, 2006.

I was in Johnson City, Tennessee, to deliver a talk at a large conference. Line after line of tornados were ravaging the state. Hourly checks with the weather bureau said we would be safe, and we were, although the very air around us "crawled" with electrical pulsations. When I stepped on the stage to speak, suddenly I could neither talk straight nor control my mouth or tongue. I had to force words, spit them out. After two hours of this, I was both exhausted and ashamed. It was the worst talk I had ever given. The crowd, fortunately, thought my long pauses and strange delivery was "for effect." I practically ran to my room to hide afterward, and turned on television news. A special bulletin interrupted the program: Ten tornados had touched down hardly minutes away during the time I was on stage. I knew then what had happened to me: The violence in the air had interfered with my body's electrical system. Electrical sensitivity had caused problems for me before during electrical storms, but this was a first. These extremes, unbelievable clusters of tornados striking simultaneously, had literally rendered me speechless. I was fine by evening, once the tornados ceased.

Mine is an isolated case, certainly, and a unique one even for me. Still, my concern here is a valid one: Perhaps weather affects near-death experiencers more than anyone previously thought.

The many puzzles to electrical sensitivity, as well as much of the psychic phenomena and healing gifts experiencers describe, are suggestive of changes in the strength factor of their access and exposure to electromagnetic fields. Something very real and very physical is going on here, and I believe it is measurable—although so far, owing to a lack of funding, only limited attempts have been made to do the necessary lab work.

The Need Factor

To help us keep things in perspective, here's more from Stephanie Johnston, whom you met in chapter 5: "After my near-death experience, dreams and visions became more pronounced. I could just touch or sense the energy of people and tell what was going on in their physical body, as well as what was mentally and emotionally stressing them. I found that I had to watch what I touched when I came out of meditation. I have touched digital clocks and radios and had them stop working. I have touched electronic equipment and watched it blow up. I have attempted to plug in small appliances and had the plug blow out of the socket. I have a terrible time getting audio equipment to record for me, and I cannot wear a wristwatch—most either stop or break within a couple of weeks."

Stephanie goes on to say: "I changed my entire life within seven years of my near-death experience. I left a very successful twenty-year career in a family-owned business. I moved from my resort home that I loved, and had never thought of leaving, to go to work in an alternative health-care profession, volunteering my time and services to help female inmates in the state prison. I am not the angry and judgmental person I once was. I love life and people. I've never again had a problem with high blood pressure. To me, I don't know if I became aware of what death means or if I became aware of what life means. I do know what awaits me, though, when it's my time to die."

Stephanie's life had been crashing in around her. In utter desperation and despair, she had attempted to kill herself. Her near-death scenario, however, introduced her to a greater reality, one that proved to be the impetus she needed to transform herself. Even though Stephanie's was an extreme case, the impact it had on her is representative of the vast majority of experiencers who say that what happened to them was needed, that it was somehow "ordered"—so their lives could be reordered.

> **New Words**
>
> A **growth event** is any kind of sudden, unexpected twist in life that twirls you around and changes your attitudes and stretches your mind. It can be positive, negative, or both.

The idea that the experience could be "needed" or "ordered" prompted me, whenever possible, to keep the individual's near-death scenario and aftereffects in context with the life he or she had previously lived. Doing this enabled me to find multiple connections, subtle correlations, and parallels between the two. I came to recognize that it's almost as if the near-death experience can be, and quite probably is, one of nature's more accelerated *growth events,* a powerful and complex dynamic that can not only foster psychological changes, but also cause physiological mutations the equal of species evolution.

If a growth event comes along and we miss it, it will quite likely come back again. And we can receive a series of them, one right after another. If we block these urges, something will happen to unblock them. Life insists on growth and change. If we forget common sense and balance, something will happen to help us remember. You can count on it. I believe the near-death experience is a growth event "reserved" for people who need an extra "shove" in life to make needed changes.

Regardless of what you think the near-death experience is, the aftereffects are undeniable. And the more intense the experience, the greater the aftereffects.

8

Startling Differences between Child and Adult Experiencers

We cannot know the truth by what seems to be true from a single point of view.

—Christian D. Larson, mystic and philosopher

It takes the average experiencer at least seven years to adjust to the aftereffects—some much longer. This adjustment period tends to be the most confusing during the first three years when everything seems somehow brand new, even if you've seen it a million times before. There's a sense of freshness about the "landscape" of your life, and you often discover details and aspects previously missed or tossed aside as unimportant.

After that third year, exploring the newness of your world gives way to a desire for more interactions with others. You want to reach out, get involved, and share. Whatever your school, business, or personal commitments, there's also an overriding sense of "mission"—the reason why you returned from death—your "real" job. This phase of approximately four years can be a time when sex takes on a new importance, or at least there is more emphasis on intimacy, and it can be money-oriented in the sense that even though materialistic needs no longer drive you, schooling and employment are still important.

The first seven years, then, can be as exciting and wonder-filled as they can be chaotic and stressful. If you think this can be a tussle for adults, imagine what it's like for kids. Child experiencers deal with the same pattern of aftereffects as do adults, but they tend to respond differently—sometimes exactly the opposite. And it takes them three to four times longer than adults to integrate their experience. I suspect this is because a child has no way to make connections between what happened to them and

Stifle That Criticism

I found that admonishing children for "lying" or for having an "overactive" imagination can not only silence children who are trying to share their near-death episode, but, in many cases, cause them to repress their experience. This can confuse their growing years and young adulthood.

their resultant behavior. A child will tend to compensate for any differences they might exhibit. They adjust, not integrate. That is the nature of childhood. It is how children cope.

Birth Trauma

Linda Silverman, PhD, one of the leading authorities on giftedness, contacted me after reading my original book on child experiencers. "Your work supports mine and my work supports yours," she offered. Dr. Silverman went on to say that a remarkable number of exceptionally and profoundly gifted children (160 to 262 IQ) were the products of excessively long labors, precipitous births (being born too quickly), overdoses of the labor-inducing drug Pitocin, or other birth traumas that might have facilitated a near-death experience during the birthing process. "They demonstrate characteristics that are very similar to those of child experiencers of near-death states."

Don't Assume Anything

The original studies about the near-death phenomenon centered entirely on adult experiencers, and all conclusions reached and models developed came from that focus. Even today, we know the most about adult experiencers, although Melvin Morse, MD, and his groundbreaking research with children has turned more attention to kids who have experienced near-death states, and inspired other researchers to follow suit.

As for me, I started paying more attention to what happens to children from the child's point of view after a confrontation I had in a station wagon filled with child experiencers and their mothers in 1994. To say our conversation was "spirited" would be an understatement. Nothing they told me matched the findings of other researchers, but was instead similar to what I had noticed with kids since my earliest days in the field. This drove me to seek additional children, as well as teenagers and adults, who could recall having had such an episode when they were young, so I could better track what was actually going on.

Concentrating on experiencers who had their episodes from birth to the age of fifteen, I studied 277 cases; about half of them were children at the time we spoke, the other half had grown to be teenagers or adults. My original premise that children never experienced extremes, either in their scenarios or in their integration of aftereffects, was proved wrong by this project. Indeed, what I, in fact, discovered—and consequently wrote about in *Children of the New Millennium* (republished as *The New Children and Near-Death Experiences*)—surprised even me.

Adult Experiencers Become More Childlike

Adult experiencers, almost to a person, become more childlike afterward. They acquire a sense of joy, laughter, and wonder that, coupled with a childlike naivete, can at times be rather disconcerting to their peers.

The majority seem blessed with the ability to "grow" younger with the passing years, and become increasingly more relaxed, friendly, creative, innovative, and intuitive. There's a certain innocence to their charm and an eagerness that can easily be labeled childish or self-absorbed—although seldom is either the case.

Most feel that not only were they given a second chance at life, but also a special opportunity to relearn and redefine themselves and their world. Without fanfare, they quietly set about doing just that.

Child Experiencers Become More Mature

Overemphasizing "out of the mouths of babes" testimonials completely misses the real child and what he or she might be feeling. Certainly, children offer the most uncluttered accounts, devoid of interpretive nuances. But relying on what they say without doing more research lays bare an unsettling truth: Kids don't have the language or the presence of mind to tell us their full story. We get "half a loaf," never realizing the scope of what was left out.

When you dig deeper, one of the first things you notice is how mature most child experiencers become after their near-death episodes. In their own words: "I felt like an adult in a child's body," and "After my episode, I lost my childhood."

Regardless of what age they were when the incident occurred—and for some it was at birth—they become "older" than their agemates afterward.

Too Much

The flamboyant, media-seeking experiencers who dominate television talk shows are not representative of the average near-death experiencer.

Second Birth

Adult experiencers claim their near-death episodes gave them a second chance at life. But the story from children differs. What happens to them has all the trappings of a "second birth" in how the phenomenon appears to "rewire" their brains and nervous systems—in a way more noticeable than with older experiencers. Perhaps the reason for this is that near-death states for the young often occur at critical junctures in brain development, when original brain circuitry is still being laid. This observation inspires evolutionary theories, especially in light of the large numbers of kids worldwide who experience near-death states. We discuss this idea in depth in chapter 22.

Observations on Forty-four Child Experiencers Reflecting Enhanced Intelligence

Observation	Percent
Faculties enhanced, altered, or experienced in multiples (synesthesia; see chapter 7)	77 percent
Mind works differently—highly creative and inventive	84 percent
Significant enhancement of intellect	68 percent
Mind tested at genius level (no genetic markers for increase)	
main group, overall figure	48 percent
subgroup, those under age 6	81 percent
Drawn to and highly proficient in math/science/history	93 percent
Professionally employed in math/science/history careers	25 percent
Unusually gifted with languages	35 percent
School –	
easier after near-death experience	34 percent
harder afterward or blocked from memory	66 percent

And decidedly so. They suddenly possess a wisdom beyond their years, and, in many cases, even beyond that of their parents. This can create discipline problems, as you can well imagine, or cause the child to become withdrawn.

Jump-Starting Intelligence

Near-death states somehow make experiencers smarter, regardless of age. I don't think that this is simply because of the unique content of their experiences, although that may be part of it. What I suspect is that the experience itself produces alterations in brain structure and brain function, especially with the young.

After a near-death episode, for instance, the average child experiencer begins to exhibit broad conceptual reasoning styles. Whereas typical cognitive development in a child progresses from detailed (concrete) thinking to abstract conceptualization, kids of all ages who undergo a near-death state come back with minds that automatically begin to think more abstractly. If they are of school age, they often have to relearn the concrete or linear style taught at their grade level.

There are other indicators too. The percentages in the chart above reveal some of my observations, and are based primarily on forty-four child experiencers who, when older, filled out an in-depth questionnaire. Their answers were compared to the larger number in my study, with a match on nearly each item.

Gifted with Genius

The typical intelligence quotient for child experiencers measured out on standard IQ tests to a range somewhere between 150 and 160—several were a few points lower, most were higher ("ordinary folk" usually score in the neighborhood of 100). But even those who did not test anywhere near that high displayed unusually creative minds, numerous faculty enhancements, unrelenting curiosity, and an exceptional ability to intuitively "know" things soon after reviving. Some were even gifted with languages.

The vast majority were natural computer whizzes. Many became top physicists and inventors, physicians, masters of the arts and humanities; a few, professional psychics. Adult experiencers are the ones who most often are drawn to some type of healing, counseling, and ministerial roles afterward. Not the kids (at least not the greater number). Mention math or science and they're all aglow. And history intrigues them, as well as anything to do with times "past."

Math and Music

In my research, 85 percent of the child experiencers with the greatest acceleration in mathematical ability also had a corresponding affection for music that was so passionate, it was like a "love affair" with the "embrace" of celestial harmonics. Many of those who were now older considered it better than sex. Intriguingly, those who showed no particular interest in or special response to music after their experience either lagged behind their agemates in math or didn't have mathematical inclinations to begin with.

An Account Often True

A fellow researcher confided to me: "I've been e-mailing a six-and-a-half-year-old every day. He's taking ancient history at the college level. He's unusually gifted with languages. He is drawn to math, science, and music. He's got the highest possible score on every single subtest on an IQ test he took when three. And he is the sweetest human being I have ever been blessed to encounter. Animals come to him. This week a woodpecker let him pet him. I asked him to ask his mother about his birth. She told him he was six weeks premature and there were complications."

Whether this boy actually had a near-death experience during birth trauma cannot be known. What can be observed is that he displays the full pattern of aftereffects and behaves as if he were a child experiencer of a near-death state.

Males and Females Alike

In my research, I've found no difference between males and females regarding intelligence enhancements and spatial and mathematical abilities. The only discrepancy I found is that in my larger study of 277 child experiencers, the figure for pursuing careers in math/science/history was 40 percent rather than the 25 percent that showed up from questionnaire tabulations.

Job Gap

The gap between child experiencers who are drawn to and are highly proficient in math/science/history (93 percent) and those who wind up actually employed in those fields (25 percent in the smaller study, 40 percent in the larger one) is exceptionally wide. A possible reason for this was offered by the experiencers themselves: the bias against creative thought in the workplace. Child experiencers, as they move up the grades and into college, most often function as abstract, creative intuitives. In most schools and on the job, this can put them at a distinct disadvantage.

A Single Unit

In the brain, the centers for math and music are located next to each other. Somehow, with the majority of children who experience near-death states, these two regions appear to accelerate together—as if they were a single unit.

Research on brain development shows that there's a link between spatial reasoning and mathematics and music, in that all three are necessary to arrange schemes that encompass the many-sidedness or wholeness of a given design. For example, melodic music imparts harmony, how things resonate or fit together; mathematics supplies measurement, the specifics of physical manifestation. But it is spatial reasoning that, through creating a specific overall pattern, gives meaning and purpose to the task or item at hand, while ensuring that all parts fit the designated whole.

This ability to create an overall pattern that's credible and valid is precisely where the kids in my research base shined. On the average, they became spatial/nonverbal/sensory-dynamic thinkers afterward—regardless of gender. I discovered that the younger the child when the near-death state occurred, the greater the chance for genius. Although such "jumps" in intelligence were also true for adult experiencers, it wasn't to the same degree as with child experiencers.

Far Apart

Responses to some of the aftereffects are nearly identical with child and adult experiencers; for instance, light and sound sensitivity. The difference with electrical sensitivity (kids 52 percent, adults 73 percent), however, is probably more a reflection of who has access to technological equipment rather than a true deviation. Yet, as you investigate further, you begin to notice startling differences.

Food Preferences

Adult experiencers are six times more likely to become vegetarians than child experiencers. Near-death kids, like kids in general, usually snub their veggies.

The average child experiencer prefers meat, and specifically red meat,

Need Drawings

IANDS is now seeking drawings done by children of their near-death experience. These drawings will occupy a special page on the IANDS' website, so everyone can see the phenomenon through the child's eyes and learn more about how a child interprets things. Contact IANDS directly to participate (see appendix B).

Abuse Issues

Forty-two percent of the children I interviewed fell victim to the tragedy of parental and *sibling abuse.* And note the sibling abuse: Big brothers and sisters can pack a mean wallop or give a nasty squeeze if goofing off or angry. But worst of all are parents who mistreat their young. Whereas such abuse is rampant throughout the general population, the additional stresses inherent with the near-death phenomenon and its aftereffects can exacerbate family conditions that are already less than ideal.

even in their later years. For those adult experiencers who still eat meat, the opposite is true—they generally turn to chicken, turkey, and fish exclusively.

For the Youngest

Parent/sibling relationships tend to be strained with child experiencers, even in the best and most tolerant of families. Additionally, kids are more likely than adults to be challenged socially and to report having regrets about what happened to them.

As mentioned in chapter 4, an astounding number of children would choose to go back to the other side of death's curtain after their experience, even if that meant suicide. Child experiencers, whether young or grown, seldom see a counselor and receive less help than an adult if they do go to one. This is not true with adult experiencers, even though they may protest otherwise.

The biggest challenge child experiencers have in therapy that I've noticed is that they don't "connect the dots" between their near-death episode and what happened to them later—nor are most counselors familiar with research on the near-death experience and its aftereffects. In chapter 24, I recommend counseling techniques that may be more helpful than standard procedures (for adult experiencers, too).

Bonds Break

The parent-child bond can break or be stretched thin after a near-death experience. There is no doubt that most children love their parents and want to be with them. Still, what parent, no matter how loving, can compare to the bright ones and angels encountered on the Other Side of death? That break can be repaired, but it may take years of patient, concerted effort to do so.

Marriage and Divorce

The majority of child experiencers, once grown, enjoy long-lasting marriages. Whether married once or twice (if twice, the first was almost always brief), 57 percent stay in the marriage. The reverse is true with adult experiencers: Easily 75 to 78 percent, sometimes more, end in divorce within about seven to ten years.

Bear in mind, though, that child experiencers seldom marry until they've reached adulthood. The transformed "self" that resulted from their near-death episode is the only one their spouses ever knew. Spouses of adult experiencers, on the other hand, have to contend with "before" and "after" personality shifts that can make it seem as if they are suddenly married to another person.

Home Sweet Home

Most adult experiencers can't wait to be rid of home mortgages; most child experiencers can't wait to have one. Even if they can't afford much in the way of furniture, curtains, or decorations, they'll sacrifice without hesitation to make certain those monthly payments are paid on time, each time, year after year. The extremes between these two reactions may seem odd, until you recall the main response both groups usually display after their near-death scenario.

Adult experiencers tend to return with a sense of freedom that is like nothing else they have ever known. Their episode "unshackles" them from restraints, attachments, obligations, and demands, and renders them free to seek out and explore new ways of doing things. Many actually do quite literally walk out on their lives, leaving everything behind—including family, friends, home, and job. There are others, of course, who remain in their present lifestyle and honor their present obligations. Yet even these more cautious types change things as much as possible. That longing to "cut loose" and "fly free" remains with most to some degree, whether acted on or not.

The attachment most child experiencers have to a sense of "home" is, I believe, a direct result of their having felt separated from their "real home" after their episode ended. And the extent to which they identify their real home with that place they encountered in their near-death state is quite remarkable. This identification is usually so strong they are unable, at least at first, to accept anything less. It's not that they cease to love their parents, but, rather, that they prefer the greater love they found "over there." Losing that can create a psychic wound that seems to "feed" a subconscious urge to make certain no one and nothing will ever again take their "home" away from them.

Money and Mission

Child experiencers, just like adult experiencers, don't give a hoot about money afterward. At least that's true for the majority. But unlike adults, the kids, once grown, do tend to squeeze pennies and pay bills in a timely fashion. (Gotta make that home mortgage, ya know.)

What amazed me is job satisfaction. Adult experiencers almost invariably change careers afterward—occasionally several times over. Nearly two-thirds of those I interviewed slipped in and out of jobs for years, never staying anywhere for too long, and often complaining about what they had to put up with. You rarely encounter this behavior with child experiencers. Some, once they become adults, do change careers, but more often than not they stay put and love their jobs. The job satisfaction rating for them is a whopping 80 percent.

If children return from their near-death episode with some sense of life purpose or *mission,* they seldom do anything about it until they are older. On the other hand, adults are almost driven to communicate their life purpose and mobilize necessary energies quickly. Yet it's the kids who wind up doing more and making a more positive and lasting contribution to society.

Perhaps this is another finding that simply reflects the age difference, but maybe not.

Remember, child experiencers seem to mature rapidly after their episodes, while adult experiencers tend to become more childlike. This might explain why kids often become cautious later on, as they ponder and plan their lives. Their seniors take all manner of risks and jump at opportunities.

The Advantage of Years

Once child experiencers mature, 57 percent in my study have long-lasting marriages, 68 percent hold home mortgages, and 80 percent report high job satisfaction (regardless of where they are employed or what their task is). This is a picture of contentment adult experiencers can't even begin to match, and one that the general population might envy. In fairness, though, adults are on the opposite end of the developmental curve, with the bulk of their lives behind them. They possess obvious advantages in dealing with their episodes, but the additional years children have "to work things out" isn't one of them.

New Word

Mission is the term given by most near-death experiencers, regardless of their age, for why they returned from death. The majority came back "knowing" that each and every person at birth was given a specific job to do, a purpose for their life on Earth (i.e., "mission"). And that, if unfulfilled, a "reminder" will set them straight. Most considered their near-death state that reminder.

Church Attendance

Child experiencers head for churches in droves afterward, or at least it seems so. And any church will do. If their parents are not already churchgoers, they usually try to drag their parents with them, cajoling and begging as they go: "Can we do this again?" or "This is a great place, I hope we can come back." Religion, per se, means nothing to a child experiencer. What matters to them is "God's House" and where they can find one.

Soon after their episode, many of these youngsters create an altar

The Boomerang Effect

After many years have passed, most adult experiencers will eventually locate a church home that feels right to them, as either members or active supporters. They seem to go full circle in their desire to explore spiritualities, ending up either back where they started from or within some type of organized religious institution, often the new metaphysical churches such as Unity or Religious Science. Child experiencers are just the opposite. If they are turned off by the people in or the beliefs of "God's House," they are most likely to withdraw from church affiliation permanently.

No Crazy Person Here

In the summer of 2005, a popular teen magazine turned down the story of a child near-death experiencer because the editor thought the kid was nuts and needed a shrink. Any properly educated psychologist or psychiatrist knows of the established diagnosis in the *DSM-IV Manual* of a religious or spiritual problem. No where does the manual pathologize such experiences beforehand; it even includes supportive responses to near-death experiences. Near-death states, clearly, are *not* a sign of madness. Whereas delusional states threaten a person's stability over time, near-death experiences do just the opposite—enriching a person's life in a consistently positive manner.

(perhaps a dresser, small table, even an upside-down box) in their bedroom and cover it with a clean, white cloth. Any items (such as a candle, Bible, cross, flowers, or a beautiful picture) placed on that cloth will be holy to them, and they will often pray there. Those who are already part of a religious tradition are no exception to this type of behavior, except that they tend to be more conscious of what they're doing and why. The rest do it as if driven by an urge they cannot explain.

Even though the majority of adult experiencers leave organized religion or claim to divorce themselves entirely from ritualized worship of God, "deity" in some form still takes center stage in their lives. Their preference gravitates to a more spiritual approach—taking on a personal relationship with God—rather than religious dogmas that state what can and cannot be believed and practiced.

Talking about It

All near-death experiencers want to talk about it. They want to tell everyone in the whole wide world what happened to them and what they think it means. Adults, however, will often quickly learn to clam up—how fast depends on the response from significant others. If they're thought of as "crazy," it may take years before they make another attempt to share their episode with anyone.

Child experiencers don't have that sense of caution. They pop off to anyone handy and "tell it like it is." Again and again. Their innocence about this can get them into all kinds of trouble.

What follows are two examples from actual case studies.

> **Please Listen**
>
> Listening to near-death experiencers of any age with interest instead of judgment is the greatest gift you can give them.

Shamed into Silence

Bill from Atlanta, Georgia, died at about two months of age when an infant chair fell over on him, cutting off his breathing. "After I learned to talk, I tried to tell my family about what happened to me. When I told my grandmother, she punished me for 'storytelling,' and told me that if I repeated stories like that I would die and go to hell (very scary) or that nobody would love me, speak to me, feed me, clothe me, or let me live with them any more (double scary). She also said the police would come and put me in the chain gang or the electric chair. And she'd hit me. I finally got tired of being slapped."

Bill goes on, "I tried to tell my brother, too, but he was five years older than I and was just beginning to hate me. He didn't want to hear about it either and made fun of me. I also tried to tell my mother but I couldn't make her understand. She'd tease me about it. Eventually, I was so hurt, scared, and upset that I put these memories aside. For a while, I wouldn't talk about anything to anyone."

The slappings Bill received from his "wrath-of God" grandmother stand out the most in his mind. He loved her but could never understand why his "journey to heaven" made her so mad at him.

The End of Caring

Nathan Kyles III, an African-American released from state prison at El Campo, Texas, was almost eleven when he and his brother Dale left home without their mother's permission and splashed around in a motel swimming pool while an older cousin applied for work. "I got out of the water and walked inside to where my cousin was. When we were ready to leave, my cousin asked me, 'Where is Dale?' The first thing that came to my mind was the pool. I ran back to the deep end and saw my brother looking up at me from the bottom. I bent over and somehow grabbed his hand, but he pulled me in." After swallowing tons of water, Nathan felt his life leave him in what was to be a vivid near-death episode. How the two boys were rescued is not exactly known, although the cousin does remember a white woman helping out. No attempt was made at the time to see if either boy needed hospitalization.

Once Nathan returned home after his close brush with death, his mother told him to shut up before he could offer a single word, then she whipped both boys for leaving the house. His later attempts at communication were also rebuked. Guilt and shame came to overlay the miracle of his experience, not because of his episode, per se, but because of the way his family treated him after he came home.

After the whipping, Nathan didn't care about anything anymore. His grades in school plummeted. His

> **Disbelief**
>
> Diane K. Corcoran, RN, PhD, a former army nurse and leading proponent of educating medical professionals about the near-death experience and its after-effects, especially with children, has this to share:
>
> "Just last week, in a workshop of nurses, a young mother said she had a two-year-old who had a near-drowning incident. She emphasized that they were not a religious family, and she and her husband did not teach about God or church; however, since the the incident, she said, the child has been talking about angels and wants to be one when she grows up. She drags the family to church now, and is very involved with all that happens at Sunday School. 'It's as if her angels are *personal friends,*' the mother remarked. 'What do you think is the matter with her?' Even after the lecture I gave on near-death states, she still was not sure that her daughter might be an experiencer."

teacher became so alarmed she called on his mother, but to no avail.

Within a span of one year, he turned from being a positive, studious, happy young man to a sullen criminal who, as he said, "didn't give a damn about anything or anyone."

Nathan explained: "Before it happened, I was never in trouble with the law. After it happened, I started stealing, burglarizing houses and buildings. My whole way of thinking changed. I was about twelve when I went to jail for the first time. I got caught stealing some old coins out of a lady's purse while playing with her son. The judge kicked me out of town for a year, and I had to live with my father 900 miles away. When I returned, I went downhill further."

A long litany of difficulties followed, beginning with a prison term at the age of nineteen for parole violation. Charges of additional burglary, terrorist threats, and harassment were later dropped because it was proved he had not committed them. When released, however, he promptly stole again and wound up back in prison. "I stayed in prison this time for nine years and two months. I was sent to a halfway house because my mom had died earlier and my parole plan was all messed up. I started smoking marijuana, I guess for comfort at my mom being dead. So, while in the halfway house, I was written up for violating their rules, which was also a violation of my parole. Again, my parole was revoked, and here I sit in prison for the fourth time." (His life is now different.)

Certainly, Nathan's mother was worried about her children and, to that degree, her being upset with him for leaving the house without her consent was understandable. Still, the question remains—would Nathan have turned out differently if she had let him speak and extended a hand of comfort instead of punishment after his near-drowning?

Although Nathan's case is an extreme example of how difficult it can sometimes be for child experiencers to communicate with their families, his and Bill's effectively illustrate the challenge faced and the different ways children respond. Unlike adults, kids tend to personalize whatever happens to them. If there are problems, they will usually blame themselves, and often to a greater degree than they deserve. Too many carry childhood guilt into their adult years. Children, especially, are feelers, not thinkers—we need to remember that.

9

Blocking Out the Experience

You are the world's light—a city on a hill, glowing in the night for all to see. Don't hide your light!

—Matthew 5:14

With all the surveys ever done on the incident rate of near-death experiences in the general population, whether a scientific poll or a news magazine survey, no attempt has been made to determine how many experiencers had their episode in childhood. The only researcher to give an educated estimate is pediatrician Melvin Morse, MD, with a figure of 70 percent for those kids who face death, nearly die, or are resuscitated. That's a lot of kids, by anyone's count. But where are their reports? You don't hear that many, and locating them for research projects can be a daunting task. Whether it's the actual child you're looking for or a child experiencer now grown, it doesn't make any difference. They are conspicuously absent from the scene. If there truly are so many of them, why are they so silent?

As you know, 277 of them did cross my path, forming the basis for research I used in writing *Children of the New Millennium* and its later version *The New Children and Near-Death Experiences.* Since the completion of both books, I have met many more. The record breaker in my studies for the individual who had the most episodes is a child experiencer who had a total of twenty-three! He will not allow me to use his name, but I can tell you this much: The man came into this world with severe physical handicaps and was not expected to live. He was in his late forties when I interviewed him. He felt he never could have survived as long as he had—having undergone countless surgeries accompanied by near-death states, starting in infancy and spread out across his lifetime—without the

Tucking It Away

A signature truism about near-death states is how vividly they are remembered over time—clearly, coherently, and accurately. But this truism applies mostly to adult experiencers. Children are six times more likely than adults to ignore, block, forget, or tuck away their near-death episode. Many never have recall, even though they currently display the full profile of aftereffects and have throughout their life.

healing strength and encouragement he gained from each episode.

And he had full memory of each one in order, and with supporting data. If he, as an individual who had twenty-three episodes, not only can remember them but keep them all straight, why can't other child experiencers recall at least one? The reasons I suggest may surprise you.

Why Adults Tend to Remember and Kids Tend to Forget

Maybe the crux of this situation is simply the age difference. Adults have greater autonomy and control; they can make the kinds of choices the average child cannot. With this in mind, about a fourth of the adult experiencers toss the whole thing off to a peculiar vision or hallucination and go on their merry way, ignoring any hint that there might be aftereffects or that maybe they should have given what happened to them a little more attention.

For a child, every event is a big event, an important NOW-KIND-OF-THING. It doesn't take long before they have invested a great deal of emotion and energy in addressing whatever occurred and at whatever age, irrespective of whether it was real or imagined, an internal or an external reality. Yet it doesn't take much to discourage them from pursuing a situation further. A child quickly learns what is allowable and what isn't, what will be tolerated from them and what will not. Their defense? Tuck the event away, or forget about it.

Of course, adults and children process life events differently. What else would you expect? Still, the simple answer of "it's the autonomy that comes with age" fails to explain what research suggests.

The Pros and Cons Adults Go Through

Near-death states initially startle, then overwhelm experiencers of any age. How long these episodes remain active in memory has a lot to do with the intensity of their impact and the degree to which details in them can be verified. Any thought that these states are dreams is shattered utterly once an experiencer is able to link what he or she witnessed while "dead" with what later proves to be true. The shock of these observations or revelations—which could not possibly have been known about in advance—leaves an indelible imprint on the individual's mind. Even if no such link between subjective experience and subsequent reality is ever made, intensity alone packs a big wallop.

Typical adult experiencers respond to this intensity by giving it their full attention. They tend to relive what happened again and again in their struggle to assess whatever meaning and value the event might have. Their quest to understand demands that they search for explanations, and they do. For some, this need becomes a driving force that pushes them over and above the experience itself into making the kind of changes in their life that correspond to what they feel their episodes mean. Notice I said "feel."

When the time finally comes to "think things through," the issue of acceptance versus denial becomes primary. Pretend you're the experiencer. This is what you must consider:

- *Accepting means taking a risk.* To accept my experience and integrate it into my daily life could well mean ridicule and scorn from others, and having to confront the issue of insanity again and again. I could be labeled undesirable or a fake since I have no proof to offer, or I could be accused of trying to be some kind of holy seer or divine prophet. Acceptance would change my life completely, necessitating that I live what I now know to be true. Since my experience challenged the validity of everything I have previously known, accepting it would mean I would have to relearn and redefine life, possibly from scratch. This means I could lose a lot. I could lose everything and everyone, but in so losing, I could also gain. I could gain everything and everyone, and possibly learn how to grow closer to God.

Feelings First

Experiencers of near-death states tend to relate to others with their feelings first, then their intellect. That's why trying to communicate with them or engage in business endeavors can be such a hassle. These people become more heart-centered and emotional, and often use their feelings to make even major decisions. They hide less and express more, which is alarming to those uncomfortable with such openness.

- *Rejecting means denial.* To reject having had the experience would mean not only denying it occurred, but also denying my own sense of integrity, honesty, and inner truth. Rejection would mean turning my back on what I know happened and pretending it away. But it would also mean I would have to take fewer risks and could retain what security and comfort I still possess. Rejection would be sensible and practical, all things considered, allowing me more time to concentrate on healing and the continuance of life as usual. No one would ever know the difference. There would be no further damage to my reputation or further insult to my family. My job and lifestyle could be preserved. But rejection would also mean I would have to deny what might have been a peek at God, and the opportunity to experience divine oneness and truth. It would mean saying no when deep down inside I want to say yes.

Either/Or

Acceptance translates as being different from your fellows and possibly alienating your own family, but having the satisfaction of remaining true to your experience, whatever that implies.

Denial translates as life as always, but the possibility of later restlessness and discontent, perhaps being haunted by or having nightmares about your experience. *Acceptance is no panacea and rejection is no escape.*

The Pressure to Fit In

Child experiencers do not process their episodes when they are children. That comes later—sometimes twenty to forty years later. Adult experiencers are more apt to recognize and explore the link between their episode and the life changes that follow. Child experiencers respond with more of a knee-jerk reaction—either the thing's useful to them right now or it isn't. Unfortunately for children, the fact that such states seldom remain "gone" if ignored can lead to recurring periods of struggle, as the youngsters deal with the difference between the greater reality they discovered and the superficiality of the one society expects them to join. Taking inordinate steps to avoid this struggle can become a self-defeating habit.

The Missing Pieces Kids Leave Behind

After I delivered a lecture about the near-death phenomenon to a group in Fairfield, New Jersey, an African-American by the name of Jerome Kirby came up and asked to speak with me. He talked nonstop, almost crying with relief to discover how normal he was, how like most other child experiencers. At the age of seven he had died and been resuscitated, and his life was forever changed by what he had witnessed while dead. He was unable to fit back into family, school, or society in any fulfilling manner. As a result, he had tucked his experience away, yet it had haunted him throughout his life, affecting the development of normal relationships with his peers.

Although Jerome became a successful bookkeeper (most child experiencers are excellent with math), he still felt lost and strangely alone. While he was telling me his story and how excited he was to hear me, he transformed in front of my eyes from a tense, suspicious, and withdrawn individual to a man at least ten years younger, relaxed, and at ease. The confusion from nearly three decades evaporated. His conflict was never with his family, per se, for they were open and receptive. His conflict was within himself. As a lad of seven, he had lacked the language skills to effectively communicate what had happened to him and especially how he felt about it. The passing years had only added to his frustration, until he quit trying to explain himself and just gave up.

Jerome's family meant well and really tried. So did he. Yet he still slid into a world apart and remained there. It never occurred to him, even as an adult, that there could possibly be a better way to handle his situation.

Kids prefer to get on with it, rather than committing time and effort toward figuring out what they feel deep inside doesn't need figuring out. This may well ensure their fitting in with their age-mates and growing along with them, but it does nothing to help them "fill in the blanks." Maturity usually solves this dilemma; and, indeed, the average child experiencer claims that he or she is able to successfully add together the various fragments from his or her memory and make helpful connections once grown. But considering the "missing voices" from childhood accounts, I seriously doubt that the number of child experiencers able to fully integrate their episode is that high.

You Be the Judge

As I relate the following case, allow yourself to see through the eyes of the psychologist, the mother, and the child experiencer. Become all three, then decide how to judge this one. These are real people who had to grapple with a real puzzle. For obvious reasons, no names can be used. The psychologist is the narrator.

"The four-year-old was born with a serious heart defect that demanded surgery within the first few weeks of life. He had undergone several more surgeries in his short life, was on medication to control heart rhythm, had to be monitored constantly, and had been rushed to emergency rooms numerous times. In spite of all the pain and suffering he had endured, he was cheerful and uncomplaining.

"I asked him to draw a picture as an 'ice breaker' and as a way to establish rapport. He drew some parallel lines with scratches wobbling between, a circle or two, and a face. When queried about the content, he replied, 'This is a person climbing a ladder to another dimension.' Please, a four-year-old? Hardly the language of the usual child, but his mother denied any chance he could have picked up such words from anyone in the family. She was as puzzled as I, and a little spooked.

"Months later she reported that this child, while riding in the car with her, had invited her attention by patting her arm and saying, 'Mom, Mom, remember when I died?' 'Oh, no, no, you've never died.' 'Yes I have, you know,' and he proceeded to describe one emergency in a particular hospital emergency room.

"His mother continued to quote his words: 'When I died the light was so bright, I thought I should have brought my sunglasses! And the angels wanted me to come with them, but I said I couldn't because I had to stay and take care of you and Daddy. But I made them promise when I did die, and you died and Daddy died, we could all be together in God's house and they said yes.' She noted that he seemed very proud and happy. It was clear, however, that his mother was not pleased with my statement that his report was typical of a genuine near-death experience. The family terminated treatment shortly thereafter."

The psychologist in this case had a near-death episode herself in the first week after her birth and displayed the full range of aftereffects throughout

Too Close to Home

Dr. Diane Corcoran, whom you met in the last chapter, has for years lectured at large gatherings of nurses on the subject of near-death experiences. At the end of her talks, she is often questioned by the nurses as to whether their own child might be an experiencer. "This happens even though I had just given the characteristics of how to recognize a child experiencer," Dr. Corcoran said. "The people can't face what they don't want to hear."

her life. She was also well-informed about the phenomenon, and was quite literally the perfect candidate to work with this boy. The youngster was ready to talk about his otherworldly adventure and was willing to make it a part of his everyday life in whatever manner his parents might approve. The mother and father, however, after talking over the situation, shut the door to this opportunity out of fear that their son might one day be labeled crazy.

Who's right and who's wrong in this case? Think it over carefully before you decide. The answer may not be as obvious as it appears.

A Child's View

As you read in chapter 8, Bill of Atlanta was slapped around by an overly protective grandmother who felt she dared not allow him to tell "stories." After all, what would the neighbors think? In a similar vein, the parents of the four-year-old you have just heard from told their son to "forget all about it" lest he, too, grow up with the "wrong" label.

Fitting back into their human family is crucial for kids. It's a matter of survival. Yet, often, whatever the family suppresses, the child represses. Once grown, how do child experiencers feel about this? Let's consider some typical comments regarding family and school, keeping in mind that it's much easier for some children to adjust than it is for others:

- "I never felt free to talk about this when I was younger. People didn't and still don't believe things like this. But I know the truth, and that's what's important."—From Clara Lane, Belmont, Ohio; near-death experience at ten, appendicitis

- "Because others cannot accept my experience as real, I have had to keep it locked up inside me for the most part, and that creates a feeling of isolation and loneliness and of 'being different,' all of which is ultimately depressing. I guess the one word to describe others' lack of belief is anguish."—Anonymous, California; near-death experience at fourteen, extreme distress in epigastric area

- "I had no childhood after my near-death experience. I felt cheated." —Beverly A. Brodsky, Philadelphia, Pennsylvania; near-death experience when nearly eight, tonsillectomy

Bill, in further sharing his story, puts into words what I have repeatedly heard from child experiencers who went on to college and then found employment:

> In my classical mechanics courses, I had what is best described as an intuitive grasp of everything I ever looked at. I would see a problem and immediately know the correct solution. Unfortunately, when I went to graduate school where you have to explain how and why, I never finished my MS in physics. A professor in my graduate-level classical mechanics class once remarked, "If you say once more that it is intuitively obvious concerning things that I and the rest of your classmates have to work out ten pages of complex equations to arrive at, I will give you not a C, but an F in this class."
>
> My analytical, mathematical, creative, and scientific skills have always been very good. I examine things and solve problems as if I had a parallel-processing system instead of a brain. This is very hard to explain, but it is almost as if most problems get broken down somewhere in my brain, the various portions of each are attacked by different subparts of my brain, and the solution is integrated and put together for me with no conscious effort or control on my part. It is particularly frustrating for me to deal with other people doing joint research or brainstorming, because other people don't think like I do. Please don't laugh—I get some of my best ideas from dreams.

So Typical

Pam Kircher, MD, had a near-death experience at the age of six during an episode of meningitis. She spent the next fifty years exploring a wide range of interests including medicine, spirituality, tai chi, and complementary modalities. Along the way, she became a family practice doctor, a hospice physician, author of *Love Is the Link: A Hospice Doctor Shares Her Experiences of Near-Death and Dying* (see appendix C), and national Tai Chi for Health master trainer of instructors. She has had no qualms about changing fields when her interest pulled her elsewhere. With a desire to be of service to others, she has done mission work in Guatemala and Fiji, as well as extensive volunteerism at home.

Aftereffects Can Take a Backseat

Children, to avoid embarrassment, will often go to extreme lengths after their near-death experience to be "just like everyone else." The fact that they may now think and feel differently from their agemates is not necessarily a good thing. Some "act out" in defiance; most shut down and quietly accommodate the situations presented to them, hoping to blend in even

Haunted by Experience

Possibly because children are more apt than adults to block or set aside the memory of their near-death episode, they are also more often subject to recurring dreams and nightmares about their experience. Most eventually outgrow these "replays," but some never do—taking into their later years an unexplained mystery that refuses to fade.

New Words

Spontaneous recall is a term used to describe the emergence of memories long hidden or locked away in an individual's mind. These memories or memory fragments can surface in unusual ways or be triggered by casual and unexpected associations. In the case of forgotten near-death experiences, the most frequent point of recall occurs after reading or hearing about someone else's episode that "feels" familiar.

though they know they don't quite "fit." This determination to fit in can block or lessen the aftereffects of their near-death state—at least for a while. Or it can "blind" them to changes that everyone else notices.

Spontaneous Recall

It's commonplace for child experiencers in their early- to mid-adult years to suddenly and without warning undergo a *spontaneous recall* of their entire childhood scenario. What was lost can return.

Once the individual is able to verify the memory that suddenly "pops" into place in his or her mind, or finds "peace" with it in the sense of knowing it is right because it explains so much of life, all kinds of strange things can begin to happen. Mysteries that could not otherwise have been explained start to unravel. Any aftereffects that were repressed reemerge—sometimes with a bang.

For instance, a fellow I know who was in his forties was surfing the Internet when he happened upon a near-death account that exactly matched an accident he had had as an infant. He had no memory of any scenario, yet he had always wondered why he was so "odd" when compared with family, friends, and coworkers. The shock of seeing the story on the Web caused a spontaneous recall, accompanied by those aftereffects he had managed to hide since childhood. He literally fell off his chair because of the "blow" he received, and is now dealing with *delayed integration*—fitting together the missing pieces of his life.

Hellish Threats Repressed

The frightening near-death episode of Judith Werner is the youngest hellish case of record. When nine days old, she was operated on for a serious staph infection and abscess. Her scenario during surgery consisted of white-robed figures devoid of emotion standing around her, with a huge light glaring down from above.

Notice in her drawing (made when she was an adult) what you and I would consider the standard layout and staff found in any modern hospital. The lower half of her drawing shows her as an older child continuing to receive treatments for the infection, which nearly killed her as an infant. These treatments consisted of a special light coming from a goose-necked lamp and administered by the same type of white-robed "zombie" as before.

Because her drawing depicts the cold sterility of ordinary medical environments, it is easy to dismiss her case as simple memory. If you really listen to experiencers with an open mind, though, study them, surprising details often emerge, as they did in Judith's case. These white-clad figures to her infant eyes were evil giants, the light a torture device, her subsequent treatment more akin to punishment than healing. Plus, there was another component to her episode. Along with the visual imagery, a heavy, deep voice spoke that sounded to her like a man hurling threats. This "Inner Stranger" (as he called himself) was exceedingly demanding of her behavior. He insisted that she must obey him or he would kill her.

Once verbal, she told her parents about the incident and about the Inner Stranger and what he said. They pooh-poohed her story. She told other friends and relatives, and was also rebuffed. She then

New Words

Delayed integration describes a situation in which an individual, for whatever reason, is unable to fully process a given event until years after it happened. Although adult experiencers are able to integrate their near-death states in about seven years or so, it can take child experiencers two to three times that long, depending on family circumstances after their episodes and the child's response to how he or she was treated.

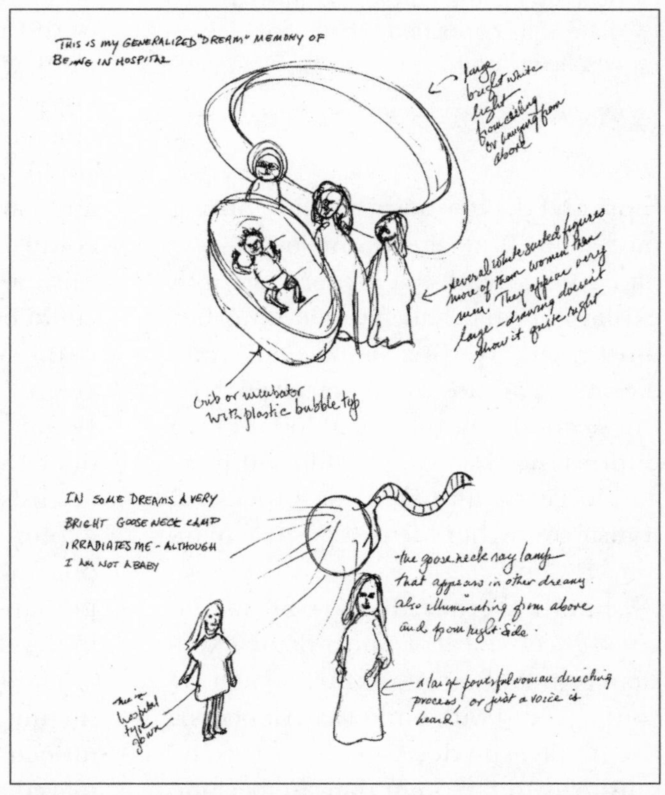

Judith Werner's memories of surgery when she was nine days old, with notations of an oval bed, large light, robed figures. Below is a depiction of further treatment when she was older, a goose-necked lamp, robed woman.

Questions

Irrespective of Judith's story and what you may think about it, how can a nine-day-old-infant remember surgery and in such detail? The shape of the operating table and other descriptions were later verified. Who was "Inner Stranger"? She told me during a session we had that "he always told me he came to save my life. He is with me still. Although demanding, he is a constant support and guide."

As a brief aside, the near-death-like state she experienced at twenty-eight was what enabled her to face and make peace with the surgical nightmare that happened when she was newly born.

repressed the episode and said nothing more, until, at age twenty-eight, she had a near-death-like experience that explained what had happened to her during surgery when she was only nine days old. The closure she received from the second episode enabled her to understand lingering childhood fears and angers, and begin the process of transforming her life in a positive manner.

Judith Werner displays all of the aftereffects typical of a near-death experience, including an unusually high IQ (often found with child experiencers). Eventually, she developed her psychic sensitivity to the point that she became professional in her ability to help others solve their problems themselves. The sternness of her early episode, even being lectured and threatened, is similar to childhood cases from Asia and various Third World countries, as well as among native peoples (regardless of tribal affiliation or tradition). Occasionally, I have come across near-death experiences like this with children in the more industrialized nations, like Judith.

Nothing to Remember

There are people, perhaps lots of them, who have never experienced a spontaneous recall and who are absolutely certain nothing as weird as a near-death scenario ever happened to them, yet they display the entire profile of aftereffects—and have since they were tots. I suspect they are part of a whole generation now being born who are somehow advanced or considerably changed from their genetic line. This could be the result of better nutrition and care for expectant mothers; or it could be environmental, the way we raise and educate today's kids. Or it could be evolution in our time—which is the subject of my book *Beyond the Indigo Children: The New Children and the Coming of the Fifth World* (refer to appendix C).

In later chapters of this book, we'll explore what appears to be signs that our human species is transforming, perhaps even taking a "quantum leap" in development.

Still, there do exist people with seemingly nothing to recall who did indeed "die" as children, then displayed altered character traits immediately after. For example, I met a woman physicist who confided to me that she had spent a lifetime avoiding mention or display of her "oddities" until she read my first book. Puzzled, she sat down with her elderly mother and lamented, "Why am I exhibiting the aftereffects of the near-death phenomenon when nothing like a close brush with death has ever happened to me?"

Her mother laughed. "Have you forgotten that high fever you had when you were four and how we had to rush you to the hospital? The doctor said you nearly died. After the crisis was over, I stood next to your bed and held your hand, and you told me all about it—about the angels who came and took you to a light-filled city and all the love you felt. We really did lose you that night, for you were never the same again. I'm surprised you've forgotten that incident. I haven't."

Nonexperience Experiencers

As you can tell from the mother's story, family members can occasionally remember a near-death episode better than the child who experienced it. For whatever reason, the physicist tossed it aside while still a youngster, but not her mother. What happened in this woman's case emphasizes that it's possible to have a near-death experience and totally erase the memory that you ever did.

Before I give specifics about how to identify *nonexperience experiencers,* I want to tell you about two cases of people who never knew they might have experienced the near-death phenomenon. Both are now deceased, yet they have left behind an ongoing legacy of love and caring.

Walter Kupchik of Louisville, Kentucky, was eighty-six when he contacted

Historical Figures

While the near-death phenomenon has not been noted historically in ways we could readily recognize, what is recorded does offer tantalizing hints that many of our most revered historical figures may indeed have experienced near-death states as children that presaged their greatness. To identify possible candidates, search through old letters and notations. Look for mention of a serious illness or accident between birth and fifteen years of age that nearly claimed the individual's life; marked differences in behavior afterward (nonconformist, thought to be socially retarded when young, creative, bold, unafraid of death, highly intuitive, aware of things future); presence of aftereffects (unique sensitivity to sun, sound, foods, medications of the time—robust health yet many complaints about stomach upsets, colds, flu, fits of depression, allergies); obsessive drive to accomplish one's mission or task.

Most of the saints in the Catholic Church had their first experience of God as children, and many of them match these indicators, as do great visionaries and prophets of all persuasions. Of more recent date, I submit the following people who match the indicators as well: Abraham Lincoln, Albert Einstein, Black Elk (and his biographer John Neihardt), Walter Russell, and Valerie Hunt. Others are: Mozart, Winston Churchill, Queen Elizabeth I, and Edward de Vere, the Seventeenth Earl of Oxford (believed by many to the *real* Shakespeare; refer to appendix V in my book *Future Memory* for a detailed examination of this claim).

New Words

The many individuals I have interviewed who fit the pattern of altered character traits soon after a childhood health crisis, yet have no memory of a near-death scenario, have given their group a name. They call themselves **nonexperience experiencers**. I now use this term as a separate category in my research.

me. He had lost his beloved wife a few years before, and was having so many visionary "visitations" from her that he found it difficult to adjust to his status as a widower. During our many conversations and letters, I became suspicious and began to ask questions about his childhood years. What had they been like? "At age eight, I had scarlet fever. My parents told me I had a very high fever for three days and I hallucinated. Ever since, I've been blessed or cursed with the ability to see very vivid images. I have or have had many of the aftereffects similar to what you describe in *Beyond the Light.*"

Walter comes from an emotional, sensitive, and sentimental family to begin with, so some of the characteristics he grew up with were probably genetic. But not all of them. The rest of his "differences" can all be directly traced to his recovery from a high fever that nearly killed him when he was eight.

Throughout his long life, Walter lived as a man of rare integrity and honor, generous, kind, loving—an individual always willing to walk that "extra mile" for another. And he was an artist and a poet.

I would like to share with you a drawing he did to illustrate a poem written by another individual, which explains Walter's understanding that we are all angels forever embraced by each other's wings.

"We are all angels forever embraced by each other's wings." Drawing done by Walter Kupchik.

I met the parents of Mark Strege of Lake Elmo, Minnesota, while attending a conference. Mark had been killed in a one-car accident when he was twenty. His mother had written a self-published book entitled *Waking Angel* about his death and all the unusual "coincidences" leading up to and surrounding that fateful day. In the book and in conversation with Glenda and Ray, the parents, I noticed a familiar pattern—that of a child experiencer of the near-death phenomenon.

You see, when Mark was just a few hours old he stopped breathing and turned blue. The same thing happened again later that day. Although, when proficient in language, Mark never mentioned anything that could be construed as a scenario, he had, since his earliest years, displayed the full profile of near-death aftereffects, which made him unlike anyone else in the family. His ability to know things increased the older he got, along with an incredible ability as an artist. He once told his mother, "I've always thought I would die young. I don't know why. Just a feeling." Many aspects of his actual death he knew in advance—including what it would feel like to die (written as poetry nine months beforehand).

Done not long before he died, and originally in blue, *Waking Angel* is a painting by Mark Strege.

His family, after much prayer, decided to make some of this art available to anyone who might be interested, via simple prints (check appendix E for details). Offered here is the black-and-white version of his masterpiece *Waking Angel,* originally done in blue. (Glenda's book takes its title from this painting because it seems like a self-portrait of Mark, an angel in the process of awakening to his true nature.)

Tips to Identify Child Experiencers Who Can't Remember

I truly believe that as more information is made available, many people will connect what happened to them in their youth with what may have been a near-death experience. To this end, here is the list of tips I promised you of how to recognize a nonexperience experiencer:

1. A life-threatening illness or accident occurred sometime during childhood, or the child had an unusually stressful delivery at birth.

2. There were behavioral changes immediately after the threatening illness, accident, or stressful delivery: becoming appreciably more somber or gregarious, exhibiting increased intelligence, a hunger for knowledge,

tending toward abstractions and a maturity beyond his or her age, having an intimacy with God or otherworldly companions, acting aloof or estranged from most family members and friends, suddenly more sensitive or allergic, disinterested in activities "normal" for his or her age group while drawn to topics like history/mythology/languages and/or math and science, infinitely more creative and inventive, vivid psychic and visionary displays, an awareness of "future."

3. If still young, doing nearly everything earlier than other children of the same age.

4. Driven to draw or write poetry about other worlds, other realms, other ways of looking at things beyond what would be expected for the child's age.

5. Evidence of a learning reversal once in school; having to go from abstract thinking (conceptualization) back to linear thinking (concrete practicality). This can confuse or threaten teachers.

6. Drawn to anything that feels like "home," and tending toward home ownership even if money is scarce.

7. Motivated by service to others or somehow making a contribution to the greater good, rather than just getting rich.

8. If married, apt to stay married. (However, this is not true if the experience happened in adulthood.)

9. During the process of maturity, begins more and more to exhibit the profile of near-death aftereffects, as if these characteristics are on the increase or expanding.

10. An inordinate attraction to material about near-death states and to people who have had such an experience, combined with a sense or feeling that something important is missing in his or her life, or somehow forgotten.

10

Medically Speaking: A Challenge to Health-Care Providers

The dead don't die. They look on and help.
—D. H. Lawrence, English novelist, poet, and essayist

The American Psychiatric Association's *Diagnostic and Statistical Manual of Mental Disorders* (DSM) has now been amended so that genuinely psychic people are no longer considered "disordered." No steps, though, have been made to give full legitimacy to near-death experiences and how people who undergo them are changed. This is becoming a major issue.

A near-death state clarifies, heightens, and enhances your thinking process. What has just happened is perceived as absolutely true. You have glimpsed a greater reality and gained from it a depth of meaningfulness and understanding unknown to you before. At last, life makes sense; the pieces of the puzzle fit.

The challenge comes when you try to convey this. Yet medical professionals are equally challenged. What diagnosis can they make if your case transcends established medical manuals? How can they even comprehend what you say when it puts them in the untenable position of having to admit you were accurate? Near-death states bring into question numerous medical procedures in a way that makes everyone uncomfortable.

Please Believe Me

Patricia Meo, administrative director at Holy Cross Hospital, Fort Lauderdale, Florida, was skeptical of near-death experiences until her husband, Tony, had one. They had traveled from their home in Florida to Milwaukee so that Tony could have open heart surgery and cardiac revascularization

New Medical Dilemmas

With anesthesia: A national doctors' group adopted new standards to help prevent patients from awakening during surgery. A reduction in near-death accounts related to surgical procedures has occurred since this deep anesthesia was introduced.

With death criteria: Many countries have expanded the definition of death used in their hospitals to include heart stoppage, as well as brain death, as a way of increasing organ donations. This puts doctors in the position of choosing between resuscitating accident victims or considering them to be organ donors. What effect this will have on near-death experiencers trying to return to their bodies is unclear.

With resuscitation techniques: A procedure has been successfully tested with animals that can return to normal neurological function a dog who has been dead for two hours and without a pulse. This flushing of the aorta with a saline solution chilled to 40 degrees Fahrenheit, preserves body organs as the critter is revived. Tests in human ER units are planned in five years. There are cases of near-death experiencers, dead for an hour or more, who revived when medical personnel changed their procedures or used different techniques.

performed by a surgeon renowned for his ability to help "hopeless" cases. After nine hours of surgery, the surgical team tried to remove Tony from the pump that was keeping his heart beating, but couldn't, so he was moved to the intensive care unit with every support device and pharmaceutical infusion imaginable. Still no luck. A few hours later, he was back in surgery, this time to determine why he continued to bleed into his chest. But while being prepped, he went into cardiac arrest.

"After the first four minutes," Patricia recalls, "the code team wanted to stop, but the physician opted to continue, later telling me that he felt a 'power' in his hands while massaging Tony's heart, and that he instinctively knew he could revive him. He was right. It wasn't until three weeks later, once his trach had been removed, that Tony told our daughter, son-in-law, and me how he had 'gone home' and 'visited heaven.' We didn't believe him. We dismissed it as a dream."

His inability to convince his family about his experience was a great frustration to Tony. He retold his story many times, explaining that he had been allowed to come back because he had a mission yet to complete while on Earth, and that he had been told the date and time he would ultimately return to heaven. Patricia says, "Tony told us that during his stop at our home [while he was supposedly dead], he had read the mail lying on the dining room table and proceeded to tell us exactly what items that mail included. He also described our house sitter's new girlfriend, whom we had never seen; to our surprise his description proved accurate. Then he said that he had visited some neighbors and family members in New Jersey during his 'trip,' and that he had seen us all crying in the hospital waiting room."

As Tony described the beauty of the "place" he had visited, his whole demeanor changed. "He was no longer afraid to die. He lived life to the fullest and taught us how to slow down, enjoy life, and savor precious moments. He taught us to value people, not possessions," Patricia says. Tony died two and a half years later, amidst incredible "coincidences" that proved to his family that his death was indeed "according to plan."

It was very important to Tony Meo that his family believe him, and that they understand his urgings on how they should live. Looking back, Patricia added, "Of one thing I am certain: Near-death experiences happen and we should believe patients when they tell us about them. Those who have such experiences are blessed with a gift from which we can all learn."

They're Not Hallucinations

There are numerous medical conditions that can cause a sudden loss of consciousness that produces hallucinations. One of them is *syncope.*

Experiments have been done with healthy young adults, through the use of techniques such as hyperventilation, to create syncopal hallucinations. The result: Internal perceptions of colors and lights intensify to a glaring brightness; familiar people and landscapes are seen but seldom with detailed features; out-of-body views are from a height looking down; sounds range from roaring noises to screaming or unintelligible human voices.

Seem familiar? Well, sort of. What's missing from these syncopal hallucinations, among other things, is the rich and vivid detail found in near-death states, along with the many independent verifications of what is seen, heard,

New Word

Syncope relates to a loss of consciousness from blood loss in the brain. It's most often caused by such things as a heart block, sudden lowering of blood pressure, or fainting. What's interesting about syncope is that it produces imagery and sounds that appear to mimic near-death states.

You Can't Compare Them

Hallucinations, no matter how they're caused (and that includes oxygen deprivation, drugs, centrifigual spinning, and blood loss), are either distorted or representative—an invention of the mind. They focus on what isn't or what could be, while deflating or inflating the ego. Their intensity fades with time or leads to increasing periods of confusion. Conversely, near-death states, regardless of type, are clear and coherent—a recentering of the mind. Consistently accurate and intense over time, these states are known to produce significant psychological and physiological aftereffects that increase with the passing years. Powerful in their ability to transform lives, the episodes are somehow "instructive" about the true reality that exists.

Not Drugs

Barney Clark, one of the first recipients of an artificial heart, is recorded to have had seven stunningly accurate out-of-body near-death episodes—and in each instance, drugs known to cause hallucinations were not used.

Mum's the Word

If people mention they once had a near-death episode on the form they fill out prior to medical treatment, the hospital can—and sometimes does—dispatch a staff counselor to interview them. Should that counselor label the person "unstable," that can affect surgical procedures (for example, the drugs used) and could cause problems with the patient's insurance carrier.

smelled, or experienced by the individual that he or she could not have otherwise known.

Don't Label 'Em Crazy

Some physicians believe that the drugs they administered to their patients caused the near-death experiences the patients had. Yet research in the field of near-death studies has shown that drugs actually depress, nullify, or prevent the phenomenon.

As a general statement, the near-death phenomenon has finally been recognized as a valid state. But as I mentioned in chapter 6, the average near-death experiencer faces the very real fear that his or her episode will be associated with drugs or some other form of hallucination—which may mean being labeled "crazy" and sent to the "nut house."

In the last chapter of my book *Coming Back to Life* (see appendix C), I tell the story of one young woman who was committed involuntarily to a mental institution just because she displayed the typical aftereffects of the average near-death experiencer. Since neither her parents nor her doctor could explain her sudden behavioral changes after the car accident she survived, they had her dragged away by armed police officers. Three years later she was released, but it wasn't until she read material about near-death states that she was able to put the nightmare of her incarceration to rest and heal.

This type of response from families and medical people still occurs today, and all too often. Apparently, news of the phenomenon's validity hasn't become well-known enough in the medical profession to reach those who most need to be updated.

Neither has it reached the insurance industry. One woman I know was declared unfit by a hospital counselor after she'd mentioned that she'd previously had a near-death experience. Understandably, she was shocked upon learning about this assessment of her, and after a lengthy appeal, she was able to get her records straightened out and her insurance coverage restored. She now says, with a smile, that she not only has had her near-death state officially recognized, but she's been deemed perfectly sane!

So You Said You Wanted Evidence

Near-death experiencers are not crazy, nor do their episodes fit any medical definition of a hallucination. Indeed, many have experiences that are embarrassingly—for others!—lucid and perceptive.

A Doctor's Mistake

Robert C. Warth, of Little Silver, New Jersey, tells of how when he was five his mother and father took him to a local doctor's office to have his tonsils removed. He was put in a room with three other children and told to sit on the bed with his jammies on until he was called. His mother told him that the doctor was going to remove something from his throat. After a while, a nurse came and took him to another room where the doctor was. She put a mask over his face. "It dripped something sickeningly sweet," he recalls.

Today, Robert knows that he was overdosed and critically near death because of the doctor's miscalculations. At the time, however, he only knew that he next found himself above the domed operating light looking down, and was surprised to see his body below him along with a layer of dust atop the light fixture. "I could see 360 degrees without moving," he noted.

Fighting back tears, Robert went on to describe a scene that still horrifies him. "My mouth was pried open and I was covered up to my neck. There was a frenzy. The nurse yelled, 'Doctor!' He swung around and said, 'Stand back!' The next thing I remember is waking up in the bed. I couldn't talk and I felt miserable."

The Seriously Uninformed

A Barnes & Noble bookstore refused a book-signing engagement for me when *Children of the New Millennium* debuted . . . because the manager didn't want his customers to know that children had near-death experiences. "This is a family store," was his excuse, "and we don't want to frighten anyone." He never stocked the book, either.

A bankers group in Phoenix, Arizona, who had previously agreed to sponsor a seminar to train nurses in how to handle possible near-death cases, suddenly cancelled all monies a few weeks before launch . . . because they feared that near-death experiences were "the work of the devil." Apparently, these bankers were fundamentalist religious types who refused to consider clinical studies.

My trip to China was axed soon after initial approval . . . because the university and hospital where I was to have spoken were concerned that I might mention an "afterlife" in my presentation. I was informed that such a topic is forbidden in China and to either mention or discuss anything about an "afterlife" would be considered a direct violation of government policy.

Robert was taken back to the doctor for a checkup two weeks later. He told the doctor everything he had seen and heard during the surgery. "The doctor winked at my mother and said, 'They tell

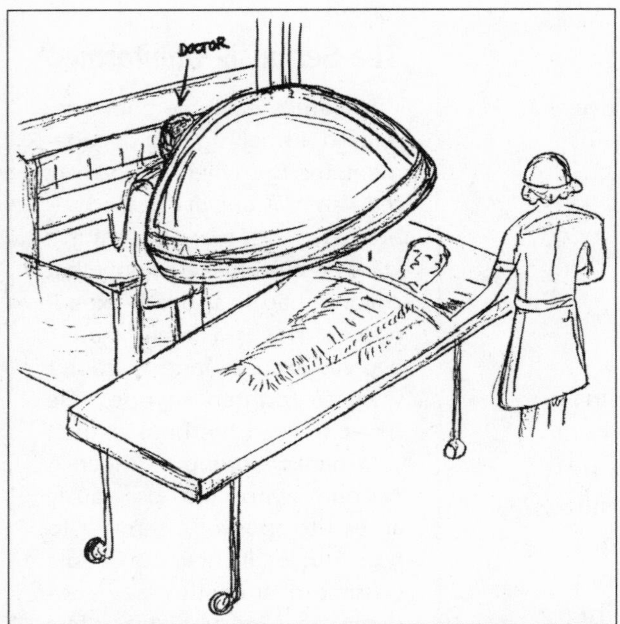

Drawing by Robert C. Warth, from the book *Children of the New Millennium* (also in the book's later version, *The New Children and Near-Death Experiences*).

me stories often. It's the ether. It makes them dream and hallucinate.' What else was the doctor going to say—that the little creep stopped breathing? I saw what he did, and he couldn't get me out of his office fast enough."

A Nurse's Mistake

'Twas the spring of 1962 in France, when a young soldier by the name of Chris Brown, from Laredo, Texas, had an angina attack that knocked him to the floor. "My heart was racing so fast I felt I couldn't breathe," Chris remembered, "and my chest was on fire." He heard people's voices, a siren, a door being banged off its hinges. He felt himself inside a speeding vehicle that took a corner on two wheels, stopped, reversed, stopped again.

The next thing Chris knew, "I'm moving, only this time feet first, bright lights overhead, then I'm under the ceiling looking down upon a doctor and a nurse. My inert body is lying on a gurney. There were two machines connected to me. One I recognized as an EKG [electrocardiogram]. The other I didn't know. It had wires around my head. The EKG had just started to make a steady beep noise. The scope trace was moving left to right with no signal. The doctor was frantically working on my heart as the nurse mostly wrung her hands. I tried to tell the doctor not to knock himself out because I'm fine and in no pain or discomfort. My primary concern is the trouble I am causing these people. Needless to say, they can't hear me.

Caution with Kids

Cherie Sutherland, PhD, an Australian researcher of near-death states, offers this caution in dealing with the medical concerns of children: "Clinic and hospital staff should tell a child what is being done to him or her and why as they go about their work. Otherwise, during out-of-body states, children will be unable to understand what is happening as they view their body from a point apart. We explain procedures to adults. We must give children the same courtesy." Dr. Sutherland has authored *Beloved Visitors: Parents Tell of After-Death Visits from Their Children* and *Children of the Light: The Near-Death Experiences of Children* (refer to appendix C).

"The doctor orders a drug from the nurse. She went around the green screen to my right, to an old-fashioned French medicine cabinet with a curved front. She opened the drawer, removed a hypo, removed the plastic wrapping, and filled it from a small bottle taken from the left side of the second shelf. She rushed around the screen handing it to the doctor. As he was about to inject it into my heart, he saw the bottle in her hand. He reached across me, grabbed the bottle from her hand, and read it. He threw the bottle and hypo across the room, knocked her down as he raced around the screen to the cabinet, screaming at the top of his lungs that she could have killed me. I thought that was ironic, and tried to tell him I was already dead.

"He searched the cabinet, found a bottle, removed a hypo, and filled it without removing all the wrapping. Still screaming at her, he vowed that she would never work as a nurse again. He returned to me, injected the medication into my heart, and started to beat and massage my heart."

Chris then began to review his life, not the chronological, nonjudgmental type of past-life review most experiencers report, but rather a deliberate assessment of his debts and responsibilities. Deciding everything was okay, he opted to go on to "the other side."

"About this time I noticed I was not alone,

Medical Goofs Revealed

Melvin Morse, MD, found that during the early to mid-1900s, doctors regularly used too much ether for tonsillectomies, and that's why so many child near-death incidents turn up in case studies during that period. My research caught the same error in medical judgment that Dr. Morse did, validating his findings. Apparently, excessive amounts of ether can trigger what causes genuine near-death states. This practice changed in the late 1970s. I also discovered that medical mistakes of varied types frequently show up in near-death scenarios, resulting in large numbers of people nearly dying from nonthreatening procedures.

The medical community should recognize this so harmful practices can be detected and corrected quickly.

Drawing by Chris Brown of the grayish and somewhat cloudy group of men who spoke to him during his lengthy near-death episode.

even though no one spoke to me. I looked at these people, they were a grayish and somewhat cloudy group of men. I didn't recognize any of them. I 'informed' them I had decided not to return to the world, but to join them. They said that I don't make those decisions. This really infuriated me and I asked, 'What is all this about then? If I am not dead or going to stay that way, why are you putting all these people through this? What purpose does it serve?' I remember that I was nowhere near as polite and reverent as I should have been."

Chris was told that he must return to do a job he had not yet done and that he must learn. When he inquired further, an entity scolded him and said, "Don't question, just do. Now go!"

"My next memory is waking up in ICU with another nurse at the foot of my bed. She went for the doctor, who examined me and pronounced me alive." Two days later, after being assured by the doctor that he could speak freely, Chris detailed everything he had seen and heard while out-of-body. The doctor asked many questions until he was satisfied that the young soldier had indeed witnessed what was seemingly physically impossible for him to, especially considering the state he was in at the time and from the position of the gurney.

Ethical Implications

Unethical or ethically questionable behavior on the part of medical staff as relates to near-death experiences, is now being called into question:

Examples of Unethical Actions

- A patient was diagnosed with a mental disorder solely on the basis of her NDE.
- A patient was medicated with a tranquilizer as a result of his postsurgery report of an NDE.
- A parishioner was discounted and ostracized as grandiose and heretical for describing his NDE.

Examples of Ethical Behavior

- A counselor without background knowledge of an NDE sought a counselor with such expertise when presented with a client whose NDE played a significant role in his life.
- A nurse regularly invites patients, both before and after surgery, to share any experience they might have had—even if unusual or bizarre.
- A rabbi listens intently to synagogue members who have NDEs, and encourages them to search for meaning as they come to appreciate the reality and inherent mystery of their experience.

(From the work of Janice Miner Holden, EdD, LPC, LMFT, NCC; Bruce Greyson, MD; and Debbie James, MSN, RN, CCRN, CNS.)

Suggestions for Health-Care Providers

The medical community has every right to be leery about the near-death phenomenon. After all, it runs counter to everything they teach and challenges them in ways that cannot be verified with a microscope or an X-ray machine. Besides that, patients say the darnedest things once they're back in their bodies after flying around the room. To a professional with a scientific mind, such stories seem just too fanciful to be true.

But, thanks to high-tech resuscitation techniques, more people are being plucked from the jaws of death than anyone could have imagined. This amazing medical advancement has brought the seldom-told stories of life after death to the forefront. In so doing, the near-death experience has become a permanent addition to the concerns of medical and emergency care. And, leery or not, as we've seen through the real-life accounts in this chapter, the medical community must not only address the phenomenon but must also champion procedures on how best to help health-care personnel aid experiencers.

In the following sections I offer a few suggestions.

Techniques for a Health-Care Provider

Kimberly Clark Sharp, MSW, president of Seattle IANDS and experiencer and social worker, has interviewed more than 2,000 near-death survivors, many in intensive care and cancer wards. In 1993, Kimberly gave a presentation to the North American Conference of IANDS in St. Louis, Missouri, in which she outlined intervention techniques for professional health-care providers.

With the permission of Kimberly, some of her recommendations are presented in a chart on pages 150–151. I think you'll find them helpful and thought-provoking.

Advice about Afterward

After the patient has recovered there is often depression or anger—either because the event happened in the first place or because it was not possible to stay in the dimension of the near-death experience. There can also be feelings of rejection that he or she was "kicked out of heaven," or a great relief that somehow he or she was "saved from hell." Invariably, there is amazement and puzzlement. There come a million questions with no ready answers. That's why it's so important to have an empathetic listener available.

THE NEAR-DEATH PHENOMENON

Immediate Intervention Techniques developed by Kimberly Clark Sharp, MSW

During Cardiopulmonary Resuscitation (CPR):

- Assume, rather than dismiss, that the patient may be having a near-death experience. At the very least, the patient will be able to hear what you say, even if he or she is unconscious.
- It is disorienting to be out-of-body, so orient the patient as to date and time, his or her location, the patient's name, and all activities related to the patient's body.
- Talk the patient through CPR either aloud or silently. Often patients report being able to "read the minds" of those in attendance and can "hear" your thoughts regarding the activities around their physical bodies. It is additionally helpful to brush the patient's body lightly with your hands, naming the parts as you touch them, so the individual can find his or her way back into the body when the out-of-body episode is over. Simply put, physical contact can act as a "beacon" to guide the patient "back in."

For the Unconscious Patient:

- Use the recommendations as previously stated, that is, orient the patient and provide light touch while naming corresponding body parts.
- As a courtesy, introduce yourself to the patient and let him or her know what you are doing.
- Tell the patient about the near-death phenomenon. Briefly mention several elements of the near-death experience while reassuring him or her that what is happening is *normal.* This will validate the near-death experience before the individual revives.

The experiencer *needs* to talk. And the experiencer *needs* to have information about the near-death phenomenon—lots of it.

A word of caution here, though, if you're involved with a near-death experiencer: They may not want your help or suggestions. Regardless of how much it's needed, support may be refused. I have yet to meet an experiencer who could adequately assess his or her personal situation with any real degree of discernment or clarity in the first three years afterward. (I was no exception.)

All experiencers need assistance at one time or another; but it's not always accepted, nor is it necessarily welcomed. Sometimes patience is the greatest gift you can give. Sometimes only the passage of time makes any difference.

For the Conscious Patient Who Cannot Verbalize:

- For the patient on a ventilator or otherwise physically restrained, remember to give your name as a courtesy and state your purpose. Verbally educate the patient about the universal elements of the near-death phenomenon, and validate for him or her that the experience is *normal.* Establish a method of nonverbal communication, such as hand squeezes or head nods, and ask if he or she remembers any near-death element.
- Promise to return when the patient can verbalize so that he or she can discuss the experience. If you cannot return, let the patient know that someone else will come in your stead to hear the story, if he or she desires.

For the Fully Conscious and Verbal Patient:

- Introduce yourself. Maintain eye contact and give your full and uninterrupted attention.
- Ask the patient if anything unusual or different happened to him or her during CPR or a close brush with death. If there's hesitation and fumbling for words, tears, and lots of "ohs" and "ahs" and "wells," that person probably had a near-death experience.
- Begin interviewing by asking the patient to describe his or her memory of events. Be nonjudgmental. Be honest about yourself and your values. Don't patronize. Near-death experiencers are *very* sensitive, and they will know a lot about you just by looking at you. Stop your interview at any sign of discomfort.
- Avoid pressure or probing. Assure the patient that you will be there to listen if wanted. Lend authority to the patient's account, as he or she (and others) will tend to discount or disbelieve. Begin to plan how the patient will integrate the near-death experience with recovery and "normalcy."
- Put the patient in touch with appropriate resources to obtain emotional support and more information about the near-death phenomenon.

Unique Health Issues

There are experiencers who are crippled or handicapped after their episodes, or are so weakened they go on to endure debilitating illnesses. The pattern of aftereffects, however, is still apparent with most of them, and their willingness to deal openly with the impact of near-death states creates a decided advantage in their overall health improvement—and how happy and at peace they can become.

A Shift in Health Options

Like the adults, child experiencers show a decided preference for *complementary* approaches to medicine as they mature. All of those in my study who claimed now to have excellent health (77 percent) credited their good

The Challenge with Kids

Children lack words to describe what they went through and cannot explain their confusion, anger, or joy. Infants must wait years before they can even begin to verbalize their stories. Allowing children to paint or draw their experiences, rather than describe them, is not only revealing, but therapeutic. Acting out episodes or using puppets is also a helpful activity for the younger set.

New Words

Complementary medicine is the term currently used to refer to health care that embraces various modalities—naturopathy, homeopathy, acupuncture, and the like, as well as allopathy. This approach weds natural healing practices with technological advances, resulting in an ideal model of illness prevention and wellness care.

fortune to a more spiritual outlook, along with having turned to things such as herbs, homeopathy, massage, and vitamin/mineral therapy for healing. The majority, irrespective of age, found pharmaceuticals difficult to tolerate.

Health-Care Concerns

Certain health issues are unique to near-death experiencers of any age, but are of special concern in raising and medicating child experiencers. Not well known, these issues hardly receive a second glance from the average person—yet they are important to know if there is an experiencer in your family or if you are a health-care provider.

Here's a list of special health precautions:

- *Blood pressure.* Current medical opinion considers long-term low blood pressure to be a major component of chronic fatigue syndrome, and therefore a disease that should be treated chemically. Adults, and sometimes children, exhibit a substantial drop in blood pressure after their episodes. Experiencers who continue to be hale, hearty, and energetic should let their doctor know that low blood pressure is normal for them.

- *Light sensitivity.* All well-meaning adults encourage everyone to be outside as much as possible. Fresh air is healthy. But if the experiencer is a child and the teacher, coach, or parent forces him or her to practice or play in bright sunlight for long periods of time, day after day, the results could be troublesome. Adult experiencers, especially those who work outside, should also be careful. Because of an experiencer's unusual sensitivity to light, he or she is subject to debilitating reactions such as fatigue, weakening immune system, or even an allergy to sunshine. It's best to wear dark sunglasses when in the sun and cut exposure time until sun tolerance can be restored (this may take a number of years, if at all).

- *Sound sensitivity.* Peer pressure for the young is hard to contend with, especially for teens. Types of music listened to and at what decibel level represent the mark of allegiance to whatever is "in." Unfortunately, if the teenager is an experiencer, any kind of loud music or noise can be painful to him or her and detrimentally affect the eardrums. This can be a special challenge to adults experiencers, as well, since sound levels once considered par for the course suddenly become intolerable. Most experiencers come to prefer nature's sounds, the classics, or the broad range of what is called "New Age" music.

- *Less tolerance to pharmaceuticals.* This is a major concern for adult experiencers, who are regularly given substantial-sized dosages for treatment of various ailments when what they usually need are smaller amounts for the same effect—like what a child would receive. With child experiencers, the situation can be more serious. That's because when youngsters are ill, they are rushed to a doctor or maybe the emergency room, where a shot is administered or pills are prescribed. This is standard procedure. But if the little one is an experiencer—suddenly more sensitive, possibly even newly allergic to the type of pharmaceuticals normally given to a child of his or her weight and age—the treatment could be more dangerous than the illness. Physicians should be alerted.

- *Sleep cycles.* The very young generally tend to nap less and have more flow states (float free of the thinking process to experience "NO THING," then return refreshed and creatively energized). Most will relive their episode or be haunted by it in vivid dream states. Adult experiencers occasionally report waking up regularly between 3:00 and 4:00 A.M. afterward, and for no apparent reason. Some claim that their breathing stops without cause, especially while they are asleep (as reported by frightened others). Many find it difficult at first to recognize the onset of sleep, which can interfere with their body clocks. (Body clock reversals, by the way, are commonplace.) None of these sleep cycle deviations seem to present health concerns. Eventually, the average experiencer will make whatever adjustments are needed to ensure healthy amounts of sleep.

> **Docs Don't Know**
>
> Because the health-care needs of near-death experiencers tend to deviate from or challenge standard medical care, physicians are generally unprepared in knowing how to treat them. That's why so many experiencers look in other directions for the help they need—regularly turning to spiritual healers and those trained in complementary medical techniques, and educating themselves in the art of self-healing, wellness, and illness prevention.

Help at Last

The International Association for Near-Death Studies (IANDS) has

Guess What?

In the famous Mayo Clinic College of Medicine, Rochester, Minnesota, first-year medical students are taught about near-death experiences as a way to learn professionalism, respect for individual patients of differing cultures, and how to work with colleagues who have varied sets of beliefs. The class features videotaped presentations, as well as small group discussions and web-based discussion boards. This program is so successful, it is being recommended for usage in any medical teaching facility. (Refer to Robert D. Sheeler, MD, Associate Professor of Family Medicine, Mayo Medical School of the Mayo Clinic College of Medicine, in appendix E.)

Available Now

A brief continuing education piece for nurses developed by Diane Corcoran, PhD (a retired military nurse) can be accessed at https://nursing.advanceweb.com/common/ce/.

recently received enough donations to develop programs that directly impact the medical community, and serve the general public in ways never before possible. As more funding is received even more programs will be made available.

Here is what currently exists:

Physicians' Advisory Committee. Formed to advise on medical matters and on how best to communicate with the medical community. Making continuing medical education (CME) credits more readily available is one of their priorities. Members are:

- Sam Parnia, MD. Originally from England, now at Cornell University Medical School, New York. Committee chair.
- Peter Fenwick, MD. England. Author of book on NDEs and NDE researcher.
- Pim van Lommel, MD. Netherlands. Cardiologist and author of study on NDEs published in the *Lancet.*
- Bruce Greyson, MD. U.S. Editor, *Journal of Near-Death Studies.* Psychiatrist at University of Virginia and author of many articles in medical journals.
- Pam Kircher, MD. U.S. Author of *Love Is the Link.* Experiencer involved with hospice and alternative medical care in Colorado.
- Jason Maclurg, MD. U.S. Psychiatrist in private practice in Washington.
- Jeff Long, MD. U.S. Radiation oncologist. Founder of NDE Research Foundation.
- Robert Cole, MD. U.S. Boston University.
- Ginette Nachman, MD, PhD. U.S. Rhine Institute in North Carolina.

• Robert Brumblay, MD. U.S. Emergency room physician in Hawaii.

Online Continuing Education credits for Medical, Mental, and Spiritual Health-Care Providers. Spearheading the creation of this five-hour "computer class" is Jan Holden, EdD, college professor and past president of IANDS. Committee members include: Bruce Greyson, MD; Diane Corcoran, PhD; Debbie James, MSN, RN, CCRN; Sarah Kreutziger, PhD, MSW; and Nadine von Daeniken (a student from the University of Basel in Switzerland). PowerPoint visuals combined with lecture and audio excerpts from previous near-death conferences and experiencer interviews with photos make up this program. Divided into five sections, it focuses on the near-death experience, aftereffects, special topics (such as children's cases), cross-cultural studies, those episodes resulting from suicide attempts, explanatory models of the phenomenon, and implications and applications for health-care providers and others who interact with experiencers.

CD-ROM—Research Bibliography, Expanded Version. This index to periodical literature through 2001 is extensive. It covers not only *Journal of Near-Death Studies* articles, but every article published in the first twenty-five years of near-death studies, a total of more than 800 articles: 703 scholarly (mostly refereed journal articles), and 123 non-scholarly (popular magazines, newspapers, and so on). Work is under way to extend CD-ROM coverage through 2005, and beyond. Reprints to articles are available by contacting IANDS, as

Even Doctors Die and Come Back

In March 1999, Roby Rogers, MD, had a near-death experience that changed the way she looked at death and dying and the role of disease in a person's life. It also changed the way she practices medicine and influenced her in many other ways.

Once Again, Nurses Are Making a Difference

The Final Entrance: Journeys Beyond Life recounts the stories of near-death experiences, gathered from twenty-five years of nursing activities, heard and recorded by a registered nurse who has attended many dying patients. Sue Schoenbeck is director of resident care at Ingleside Skilled Nursing and Rehabilitation Center in Mount Horeb, Wisconsin. She is also a nursing home administrator and associate clinical professor at the University of Wisconsin in Madison. "The intent of this book," Schoenbeck explains, "is to provide for nursing and other medical professionals a perspective on what near-death experiences are and how to counsel patients who entrust such experiences to them. The time is not too far past when people who told their nurse or doctor that they were floating in and out of their body or were talking with deceased relatives were whisked off to some special ward to be 'cured.'" Tragic, but true.

are recordings from previous conference lectures and panels.

Introductory Bibliography of Near-Death Experiences. A handy guide to a list of books that cover the various aspects of the near-death phenomenon.

NDE of the Month, Member Service. Each month, IANDS sends to its members via e-mail a near-death account from their archives. All accounts are anonymous. The purpose is to help people better understand near-death experiences and gain insight from them.

Digital Audio Archive Project. A large archive of near-death experiencer accounts already exists. The purpose of this project is to digitize all past IANDS conference audio recordings (which up until now have only been available as audiotapes), and make them readily available to anyone so interested.

IANDS Speakers Bureau. Rev. Jerry Shields has been charged with the development of a bureau of people qualified to speak on topics covering or related to the near-death phenomenon. For those wishing to schedule any of these speakers, contact Rev. Shields at JKShields@mar.med.navy.mil.

Please refer to appendix B for more information and contacts concerning the International Association for Near-Death Studies (IANDS).

Part 3

Time Out for Questions

We've learned a lot about the near-death experience, and perhaps you think that by now, more than two decades after the publication of Moody's groundbreaking book *Life After Life,* the story would be winding down. But the story isn't winding down; indeed, since it began being told, many have challenged it, even rejected it. "A fabrication of the mind," they say, "of the dying brain."

The voices of those who challenge the validity of the near-death experience are important. Like the river that rubs against the rock and smooths it, the voices of dissent help shape the story and make sure it stays truthful.

In these chapters, we'll listen to what the challengers have to say, and we'll learn how near-death researchers have responded to these voices of dissent.

11

Are the Dead Really Dead?

I shall have more to say when I am dead.

—Edwin Arlington Robinson, U.S. poet

Old mystical and spiritual texts speak about the proper way to determine if the dead really are dead. Most of them warn that three days must lapse before a corpse can be burned or tampered with. The warning explains that the departing soul (that regulating force that directs the mind) needs this time to remove all its history from the body parts, and is somehow energized by early stages of decay from the vacated corpse.

The warning further states that during these three days, it's possible for the departing soul to change its mind about leaving. In case this might occur, the body should be left intact and available for reinhabitation. After the full three days have passed, it seems not to matter what becomes of the corpse. If the three-day time frame could not be respected, then natural, at-home burials were preferred to burning or any method that would violate the body. It was cautioned that premature destruction of the body (on purpose or accidentally) meant premature return to another life before the soul could be fully readied.

Of course, no one can prove the claims of these traditional teachings; but in light of recent findings that establish death as a process, not an event, there could be some truth to these old warnings. Let's explore this further. And while we're at it, we'll take a look at a couple of actual accounts that show how difficult it can be to determine if the dead really *are* dead.

Back from the Dead

Pim van Lommel, senior cardiologist at a hospital in the Netherlands, and his associates Ruud van Wees, V. Meyers, and I. Elfferich, spent twelve years doing clinical studies of cardiac patients in ten Dutch hospitals who had reported near-death episodes. Every person studied had passed the clinical death tests mentioned here, then revived. And 18 percent had a remarkable story to tell about how alive they were while dead.

Real Tales from the Crypt

Cessation of vital signs used to be the criteria for determining death. To double-check, a mirror or piece of glass was held under the individual's nose as a test for condensation (a cloud of moisture meant life remained), and the pupils of the eyes were flashed with something bright to test for a reaction to light (a response signaled active body involvement).

The invention of the stethoscope in the 1800s enabled doctors to more specifically monitor heart sounds. Electrocardiograms (EKGs), which made the scene in the 1900s, opened the door to mapping electrical activity in the heart. Both of these advancements were a boon to the medical community and helped make death pronouncements more secure. Then along came CPR (cardiopulmonary resuscitation). This did away with the old heart-lung criteria, and instituted "brain death" as the only acceptable protocol to determine if someone had died.

It didn't take long, however, for brain death to also be deemed unsuitable as a dependable criterion. That's because too many patients who were brain dead tested with biologic activity for up to seven days afterward, and too many of those used for organ donations showed increased blood pressure and heart rate as the organ was being removed. Medical science then made a stunning discovery: Death is a process, not a definitive event. That discovery led to the current three-fold testing method used to establish death:

www.sacredcowsonline.com www.cafepress.com/sacredcows

1. An EEG (electroencephalogram) check for brain-wave activity

2. Auditory-evoked procedures to measure brain-stem viability

3. Documentation from other tests to show the absence of blood flow to the brain

But people who meet the criteria of all three tests can still have a near-death experience and return to life.

So Much for Quiet Corpses

The average length of time a near-death experiencer is "dead" usually clocks out at between five and twenty minutes. It's not uncommon, however, to find clinically dead experiencers who revived thirty minutes to an hour later, or several hours later. I came across one woman who was dead for twelve hours, another for sixteen. Both "awakened" in the morgue. This is amazing since the medical community cautions that without sufficient oxygen, the brain can be permanently damaged in three to five minutes. By the way, neither of these people suffered any ill effects—in fact, they returned smarter and more creative than they had been before!

Indeed, several embalmers I've spoken with have had stories to tell about dead people "waking up"—about the so-called "deceased" occasionally moving around and asserting that they are quite alive once the embalming procedure begins. One particular story I was told is of a "corpse" who swatted morgue personnel when the syringe was inserted to drain his blood.

The Corpse Who Changed History

We can't go into the past and change history, but some who have "passed" have come back and did indeed change history. Robert E. Lee's mother "succumbed" to an illness, was given a proper funeral, and then interred in the family vault. A relative who arrived too late for the service requested that he be shown the body. When he looked at her, he saw her chest move. After regaining consciousness, a very indignant "corpse" scolded everyone for jumping to conclusions. Three years later, Mrs. Lee gave birth to the child who would someday lead the South in the Civil War.

Get Me Outta This Coffin!

You'd think that with the technology available today, there would be fewer accounts of "faulty funerals," but that's not true. Many countries simply cannot afford the luxury of new equipment; in others, religious restrictions prevent medical intervention. Even in industrialized nations, health-care givers still goof.

Case in point: A London newspaper in 1992 carried a gruesome story about a seventy-one-year-old Romanian man who had been buried alive. Apparently, the man had choked on a chicken bone, collapsed, was thought dead of a coronary, given a funeral, and buried. Three days later, gravediggers heard knocking from inside his

New Words

Code blue is a term used in the medical community to signal a cardiopulmonary arrest, that is to say, a life-threatening heart rhythm that may or may not involve the cessation of breath. The key here is speed. By calling a code blue, a medical team rushes to deliver the type of intervention that, it is hoped, will prevent a full-blown heart attack from occurring.

wooden coffin. Unsealing it, they found the man quite alive. But when he arrived home, his wife refused to see him. It took the poor fellow three weeks to convince priests, bank clerks, doctors, town hall officials, and police to cancel his death certificate.

Still skeptical? Here's another case, this one from Cairo, Egypt: In 1997, a man who was pronounced dead regained consciousness after spending twelve hours in a coffin stored in a morgue refrigerator. Upon hearing the man's shouts for help and discovering him alive, a paramedic collapsed in shock and died, the daily *Al-Akhbar* newspaper reported. It was the cold of the refrigerator that revived Abdel-Sattar Badawi, after he'd been declared dead and placed inside a coffin in a hospital in Menoufia, sixty-five miles northwest of Cairo. "I opened my eyes but couldn't see anything. I moved my hands and pushed the coffin's lid to find myself among the dead," Badawi was quoted as saying.

The Newly Dead Who Greet the Newly Dead

We've taken a look at how difficult it can be to determine if someone is really dead. Now we need to broaden our discussion by asking the question: How dead are near-death experiencers? We have all these reports, but were the people fully and completely dead when they had their episodes?

Obviously, some were not that close. With others, death consisted of hardly more than a few missing bleeps on a machine before medical personnel "shocked" the individual back to life. For those who revived hours later in a morgue, the question is moot.

Therefore, perhaps the best way to approach the death question is to examine it from various angles. What follows are some intriguing, real-life stories that challenge our notions about death.

A Bird Named "Doolittle"

Lloyd L. Haymon of Friendswood, Texas, had a typical near-death experience—but with a twist. Lloyd did not recognize the signs that a coronary was about to happen. He drove home with a tremendous pain in his lower right side, consulted a medical self-help book for advice, then called his wife. The next thing he remembered was lying on his living room floor with paramedics all around him and the rush to reach a hospital, with his wife sitting on the passenger side of the ambulance. His was a *code blue.*

While in the ambulance, Lloyd left his body and had a vision of his wife dressed in the clothes she wore when he first met her. The vision faded as he "yo-yoed" from a space near the ambulance ceiling to being inside his body and then back out again. But, as Lloyd later tells it, his biggest shock was when he finally returned to and stayed in this body: "At my feet is my younger brother who had died years before of cancer at the age of thirty. He is shaking his head as if to say 'No, no, it's not your time.' On my brother's shoulder is a bird. I look closer and it is my bird, Doolittle the parakeet. I can't take my eyes off Doolittle, and I want to ask someone why Doolittle is on my brother's shoulder." (Doolittle was very much alive when Lloyd had last seen him, which was only minutes before.)

After the crisis was over, Lloyd recalls: "As my wife and I head home from the hospital, I ask her if my bird is home. She said no, so I say to her 'Take me to Wal-Mart because I need to get another bird.' She refuses at first, but I get my bird, Sailor. We let him out of the box once home, and he flies up to the curtain and sits. My wife then tells me that Doolittle died for no apparent reason the day I had my heart attack. He died while the paramedics were working on me. She let him lie on the bed for three days before she buried him.

"After she speaks, the new parakeet flies down and lands on my shoulder. Young, untrained wild birds do not do this. I put out my finger and Sailor jumps on it. The little guy says, 'Doolittle.' My wife and I both come unglued. Sailor became tame right then, and began to talk, just like Doolittle did. When he died, we buried him next to Doolittle. My life changed forever. I became creative and started building furniture. I went back to school and became a clinical hypnotherapist. My attitudes, the way I treat people, have changed 100 percent. I know this happened, and I no longer fear death."

Even with Pets

In Lloyd Haymon's case, the fact that the new parakeet immediately said "Doolittle," then mimicked the deceased bird's behavioral traits, illustrates more than the bond that exists between pets and their owners. It implies, and quite persuasively, that loving concern for another can be communicated between the dead and the living—*even from pet to pet!*

Doolittle died within minutes of Lloyd Haymon. There is no way he could have known this. Although the appearance of the deceased—like that of Lloyd's brother who had died years before—is typical of near-death states, being greeted by a loved one thought to be very much alive but who had just died harkens back to the medical discovery that death is a process.

Could it be that "death by degrees" sets the stage for a possible comingling of the newly dead? Could this be evidence that indeed the near-death phenomenon treads the same pathways as does death itself?

Of course, it's possible that Sailor said the name "Doolittle" simply because Lloyd's wife had spoken it while she was explaining the older bird's death. Lloyd, however, disputes this, because of the unusual way Sailor

Write It Down

Always check every source possible when trying to verify experiencer accounts, then record what you find on paper that's dated and signed, not only by yourself, but by everyone else involved. Too often, people wait until years later to verify details, only to discover witnesses have died or moved away and cannot be located.

behaved from the moment they got him at Wal-Mart. An experienced bird trainer, Lloyd insists that Sailor's actions were like nothing he had ever seen before.

The Father Who Intervened

In another case, a young woman died on the operating table from injuries received in a car/truck accident, but was resuscitated. Immediately and with great animation she described meeting her father while she was dead. She said her father had told her why he had been born, and why and how he had died. He then told her why she had been born, and that she must return to the land of the living for she had not yet completed all that she must do. She was so excited about her father's "visit" that the surgical personnel had a tough time finishing the medical procedures she needed.

A gathering of relatives in the waiting room pooh-poohed her entire story when a physician told them about it, asserting that the father was healthy and robust. One of them offered that he had spoken that very morning with the father on the phone. After several more unsuccessful attempts to convince the woman she was hallucinating, the doctor returned to the waiting room and insisted that the father be called. Many phone calls later, it was discovered that the father had died exactly as he had told his daughter he did—five minutes before she died. No one could have known this in advance, much less the daughter.

As Dead as You Can Get

Near-death states most often emerge from close calls at the edge of death, where it's difficult to determine if the individual actually died or was about to. Few have been issued signed certificates to prove they were ever dead, even though eyewitnesses, medical or otherwise, can and do testify to just that. Yet the combination of a lack of vital signs and the patterning identified with near-death states (the scenario and the aftereffects) convinces the majority that the experiencers really did die.

There are a fair number of cases, though, that are so striking they completely dissolve the notion of a border between life and death. Even considering "death by degrees," these people were as dead as it gets—and then came back. Let's take a look at their stories.

Hold on to Your Socks for This One

In *Beyond the Light,* I tell the story of George Rodonaia, a vocal Soviet dissident during the Cold War who had earned his master's degree in research psychology and was working toward his doctorate when he was assassinated by the KGB. He felt the pain of being crushed beneath car wheels as he was run over twice by the same vehicle. But what bothered him most was the feeling of an unknown darkness that came to envelop him.

> **Note This**
>
> What makes the cases you are about to read so important is that they support the hypothesis that consciousness can function apart from the brain.

As he focused on what was occurring, he was surprised to discover the range and power of his thoughts and what he could do with them. A pinprick of light appeared, then bubbles like balls of molecules and atoms, life-making cells moving in spirals, revealing to him higher and higher levels of power with God as the highest. He found he could project himself anywhere on Earth he wanted to go and experience what was there, and that he could do the same thing regarding events in history. Being extremely curious, he did just that, amusing himself by projecting invisibly into various times and places to find out what he'd see and learn. Among other things, he discovered that he could get inside people's heads and hear and see what they did.

He returned to the morgue, saw his body, then was drawn to the newborn section of the adjacent hospital where a friend's wife had just given birth to a daughter. The baby cried incessantly. As if possessed of X-ray vision, George scanned her body and noted that her hip had been broken shortly after birth (a nurse had dropped her). He "spoke" to the infant and told her not to cry, as no one would understand her. The infant was so surprised at his presence that she stopped crying. He claims that children can see and hear spirit beings; that's why she responded. After that, he experienced a life review that involved reliving not only his own life, but the death of his parents at the hands of the KGB—something he had not known as he'd been raised by relatives who had withheld the truth about what had happened to his mother and father.

George's corpse was stored in a freezer vault in the hospital morgue for three days (he doesn't know what the exact temperature was). He revived while the trunk of his body was being split open during autopsy. The shock of seeing this sent the physician in charge screaming from the unit. (His own uncle was one of the doctors in attendance.) All his ribs were broken, his muscles destroyed, his feet a horrible mess. It took three days before the swelling in his tongue went down enough for him to speak. His first words warned the doctors about the child with the broken hip. X-rays of the newborn were taken, the nurse who dropped her questioned, and he was proved right on both counts. During the nine months he was hospitalized, he became something of a celebrity.

For a year afterward, his wife, Nino, would not sleep in the same room with him. She had great difficulty dealing with his miraculous return and the fact that he had correctly "seen" everything she had while selecting his gravesite—

The Blind Can See

Vicki Noratuk has been blind since birth, but has had two episodes of seeing when she left her body through near-death experiences. As a premature baby, Vicki was given the accepted medical care and support of the 1950s, which was to be placed in an incubator that had high levels of oxygen. Only later was it discovered that this destroyed the optic nerves of children. At an early age, Vicki had her first near-death experience in which she was able to leave her body and be aware of the hospital environment. Many years later, a traffic accident at the foot of Queen Anne Hill in Seattle, Washington, again led to her leaving her body and seeing, not only the accident scene below, but her encountering deceased friends in spiritual realms. Vicki had normal vision during both episodes, and recognized who and what she saw, even though she had never seen before, and still cannot.

Rev. Juliet Nightingale has had several near-death experiences as a result of life-threatening illnesses since childhood. Even though she has severely restricted vision (legally blind), she had no trouble seeing colors, shapes, beings, even recognizing minute details during each episode. "I experienced no blindness then," she claimed. "What a sense of awe and wonder—to be able to see!"

New Word

Standstill is a nickname given to an operation called hypothermic cardiac arrest. It renders a patient "dead" by all known clinical standards. During the surgery, body temperature is lowered 60 degrees, heartbeat and breathing are stopped, brain waves are flattened, and blood is drained from the head. The procedure is only performed when other medical techniques cannot be used.

even quoting back to her all her thoughts when she was considering other men to marry now that she was a widow. I asked Nino about this, and she said, "How would you like it if you had no privacy, not even in your own mind?"

A Medically Documented Flatline

One argument used to invalidate near-death states as being anything other than hallucinations is the claim that no one who was totally flatlined has ever returned, much less with an otherworldly tale to tell. Here's a case that proves the falsehood of that claim.

Cardiologist Michael Sabom's book *Light and Death* documents the medical flatline (brain death) of a woman who, upon being resuscitated, reported a long and detailed near-death experience. Dr. Sabom is one of the top researchers in the field, and his work spans more than twenty years of careful observation and analysis. His story of Pam Reynolds centers around what is known as *standstill*—a radically risky new surgical technique for correcting blood clots and damaged blood vessels located in places that could not previously have been operated on.

The daring surgery performed by Robert Spetzler, MD, was used to remove an aneurysm (a damaged and inflated section of an artery) that had been found in Pam's head. Once she had flatlined, a large section of her brain was carved out so the aneurysm could be located, excised, and a new vessel sewn in place (obtained from her groin area). Complications arose, however, when the damaged area turned out to be extremely large and extended up into the brain.

After 11:25 A.M., medical monitoring equipment declared Pam dead. The aneurysm sac had collapsed like a deflated balloon and was clipped out and replaced, then the cardiopulmonary bypass machine was turned back on so warm blood could once again course through her body. At noon, the heart monitor began to register a disorganized rhythm. After two jolts of electricity, normal rhythm returned. By 12:32 P.M., her temperature had reached a low but life-sustainable degree, instruments were removed, and her surgical wound closed. At 2:10 P.M., she was taken to the recovery room.

For more than half an hour, Pam's brain was completely and absolutely dead. Yet afterward, Pam recounted that from a point "sitting" on the shoulder of Dr. Spetzler, she could see, hear, and feel what was going on. What she described proved to be accurate. As well as the out-of-body component, she experienced a lengthy near-death scenario that deeply impacted her and

What Pam Saw in Surgery

After loss of consciousness, she heard the piercing sound of the cranial saw. She said it emitted a natural D tone as it pulled her out of the top of her head. She came to rest on Dr. Spetzler's shoulder. From there, she saw with clarity and in detail the cranial saw, her head, the operating room, and the surgical team.

She was somewhat dismayed to see someone conducting a procedure in her groin area when this was supposedly brain surgery. She heard a female voice report that veins and arteries were too small, and a male voice directing her to try the other side.

What Pam Saw on the Other Side

She moved through a tunnel-like area and joyfully encountered several deceased relatives. That incredible, ineffable light bathed her. While in the light, she communicated via telepathy with her family members, and was told she was not to go any further into the light. Her deceased uncle accompanied her back to her body, but when she saw how bad it looked, she became frightened and didn't want to reenter it. Her body "jumped" several times, then she felt her uncle push her back in. She described reentry as "like diving into a pool of ice water—it hurt!"

Shared Accounts

Occasionally in research you run across cases of multiple deaths and multiple miracles, where, somehow, all of those who were dead revive. I have noticed a fascinating peculiarity in those I have investigated, and that is, if one of the people involved reported having had a near-death episode, they all did—even if the multiple parties had not spoken to the others nor divulged what had happened to them with anyone else. Once they did get together and compared accounts, they were shocked to discover they each had experienced a near-death state and how similar each one had been to the other (although precise details sometimes varied).

touched everyone who heard about it, especially Dr. Sabom. (The account just given was paraphrased from Dr. Sabom's book with permission from his publisher, Zondervan Publishing House.)

When Two or More Die Together

Another variant on "death by degrees" concerns shared experiences between experiencers. These incidents challenge the overall significance of any "need" factor a sole individual might have, and threaten the underpinning of any scientific argument that body processes explain near-death states.

From time to time you hear about a couple who both die—in a car accident, for example—and have a near-death episode in which they see one another, and one says to the other, "I must stay, but you need to return." And, indeed, only one comes back. I've encountered this with married couples and with parent-child duos. Since only one lives, it's impossible to verify the full account. All you can deal with is the single survivor and his or her response to the event and the ensuing aftereffects.

I have encountered other people, though, who reported scenarios that appeared so similar it's as if they were shared. This oddity happened in two ways: They were either all at the same location within the same time span, or they were miles and years apart. In my own case, two of my "deaths" happened in January of 1977, the other in March. I have since met a dozen other people whose experiences were so akin to my first and last one it's as if we each lived through exactly the same thing. Later, I met fifty-one other individuals who also had three near-death episodes in 1977, with before and after conditions similar to mine—even though we "died" in different months and experienced different scenarios.

Save Me, I Can't Swim

Steven B. Ridenhour of Charlottesville, Virginia, and his girlfriend, Debbie, decided to "run" the rapids at the "bullhole" part of the river that flows behind an old cotton mill in Cooleemee, North Carolina. Both had been smoking pot and were bored. Their decision to run the knee-high rapids meant that they had to start at the beginning of the rock incline, run down about twenty feet, and start skiing barefooted until they reached the moss beds. Overtaken by laughter, they were easily swept off their feet and dragged downriver before they could react.

Steven recalls Debbie screaming, "I can't swim, I'm drowning!" He rushed to reach her, but the water was too much for him. At that moment, he said the water took on a golden glow and time stopped. He experienced floating in a vertical position, his arms outstretched, and his head lying on one shoulder.

He experienced total peace and serenity—until his life review started. "It was like looking at a very fast slide show of my past, and I do mean fast, like seconds." He didn't understand the significance of all that was shown to him, but he was certain there was some importance. "When this ended, it was as if I was floating very high up and looking down at a funeral. Suddenly, I realized that I was looking at myself in a casket. I saw myself dressed in a black tux with a white shirt and a red rose on my left lapel. Standing around me were my immediate family and significant friends."

Then, as if some powerful force wrapped around him, Steven was thrust out of the water, gasping for air. He made a grab for Debbie's hair and swam for the rocks. "After lying on the rocks for a while, I glance over at Debbie and it's like looking at a ghost. As she describes what she went through, it became apparent that we both had the same experience underwater—the golden glow, the serenity, seeing our lives flash before us, floating over a funeral, and seeing ourselves in a casket. That's the only time we ever talked about it. I haven't seen or talked with her since."

> **Two for One**
>
> Debbie and Steve were reunited many years later when they were both guests on a television show. In front of the cameras, Debbie confirmed Steve's memories of the incident—including that their separate near-death episodes were virtually *identical.*

Hotshots in Hell

A fellow researcher, Arvin S. Gibson, has allowed me to share with you a most amazing account that appears in his book *The Fingerprints of God* (see appendix C). It concerns a firefighter, a man by the name of Jake, who contacted him after reading Arvin's *Glimpses of Eternity.*

Jake was a member of an elite firefighting group called the "Hotshots," who specialized in fighting the most troublesome forest fires and bringing them under control. In 1989, Jake, as crew boss, and two twenty-person units were dropped onto the peak of a steep mountain. Because of where the fire was burning and the way the wind was blowing, a decision was made to create a back-fire. Just as they had done so, the wind changed direction and trees in front of the Hotshots erupted into flames with explosive force. Firefighters like the Hotshots are normally prepared for such a crisis and carry a fire-resistant pack with their gear, which includes an

Told the Reasons Why

Often, as part of their near-death scenario, experiencers are given instructions from On High, or told by a voice they believe to be that of God the reason why a certain action is necessary. These communications take on a deeply felt, religious or spiritual significance for the near-death experiencer—and for many others who hear of it.

aluminum foil–type of material they can use to cover themselves. This time, however, nobody had their coverlets.

"The panic-stricken crews started to try and go back up the trench-trail they had built," recalled Jake. "Trees exploded and fire engulfed the immediate area, and oxygen feeding the conflagration was sucked from near the ground where the people struggled to breathe. One by one, the men and women fell to the earth suffocating from lack of oxygen. They were reduced to crawling on their hands and knees while they attempted to get back up the hill to a more safe area."

Jake thought, "This is it. I am going to die." And with that thought, he found himself in the air looking down on his body lying in a trench. He looked around and saw the other firefighters also standing above their bodies in the air. One of Jake's crew members had been born with a defective foot. As he came out of his body, Jake looked at him and said, "Look, Jose, your foot is straight."

A light brighter than sun shining on a field of snow appeared. Then Jake was met by his deceased great-grandfather, who acted as a guide throughout a long and extensive near-death scenario that followed. His great-grandfather communicated nonverbally and said it was up to Jake whether or not he returned. Jake pleaded to stay, as he did not want to revive in a horribly burned body. According to Arvin: "Jake was informed that neither he nor any of his crew who chose to return would suffer ill effects from the fire. This would be done so that God's power over the elements would be made manifest."

Coming back to life was painful to Jake, not because he was hurt, but because being in spirit was such a perfect state that anything else paled by comparison. He noted, as he walked back up the hill protected in a "bubble" from the intense heat, that some of his metal tools had melted. Upon reaching safety, he saw the other members of his crew gathering. They were all so profoundly affected by their deliverance that the group knelt in prayer and thanked the Lord.

Arvin continued: "Jake said that in comparing accounts of their different episodes, the men and women were astonished that they had each undergone some type of near-death experience. And this happened to a diverse ethnic and religious group of Hispanics, Caucasians, and American Indians. Throughout the summer as the crew worked together, they continued to discuss the miraculous adventure which they had all lived through."

Crew members confirmed that they too had experienced discomfort reinhabiting their bodies, that they had met with deceased family members, and had been given the choice of remaining where they were or returning to Earth. Some had seen each other and conversed during their episode.

Even Movie Stars

Some famous entertainers who have had a near-death experience: Peter Fonda, Elizabeth Taylor, Christopher Reeve, Sharon Stone, David Letterman, R. Carlos Nakai, Johnny Cash, and Burt Reynolds.

Symbols Surface

While discussing degrees of death, variants to the death process, and possible stages immediately thereafter, there is yet another area we need to broach. And that is, the presence of symbolic revelations that surface from this venue to further inform us about what is important and what isn't relative to the "death" near-death experiencers appear to undergo. These symbols are gleaned from what seems to be research trivia.

How the Children Died

Speaking of what caused their deaths, in my study of child experiencers, by far the most frequent cause was drowning. Large numbers also "died" during or after surgery, from suffocation, tonsillectomies, and abuse at the hands of their parents or siblings. Other traumas were described, like those from high fever, being hit by lightning, or, sometimes, an unusually precarious birth.

For instance, while interviewing child experiencers as youngsters or when they were older, I kept seeing correlations between what the child went through and how that affected significant others. Sometimes family members, or even the doctors and nurses, were so touched by what they witnessed that the affair changed their whole life, literally transformed them. I got the feeling sometimes that the youngster was a conduit for what the other people needed in their lives at that time. Invariably, though, when the child was grown, the near-death experience proved to be of immense importance to him or her as well. The cause of death, however, didn't seem to matter at all.

Adult experiencers differed in that the cause of their deaths *did* seem to matter. What threatened their lives was more gender-specific in how it linked directly to what affects men versus what affects women. When I studied this, comparing simple statistics to how people changed afterward, I began to recognize patterns that struck me as significant. I had noticed a subtle "need factor" before with types of scenarios experienced; the individual would say, "I got what I needed" (I discuss this in depth in chapter 16). Now I was seeing all kinds of tie-ins, especially symbolic ones. Consider that a little over half the men I contacted had died because of what happens to more men than women—heart-related ailments—while another 25 percent or so were involved in violence—either accidentally or on

Dr. Quinn "Medicine Woman" Returns

In 1968, while filming *Onassis: The Richest Man in the World* in Madrid, actress Jane Seymour developed a bronchial infection. While giving her an injection of antibiotics for the infection, a nurse missed the muscle and hit an artery or vein. "My mouth and throat closed up, and I could feel myself losing consciousness," recalls Jane. "The next thing I knew, I had a view from the top of my room. I could see a man crying and screaming on the phone and then trying to resuscitate me. I knew that I had left my body. I actually saw a white light. I was very calm, but I remember thinking, 'I have children that need me.'" The actress had gone into anaphylactic shock and had to be given shots of adrenaline and cortisone. "The doctors told me later that I nearly died," she says, "but I think I made it clear to whoever was listening that I was not ready to give up."

The Best Film Ever

The most compelling film ever made on near-death experiences is *The Day I Died,* produced by the British Broadcasting Company (BBC) in 2002. The film features in-depth case studies (including that of Pam Reynolds), recent research, and balanced interpretations from both skeptical and "believer" perspectives. Distributed by Films for the Humanities and Sciences, it is available from IANDS for showings at schools, universities, houses of worship, hospitals, hospices, community agencies, and other public venues. (Refer to appendix B for further details.)

purpose. But a whopping 70 percent of the women experienced their episode in female-related crises—during childbirth, miscarriages, hemorrhages, or hysterectomies—all of which relate to the uterus and the act of procreation.

If viewed symbolically, I take these figures to be indicative of the fact that in our society men are not encouraged to express their "heart" or emotions openly. Aggressive, athletic behavior is promoted, but not gentleness or loving kindness. Men are expected to perform as stalwart paragons of strength and success. Weakness is not tolerated. It should come as no surprise, then, that so many men suffer heart stress, commit acts of violence, or are involved in accidents. By repressing or holding in their emotions, they build up pressure that must be either externally or internally released.

The process of pregnancy and childbirth has always signaled a time when a woman is completely transformed through the high drama of procreation, which carries with it the ever-present possibility of either death or disfigurement for herself or her child. The opposites of fear and love fuse together into a single raw edge during this time. Ego vanishes. Goals, dreams, and wishes dissolve. Traditionally, it is held that birthing a child and all that goes with it requires that a woman be consumed by a force beyond her control. Although women physically died more often in the past from childbirth and related conditions, women still today "die" in the sense that the birth of a child demands both the surrender and the rebirth of the mother.

Image of film cover of *The Day I Died,* courtesy of Films for the Humanities and Sciences, Princeton, New Jersey.

So far in this book, we've been able to learn that near-death states produce evidence that strongly suggests there may indeed be stages to the death process, and that life itself begins before birth and continues after death. We have also learned that our faculties and brains and bodies may be capable of more than we think, that reality may be measured more by how well we "attune" to energy fields than by what we can hear, see, feel, and touch.

Yet the deeper you dig into research, the more convincing it becomes that the near-death experience is far more complex and revealing than what has been portrayed for the thirty years of its history. As far as I'm concerned, research to date has only covered the tip of a giant iceberg. We have just begun.

12

Heavy on Research

Death meets us everywhere and enters in at many doors.
—Jeremy Taylor, English bishop, theologian, and devotional writer

There was a time when only philosophers and theologians pondered the deeper questions of life, death, and the hereafter. These days, psychologists, medical doctors, biologists, sociologists, and the like are not only discussing these issues, they're researching them. What prompted this? The publication of one man's book. This man didn't just introduce a previously all-but-unknown phenomenon into our lives, he also expanded our vocabulary with the term "near-death experience." As a result, near-death states today have become the most researched of all subjective experiences.

To give you an overview of the breadth and depth of the research that's been done, here is a list of the top researchers in the field—complete with stories about each. I present them to you chronologically, in the order of their first publications, to create a feel for how the research has grown. Each researcher deserves more attention than can be given here. Therefore, I urge you to treat yourself to a further exploration of their work. (All books and papers mentioned are referenced in appendix C.)

We begin with the man who published the first academic articles on the near-death experience—and he wasn't Moody.

Russell Noyes, MD

Even before 1975 when Raymond Moody introduced the term "near-death experience" to the public and to professionals with his seminal work *Life*

Admiration

During his early years in the field of near-death studies, Bruce Greyson, MD, learned a great deal from Dr. Noyes. "He takes near-death experiences seriously, approaches them with an open mind, and isn't afraid to talk about their spiritual aftereffects. He's a researcher's researcher," stated Dr. Greyson.

New Word

Nonlocal means not bound or restricted to any particular place, location, function, or event. Used mostly in references to prayer, healing states, and mind/consciousness not being held synonymous with the brain organ. A scientific term in physics.

After Life, Russell Noyes had authored four scholarly journal articles about the phenomenon. Dr. Noyes is a psychiatrist who spent his entire academic career on faculty at the University of Iowa's Carver College of Medicine. Between 1971 and 1989, he wrote more than fifteen articles in mainstream academic journals, and one important book chapter on the topic of near-death experiences. Although he retired in 2002, he remains committed to scholarly investigations of the phenomenon.

A Model Others Could Follow

Dr. Noyes' attention to detail and the way he approached investigating the phenomenon became an invaluable guide for others—alerting them to the value of the experiences patients were having at the edge of death. He recognized early on that accounts about life on the other side of death were valid contributions to the ongoing study of consciousness and the notion that mind and brain were not the same, and that mind was *nonlocal.*

Medical Staff, Take Heed

Regardless of clinical setting, Dr. Noyes believes that medical personnel should be alert to the possibility that the patient may have had or be having a near-death experience. He urges staff to be aware and accepting of near-death states, to be informed, trained in how to listen to patients, and ready to provide references and referrals for further support.

He found that the loss of the fear of death that experiencers report afterward yields a greater vitality and aliveness to the individual's life in the years that follow. Many take on a sense of invulnerability because of it. Dr. Noyes points out that two important consequences arise from this: a crisis of existence (needing to develop a philosophy of personal worth), and the challenge of a spiritual encounter (discovering the reality of spiritual realms and spirit beings).

Raymond A. Moody Jr., PhD, MD

"What is it like to die?" That's the opening sentence of psychiatrist and philosopher Raymond Moody's 1975 book, *Life After Life.* It's an age-old question, but with the publication of his book, Dr. Moody was to reinvigorate the subject in a way nobody could have predicted. Consisting of the accounts of fifty people who had undergone what Dr. Moody termed a "near-death experience" and who had told him their stories, his book was—and Dr. Moody was quick to acknowledge this—not a scientific work, but an anecdotal collection.

At the outset of his book, Dr. Moody created a composite near-death scenario. He hastened to add that it wasn't meant to be representative, as no experiencer he had found reported all the components he had listed. This fictitious account was to be nothing more than a "model"—Dr. Moody's word. Unfortunately, the composite illustration he created of various elements and possible scenarios was taken literally by the media, and used to sensationalize his book.

This media ploy made *Life After Life* a best-seller, but it misled and misdirected public discourse about the phenomenon in the years that followed—a situation Dr. Moody attempts to correct in *The Last Laugh,* a book in which he admits the folly that occurred and urges people to "lighten up" about the situation.

Outgrowing Medical Criteria

Regarding the question of whether or not experiencers had really died, Dr. Moody said it all depended on how "death" is defined. The notion that death is not a particular moment but a process of "shifting" moments is more appropriate to actual facts. Modern technology, he points out, has complicated the definition of death by extending or restoring a person's life beyond previous medical criteria.

Off to China

Dr. Moody, a perennially popular speaker, is now busier than ever. Since the medical community has recognized the validity and importance of near-death experiences, his many travels increasingly take him to medical universities and research centers. His most exciting trip thus far occurred in the late fall of 2006 when he and his wife went to China. The Chinese government had turned a deaf ear to requests for such speakers for years, fearing any mention of an afterlife. Because of the perseverance of Eunice Brock, the taboo was lifted. Brock, born in China of missionary parents, returned there after being widowed and retired from her career stateside, for the purpose of helping the Chinese people. She not only sponsored Dr. Moody and arranged for him to give numerous talks, but she saw to it that the Chinese media was included and encouraged. The result was favorable coverage—with no censorship.

Kenneth Ring, PhD

A professor of psychology at the University of Connecticut, Kenneth Ring wrote *Life at Death: A Scientific Investigation of the Near-Death Experience* (1980), which examined Raymond Moody's anecdotal findings and explored aspects of the phenomenon

New Word

Omega literally means "great." Yet, as the final letter in the Greek alphabet, it has come to represent "the end," "the last in a series," or "death." Kenneth Ring explains that as "the end," omega has a second meaning—that of an "ultimate outcome"—or, as he used it, "the destination toward which humanity is inexorably bound."

Dr. Moody had not discussed. In his scientific approach, he was able to confirm all the core experiential components that Dr. Moody had reported, but like him, he did not come across hellish experiences. Dr. Ring's research resulted in his positing five stages to the near-death model:

1. A sense of peace and well-being
2. An out-of-body experience
3. A feeling of floating into a darkness (a void or tunnel)
4. An encounter with a presence that elicits a life review and the decision as to whether to live or die—the decision terminating the experience
5. If stage four does not occur after stage three, the experiencer moves from darkness into a loving light (an exquisitely beautiful "world of light"), where he or she may be reunited with deceased loved ones before being told "It is not your time."

Dr. Ring further discovered that there's no correlation between how someone dies (whether suicide, medical problems, accident, illness, murder) or an individual's sex, age, race, personality, social class, occupation, and so forth, and the content of a near-death experience or the likelihood of ever having one.

An Evolutionary Phenomenon

In his second book, *Heading Toward Omega: In Search of the Meaning of the Near-Death Experience* (1984), Dr. Ring shifted his focus to the aftereffects: "The key to the meaning of near-death experiences," he wrote, "lies in the study of their aftereffects." He concluded that the phenomenon is a spiritual experience that becomes a catalyst for spiritual development, and, as such, imparts spiritual meaning to life and death.

The deep awakenings, transformations, and value changes described by near-death experiencers, Dr. Ring says, highlight evolutionary changes for all humankind—heading us toward the higher consciousness traits of cooperation, compassion, and caring. Borrowing from the writings of Jesuit priest and paleontologist Pierre Teilhard de Chardin, Dr. Ring calls this "the *Omega* Point."

Interestingly, Dr. Ring published a study in 1992 comparing near-death experiencers with UFO abductees. His study became the basis of his book *The Omega Project: Near-Death Experiences, UFO Encounters, and Mind at Large.* In it, he developed a theory that these experiences change people so powerfully, and at such a fundamental level, that a new prototype in human evolution seems to be emerging as a result of undergoing them. He noted, though, that while near-death aftereffects tend to be positive and uplifting over time, those from the abduction scenario are all too often just the opposite.

Lessons from the Blind

Always the innovative researcher, in 1999, Dr. Ring published his study of near-death experiences among the blind in the book *Mindsight: Near-Death and Out-Of-Body Experiences in the Blind* (written with Sharon Cooper). Prior to this, he had published, along with his cowriter Evelyn Elsaesser Valarino, *Lessons from the Light: What We Can Learn from the Near-Death Experience* (1998), in which he introduced his initial findings about the blind. And his findings are quite spectacular:

- The near-death experiences of blind people—even those blind since birth—are no different from those of sighted people, including being able to see.
- Near-death experiences are different from dreams, in that in the near-death state, blind people can have visual perceptions, but are not always able to in their dreams.
- In a near-death experience, partially sighted people can acquire enhanced visual acuity—even perfect sight.

Yet are the blind truly "seeing"? Are they engaging in what we might call "retinal vision"? Dr. Ring contends that while the blind use "a language of vision" in their near-death accounts, this is more likely because they're engaging in certain linguistic conventions, like a deaf person saying "I heard so-and-so got married." We should not understand their words to suggest that they acquire "anything like physical vision per se."

What, then, is occurring? Dr. Ring suggests that the blind "have access to a kind of expanded supersensory awareness." This conclusion has profound implications, because what he implies is that the near-death experience offers us a different way of perceiving reality—a way, as is evident from the studies of the blind, that is not dependent on the senses of a physical body. Indeed, it's a way of perceiving that only comes into play "when the senses are defunct." We supposedly acquire a "transcendental awareness" or *mindsight* when this happens.

> **New Word**
>
> **Mindsight** is a state of transcendental awareness that enables an individual, sighted or blind, to access a realm of knowledge not available through a normal waking state. This awareness is described as omnidirectional—360 degrees of spherical vision—the ability to see with whole consciousness rather than depending on physical eyes.

Michael Sabom, MD

A cardiologist in private practice and on staff at Northside and Saint

Clash of the Titans

Dr. Sabom, in his book *Light & Death,* accused Dr. Ring of slanting his findings toward a humanistic, secular view of what can be learned from near-death experiences, to the exclusion of religious doctrine. An entire issue of *Journal of Near-Death Studies,* Vol. 18, No. 4, Summer 2000, was devoted to what became the "religious wars," including a counterpoint from Dr. Ring in which he noted how fundamentalistic Dr. Sabom had become in his Christian belief. Discourse between the two men "calmed the waters," so to speak, yet at the same time, their mutual criticism of each other highlighted a very important aspect of near-death research: findings need to reflect objective, unbiased reporting. Personal opinions are fine, as long as they are so stated.

Joseph's Hospitals in Atlanta, Georgia, Dr. Sabom is the founder of the now-famous 1994 "Atlanta Study." Like many researchers, Dr. Sabom first heard of the near-death experience through Raymond Moody's book *Life After Life.* And like many others, when asked what he thought, he said, "I don't believe it."

Dr. Sabom had never heard such stories from his own patients, and he "truly believed Raymond Moody was pulling a fast one." Challenged to ask around, he was stunned when the third patient he spoke with told him a story that was strikingly similar to the many accounts Dr. Moody had collected. Dr. Sabom became a believer and has gone on to publish his findings in *Recollections of Death: A Medical Investigation* (1982) and *Light & Death: One Doctor's Fascinating Account of Near-Death Experiences* (1998), in which he detailed the Pam Reynolds' case.

No Proof of Life after Death

Michael Sabom was a religious man prior to his encounters with near-death experiences, whose faith deepened afterward. He maintains that, although many experiencers claim to have been to "the other side," the Bible clearly states that we only die once. So, other than exceptional instances—when God (not medical doctors) reanimates the dead (e.g., Lazarus)—"the dead do not report back to the living." Consequently, he believes that "modern-day descriptions of near-death experiences are not accounts of life after death."

What, Then, Is the Near-Death Experience?

Dr. Sabom thinks that the phenomenon is an occurrence that hints at an afterlife, but is not a direct experience of it. He concludes that:

- It is a spiritual experience consisting of four aspects: It does not take place in the physical realm but in the realm of the soul; it is about religious experience and not material; it is responsive to spiritual scrutiny, not scientific; it is real and not imaginary.

- It is an out-of-body experience but not related to death, because there is no return from death.

- Since the Bible says no one can see God and live (Exodus 33:20), and as Jesus acknowledges being the Christ (Mark 14:61)—a facet of the triune God—then, contrary to reports that experiencers see God and/or Jesus, what they're actually having is a confirmation that God and Jesus exist. They see neither.

Bruce Greyson, MD

Dr. Greyson is the "central hub" the rest of us turn to. He's the researcher whose writings appear in most medical journals and who's consulted by encyclopedias (including *Encyclopaedia Britannica*).

Kenneth Ring was the editor of *Anabiosis—The Journal for Near-Death Studies* at its 1981 inception. But from 1982 to the present, Bruce Greyson has held the top spot, seeing the publication through a name change to *Journal of Near-Death Studies,* and to the respect it has achieved as a peer-reviewed journal of importance and merit.

A graduate from Cornell University with a major in psychology, Dr. Greyson received his medical degree from the SUNY Upstate University College of Medicine, and completed his psychiatric residency at the University of Virginia. He practiced and taught psychiatry at the University of Michigan and the University of Connecticut, where he was Clinical Chief of Psychiatry, before returning to the University of Virginia ten years ago, where he is now the Carlson Professor of Psychiatry and director of the Division of Perceptual Studies.

One of the Founding Fathers

Dr. Greyson was one of IANDS' founders and served for many years on its board of directors, including a term as president. He also served as director of research, and facilitator of a local near-death support group in Connecticut.

Lots and Lots of Writing

His near-death research for more than three decades has focused on the aftereffects of the experience, and has resulted in seventy presentations to national scientific conferences, one hundred publications in academic medical and psychological journals, and several research grants and awards.

A few of his accomplishments:

- In 1984, Dr. Greyson coedited *The Near-Death Experience: Problems, Prospects, Perspectives,* with Charles P. Flynn.

- In his 1992 *Encyclopaedia Britannica* article, Dr. Greyson states that patients who were given drugs "report *fewer* and *briefer* near-death experiences" than those not given drugs. This suggests, as he emphasizes in the article, that instead of causing near-death states—as many have hypothesized—drugs either prevent their occurrence or cloud the patient's ability to recall them.

The Classical Model Isn't That Classical

The work of Margot Grey, PhD, added to the growing data showing that elements in near-death scenarios seldom matched the so-called "classical model." She did find, however, consistent indications of a core pattern underlying the experience, but not that the elements occur in any particular sequence.

- In a 1998 article in the *Journal of Scientific Exploration,* Emily Williams Cook, Bruce Greyson, and Ian Stevenson proposed that while the evidence isn't yet conclusive, the existence of "enhanced mentation" (use of the mind), out-of-body experiences, and "paranormal perceptions" (perceiving events out of sight from normal vision), "might provide convergent evidence" that human personality survives death.

Margot Grey, PhD

A humanistic psychologist, Margot Grey not only underwent a near-death experience herself, but in 1985 she published her research about the phenomenon—the first book by an experiencer—called *Return from Death: An Exploration of the Near-Death Experience.* Response to her work was so great, she was inspired to initiate the U.K. branch of IANDS.

Her research, as part of her thesis, scientifically validated Kenneth Ring's findings, but she deviated in important and interesting ways. She found that Dr. Ring's phases of the near-death experience aren't sequential, occurring neither chronologically nor in any other predetermined order, but more often as a "simultaneous matrix of impressions."

Her other discoveries:

- Consciousness survives death.

- Not all experiences are pleasant; but the hellish ones appear to follow a pattern similar to those that are pleasant—with experiencers of hellish episodes just as convinced that there's an afterlife and that they should improve their lives. This suggests that the intriguing theory that there's a core pattern and an underlying transformational purpose to the near-death experience may indeed be true.

- If met by a deceased spirit, experiencers are almost always told to return to earthly life, that it's not their time; if met by a "presence" ("being of light"), they are encouraged to decide for themselves what course they want to follow—return or continue on into death.

P.M.H. Atwater, LHD

Although my first book, *Coming Back to Life: The After Effects of the Near-Death Experience,* wasn't published until 1988, I began my research in 1978, having had three near-death episodes the previous year. My initial work was followed by *Beyond the Light: What Isn't Being Said about the Near-Death Experience* in 1994; *Future Memory* in 1996 (reissued in 1999); *Brain Shift/Spirit Shift: Using the Near-Death Experience as a Theoretical Model to Explore the Transformation of Consciousness* in 1998; *Children of the New Millennium: Children's Near-Death Experiences and the Evolution of Humankind* in 1999; *The Complete Idiot's Guide to Near-Death Experiences* (with David Morgan) in 2000; *The New Children and Near-Death Experiences* in 2003; and *We Live Forever: The Real Truth about Death* in 2004. As my various published works and findings serve as sources for the book you are now reading, in keeping with the subject of this chapter, focus here is on my research methods.

Odd One Out

The research methods I use are not considered scientific by many professionals, even though I employ objective methods. Also, my advanced degree was often snubbed, because my Letters of Humanities doctorate was earned in Montreal, Quebec, at an unaccredited institution. The bulk of my work received little in the way of comments during two decades of scrutiny. Now that some of my findings have been verified in clinical studies (including in the *Lancet*), this situation has finally changed.

Like Father, Like Daughter

After a meeting with Dr. Elisabeth Kübler-Ross in July 1978, I learned that the experiences I had had the year before had both an official name and description. Yet, during our conversation, she did not mention Raymond Moody nor his book; so for all intents and purposes, I was left pondering more questions than answers and launched my own research study that November. Three years later, Kenneth Ring purchased my self-published book, *I Died Three Times in 1977*. He located me via phone and arranged a meeting. It was then that I was invited to "join" the field of near-death studies and meet my peer group.

My research was extensive by that time; my style, distinctly my own. Growing up the daughter of a police officer, I had been trained to ask non-leading questions. This meant that during an interview, I would simply say, "What happened to you?" Never would I use any word or phrase until the experiencer used it first. Additionally, as my father had instructed me to do, I paid close attention to people's body language and facial expressions, especially when others were around, to pick up what clues I could from the nonverbal language we all "speak."

Not Just Gathering Stories

To say that I listened to experiencers tell their stories should not be construed to mean that my research is dependent on anecdotes. It is not. My work is far more structured and probing than that, consisting of an amalgam of interview, observation, and questionnaire techniques. This multifaceted approach enabled me to look at the near-death experience and its aftereffects from 360 degrees. Whenever possible, I also had sessions with "significant others" such as experiencers' relatives, spouses, health-care providers, and coworkers.

A Surprise Turnaround

Think that the near-death experience transforms only the experiencer? In a 1992 article in *Life* magazine, Dr. Morse admitted that regarding belief in God and an afterlife, he had "a tremendous emotional barrier to all of this." Then, when in a plane that was encountering a lot of scary turbulence, he found himself thinking, "Now I'll get to see the light!"

Everything I did I cross-checked at least four times with different people in different parts of the country. Because I use police investigative techniques as my protocol, today I am often referred to as "the gumshoe of near-death."

Melvin Morse, MD

While serving his internship in pediatrics in a small Idaho hospital, Melvin Morse resuscitated a nine-year-old girl named Katie who, several hours before, had been found drifting face down in a YMCA swimming pool. After she recovered and felt well enough, Dr. Morse scheduled a follow-up examination. She accurately recounted many incidents that had taken place during her medical treatment, despite having been "extremely comatose" at the time.

But it was when Dr. Morse asked her what she remembered about being in the pool that he got his most startling answer: "Do you mean when I visited the Heavenly Father?" Taken by surprise, he registered shock, which caused Katie to become embarrassed and grow silent. The next week, when they met again, Katie said she remembered nothing about the drowning, only of being in darkness, being too heavy to move, and then having a tunnel open and being greeted by a "tall and nice" woman named Elizabeth who escorted her through the tunnel into "heaven."

After drawing pictures of people she met on "the other side," neither Katie nor Dr. Morse could be certain what had happened to her, but the incident inspired him to investigate other children's stories. As a result, he wrote an article about Katie for a medical journal—to his knowledge the first ever of a child's experience—and his 1990 book *Closer to the Light: Learning from Children's Near-Death Experiences* (cowritten with scholar and science writer Paul Perry, who also cowrote books with Raymond Moody and Dannion Brinkley).

Although his stories of children's near-death experiences are fascinating and delightfully guileless, it is not in regarding children's accounts, per se, that Dr. Morse makes his most thought-provoking pronouncements:

- Research of neuroscientists supports the idea that within the brain there is an area "genetically coded for out-of-body experiences, tunnel experiences, and much of what we know as the near-death experience." That area is the right temporal lobe.

- The near-death component of "the light" cannot be explained by brain research. As the testimonies of children attest, the light is the key aspect of the experience—the transforming element that originates outside our bodies. It is, claims Dr. Morse, identical to the light experienced, spoken of, and written about by mystics.

In his second book, *Transformed by the Light: The Powerful Effect of Near-Death Experiences on People's Lives* (also cowritten with Paul Perry, published in 1992), Dr. Morse went on to say that those who had experiences of light in their near-death episodes were transformed the most—"and the deeper that experience of light, the greater the transformation."

Besides His Work with Kids

Dr. Morse is highly critical of what he considers to be excessive costs with end-of-life care, and he speaks openly to this issue in both *Closer to the Light* and *Transformed by the Light.*

His most controversial work, however, is *Where God Lives: The Science of the Paranormal and How Our Brains are Linked to the Universe* (2001, coauthored with Paul Perry). In this book, he develops his idea that the right temporal lobe in the brain, specifically the sylvian fissure, is "the God spot," that place where all the imagery, sounds, and sensations of ecstatic, spiritual experiences originate.

Arvin S. Gibson, BSME

Arvin Gibson's father died in 1963, but it was an experience that his father had in 1922 that spurred Arvin's exploration of the near-death phenomenon. That was the year his father suffered a massive heart attack and had a near-death experience. Because of its profound religious content and the way it affected him, Arvin's father decided to share his story with his son as he wrestled with his beliefs while a student at the University of California at Berkeley.

This account made an indelible impression on Arvin, yet he gave it no more attention until he read Raymond Moody's book in 1978. As a Mormon, he was stimulated to examine near-death states in conjunction with Latter-day Saints scripture and teachings. With this intention in mind, he wrote *Glimpses of Eternity: New Near-Death Experiences Examined* (1992). In his book, he stated:

- Near-death experiences are not proof of life after death, as that would compromise "the Plan of Salvation." Salvation is dependent on faith and free will—faith that how we live matters, and free will to make the right choices of how to live and earn salvation.

- Near-death experiences are not evidence of reincarnation. For one thing, the prophet Joseph Smith taught that reincarnation was a false doctrine. Moreover, belief in reincarnation diminishes the urgency of leading righteous lives and repenting for our sins in this life, as it suggests that we could "ultimately achieve nirvana simply by living enough lives." Finally, unless they are Latter-day Saints, who embrace the teaching that "we have existed as individual beings for eternity," near-death experiencers mistake being in their spirit bodies during their episode as evidence of cyclic existence.

Testy Connections

Arvin Gibson noticed a correlation few others did: There seems to be a cause-and-effect relationship between many a person's life activities and hellish near-death states. Those he interviewed claimed that they could identify the causal condition—an unkind, abusive, immoral circumstance—that led to their experience being unpleasant.

- Near-death experiences confirm the literalness of scripture.

- Near-death experiences are ultimately about God's love.

In his subsequent books—*Echoes from Eternity: Near-Death Experiences Examined* (1993); *Journeys Beyond Life: True Accounts of Next-World Experiences* (1994); and *The Fingerprints of God: Evidences from Near-Death Studies, Scientific Research on Creation and Mormon Theology* (1999)—Gibson continued to explore the religious aspects of the phenomenon. He was only a few weeks short of his eightieth birthday when he passed away on the eve of Thanksgiving 2004.

Peter Fenwick, MD, FRCPsych

We would expect that, as a neurophysiologist, neuropsychiatrist, and Fellow of the Royal College of Psychiatrists in England, Peter Fenwick would have an interest in different states of consciousness—and indeed he does. But when he read Raymond Moody's book, he was both intrigued and skeptical. The fact that Dr. Moody's book was exclusively anecdotal, and that it was published in the United States (a perceived haven for New Age flakiness), made him hesitate.

Then, one of his patients, a man named Peter Thompson, told him about an experience he'd had moments before undergoing an operation. As Peter relayed his story, his eyes dropped, for he was embarrassed to speak of such a preposterous tale. Dr. Fenwick listened intently, nonetheless. This incident changed his mind.

As Dr. Fenwick would later say in

Thorough Physicians

Sam Parnia, MD, PhD, in collaboration with Dr. Fenwick, conducted a landmark prospective study of near-death experiences at Southampton General Hospital in England. Results were published in the journal *Resuscitation.* Their work received widespread coverage in the national and international press. He has described that study of sixty-three survivors, 11 percent of whom reported an NDE, and its implications in his 2006 book *What Happens When We Die: A Groundbreaking Study into the Nature of Life and Death.* Dr. Parnia is currently pursuing a fellowship in pulmonary and critical care medicine at Weill Cornell Medical Center in New York and is the founder of the Consciousness Research Group there.

the 1995 book he cowrote with his wife Elizabeth—*The Truth in the Light*—"Peter Thompson was a man I liked and respected, and there was no doubt in my mind that he was telling the truth."

Dr. Fenwick, determined to research and investigate such states, met with Margot Grey. She invited him, along with several others, to help her form IANDS-UK. Through numerous media opportunities, he and David Lorimer, then chairman of the new group, received firsthand accounts of near-death experiences from all over England, as well as a few from Scotland, Wales, and Ireland. These became the basis of Dr. Fenwick's book.

An Out-of-Body Brain Test

Peter Fenwick supports the recommendation of U.S. scientist Charles Tart that a specific object be placed above the sight line of patients in hospital rooms and left there. It must be a visual illusion, as such images can only be perceived when the brain and eyes are connected. This object might be a sequence of stripes that appear to shimmer when looked at by the physical eye. Because of the way our sight occurs, in a succession of minute flicks, this shimmering effect, if ever seen, would show that an experiencer while out-of-body could still be using normal eye/brain processes.

Mind and Brain

Near-death episodes provoked Dr. Fenwick to wonder about the nonlocality of the mind. Can it truly exist outside the brain? He acknowledges that though there are intriguing studies exploring this question, no conclusions can yet be reached. He also says that even if the nonlocality of the mind could be proven, it would not, in and of itself, prove the existence of a soul, nor that individual consciousness can continue after brain death.

"Our individual consciousness," he points out, "entails memory—indeed, my memories are what contribute to my individual consciousness versus your memories which contribute to yours. To prove that personal consciousness survives death, we have to then show that memory, too, can exist independent of the physical brain."

Dr. Fenwick explains that the account most commonly cited to show that memory can exist separate from the brain is a checkered one. It's the story of a Seattle woman named Maria, who suffered a cardiac arrest. Maria later told her social worker, Kimberly Clark Sharp, that while in the hospital she had an out-of-body experience and saw, among other things, a shoe—describing it quite vividly—that was on a third-floor window ledge of the hospital. Skeptical, Kimberly went to look for the shoe. Not only did she find the shoe, it had the exact characteristics Maria had described. Since no one has ever been able to find Maria after she left and talk to her about this, the tale remains hearsay. (For Kimberly Clark Sharp's version of this story, refer to chapter 17.)

Back to the Death Question

Dr. Fenwick refers to Tibetan Buddhism's notion of the *bardo,* explaining

New Word

Bardo is a Sanskrit word meaning "intermediate" or "inbetween state." In Tibetan Buddhism, it refers to the forty-nine-day period between death and rebirth, during which the individual exists as an ever-changing continuum of consciousness experiencing either enhancement or confusion, while separated from the body. (The concept of an unchanging soul does not exist in Buddhism.)

that there are two bardo states: the bardo of dying and the bardo of becoming (the state an individual enters after death). The Tibetan Book of the Dead tells that during the bardo of becoming, the person is able to hear and see living relatives. Although this sounds like a near-death experience, cautions Dr. Fenwick, an individual must in fact die to enter a bardo state. "Near-death experiencers do not actually die, though they may briefly appear to be dead."

Gender Differences in Research

Among top researchers in the field, only the women have actually experienced near-death episodes. Intriguingly, women researchers have concentrated more on the aftereffects—how the phenomenon transformed the experiencer's relationship to life and others. Although the men too have examined aftereffects, most of them have specialized in the experience itself along with medical/philosophical implications.

We may never find "a logical and scientific" explanation for the near-death phenomenon, according to Peter Fenwick, but that's not necessarily a shortcoming. He thinks these events offer "enormously meaningful and powerful lessons" for experiencers and for the rest of us.

Cherie Sutherland, PhD

While Australian sociologist Cherie Sutherland was giving birth, she had a near-death experience. In her 1995 book *Reborn in the Light: Life After Near-Death Experiences* (published in 1992 for Australia and New Zealand as *Transformed by the Light*), she states that at the moment of her "movement—into self-consciousness," she focused her attention not on the meaning of the near-death experience as it comments on life after death, but on what it says about life.

Among Dr. Sutherland's findings are the following:

- Attitudes about death and an afterlife changed dramatically after a near-death experience. In a related finding, 80 percent of the experiencers in her study acquired a belief in reincarnation.

- After having a near-death episode, experiencers felt strongly that they'd never commit suicide, and expressed sadness for those who did seek to end their lives.

- Experiencers thought their episode was spiritual rather than religious, as it enabled them to attain direct contact with God.
- Experiencers often acquired psychic abilities afterward.
- Self-esteem increased, along with a stronger sense of purpose, after such an episode.
- While feeling more loving and compassionate toward others, half of the individuals in her study expressed having difficulty with personal relationships.
- Changes in diet and lifestyle habits included less television watching and newspaper reading, more concern about eating nutritious food, and a preference for alternative medical and self-healing procedures.

Across the Big Pond

What makes the work of Margot Grey, Peter Fenwick, and Cherie Sutherland important is that it acquaints us with data from outside the United States. Although the experiences they report may not differ that much from those found in this country, their findings give us a greater understanding of the widespread nature of the near-death phenomenon.

Why So Important

"In my view," relates Dr. van Lommel, "the only possible empirical approach to evaluate theories about consciousness is research on NDE. Because, in studying the several universal elements that are reported during NDE, we get the opportunity to verify all the existing theories about consciousness that have been discussed until now. Consciousness presents temporal as well as everlasting experiences. Is there a start or an end to consciousness?"

Pim van Lommel, MD

A cardiologist trained in the Netherlands and in London, Dr. van Lommel, during his internship rotation in 1969, cared for a patient who was successfully resuscitated using electrical defibrillation. The patient regained consciousness, and was very, very disappointed. He told Dr. van Lommel about going through a tunnel, seeing a light and beautiful colors, and hearing music. He didn't want to come back. This caring physician never forgot the event, but also did nothing further with it. In 1986, he read about this type of experience and started to interview patients who had survived a cardiac arrest. To his great surprise, within two years, twelve patients out of fifty survivors of cardiac arrest had told him about their near-death experiences.

The Study That Electrified the World

In 1988, a prospective study of 344 consecutive survivors of cardiac arrest

Wow!

In three prospective studies with identical study design, approximately the same percentage of NDE was found: 18 percent of 344 Dutch survivors of cardiac arrest (van Lommel, et al., 2001); 15.5 percent of 116 American survivors of cardiac arrest (Greyson, 2003); and 11 percent of 63 British survivors of cardiac arrest (Parnia, et al., 2001). Of these three, the Dutch study went further in researching possible factors that can influence the occurrence of near-death experiences.

"No one physiological or psychological model by itself could explain all the common features of NDE," states Bruce Greyson, MD. "The paradoxical occurrence of heightened, lucid awareness and logical thought processes during a period of impaired cerebral perfusion raises particular perplexing questions for our current understanding of consciousness and its relation to brain function."

in ten Dutch hospitals began with the aim to investigate the frequency, the cause, and the content of near-death states. This landmark study was published December 15, 2001, in the *Lancet* medical journal. Dr. van Lommel was assisted in this work by the expertise of Ruud van Wees, Vincent Meyers, and Ingrid Elfferich.

According to Dr. van Lommel: "We studied patients who survived cardiac arrest, because this is a well-described life threatening medical situation, where patients will ultimately die from irreversible damage to the brain if cardiopulmonary resuscitation (CPR) is not initiated within five to ten minutes. It is the closest model of the process of dying. We [also] performed a longitudinal study with taped interviews of all late survivors with NDE two and eight years following the cardiac arrest, along with a matched control group of survivors of cardiac arrest who did not report an NDE. This study was designed to assess whether the transformation in attitude toward life and death following an NDE is the result of having an NDE or the result of the cardiac arrest itself. In this follow-up research into transformational processes, we found a significant difference between patients with and without an NDE." (From the article, "About the Continuity of Our Consciousness," by Pim van Lommel, MD. See appendix C.)

Groundbreaking Early Projects

Two projects of significant interest were conducted before the rush of books that followed *Life After Life.* They deserve mention.

The Evergreen Study

Known by its shortened name, the Evergreen Study, the proper title, as published in *Anabiosis—The Journal for Near-Death Studies,* is "Near-Death Experiences in a Pacific-Northwest American Population: The Evergreen Study." While we associate the Pacific Northwest with logging country, the "Evergreen" in the title actually refers to Evergreen State College in Olympia, Washington, where the study was conducted over a five-month period, beginning in January 1981. The researchers were James H. Lindley, Sethryn Bryan, and Bob Conley. Forty-nine people who had fifty-five encounters with death were included in the study.

The researchers designed their investigation around the five stages of the near-death experience that Raymond Moody and Kenneth Ring identified:

1. A feeling of overwhelming peace
2. An out-of-body experience
3. Entrance into a dark tunnel or just darkness
4. Encountering a light
5. Entering the light

As had Drs. Moody and Ring, the researchers noted that these five stages are not experienced by every individual, nor should they be thought of as "consecutive levels." The fifth stage proved troublesome, as it implied that experiencers not only saw a light, but entered into it. Stage 5 also carried the meaning that within this light were "worlds" from which the light originated. The researchers received no report confirming this. Instead, the light seemed to be nonphysical; and if anything, the "worlds" had their origin in the light, not vice versa. They suggested renaming the fifth stage "the inner setting"—"a location of great natural beauty such as a garden, valley, or meadow." This "inner setting" was where the experiencer spent time before deciding whether or not to return.

Few Had a Life Review

Although we often hear that when experiencers are in a life-threatening situation their life flashes before them, in the Evergreen Study, only 9 percent of the subjects had a panoramic life review. And, in each instance, the cause of death was an accident.

Following are the results obtained from those in the study:

- 74.5 percent experienced Stage 1 (serenity)
- 70.9 percent experienced Stage 2 (out-of-body experience)
- 38.2 percent experienced Stage 3 (tunnel or darkness)
- 56.4 percent experienced Stage 4 (seeing a light)
- 34.5 percent experienced Stage 5 (entering an "inner setting")

Interestingly, during this early phase of inquiry into the phenomenon, the researchers found that 20 percent of the experiencers had accounts of "hellish" experiences—an episode type not mentioned in early books or articles—which the researchers defined as "one that contains extreme fear, panic, or anger."

Typically, they said, it "begins with a rush of fear and panic or with a vision of wrathful or fearful creatures." Negative aspects often changed to positive ones, though, during the episode.

They also found that it was common for unpleasant sensations to come

Watch Those Returns

Concerning "reentry," subjects in the Evergreen Study claimed that their return to their bodies was much more rapid than their departure; the dying process, in other words, occurred more gradually than coming back to life. The return process could be voluntary (many women wanted to return to raise their children) or involuntary (resulting in the individual being angry or resentful at having to leave so peaceful a place and/or come back to an impaired or pain-filled body). For some, the process of return involved bargaining, and for others the decision to return was not theirs but made by a "tribunal" who decided their fate.

at the end of a positive experience, suggesting to them a "fall from grace" as the individual returns from otherworldly tranquility to ordinary consciousness. Many experiencers supported this assumption by admitting that they didn't want to return and fought back.

Finally, the researchers made the intriguing suggestion that Stage 1—a feeling of peace—has a biological origin. At the onset of death and the breakdown of vital systems, the hypothalamus might release morphine-like substances (for example, endorphins or enkephalins) into our brains as a final biological attempt to produce a state of well-being. They found no biological basis for the remaining stages, however.

The Southern California Study

Published in *Anabiosis—The Journal for Near-Death Studies* in 1983 and formally known as "Near-Death Experiences in a Southern California Population," this study was conducted by J. Timothy Green and Penelope Friedman. It took place at California State University, Northridge, and consisted of in-depth interviews of forty-one persons having had a total of fifty near-death experiences.

Beginning in January and concluding in December 1981, the researchers placed ads in various Los Angeles area newspapers asking to interview "persons who have been close to death or clinically dead." It was only after inquiries were received that the researchers revealed their deeper concerns: Had the person "had an experience while unconscious"? By initially withholding their true intention, they had also hoped to arrive at better percentages across the board of people who were once at death's door and survived.

As with the Evergreen Study, the Southern California Study examined reports in terms of the Moody/Ring stages. Here are the results:

- 70 percent experienced Stage 1
- 66 percent experienced Stage 2
- 32 percent experienced Stage 3
- 62 percent experienced Stage 4
- 18 percent experienced Stage 5

In addition, 48 percent of the respondents said they encountered spirit beings, deceased friends or relatives, or religious figures; and 12 percent had a life review. Ninety-six percent considered the experience real and not a dream, claiming that the contents of the experience were unlike anything they'd ever had in a dream.

In summary, the researchers of the Southern California Study suggested that rather than contradicting or undermining science, this newly discovered human experience "extends rather than refutes what we already know much in the same way that Einstein's view of the universe extended Newton's." They observed that: "The implications the near-death experience presents . . . are potentially so revolutionary that at this point in history, when mankind has harnessed enough energy to destroy itself many times over, a deeper understanding of ourselves and our continuum might be crucial."

Not Sure about Light

The Southern California Study, like that at Evergreen, found that many experiencers did not feel they had actually entered a light (Stage 5). Some said the light was all around them, but they weren't sure that constituted being in it. Others found themselves in a pastoral setting, but had not entered a light to get there.

13

Scientific Naysayers

If one regards oneself as a skeptic, it is a good plan to have occasional doubts about one's skepticism.

—Sigmund Freud, Austrian neurologist and the founder of psychoanalysis

You would expect there to be opponents to acknowledgment of the near-death phenomenon. Every new claim of human experience is met with naysayers. Columbus didn't have an easy time gaining permission to sail out to sea; Galileo had to renounce all his claims supporting Copernicus's theories. And these were views about an objective, physical world. So how much more ruckus would a claim cause that addresses an entirely internal, subjective state that seems in opposition to external reality?

What's important to note, though, is that none of the skeptics of the near-death experience have doubted that experiencers are having an experience. As you'll see, what they've questioned are the alleged causes of the phenomenon and meanings associated with it. Roughly, these challenges can be broken down into two types: the biological/physiological challenge, and the psychological challenge. That's how I have divided this chapter, adding at the end certain skeptical notations that don't fit these basic two categories.

With few exceptions, I've not named names, as few challenges to the phenomenon are exclusive to any one person or group. My aim, instead, has been to set out most, if not all, of the arguments against the existence of the near-death experience. In the next chapter, I'll let the specific researchers argue with one another—and let you decide the outcome.

www.sacredcowsonline.com www.cafepress.com/sacredcows © 2006 SpiritPainter

It's All in the Brain: Biological/Physiological Causes

Biological/physiological arguments against near-death origins and claims all basically center around what has been called "the dying brain theory," as well as the administration of drugs in the treatment of the critically ill or injured.

Oxygen Deprivation

Perhaps the most common argument against the veracity of near-death experiences is that they're simply the result of hypoxia (a significant decrease in oxygen) or anoxia (a severe form of hypoxia, resulting from complete or severe oxygen loss). Studies have demonstrated that loss of oxygen to the brain can bring about memory alterations and a visual distortion which, interestingly, leads to tunnel vision (a narrow focus in one's vision)—and, of course, perceiving oneself to be in a tunnel (a particular narrowing of the visual field that some have compared to the tunnel component in near-death scenarios).

Test pilots undergoing acceleration-induced unconsciousness (for example, from centrifugal force tests or g-force tests) often undergo oxygen deprivation, and report many of the same characteristics of a near-death experience. Their accounts include tunnel vision, bright lights, floating, out-of-body experiences, and pleasurable sensations, including being in beautiful places and seeing family members and close friends.

The claim, then, is that a near-death experience is simply a dying brain's reaction to the loss of oxygen.

> **A Closed Mind**
>
> Dean Edell, MD, "America's Favorite Doctor," is well-known for his position on the phenomenon. During his radio show broadcast on January 20, 1999, he stated that, "Near-death experiences are the result of oxygen deprivation. Nothing more."

Hypercarbia

In the 1950s, American psychiatrist L. J. Meduna treated psychiatric patients with mixtures of oxygen and carbon dioxide. As a result, many of his subjects had what appeared to be experiences identical to near-death states: tunnels, lights, a feeling of cosmic importance and oneness with God, reliving of past memories, and love. Additionally, while most said that their episodes were positive, many said that what they perceived was real.

Some of Dr. Meduna's subjects even reported that their episodes were terrifying—as do some near-death experiencers—giving further support to the similarities between *hypercarbia* and near-death states.

New Word

Hypercarbia is a condition in which there is an increased amount of carbon dioxide in the blood. When the oxygen level in our blood decreases, such as during the last stages of the death process, our carbon dioxide level increases. Some have stated that near-death states are nothing other than this experience of hypercarbia, first discovered several decades ago.

Optical Illusions

Lights and tunnels are often associated with near-death states. One theory for this is that, as oxygen supply diminishes and the visual cortex becomes disinhibited, the optical cells not only start firing randomly, they do so more toward the center of an individual's visual field than the periphery, creating tunnel vision.

In a computer simulation of this phenomenon, the result was a tunnel-like effect that formed as the visual field steadily reduced. But if the cells in the cortex began firing rapidly, the perception of light increased until the individual was engulfed by it. If resuscitation continues, though, and the person is "brought back to life," oxygen is restored to the body. Once that happens, disinhibition stops, normal cortical activity resumes, and the narrowing of movement toward the center of the focal field reverses. The individual would then feel as if the tunnel had gone, and he or she had returned back down or through its expanse.

The Scientific Method

"Science is a system of knowledge covering general truths or the operation of general laws tested through the scientific method, which is the collection of data, through observation and experiment, and the formulation and testing of hypotheses. Proof is not absolute. It is rarely cut and dried. Proof is merely a consensus among humans as to the meaning of the evidence. It can change with additional evidence and with different researchers."

—Donald R. Morse, DDS, PhD

Temporal Lobe Excitation and Seizures

Studies in which electrical shock was applied to the brain's right temporal lobe have been shown to produce many of the characteristics of a near-death experience: being drawn toward a light, out-of-body experiences, hearing

Her Head Hurts

Melvin Morse, MD, tells of a young girl who, suffering an "intense headache," laid down and felt herself being "sucked out" of her body into a "long tunnel." She drifted to the ceiling and saw herself "all miserable and in pain." She then traveled through the tunnel and into a celestial realm of bright flower-like lights and a shimmering castle. She saw no spiritual beings or spiritual light. She felt if she stayed in this place she would die and her mother would be sad, so she returned to her body. She was in otherwise good health, was not near death, and experienced this in "real-time." A subsequent electroencephalogram revealed "abnormal right-temporal-lobe activity."

A Ghostly Double

The condition of autoscopy is similar to stories of a "Doppelganger" (German for "double-walker"), which traditionally is said to be "a ghostly double or counterpart of a living person." History is filled with actual sightings of these double-walkers; some such events have even been confirmed by independent witnesses. As yet, no explanation has been found to explain the phenomenon.

unusual music, and having the sense of a profoundly meaningful experience.

In addition, the combination of reduced oxygen and the release of "endogenous neuropeptides" (for example, endorphins) can produce epileptic-like seizures in the temporal lobe regions. One form of epilepsy is known as temporal lobe epilepsy—which, again, can initiate near-death-like sensations that include a life review. The theory has been proposed from this that the stress of being near death stimulates the temporal lobes, and brings about the so-called "near-death experience."

Autoscopy

Various brain lesions, migraine headaches, strokes, and tumors have been known to produce what are called "autoscopic" hallucinations—the occurrence of seeing your own double. Some skeptics claim that this condition is what happens to near-death experiencers when, during their episode, they gaze upon themselves from an external point in the room.

Drug-Induced Hallucinations

Another widely argued and extensively researched response is that the near-death experience is the result of either drugs administered during a medical procedure, or morphine-like substances released by the brain during stress.

1. *Endorphins.* Morphine—an opiate, or drug derived from the opium poppy—was first synthesized from opium in 1806. Because morphine can be injected into the body in controlled amounts and lacks the side effects of opium, it was well-received

in medical circles as a great advance in pain relief for patients. The problem was it was highly addictive. Then, in the 1970s, it was discovered that the body produces its own analgesics (painkillers) that resemble, in their analgesic effect, morphine. Among these are endorphins (short for "endogenous morphine," or morphine produced by the body). One theory is that the euphoric sensations of the near-death experience are a result of the dying brain producing opioid-type peptides—among which are endorphins—in order to ease the pain or stress of an individual in physical pain or upset emotionally (or both), such as when nearing death.

2. *Ketamine.* Arguably, the most challenging claim for a drug-induced explanation to the near-death experience revolves around the drug ketamine, used principally as an anesthetic, but which has been found to have short-acting hallucinogenic properties. Ketamine can produce an altered state of consciousness that has the characteristics of near-death states: the tunnel, entry into a light, and telepathic communication with spirit beings and with God. Certain situations of stress release the neurotransmitter glutamate, which can kill neurons by stimulating a receptor in the brain known as the NMDA (N-methyl-D-aspartate) receptor. Ketamine blocks this process and protects the cells. But in addition to being an anesthetic, it's a psychoactive drug, producing the sensations commonly associated with near-death episodes, including the life review, as a side effect.

   Because the NMDA receptor is involved in memory, blocking the receptor closes off its accessibility to outside sensations. This allows only previously stored memories to be released into consciousness.

The Drug Did It

Another argument in support of near-death states being hallucinations resulting from drugs, medically administered or otherwise, is that people smoking hashish or taking LSD have experienced many of the identical experiences: entering a tunnel, seeing and entering a light, out-of-body travel, a sense of timelessness and vastness, and euphoria.

The "ketamine model" has proved to be so provocative that an entire issue of the *Journal of Near-Death Studies* was devoted to its discussion: Vol. 16, No. 1, Fall 1997. From that particular edition of the journal comes the following response to critics of the "ketamine model," given by Karl L. R. Jansen, PhD, MD, MRCPsych, psychiatrist at Maudsley Hospital in London. "With respect to the 'reality' of ketamine experiences, almost all persons believe their experiences to be real while under the influence of the drug. In one study, 30 percent of the subjects continued to insist on the reality of their experiences once the drug had worn off."

Can't Happen

Neuroscience maintains that conscious experience is not possible during physical unconsciousness.

Pam Spam

You might think that tight medical controls used during Pam Reynolds' surgery would render her case beyond reproach and skepticism. Not so! Her account was not documented until three years after its occurrence. G. W. Woerlee, an anesthesiologist in the Netherlands, has gone to great lengths to show that every aspect of Pam's near-death episode can be explained by natural laws, the functioning of the human body, and the effects of anesthesia.

He is convinced she was "awake" because of insufficient anesthesia, that the drugs alone induced her sense of being out of her body, and that she was not on bypass soon enough, therefore her body was not cooled sufficiently. He states that her "typically American transcendental NDE of someone expecting to die" had to occur somewhere between her OBE and being awakened when the surgery was over.

Dr. Woerlee asserts: "[I]t could not have occurred during her period of hypothermic cardiac arrest, because people are definitely unconscious at 15 degrees C, and unconscious people have no conscious experiences." (Refer to appendix D for Dr. Woerlee's website address where he has posted a detailed critique of the Pam Reynolds' case.)

The Mind-Body Question

Many state that while verified claims about what near-death experiencers saw during the out-of-body component to their episode are evidence that these experiences are not merely dreams, the sightings in themselves are not proof of out-of-body experiences. Indeed, they fly (no pun intended!) in the face of what we know about sense perceptions, that is, that they require a physical body. A person needs eyes to see, ears to hear, and the like—yet out-of-body experiencers agree that they are outside their bodies and, in fact, no longer inhabit material form.

That would make their confirmed sightings contradictory to what we know about the physical requirement for sensation. So, while near-death experiences are suspect in and of themselves, the out-of-body component may evidence that the experiencer has extrasensory perception (ESP). It may be through that means that he or she is able to "see" events around and outside the body physical.

Related to the issue of needing eyes to see and ears to hear is the argument that a person needs a physical brain to store memories. If near-death experiencers are not in their physical bodies—if they're having out-of-body episodes—then by what means are they acquiring memorable and sensory experiences? This simply cannot happen as described.

They're All Basically the Same

Ironically, what near-death experiencers most commonly cite as validation of the out-of-body component of their scenario—that independent, unrelated individuals have had virtually identical experiences—becomes at once a weakness, according to this argument. If so many diverse people can have relatively the same experience, the argument continues, then there must be a shared cause: the dying brain.

All brains the world over, in other words, die the same way. The experience, then, is not a testimonial of some external event, but of the fact that brains are brains, and when they die, neurotransmitters are shutting down and producing near-death-like imagery and occurrences in the dying.

Utter Nonsense

Some proponents of the argument against being able to have non-corporeal (out-of-body) sensations claim that many of the alleged out-of-body sightings have later proven to be false or were unverifiable. They further state that none have been replicated, and that no test has successfully been conducted in which objects were hidden and a patient saw them while in an out-of-body, near-death state.

It's All in the Mind: Psychological Causes

Imagine someone coming up to you and saying, "You know that date I had the other night? Well, I'm in love!" More than likely, your first reaction would be to think that this person is fantasizing. None of the so-called "objective" criteria are present: The person has only been known for one date; the two have not had time to discover each other—their likes and dislikes, their ways of settling disagreements, their temperaments, their lifestyles and values. They've not even experimented with ways of living together.

Quite likely, you're going to be concerned about your friend, asking questions like: "Have you lost your marbles? How can you know if you love this person, you've only been on one date together." You'll feel certain that your friend's avowed love is nothing more than fantasy, or maybe wish fulfillment, or delusion.

What's important about all this is that it's not the notion of love you're questioning. That's something you most likely know something about. Your concern is that you have serious doubts about the reliability of your friend's *subjective* assessment about this thing called love.

Now, imagine that you've had a near-death experience—an experience for which there still aren't any universally agreed-upon *objective* criteria—an experience for which proof of authenticity is mostly subjective. How can others determine the veracity of your claim? The likelihood is they'll act exactly as you reacted to your friend: saying it's nothing but fantasy, wish fulfillment, delusion. And skeptics do just that.

Reliving Birth Trauma

In the assumption that it must be a fantasy, one theory posits that what might be occurring during a near-death scenario is that the experiencer is simply recollecting the experience of

Born Again

The near-death scenario as a recollection of the birth experience is an idea that has been tossed around by numerous researchers. Carl Sagan, PhD, popularized the theory in his book *Broca's Brain: Reflections on the Romance of Science.*

Just a Hallucination

Supporters of the near-death phenomenon as being a hallucination often recount two well-known characteristics of the mind to support their theory: its predisposition to make order out of what it perceives, and its inability to distinguish between what's real and what's imagined. They assert that near-death states must indeed be reactions of the mind falsely attributed to the external world.

birth: the movement from the womb through the birth canal (a tunnel), toward the light (birth), and the love and warmth received in the light (from the attending medical team and parents). The dying brain, then, simply reenacts the transition from the womb through the birth canal into life.

Depersonalization

Another argument is that when faced with a situation perceived as inescapably dangerous or life-threatening, many will "die unto themselves."

That is to say, they will abandon any sense of their own identity as an independent and separate entity, in order to completely detach from the frightening perception. In doing so, the person replaces the terrifying experience with a pleasurable, dreamlike, fantasy scenario that is more bearable.

This theory holds, therefore, that the near-death experience is a mimicry of death: the mind's reaction of shutting down the personal self ("death") and inventing a more desirable, dreamlike scenario. One characteristic of depersonalization is the feeling of "walking in a dream," in the face of an actual situation that is perceived to involve imminent death.

Dissociation

Another charge is that the near-death state is brought about as a result of "withdrawing" or detaching from certain unwanted feelings or body sensations in order to defer or avoid experiencing the emotional impact of them.

According to this notion, the phenomenon is an unconscious defense mechanism in which an individual separates himself or herself—dissociates—from specific activities, behaviors, or emotions to avoid their reality. This urge or instinct to withdraw could be triggered by such situations as a seemingly fatal accident or illness, the body losing its vital signs in readiness for death, or the fear of death itself.

They're Culture-Dependent

Many who refute the veracity of near-death states emphasize the fact that most of the research is done in the United States, where despite certain diversities among the population, there is nonetheless a general similarity in American culture and beliefs. Although such aspects as encountering other beings and entering into other realms appear in accounts from different countries, proponents of this theory point out that the life review and tunnel components are primarily a feature of cases from Christian and Buddhist cultures.

A Lack of Consistency

Additionally, refuters explain that even within one culture there is a lack of consistency in the accounts—a fact that is even acknowledged by pro-near-death researchers. Not all people have the tunnel experience, not all people describe the tunnel identically, not all people enter a light, and so on.

A Self-Fulfilling Prophecy

Studies have shown, say the scientific naysayers, that those who are not nearing death but who think they are can have near-death experiences—including the mystical effects and positive aftereffects. The belief that they're going to die seems to be enough to trigger the phenomenon.

Visual Deception

Although many near-death experiencers report seeing spirit beings and beings of light, in some instances, these have turned out to be none other than the attending medical team. Because of this, the theory has been proposed that owing to the abnormal activity in the temporal lobes, sensory impressions are impaired and what are taken to be beings of light are real-life medical personnel hovering over the experiencer's body.

The Dualistic Illusion of Self

Another theory that has been proposed is that as an individual nears death, he or she begins to entertain the notion that perhaps, after all, there isn't a permanent, immaterial self that separates itself at death from what is physical. Such a dual conception (that of soul and body) is nothing more than a mental construction. Nearing death and gaining that insight enables an individual to let go of the mental construction and, with it, let go of the fear of death.

According to the theory, there is no permanent, ongoing self; there never was such a self, and so there literally is "no one" to die. Hence, no self remains after death—no life after death.

The transformative effects of the near-death experience, then, could not be a result of the experiencer having an otherworldly spiritual encounter. The close call with death, of itself, is simply a wake-up alarm inspiring the

> **No Nothin'**
>
> In *Dying to Live: Near-Death Experiences* (see appendix C), psychology lecturer and parapsychologist Susan Blackmore writes that we are "biological organisms," evolving "for no purpose at all and with no end in mind. We are simply here and this is how it is. I have no self and 'I' own nothing. There is no one to die. There is just this moment, and now this, and now this."

individual to reevaluate the way he or she is presently living. Nothing more.

Having an Experience Is Not Proof

Regardless of their prior views on religious matters, most near-death experiencers return from their experience with not only renewed or newfound faith, but also a renewed or newfound conviction in the existence of God and life after death.

Yet, say critics, the subjective awareness of having undergone an episode is not itself a verification of the experience. After all, haven't we all "seen" a body of water shimmering ahead of us as we're out walking on a hot summer day, only to learn that the water was just a mirage? And didn't people once view sailing ships sail toward the horizon and disappear, and conclude that such a sight was proof that the earth was flat? In each instance, what was seen was an illusion.

Although subjective experiences might well tell us something about the experiencer, say those who refute near-death claims, they tell us nothing about the world.

There's No Proof in Numbers

Sometimes, when we see a mirage, we're with a group of people and each of them see it too. And it wasn't just one person who stood on the shoreline and saw a sailing ship appear to slip off the edge of the world, it was thousands. Each time, what these people insisted was true turned out to be their imagination.

The fact that a subjective experience is shared by hundreds of people,

It's a Sleep Disorder

Kevin Nelson, a neurophysiologist at the University of Kentucky, compared the sleep patterns of fifty-five people who had reported unusual sensations during a near-death experience to fifty-five people who hadn't. He and his team of researchers discovered that the near-death group had a significantly higher rate (60 percent compared with 24 percent) of a sleep disorder known as rapid eye movement (REM) intrusion. This disorder causes one of the most active dream states of sleep (REM) to intrude into wakefulness. Once awake, people can feel paralyzed, hear sounds other people didn't, and experience leg muscle weakness. The implication from Dr. Nelson's research is that near-death experiencers are more likely to have different sleep-wake mechanisms in their brains than those of the general public.

Primitive Logic

Rejection of the cause-and-effect argument for the validity of near-death reports can be illustrated in this example: Many primitive peoples believed that if they sacrificed an animal or person to the gods, there would be rain the next year. They conducted the sacrifice, and sure enough, the rain came. The fallacy, though, was in assuming that the effect (rain) came from the cause (sacrifices).

even thousands, does not increase its likelihood of truthfulness.

Where There's Smoke, There's Fire

One argument for the validity of experiencer reports, where so many people see God and receive affirmations of an afterlife, states that there must be some authenticity to the claim—there must be a genuine cause for that effect.

But, say those who criticize near-death states, they're not refuting that there is a cause, they're just saying that there's no evidence for the cause that experiencers insist upon—while there is considerable evidence for other causes.

The Revelation of an Afterlife

Having read this far in the book, you already know this argument. It's the one that even researchers who are proponents of the near-death experience concur with: The anecdotal account of an afterlife is not proof of an afterlife. To put it another way, the subjective experience of an experience is not, in and of itself, proof of the experience. Although you're familiar by now with this argument, I have included it here for these reasons:

- To be unbiased and thorough, and set before you as many well-considered opposing arguments as possible so you will see how truly engaging, thought-provoking, and intellectually stimulating this phenomenon has become in scientific circles.

- To relatedly show you the fascinating philosophical, scientific, and humanistic issues near-death states have raised.

- Because while independent researchers on both sides agree with the argument that subjective experiences don't prove the existence of an afterlife, experiencers themselves believe that the subjective experience of an afterlife is truthful.

Obviously, we're not yet finished with this argument.

A Perceptual Bias

As I've mentioned in earlier chapters, authentic spiritual and religious experiences have long been labeled by the medical and lay community as psychotic or neurotic episodes, delusions. Hence, people who undergo near-death states and return to speak of

Remember . . .

Yesterday's dogma is today's heresy.

Our Fear of the Mystical

It's an interesting paradox that although we as a nation affirm religious belief, we're simultaneously ambivalent about others' assertions of spiritual or religious experiences. We read the Bible, which contains stories of individuals having such occurrences, yet if someone were to stand up in our churches or temples and claim to have directly seen or heard the voice of God, we'd likely shy away from that person.

directly experiencing beings of light, God, and an afterlife, are often branded as "loony."

The general suspiciousness society has regarding "otherworldly journeys" remains unchanged.

The Investigator Effect

"It is true that the researcher's belief system can affect the results of a study, even in so-called double-blind studies (known as the "investigator effect"). The study participants receive hidden or subtle messages about the researcher's belief about the outcome or their own beliefs that can then affect the outcome. There may even be telepathic connections between the researcher and the participants, even if the researcher and the participants are not aware of it."

—Donald R. Morse, DDS, PhD

Surprising Reversals

"Charles Tart, a psychologist at the University of California at Davis, who did the first major study of out-of-body experiences in 1969, and Raymond Moody, a psychiatrist recently retired from the University of Nevada at Las Vegas, who did the same for near-death experiences in the early 1970s, designed experiments of questionable rigor and made matters worse by ignoring the peer-review process and publishing their results in best-selling books. Both Tart and Moody later wrote follow-up books partially debunking and partially recanting their previous ones."

—Steven Kotler, "Extreme States," *Discover,* July 2005.

A Lack of Agreement among Researchers

Another argument against the validity of near-death states is that near-death researchers cannot yet clearly define what they mean by "death," what method is best for studying the phenomenon, or what the components are of its overall pattern. To a certain degree, anything and everything is allowed—even the so-called "near-death-like" experience, in which someone undergoes a scenario and is transformed by the experience (without or with only the threat of pending death).

The definition of the experience, therefore, lacks clear boundaries that would separate it from mystical states or other transformative experiences.

So, Where Are We?

Some of the physical/biological and psychological arguments I've mentioned seem quite reasonable. Others are easily dismissed. But all of them suffer the same problem that the supporters face: The near-death experience is a subjective phenomenon that has no objective criteria for validity.

Both the refutations and the explanations are simply theories. And the problem with theories is that while they may have powerful explanatory features, they ultimately lack causative

CARTOON by Bruce Greyson, MD: There's an Elephant in the Room

As with the ancient Hindu parable of the blind men who identify what the elephant looks like according to the particular parts of its body they grab, some scientists have tried to explain the near-death experience by analyzing certain physical and psychological aspects, such as what occurs in hypoxia, temporal-lobe seizures, psychological defense mechanisms, wishful thinking, and so on. But none of these theories include the spiritual or mystical aftereffects of near-death states. Dr. Bruce Greyson asserts: "The only way a materialist can explain NDEs is to deny that the spiritual and mystical elements are real. Is that the scientific approach to NDEs? I would suggest that refusing to consider those elements which you cannot explain is about as unscientific as you can get."

ones. In other words, while they provide engaging explanations, they can't demonstrate actual causes.

To illustrate what I'm getting at, although it can be demonstrated that ketamine can produce what seems to be a subjective experience identical to a near-death state, that doesn't prove that ketamine is the cause of a near-death experience. Or to take another example: The Big Bang theory of the origin of the universe seems scientifically plausible. But no matter how plausible it seems, it cannot be demonstrated that it's the way the universe in fact came into being. The best it can be is a plausible hypothesis, a theory. To know how the universe actually came into being, we would have to have been there.

Perhaps in the end, that's the only way we will ever know the truth about the near-death experience: We'll just have to be there for ourselves. This doesn't mean, however, that we can't weigh various skeptical theories in terms of their plausibility. So, having now heard the theories of the scientific naysayers, let's move on, and in the next chapter give the proponents their day in court and a chance to respond.

14

Debunking the Debunkers

Where there is an open mind, there will always be a frontier.
—Charles F. Kettering, U.S. engineer and inventor

Researchers and near-death experiencers claim that the problem with the evidence against the near-death experience is that all of it focuses on only one element, or a few of the elements, of the experience, for example, the seeing of light or the tunnel.

Skeptics claim that this is not a valid argument against their findings. Indeed, they say, researchers of the near-death experience admit that there isn't yet any mutually agreed-upon set of criteria for what would even minimally be accepted as a definition of near-death states. So how, they ask, can they come up with research that addresses the complete range of pertinent near-death experience elements when no one has yet determined what those elements are? Moreover, they say, the lack of any standard definition of the components of a near-death episode leaves them unable to—in fact, makes it perfectly acceptable for them not to—do more than find fault with experiencers' explanations for the individual components.

Here, the debunkers have a strong argument that for the time being—until an agreed-upon criteria for what constitutes a near-death episode can be arrived at—those of us in the field of near-death research will have to yield on this point. Yet, as we shall see, this doesn't mean that we must accept the explanations the debunkers have cited for the various aspects of the near-death scenarios they've looked into.

It's All Subjective

One of the most common arguments against the near-death experience is that it's subjective, idiosyncratic. Nonbelievers point out, for example, that not everyone in the same culture has the same elements in his or her near-death episode and that there are cross-cultural differences that suggest cultural influences. Having a life review and seeing a tunnel, for instance, are often part of the near-death experience in Christian and Buddhist cultures, but are seldom if ever found in the scenarios of native peoples of North America, Australia, or the Pacific Islands.

It's true that not everyone has the same experience—remember in chapter 1, I pointed out that even the popular tunnel component isn't that common, occurring in less than one-third of actual scenarios. This does not, however, deny the validity of the experience itself. Subjective differences in responding to or in having an episode do not negate the truth of near-death states. Not everyone, for example, falls in love with the same person. Not everyone agrees on the merits of a particular movie. Not everyone responds to modern art or modern jazz the same way—some don't even consider it art or music! But in each of these instances, the experience the person is having is, in fact, a real experience.

Subjective responses to an experience don't make the experience itself subjective.

Update

As of 2007, we now have dynamic, verified research in the field of near-death studies to show clearly what a near-death experience is *not* (such as oxygen deprivation) and what it *is* (a physically real and valid experience that implies that consciousness survives death).

Research on the aftereffects is also more advanced than before, indicating that the pattern of aftereffects includes physiological changes as well as psychological ones—and that the aftereffects are what validate the near-death experience.

So Much for Subjectivity

While there are admittedly some cross-cultural differences and variations in individual scenarios, the claim that near-death responses are biased because of personal or cultural expectations doesn't hold up. As we've seen, many who were atheists and then had near-death experiences became believers in God. And many report having episodes that differed from—and profoundly changed their attitudes about—their religious beliefs and notions about death. Also, those who have never heard or read about near-death states report the same scenarios as those who are familiar with them. And children too young to have received religious or cultural conditioning—or to have developed a concept of death—have basically the same scenarios as adults.

But I Don't Want to Die

One group of arguments against the near-death phenomenon is that it's a fabrication of the mind or brain at the time of death, created in order to protect the individual from the terrible trauma of the impending end of his or her life. These arguments are either psychological or physiological—claiming to be either the result of the mind (psychological) or the brain (physiological) erecting some defense mechanism against the shock of dying.

Let's look at some of these arguments.

Science, Too!

Ironically, the argument of subjectivity and lack of agreement could equally be leveled against science. The history of science is filled with subjective and opposing conclusions. Einstein, for instance, refused to accept quantum mechanics, not for scientific reasons but for subjective ones. "I shall never believe," he said, "that God plays dice with the world."

They're Just Taking It Too Personally

One theory is that in response to the unwanted onset of death, we separate ourselves from that state—*depersonalize* it—and create pleasurable fantasies that protect us. These pleasurable fantasies, the argument goes, are what near-death experiencers report in their near-death scenarios.

Although it's true that we can depersonalize when faced with a traumatic situation, research on depersonalization shows that it typically does not include such near-death elements as "hyperalertness," mystical consciousness, or out-of-body sensations. Additionally, depersonalization is usually experienced as dreamlike, which, as we've seen, is not how near-death experiencers describe their scenarios. On the contrary, they claim that their episodes are anything but like their dreams—being more vivid, more real, and having a far more lasting influence on their lives and beliefs.

I Can't Associate

A variation on the theory of depersonalization is that, when faced with a stressful situation, we develop an unconscious defensive coping response in which we detach (dissociate) ourselves from our bodily sensations and emotions. "Tuning out" to what's emotionally frightening and physically occurring to our bodies, we "tune in" to something imaginative and pleasant. Several near-death researchers have suggested that because near-death experiencers seem to have undergone more childhood traumas than the general population—during which time they may have created alternate childhood realities—they could have a tendency toward dissociation.

Not True

There is no conclusive evidence to indicate that incidences of childhood trauma are more prevalent among near-death experiencers than nonexperiencers. Dr. Bruce Greyson, for example, has been unable to support this theory in his work. I, too, have not found such a correlation in the thousands I have interviewed.

So Much for Stress

Willoughby Britton, a doctoral candidate in clinical psychology at the University of Arizona, was interested in posttraumatic stress disorder. Britton knew that most people who have a close brush with death tend to have some form of posttraumatic stress disorder, whereas people who get that close and have a near-death experience have none. In other words, people who have a near-death experience have an atypical response to life-threatening trauma. No one knows why.

(From Steven Kotler, "Extreme States," *Discover,* July 2005.)

Figure Out This One

"In our prospective study, we did not show that psychological, physiological, or pharmacological factors caused these experiences after cardiac arrest. With a purely physiological explanation such as cerebral anoxia, most patients who had been clinically dead should report an NDE. All 344 patients [in my study] had been unconscious because of anoxia of the brain resulting from their cardiac arrest. Why should only 18 percent of the survivors of cardiac arrest report an NDE?"

—Pim van Lommel, MD, "About the Continuity of Our Consciousness," in *Brain Death and Disorders of Consciousness,* edited by C. Machado and D. A. Shewmon

Saying that near-death experiencers might have a tendency toward dissociation is not the same thing as saying that a near-death experience is itself an instance of dissociation or a dissociative disorder. Those suffering from the latter state of persistent, recurrent, and chronic dissociation don't match the conditions found with near-death experiencers.

To Air Is Human

Various people have contended that there's a correlation between oxygen loss (hypoxia) or deprivation (anoxia) at the time of death and the near-death state. Studies of fighter pilots undergoing rapid acceleration, which reduces blood flow—and thus, oxygen to the brain, resulting in unconsciousness—have been offered to demonstrate this theory.

It's certainly true that fighter pilots experiencing acceleration-induced unconsciousness do report tunnel vision, bright lights, floating sensations, out-of-body experiences, "dreamlets" of beautiful places (which often include family members and friends), euphoria, and the like. But there have been no reports of fighter pilots having life reviews or panoramic memory, or of details that could not have been known before that were later verified. Nor do they exhibit the pattern of life-changing aftereffects that near-death experiencers do—changes in physiology and behavioral traits that increase with time, not decrease.

Also, the argument completely misses the scientifically proven fact that tunnel vision is a narrowing of the visual field down to a small area in the center, with no visual experience of the periphery; that is to say, there is not just a perception of darkness in the periphery, but no perception at all. By contrast, in the tunnel experience, there is usually a bright light at the end of a long, dark, yet complexly structured tunnel and even peripheral imagery in precisely remembered detail.

Just Numb Me

One theory is that at the time of death, our brain produces an increase of endorphins that flood our bodies, literally drugging us with pleasant sensations in order to reduce the effect of the shock of dying.

There's no evidence, though, that the brain produces a greater quantity of endorphins prior to dying than at other times of stress. So why aren't we having "near-death experiences" at other times when endorphins are present?

Take Me Home Again, Ketamine

The most compelling theory relating the near-death experience to medical intervention is the ketamine model. As I mentioned in chapter 13, ketamine is an anesthetic that has been found to have short-acting, hallucinogenic properties that surprisingly mirror many of the elements of a near-death scenario: the tunnel, entry into a light, telepathic communication with spirit beings and with God, and life review. Additionally, in one particular study, 30 percent of those who had ketamine episodes maintained afterward that what they experienced was real—just as do near-death experiencers.

This makes the ketamine model an intriguing one, but one that is not without its problems. Again, what about those near-death experiencers who don't have their experience while on the operating table, under the influence of

Narrow Tunnels

As blood flow to the retina diminishes, the visual field contracts, producing tunnel vision, sight loss, and blackout. Proponents of the oxygen-deprivation theory regard this as evidence of phenomena mistakenly attributed to a near-death episode. Or, more precisely, they maintain that it's an explanation of what occurs as death nears, and one that's more accurate than the explanations near-death experiencers give.

Induced Experiences Fall Flat

Neurophysiological processes such as epilepsy, hypercarbia, cerebral hypoxia, and hyperventilation and the use of drugs such as ketamine, LSD, or mushrooms can indeed result in unconsciousness and reports of out-of-body experiences, sounds, lights, and flashes from one's past. Yet the reports describe only fragmented and random memories, unlike the panoramic life reviews/previews of near-death experiences, and there are rarely aftereffects on a par with the transformational changes that follow near-death experiences.

Can You Explain This?

Experiencers, especially infants and toddlers, often describe the deceased people they have met during their near-death episodes—giving details of personal features, objects held, clothing, even naming names. In many cases, the experiencers have never seen or heard of the person before and are surprised later on to learn that the deceased is a relative. Couple this with the consistency of physiological and psychological aftereffects that occur and you have a phenomenon that defies being linked to any known drug hallucination, including ketamine. Just the reports from children alone run counter to the medical understanding of drug effects.

the anesthetic ketamine? The response is that the ketamine model is not, in and of itself, intended to explain the near-death phenomenon, but to explain what occurs within the brain at the time of death. Just as the brain produces morphine-like endorphins, the brain, at the time of death (this theory maintains) produces its own ketamine-like, anesthetizing substance that leads to a person having what is labeled "a near-death experience."

So far, though, that's only true in theory.

Moreover, whereas 30 percent of those in the study who used ketamine maintained afterward that their experiences were real, almost every single near-death experiencer made the same claim—an almost unheard-of response. Furthermore, ketamine produces its effects by temporarily altering cerebral functioning. With the near-death experience, research (my own included) suggests that structural, chemical, and functionary changes may occur in the brain during these states, especially if the near-death episode is intense. These changes seem to increase steadily and expand over time.

As I've noted in earlier chapters, research in the field of near-death studies has shown that drugs actually depress, nullify, or prevent near-death experiences. We must also consider that scenario details previously unknown often prove to be accurate, and that the complex pattern of aftereffects clearly sets the phenomenon apart from any known drug effect.

Who's That Knocking on My Head?

Neurosurgeon and Nobel prize–winner Wilder Penfield is the pioneer in experiments directly stimulating the brain with electrodes and producing vivid, long-forgotten memories. We all know the stories: Someone has a certain sector of his brain poked with an electrode and suddenly remembers everyone who was at his fifth birthday party. Or begins hearing a song sung to her by a deceased family member.

Today, magnetic resonance imaging (MRI) has been used to monitor temporal lobe activity in, among other studies, schizophrenics who are experiencing auditory hallucinations.

Some researchers claim that at the time of death, some similar neuroelectrical activity is going on, creating the narratives we know as "the near-death experience." The randomness of recollected memories in temporal lobe stimulation, compared to the cohesiveness and similarity of near-death scenarios and their aftereffects, however, strongly argue against this theory.

Doesn't Match Up

According to Pim van Lommel, MD, Wilder Penfield could sometimes induce flashes of recollection of the past (never a complete life review), experiences of light, sound, or music, and rarely a kind of out-of-body experience. Yet none of these effects produced life-attitude transformations.

Mr. Sandman, Send Me a Dream

Skeptics of the near-death experience frequently claim that the episodes are nothing but dreamlike variations or fabrications of an overactive mind. In a word or two, wishful thinking. As we shall see, however, there are differences between near-death scenarios and both dreams and hallucinations.

I Can See

As we saw in chapter 12, Dr. Kenneth Ring's studies of the blind indicated that blind people who experience a near-death episode often have visual perception—even though they may have been unable to experience this same ability in their dreams.

I Must Be Dreaming

Unlike near-death episodes, dreams are usually quite surreal, having no cohesive storyline outside of how the symbols present in them are interpreted. Although near-death scenarios may not contain events commonly occurring within the experiencer's real life, they nevertheless develop around an explainable sequence of events that not only has meaning but immediate significance.

Dream content varies from person to person. Although there isn't a single, uniformly experienced near-death scenario, there are common elements that appear in episodes regardless of culture or belief. Dreams are frequently forgotten. We usually remember that we had a dream or two, but we don't always recall what it was about. With the exception of near-death experiences that happened in childhood but were then repressed, only to be remembered later in adult life, the vast majority of near-death experiences are vividly remembered and seldom ever forgotten.

Dreams can be veridical, but when they are, they're typically dreamt by people considered to have psychic abilities. On the other hand, and as the numerous stories I've presented in this book have shown, people who have out-of-body experiences as part of their near-death episodes tend to report, and accurately, activities that occurred

So Much for Sleep Disorders

There are many problems with the sleep disorder research of Dr. Kevin Nelson and his associates (mentioned in the previous chapter). Among them are: Questions asked of participants were so ambiguous they missed the point of the study; and the control group consisted of friends and colleagues of Dr. Nelson, not those more representative of the public at large. The most serious, though, concerns a well-known finding that sleep patterning and dream states change afterward for the vast majority of near-death experiencers. He would have had to conduct before-and-after investigations of experiencers previous to his study in order to have a valid baseline for measurement.

Pure Fantasy

Sometimes people in real life do make up near-death experiences. In his book *Raising the Dead: A Doctor's Encounter with His Own Mortality,* surgeon and popular author Richard Selzer claimed that he had a near-death experience, complete with an out-of-body episode. He later acknowledged that he was never pronounced dead (he was in a coma), and his out-of-body account was complete invention: "I just wanted to tell a ripping good story."

around them as well as outside their physical field of vision—people who were otherwise not considered to be telepathic or psychic. (Go back to chapter 11, for instance, and reread the story of the young woman who while in a near-death state saw her father, and when she was resuscitated, told everyone that she'd spoken with her father and that he said he had died. No one believed her. But after making several calls, it was learned that he had in fact died—five minutes before her near-death experience!)

And the testimonies of experiencers themselves argue against near-death episodes being dreams: Almost all of them maintain that the imagery, vividness, content, and sense of authenticity of their near-death scenarios are completely different from what they experience when dreaming.

No, Your Honor, I Wasn't Under the Influence

A certain type of personality has been identified as the "fantasy-prone personality," and the suggestion has been made that there's a correlation between this personality type and near-death experiencers.

The fantasy-prone person is deeply invested in fantasy life, has a vivid hallucinatory ability, intense sensory experiences, and a strong visual memory. Comparative studies between fantasy-prone people and near-death experiencers, though, have been inconclusive. In one study, for example, fantasizers—in contrast to near-death experiencers—said that their hallucinatory fantasies were not "as real as real" and were not lifelike, detailed, or stable. Two other studies came out showing substantial differences between fantasy proneness and those who experience near-death states.

And whereas psychedelic drugs have been shown to produce experiences similar to the subjective scenarios of the near-death state (tunnels, lights, heavenly music, mystical consciousness, and childhood memories, among others), the drug user is aware afterward that his or her experience was not real, even if at the time it felt as though it were. Near-death experiencers maintain that their episodes were real. The vast majority live their lives afterward—in one way or another—on the basis of this conviction. Most make significant life changes because of what happened to them.

Though there have been near-death reports that later proved to be false, there's generally too much veracity in near-death experiences for them to be easily labeled as hallucinations. To cite just one example, recall Lloyd L. Haymon's story in chapter 11: He saw his pet parakeet in his near-death scenario and realized that the parakeet had died. No hallucination here. Lloyd's wife later confirmed that the bird had died "for no apparent reason" at the same moment that Lloyd suffered his heart attack and was being treated by paramedics—minutes before he was in the ambulance in which he had his near-death experience.

The intensity of hallucinations, no matter how they're caused (and that includes oxygen deprivation, blood loss, drugs, and centrifugal spinning), fade with time or lead to increasing periods of confusion. Conversely, near-death states, regardless of type, are clear and coherent—a recentering of the mind. Consistently accurate and intense over time, these stories are known to produce significant psychological and physiological aftereffects that expand with the passing years. Powerful in their ability to transform lives, the episodes are "instructive" about reality as it truly exists. Hallucinations don't exhibit such characteristics.

On the Question of Realness

We often mistakenly think of hallucinations as false experiences. In fact, at the time of their occurrence, hallucinations are taken to be true perceptions, immediate sensations of reality. It's only afterward that they're seen for what they are—except by those with severe psychological disorders, such as paranoid schizophrenics. Although sharing the belief in the realness of the experience long after it's over with those who have psychological disorders, near-death experiencers don't exhibit mental problems as a result of their belief in their experience (contrary to the opinion of some physicians).

No Confusion

"No epileptic seizure has the clarity and narrative style of an NDE. And this is because *all* epilepsy is confusional."
—Peter Fenwick, MD, FRCPsych

A Counter Message

Instead of the dying brain creating measures to help the individual cope with death, some theories say it appears to enhance intelligence and reenergize the body during near-death states in a manner suggestive of preparation for reviving. It's as if, at the point of death, the brain can receive a counter message: Don't shut down, speed up!

The Dying Brain Theory

This theory comes in many versions. The notion is that the dying brain creates some sort of defensive coping mechanism to ward off the shock of impending death. This could include neuronal and physiological activity occurring near the time of death that brings about the sensory experiences often associated with a near-death episode. The idea is that near-death experiences must surely be the response of a dying brain/body, and not any kind of authentic, spiritual, or otherworldly experience.

Although I've already mentioned in the previous chapter some of the theories that come under the "dying brain" category—the endorphin and the ketamine model theory, to mention two—I'm returning to the subject because of the writings of Susan Blackmore. A parapsychologist at the time of her original work, but now focusing on psychological research, Blackmore has written one of the most influential books on the near-death experience, *Dying to Live: Science and Near-Death Experiences,* in which she presents a detailed version of the dying brain theory. Her aim is to provide a materialistic interpretation of near-death states.

Blackmore's theory is too complex to present in its entirety here, but the following is a summary of it:

- Anoxia can cause the occurrences of hearing music (by stimulating the cochlear region of the ear), seeing tunnels, and seeing a light.

- An inordinate release of endorphins at the time of death is the source of the euphoria associated with a near-death episode.

- The actions of endorphins and neurotransmitters cause such cerebral structures as the hippocampus (associated with memory) to release stored memories, resulting in the life review.

- The sense of timelessness is the result of the breakdown of one's sense of self at death (the self being the basis for distinguishing moments of time).

To respond to each of these points is not necessary. Instead, we can offer a rebuttal to the whole by quoting Dr. Kenneth Ring's criticism from his excellent review of Blackmore's book in the *Journal of Near-Death Studies* (Winter 1995, p. 123): "Does the brain state associated with the onset of an NDE explain the experience or does it merely afford access to it?" In other words, although many of the near-death-related phenomena may be traceable to our body's responses to dying, does that mean that those responses explain the phenomena, or do they simply provide clues to an even deeper and more provocative mystery?

Clear Consciousness

Pim van Lommel, MD, has a point to make that applies here. Cardiac-arrest patients with a near-death experience can report a clear consciousness during the period of unconsciousness when there is total lack of electrical activity in the cortex, and brain-stem activity has ceased. He asks the question, "How could a clear consciousness outside one's body be experienced at the moment that the brain no longer functions during a period of clinical death, with a flat EEG?" He believes that the function of science is the search to explain new mysteries, rather than stick with old facts and concepts.

And Here's Another Point to Make

The assumptions made by Dr. G. W. Woerlee about the Pam Reynolds' case in the last chapter—that anesthesia was insufficient, that drugs alone induced her sense of being out-of-body, that she was not on bypass soon enough, therefore her body was not sufficiently cooled—have been vigorously denied by the attending physicians. In discussing this case, Dr. Peter Fenwick emphasized an important fact: Her clear consciousness was continuous from beginning to end, including during the period of hypothermic cardiac arrest, which Dr. Woerlee says is impossible.

A Few Extras

Not all theories attempting to explain away the near-death experience fit neatly into categories. Here are a few such theories.

I'm Seeing Double

As I mentioned in the last chapter, autoscopy is a term for seeing your own double. It occurs in the presence of certain brain lesions, migraine headaches,

Like a Run-Down Computer?

At the 1993 World Congress of Neural Networks, Dr. Stephen Thaler presented the results of an experiment: When 90 percent of the connections were severed in sophisticated, "trained" computers modeled after the human neural network, the computers began to spew out information based in part on previous programming and the rest "whimsical" invention. "Time" also slowed down. Dr. Thaler suggested that the computers' response to "dying" may well be analogous to the human brain's neurological, near-death-experience responses.

Sage Advice

The famous Dutch doctor, Frederik van Eeden, in his 1890 lecture about scientific progress, said: "Personally, I am more than ever convinced that the largest enemy of scientific progress is to reject and to refuse to study beforehand and out of prejudice seeming incomprehensible, strange and unknown facts."

> **New Words**
>
> The term **anecdote**, which means a short, entertaining tale, is being discarded in near-death research as a reference to near-death experiences. In its place, **narrative** is favored, as the term recognizes that near-death experiences are stories, literally, narratives from a person's life, that have deep and profound meaning, and are intimate to the experiencer.

brain tumors, and strokes. Many have claimed that this is what's occurring when near-death experiencers report having an out-of-body episode.

But autoscopy and out-of-body experiences differ in a significant way: In autoscopy, the viewer is within his or her body, looking at his or her double; in out-of-body experiences, the viewer is outside of his or her body, looking back onto it. Also, more exact verifiable details emerge from reports of out-of-body episodes than from autoscopy.

You Must Have Been a Beautiful Baby

The argument has been put forth, particularly in consideration of the famous tunnel component of some near-death scenarios, that the near-death experience is nothing but a recollection, or reenactment, of the birth experience.

Research to test this divided experiencer accounts that featured tunnels into two groups: those born vaginally, and those who were taken directly from their mother's womb via C-sections (cesarean births). No statistical difference between the groups was found, proving that "tunnels" are not in any way a recollection of birth.

Mind over Matter

This is a philosophical argument that would come under the heading of "the mind-body issue." The argument is that near-death episodes cannot be real because experiencers claim to have sensory experiences while outside of their bodies, and there's no evidence that sensory experience can occur in the absence of some physical sense organ (eyes, ears, skin, and so on).

The occurrence of incredible intuitions and psychic readings—to say nothing of the equally incredible out-of-body reports of near-death experiencers—argues against this claim. Suggested instead, contrary to its intent, is that this argument may, in fact, more properly be calling for a reexamination of our long-held notions about how we acquire sensory experience.

One Last Time

In wrapping up what we just discussed:

- The theory that near-death episodes are the result of medicines given prior to surgery ignores the fact that the majority of near-death reports come from people who had their episode at the scene of automobile accidents, near-drownings, and the like—when they were not in surgery, sedated, or under the influence of any drugs (medical or otherwise).

- Associating near-death experiences with depersonalization or dissociation misses completely the finding that near-death experiencers undergo their episodes with intact ego identities.

- Claiming that near-death experiences resemble other sorts of experiences—neurological, physiological, or drug-induced—is not the same thing as proving that the near-death experience is the same as those other experiences. That two events can share certain characteristics is not the same thing as saying that the two events are identical.

Where does all this leave us?

Although we can't determine on the basis of their subjectivity alone the truth or plausibility of near-death experiences, we can test for a certain degree of truth and plausibility on the basis of how the episode is reported. If someone says that he or she saw or heard something during a near-death state, we can, like Kimberly Clark Sharp did (see chapter 12), check that person's claim. Or, if a child says that in a near-death scenario he or she encountered a previously deceased relative that the child never saw or heard of in real life, we can confirm that based on the child's description of the individual.

And we can test for the truth or plausibility of the experience on the basis of the fact that those who have never heard of near-death states nonetheless report identical scenario components as those who have heard of them, irrespective of culture or country, and exhibit the same pattern of aftereffects.

Even Researchers Are Changed

Called the "compassionate coroner," Janis Amatuzio, MD, has written two books that draw on her more than twenty-five years of forensic investigations. Both *Beyond Knowing* and *Forever Ours* chronicle cases in which she encountered unexpected happenings for which she was not professionally prepared. Cases with messages from the dead, near-death experiences, and mysteries suggestive of immortality caused her to reconsider life and the existence of the soul. (Refer to appendix C for more information about both of her books.)

Most important, though, is the response factor. We can examine the extent to which the experiencer was affected by what happened to him or her. Here's what my research indicates:

- 21 percent claimed no discernible differences afterward
- 60 percent reported significant life changes
- 19 percent noted radical shifts, almost as if they had become another person

If you add the last two figures, that makes 79 percent who were affected in a significantly profound way!

On the minus side: Nearly a quarter of them, mostly children, were pulled so strongly to return "Home" that they attempted suicide to get back. Depression and divorce plagued large

An Updated Tool

The Life Changes Inventory (LCI) was an instrument originally developed by Kenneth Ring, PhD, to quantify value changes following an NDE. Over time, this scale has been updated to reflect accumulated knowledge from administering the instrument to disparate samples and from qualitative research into attitudinal changes reported by NDErs. This latest version detailed in *Journal of Near-Death Studies* is now dubbed the Life Changes Inventory–Revised (LCI-R). Drs. Ring and Greyson hope it will become the instrument of choice for future research into value changes and personal transformations associated with near-death experiences. Request *Journal of Near-Death Studies,* Vol. 23, No. 1, Fall 2004, from IANDS. The LCI-R plus full explanatory information can be found on pages 41–53.

numbers who had difficulty integrating their experience into their daily lives. Even being able to talk about what they encountered, without being met with scorn, more than a third of the child experiencers became alcoholics within five to eight years afterward for the same reason.

On the plus side: A sense of love and forgiveness, a spiritual strength, empowered the majority to make strikingly positive changes in their lives. Latent talents readily surfaced, coupled with an unusual increase in intellect and hunger for knowledge. Enhanced creative and intuitive abilities, a deep desire for classical or melodious music, and a dedication to service were commonplace—many entered the public sector as reformers or agents for change.

What hallucination, temporal lobe seizure, or drug or laboratory-induced episode can match the depth of this response?

Hi-Ho, Forward We Go

There are many projects in the offing for near-death research. Here are a few:

Col. Diane Corcoran Military Research Fund

As part of IANDS, this fund has been developed for educating military and veteran hospitals, and the veterans themselves, about near-death experiences. Col. Corcoran was in the Army Nurse Corps and had early experiences of patients in Vietnam telling her about their near-death episodes. She has since presented lectures at all major nursing conferences and written articles for nursing journals about the phenomenon. Today, military personnel are having near-death experiences in record numbers. Yet, because military hospitals and rehabilitation facilities are being privatized, there is no longer a central source for information about near-death experiences, or a way to contact veterans directly to obtain their stories, form focus groups, or provide support if needed.

To contribute to the fund or to help in this effort, contact IANDS (see appendix B). To contact Col. Diane Corcoran, e-mail her at Dcorcoran@nc.rr.com. She is actively soliciting narratives from veterans (see appendix E).

Dr. Bruce Greyson and Associates Research Project

If you have had a near-death experience or other unexplained experience, you are invited to contact Dr. Greyson and his team of researchers. This project covers not only near-death experiences, but also deathbed visions and other phenomena that suggest we may survive bodily death. Follow-up contact involves getting an account of the near-death experience itself, supplemented by a rather detailed and comprehensive questionnaire that addresses a lot of aspects people often don't think to include in their narratives, and finally a host of short questionnaires that address spirituality, attitudes, and personality traits. If you respond to Dr. Greyson or to anyone on his team, you can be assured that everything you tell will be completely confidential.

Their website is www.healthsystem.virginia.edu/personalitystudies. To contact Dr. Bruce Greyson to report near-death experiences, you can e-mail him at cbg4d@virginia.edu. Contact Dr. Jim Tucker to report children with memories of past lives: jbt8n@virginia.edu. Contact Dr. Emily Kelly to report anything else, such as apparitions, deathbed visions, and communications from deceased loved ones: ewa2r@virginia.edu. (Refer to appendix E.)

Todd Murphy and Allan Kellehear, PhD

A concerted effort is being launched by a number of researchers to obtain near-death experience narratives from other cultures. Only in Western countries are tunnels and life reviews reported, suggesting that these particular features may be culture–specific. For instance, Japanese near-death experiencers frequently report going into a cave, which is the entrance for them to a new reality. Sometimes experiencers in other areas of the world speak of coming to a dark river in their episodes, where there is a boatman waiting for them.

I've traveled to several countries "off the beaten path"—I am reminded here of Korea—where locals were enthusiastic about doing research on the phenomenon but were unsure of how to begin, what to do, or where to report their findings. I've urged IANDS to design a "Research Instruction Packet" to fill this need, and they are. It is my hope that this packet will have wide distribution. By the brief outline of my proposal to them that I've included here, you will be able to recognize the many fronts of near-death research present today.

Proposal for Research Instruction Packet

I. Different ways of doing research
  - A. Clinical
    1. Prospective
    2. Retrospective
    3. Greyson Scale and Life Changes Inventory–Revised
  - B. Observational (which is what I do)
    1. Police science
    2. Neurolinguistic style
  - C. Narrative collection
    1. Personal interviews
    2. By-mail collections
    3. Questionnaires to use if applicable (samples given),

II. How to record case studies

III. Submitting case studies

  A. Research papers

    1. Articles

    2. Archival data collections

IV. Where to send finished work, how to use it

  A. IANDS archives

  B. Journal of Near-Death Studies

  C. Universities, medical schools, etc.

  D. Media

It is my belief that once a packet like this is readily available, more people will participate in near-death research worldwide, and because of that we will have better information to use in addressing the life and death issues associated with the phenomenon.

15

Religion's Got a Gripe, Too

I leave this rule for others when I'm dead/Be always sure you're right—then go ahead.

—David "Davy" Crockett, *Autobiography*

In the beginning of near-death research, people such as myself were excited by the findings we were getting and looked forward to the religious community being equally excited. We were not only surprised but shocked to discover that, in many religions, "people of the cloth" turned against our work and condemned or heavily criticized the entire phenomenon.

Here we were working within a highly charged religious and spiritual setting, investigating and supporting a deeply religious and spiritual experience, and religions and religious leaders—those we thought would be most encouraged and encouraging—were, more often than not, condemning us, the experiencers, and what we were researching. We felt as if we'd "met the enemy, and the enemy is us," as the saying goes.

Why and how did this come about?

It's in the Bible

Every religion has its holy literature that is the philosophical, spiritual, theological, and moral foundation of the faith. In the West, the two religious writings that inspire and inform us are the Old Testament and the New Testament, collectively referred to as the "Holy Bible."

Even though the two books are called by one name, and we speak of a Judeo-Christian culture as if it were one ethic, in fact the teachings of the Old Testament and the New Testament aren't the same. Nor are the beliefs of the followers of the Old Testament and

Which One, God?

"Christendom has 243 different denominations, and it is almost impossible to find a single belief all have in common. One man's heresy is another man's dogma. This is precisely why the early church was forced to embrace creeds to solidify the mainstream of Christian thought."

—John Tomlinson, Director of Research, American Institute of Health and Science (see appendix C)

New Words

Necrolatry is worship of or excessive reverence for the dead. Practice in **necromancy** entails communing or conjuring up the dead in order to learn about or influence the outcome of forthcoming events in this life.

the New Testament. And when it comes to as important a phenomenon as death and how it figures into our lives, those differences and how they're expressed can be of great consequence, especially when a generation arises that claims to have been able to see beyond death.

A Speck of Dust, a Moment in Time

As I mentioned in chapter 1, Old Testament writings caution us against mediums, wizards, *necrolatry, necromancy,* or the practice of any cult of the dead. A medium was defined as "anyone who has inside him an ancestral spirit." The punishment for professing to be a medium or wizard was quite harsh:

> "A man also or a woman that divineth by a ghost or a familiar spirit [that is, a medium or a wizard] shall surely be put to death: they shall stone them with stones; their blood shall be upon." (Lev. 20:27)
>
> "There shall not be found among you anyone that maketh his son or his daughter to pass through the fire, one that useth divination, a soothsayer, or an enchanter, or a sorcerer, or a necromancer. For whosoever doeth these things is an abomination unto the Lord; and because of these abominations the Lord thy God is driving them out from before thee." (Deut. 18:10–12)

When we die, we are dead. There is nothing left, nothing to consult:

> "For dust thou art, and unto dust shalt thou return." (Gen. 3:19)
>
> "For we must needs die, and are as water spilt on the ground, which cannot be gathered up again." (2 Sam. 14:14)

Indeed, one message in the Old Testament is that death is actually a punishment. Accordingly, because Adam and Eve disobeyed God and ate from the tree of the knowledge of good and evil, both were banished from the Garden of Eden, denied access to the tree of life within the Garden, and would now live out their lives and then return to the ground from which they were made.

Obviously, the near-death experiencer who tells us that death is not a punishment but one of life's passages, and that, though not a medium, sorcerer, or wizard, he or she nonetheless met with previously departed souls, clearly speaks of things that run counter to these Old Testament teachings.

The unkindest treatment of near-death experiencers came less from those whose faith is based on the Old Testament than those whose faith is based on the New Testament.

Death's Sting Gets Removed

In Romans 5:12–21, Paul expresses the belief that has become the basis of much of contemporary church thinking: Adam's eating of the tree of the knowledge of good and evil represented the Fall of Man. Sin entered the world, and humans were now condemned to die. "Just as sin came into the world through one man," Paul wrote, "and death came through sin—so death spread to all, because all have sinned." (Rom. 5:12)

The sin of the father, in other words, was passed on to the children.

Death, then, was not part of the Divine Plan, but came about through a human act of deceit and disobedience. Death was not part of the Creator's design, it was an event in the history of human beings. Another historical event, therefore, might be able to undo it. And indeed it can. Jesus has come as the new Adam. And just as the actions of the "old" Adam affected humankind, so, too, do the actions of the new Adam:

What About God's Mind?

A cosmology think tank called "Beyond" has been established at Arizona State University. ASU president Michael Crow wants the new department to ask tough questions like "Why are the laws of nature mathematical? What about the origin of the universe, life, consciousness, and the emergence of humans? The core goal with "Beyond" is to "search for the mind of God."

An Earthy Guy

There are two Old Testament stories about the creation of man and woman. In one story, man (Adam) is created from the earth. The Hebrew word for "earth" is *adamah.* "Adam," then, is literally derived from the earth *(adamah).*

Look Away, Quick

A further Biblical argument against near-death experiencers' claims of transcendent religious experiences and an afterlife is that the Bible explicitly states that no one is to see the face of God and live.

It's a Matter of Opinion

The idea that an individual has to wait until the end of the world to awaken in spirit and in truth is a peculiarity of the Seventh Day Adventists' teachings, and not held by mainstream Christians. The teaching is referred to as "soul sleep." In Biblical Christianity, the understanding is "to be absent from the body is to be present with Christ." Thus, if we are born again (renewed by our faith, transformed by God's Love), we go immediately to heaven when we die.

Boos from the Clergy

Because of Jesus' words "everyone who lives and believes in me will never die," many Christian clergymen, clergywomen, and congregants reject near-death experiencers' claims of having seen an afterlife on the grounds that it's only through faith in and the grace of Jesus that one can enter the afterlife—and many experiencers didn't believe in Jesus before their episodes. Relatedly, some researchers (as we saw in chapter 12) and religions refute the claims of near-death experiencers regarding an afterlife by maintaining that entrance into the afterlife is only attainable through faith and deeds.

> "Thus it is written: The first man, Adam, became a living being; the last Adam became a life-giving spirit. The first man was from the earth, a man of dust; the second man is from heaven. Just as we have borne the image of the man of dust, we will also bear the image of the man of heaven." (1 Cor. 15:45–49)

We are like the "old" Adam in that we are physical and we sin and die, but we are also like the new Adam, in that we are spiritual and can acquire eternal life.

Yet that eternal life will come only at the end of days:

> "Listen, I will tell you a mystery! We will not all die, but we will all be changed in a moment, in the twinkling of an eye, at the last trumpet. For the trumpet will sound, and the dead will be raised imperishable, and we will be changed." (1 Cor. 15:51–52)

Jesus has come as the new Adam, and through his resurrection, Jesus has eliminated the power of death. "Death has been swallowed up in victory." (1 Cor. 15:54) But this "victory" comes exclusively through belief in Jesus, the Christ: "I am the resurrection and the life. Those who believe in me, even though they die, will live, and everyone who lives and believes in me will never die." (John 11:25–26)

Near-death experiencers, however, tell about experiencing the afterlife here and now—not having to wait until the end of days. And not only aren't all near-death experiencers believers in Jesus—they come from all religions and spiritual practices—many were atheists prior to their episode!

Not So Fast

Besides the quote from 2 Sam. 14:14 given previously, that same passage goes on to promise that no one can be expelled from God, not even those who are banished.

Repercussions

Unfortunately, with these Biblical teachings having become ingrained in formal religious beliefs, near-death experiencers get more than they bargained for when they begin to share their stories.

One of the adult cases I investigated involved a man in his mid-forties, married, with several children and a successful business. He had been very active in his church before his near-death experience. During my session with him he was literally down on his hands and knees begging me, saying "Please tell me I am not psychic. It's against my religion. It's the work of the devil." What could I say to him? The Truth. "Not only are you psychic, you will become more so. Psychic abilities have nothing to do with the devil or your Christian beliefs. They are simply extensions of faculties normal to us. You're okay. What's happening to you is normal for what you've been through."

Another case (which I've written about earlier in this book) involved a young mother of two who was married to a minister of a fundamentalist Christian church. She told me that after her near-death experience she became uncomfortable with her husband's sermons. "He's wrong," she told me. "I know he's wrong. What he's preaching isn't the truth. I love my husband and I love our children and being his wife. I don't want to leave him or change our life together. It's just that I can't listen to his sermons any more. They bother me." So, on Sunday mornings, while her husband preached from the pulpit, she stayed home with the kids. How long she was able to continue this I don't know, as I've lost track of her. But I'll never forget the look of distress on her face when she spoke with me.

I know of two ministers of Protestant churches who were fired by their superiors because they dared to speak

Punishing Ministers

Some ministers who have either had near-death experiences or support the claims of near-death experiencers have had to leave their professions altogether because of the treatment they suffered. One clergyman I met was forced to move to a more liberal state and apply for a position with his denomination there—a more open-minded congregation and supervisory board.

Devil's Gonna Get Ya

The most familiar response from frightened families who don't understand near-death states is, "You are possessed by the devil, and you will go to hell if you don't repent and save your soul."

Satan Is Bad News

Identifying Satan as "the evil one" has an interesting biblical connection. There are biblical scholars who believe that the passage in the Lord's Prayer that says "deliver us from evil" (Matt. 6:13), originally meant "deliver us from the evil one." Some editions of the New Testament use this translation (for example, *The HarperCollins Study Bible: New Revised Standard Version*).

during their church sermons about near-death experiences and what can be learned from them. Both of these men were nonexperiencers, but they were deeply affected by the stories experiencers told and the findings from near-death research.

Inarguably, the most tragic instances of scorn are those that occur to child near-death experiencers. One nine-year-old boy I interviewed was visited by the family minister weekly over a period of several months. The minister told the boy—and his mother—that the boy would rot in hell if he did not publicly recant what he claimed to have seen when he "died." The mother was terrified and the boy terribly confused.

One large Catholic church, in a special section on the website they sponsor, state that "Not all angels are of God." Warnings about "counterfeit angels" are lengthy and backed up with scripture. Angels seen by people who have near-death experiences, even child experiencers, are especially considered counterfeit and are denounced.

My files are filled with similar stories—of experiencers who were disinherited by their families because they were thought to be "possessed," who were chastised because their behavioral changes were such an "embarrassment," who felt driven from their community because of religious intolerance and the characterization they had been given of being "cursed by Satan" because they had a near-death experience. Many have been labeled "witches" or told they were going crazy.

The Devil's Handiwork

So many near-death experiencers have been accused of being possessed, of themselves being agents of the devil and their near-death episodes products of his handiwork. Let's take a closer look at the devil.

The True Light at the End of the Tunnel

As we've seen, even in the Old Testament there was the message that there was an evil force at work in anyone claiming to have knowledge of or to have visited or communed with the dead. But the notion of an evil agent—of an archenemy of God—didn't truly acquire prominence until the time of New Testament writings and teachings.

Referred to by various names in the New Testament—Satan, Devil, Beelzebul (or Beelzebub), Beliar (or Belial)—evil in the world became personified. It was "the tempter" (Matt. 4:3), "the prince of demons/devils" (Matt. 12:24), "the evil/wicked one" (1 John 5:18).

As the devil is the archenemy of God, and as Jesus said, "He that is not with me is against me" (Matt. 12:30), then those who express views contrary to the views of the New Testament, contrary to the alleged teachings of Jesus, are considered by many to be against God, against Jesus. Unfortunately, it is considered right to banish these people from congregations, humiliate them, reproach them, or censor them. They are agents of and possessed by "the prince of demons," and are voicing evil.

Moreover, as Satan is "the tempter," near-death experiencers don't realize that they are being used by him. So it is often thought that there's a certain spiritual/religious obligation to help experiencers—to show them the true light and cast out their wrong-minded thinkings.

Or, not succeeding at that, to cast the experiencers themselves out.

Possessing People

According to St. Luke, Satan can enter into people and cause them to perform evil: "Then Satan entered into Judas, called Iscariot." (Luke 22:3)

The Truth about Satan

"He's not the enemy of God, his name really isn't Lucifer, and he isn't even evil. And as far as leading Adam and Eve astray, that was a bad rap stemming from a case of mistaken identity . . ." So says University of California at Los Angeles professor Henry Ansgar Kelly. His book *Satan: A Biography* sets the record straight according to historical renderings and religious teachings. "Satan's basic intention," claims Professor Kelly, "is to uncover wrongdoing and treachery, however overzealous and unscrupulous the means. But he's still part of God's administration." (See appendix C for the book's reference.)

The False Light, or What's in a Name?

Another name for Satan/the Devil that we are all familiar with is Lucifer—a name that became popular in the Middle Ages. But what may not be familiar, and what's of particular interest in this chapter, is the meaning of the name. "Lucifer" means "light-bearing." Because of two Biblical passages, one from the Old Testament and one from the New, plus the image of the Devil as a fallen angel, he has been identified with the morning (or day) star:

> "How are thou fallen from heaven, O Day Star, son of the morning." (Isa. 14:12)
>
> "He said unto them, 'I watched Satan fall from heaven like a flash of lightning.'" (Luke 10:18)

Watch Out for Disguises

Why does Satan disguise himself as light? Because he often takes on the appearance of God in order to deceive, and light is God's most common characteristic. It's as some form of light (in this case, fire) that God appears before Moses (Exod. 3:2–4, 19:18), and Jesus refers to himself as "the light of the world" who brings "the light of life" (John 8:12).

The Voice of God

In the Old Testament, Abraham is said to have heard the voice of God telling him to bring his "only son Isaac" to a mountaintop and "offer him there [to God] as a burnt offering" (Gen. 22:2). Without delay—without even conferring with his wife, Isaac's mother!—Abraham prepared to do so. How many of us, upon meeting Abraham on the road and learning what he was about to do, and why, would have casually accepted what Abraham would have told us and gone about our way? And yet, Abraham's actions proved to be correct.

In the Christian Church, Isaiah's Old Testament figurative reference to a Babylonian king who had fallen from power came to be connected with Luke's New Testament reference to Satan, whom legend said had fallen from heaven when he rebelled against God. Lucifer and Satan became mistakenly synonymous once this connection occurred.

Add to this the reference in 2 Cor. 11:14 of Satan as being able to disguise himself as an "angel of light" and you have the basis for fundamentalist claims that the light seen by near-death experiencers in their episodes is in fact "the tempter" tempting them.

Remember, according to New Testament and many church teachings, one doesn't get to go to heaven and see the afterlife until the end of days, and then only through the grace and faith in Jesus. So, if near-death experiencers are seeing heaven and the afterlife now, and they're not even all Christians, obviously the light that's beckoning them must be the doings of the accursed "angel of light."

We Got Here First

Another bone of contention that many religions have with near-death experiencers is the experiencers' explicit claim of direct revelation. In part, resistance to accepting these claims is understandable. If someone stood up in your place of worship, or approached you at the office, and said, "Last night I spoke with God and God told me to [fill in the blank]," you—and probably everyone else within earshot—would most likely be wary. And with good reason. After all, we hear enough stories on the news about sociopaths and psychopaths who claim that their deeds were prompted by direct communion with God.

But there's a difference. Near-death experiencers aren't killing in the name of God, hating in the name of God, posing as cult leaders in the name of God, and so on.

New Word

Sacerdotalism is the teaching of and belief in the divine authority of the priesthood, of priests as being the essential mediators between humans and God.

The Privileged Possession of Clergy

Near-death experiencers are saying that love is the cornerstone of life—and that death isn't the end of life. These are messages that are at the core of most religions. So why do so many of the clergy revile experiencers?

Because, unfortunately, some things have gotten out of hand in many religions and among their representatives. Since "possession is nine-tenths of the law," members of the clergy want to claim and preserve privileged possession of the right to commune directly with God. It's called *sacerdotalism.*

What Would Jesus Say?

Ironically, the clergy's behavior runs counter to what Jesus said, when he instructed us that we could do what he did and even more (John 14:12). Even though we are further instructed to believe in Jesus in order to be able to do this, the inference is quite clear—it is within our power to commune directly with God, to have direct revelation.

A recent development within the Catholic Church points to a growing change in theological thinking as concerns direct contact with the dead and the helpful guidance that can result. Reverend Gino Concetti, chief theological commentator for the Vatican newspaper, *L'Osservatore Romano,* wrote at length in a news article that "Communication is possible between those who live on this Earth and those who live in a state of eternal repose, in heaven or purgatory. It may even be that God lets our loved ones send us messages to guide us at certain moments in our life."

Rev. Concetti wrote in support of an American theologian whose friend had seen a ghost. The reverend said there were various explanations, but the important thing "is not to deny such things a priori." The key to the church's attitude, he explained, was the "Communion of Saints"—a belief in the communication possible between Christians, whether living or dead.

According to Rev. Concetti, the new

Intuition: Spirit's Gift

Interestingly, the early Christian Church valued intuitive gifts. Receiving or "channeling" guidance directly from the Holy Spirit was so prized, it was considered a necessary part of being a good Christian, according to Alan Vaughan in his book *Doorways to Higher Consciousness* (see appendix C). Saint Paul encouraged it; every male member of a congregation was expected to participate, as well as prophesy.

Basic Truths Revealed

John Tomlinson, director of research at American Institute of Health and Science (quoted early in this chapter), has a lot of say about what is emerging from near-death studies. He looks at the various stages many episodes appear to follow and recognizes in doing so the revelation of basic truths. He defines these as: We have a soul, there is life after death, we are held accountable for our conduct on Earth, beings exist beyond time and space who play an active role in our lives, and we are implored to foster Godliness at every turn irrespective of circumstances. He believes these extrapolated truths from near-death experiencer stories offer a basis for common ground we can all live with—to our mutual benefit.

I would add to this: each near-death experiencer's episode and what can be learned from it, belongs to the entire human family—not just to that person, nor to that person's religion or personal philosophy.

Catholic catechism specifically endorsed the view that the dead could intercede on Earth and quotes the dying Saint Dominic telling his brothers: "Do not weep, for I shall be more useful to you after my death and I shall help you then more effectively than during my life."

Direct revelation from On High, direct communication via the Holy Spirit, direct communication between the living and the dead—religious doctrine is slowly acknowledging the value of what has always been done, and still is.

I must admit, though, that before I had my near-death experiences or heard of the phenomenon, had someone stood up in my church and made such a claim, I would have been hesitant to accept what he or she had to say. And there's nothing wrong with that. A healthy skepticism is wise to have.

But that's not the real issue. The problem is that near-death experiencers and those who study and are intrigued by the experience—adults as well as children—are often scorned, ridiculed, and shamed. To question in the name of objectivity is one thing, but to condemn in the name of piety is quite another.

It's reasonable to ask questions, to hold near-death experiencers and researchers accountable for their claims. Still, while we're doing this, let's also remember two other sayings of Jesus:

> "It is not what goes into the mouth that defiles a person, but it is what comes out of the mouth that defiles." (Matt. 15:11)
>
> "Do not judge so that you may not be judged." (Matt. 7:1)

The Forgotten and Underreported

Remember what has just been said as you consider this statement: There's another way to look at hell.

Hell's Other Side

In this chapter, we've been delving into religious thought, the ministry, and the various complaints people of faith can have about near-death experiences. And we've talked a lot about the devil, Satan, and hell. Nancy Evans Bush, a pastoral counselor and specialist in unpleasant near-death states advises: "Near-death experiences, both radiant and distressing, belong to a family of experiences of the deep psyche; the family that includes experiences of prayer, meditation, shamanic initiation, near-death, and other circumstances . . . Distressing experiences are more common than has been thought . . . They are underreported out of fear, shame, social stigma, the sense that the person cannot burden others with such horrific information, or other reasons."

Unpleasant near-death experiences speak to the very heart of religious belief in regard to the existence of heaven and hell, and far more powerfully than do the pleasant type. The book *Blessings in Disguise,* by Barbara R. Rommer, MD (see appendix C), presents us with one of the largest studies yet done on this subject. Some of her comments will help us prepare ourselves for part 4 of this book—"Taking a Leap Beyond."

Dr. Rommer has this to say in summarizing her study:

"First, the Less-Than-Positive [unpleasant] event is an impetus to reevaluate previous choices, actions, reactions, thoughts, and belief systems. Second, an LTP event may occur because the person's mindset immediately prior to the experience was less

Churches Are Changing

A Vatican-endorsed editorial says we no longer need to fear an afterlife of fire, brimstone, and Satan-organized torture. The *Christian Century* (Sept. 22, 1999) reports that a kinder, gentler hell is in vogue among those who know. "Hell exists not as a place but as a state, a way of being of the person who suffers the pain of the deprivation of God," according to the editorial in *Civilta Cattolica.*

Heaven and Hell

The term "kingdom of heaven" in Aramaic is *malkutha dashmaya.* This phrase does not refer to a heavenly state after death. It means "the kingdom of God," that is, God's sovereign counsel. Jesus used the term "heaven" euphemistically to refer to "God." Jesus' mission was to bring a heavenly state here on Earth. His message was never about going to heaven after one had become deceased. Even the expression *gehenna dnoohra,* "hellfire," is not a place where supposedly evil people go after death for eternal punishment. In Aramaic, "hellfire" is an idiomatic term and means "mental torment and regret." (From Rocco Errico, ThD, PhD, an expert in the language of Jesus and Biblical idioms. Refer to his article "Heaven & Leaven," *Science of Mind,* November 2005.)

than loving. Third, I feel that many of the examples have proven that an LTP may occur secondary to negative programming during childhood. When one grows up programmed to expect hellfire and brimstone, then that is what projected to the cosmos and that is exactly what one may experience.

"We are the ones who determine this. It is our very consciousness, essence, soul, spirit, or life force, that projects what it is that we *need* to endure. If it is something that we need to *shock* us into change, then that is what we project and that is what we are shown. Remember, the cosmic forces, including a supreme entity, can certainly 'read' our needs.

"Our needs will far outweigh and take precedence over our wants . . . Our ultimate need (that which will make a significant difference in how we continue to live this present life time more meaningfully) is ultimately what we are shown."

An Important Message

"All features of the near-death experience suggest an urgent need in society to include the extraordinary."

—Allan Kellehear, PhD

Part 4

Taking a Leap Beyond

The stories we tell each other are often richer than our vocabularies. That's why some stories suffer and their meanings become fuzzy because the words we have available fall short. And sometimes we fail to communicate at all because we're shy about telling our stories, fearing that we'll be laughed at or rebuked.

If you've had an otherworldly experience, you can't keep it to yourself. You feel like you've had some breakthrough in life into other realms and planes of existence—other realities beyond the ordinary.

In these chapters, we'll look at spiritual experiences—which include near-death experiences—and we'll stretch all definitions of what's possible and what's impossible. Language isn't always adequate to describe such things, but I'll do my best.

16

Viewing Storylines in Different Ways

There are more things in heaven and earth, Horatio, than are dreamt of in your philosophy.

—Shakespeare, *Hamlet*

Consciousness researcher and philosopher Ken Wilber almost single-handedly launched the transpersonal revolution in psychology several decades ago with the publication of *The Spectrum of Consciousness* (see appendix C). His comments about the rift between science and religion are notable: "When you take into account that 90 percent of the world's population has a religious outlook based on some kind of mythology—God the Father and so on—and that the standard scientific view gives these myths as much credibility as they give the tooth fairy—you see the problem clearly. There's an enormous split between reason and meaning that must be healed."

You've had a good taste of this split and its many ramifications in the previous part of this book. We now step beyond the "party lines" of either science or religion to view near-death scenarios differently.

What has recently occurred in the field of anthropology reflects what happens when experiencer storylines are reconsidered. I refer here to the April 26, 1999, *Newsweek* article "The First Americans," by Sharon Begley and Andrew Murr. This article reports that the old theory about the first Americans being East Asians of Mongoloid descent who trekked across the Bering Straits has been proven untrue. A melting pot of migrants, some from Europe and Polynesia, were here, and in large numbers, thousands of years before. And they bore no resemblance, genetic or otherwise, to American Indians. Both the spiritual traditions of native peoples (the subjective view) and decades of meticulous

scientific fieldwork (the objective view) are called into question by this finding.

We must have the courage to do the same thing regarding near-death states as has been done in the field of anthropology—look again, only this time through a broader lens. Our understanding of near-death scenarios and how they are described hinges on our willingness to consider all the variables.

Sometimes We Can Mix Things Up

I have yet to meet a single near-death experiencer who consciously stretched the truth or exaggerated about anything—at least at first. I have met many adult and teenage experiencers, though, who either twisted their story around or changed parts of it once they made the discovery that their episode didn't match the "classical model" or follow what has become "standard fare." Any perceived deviation in their episode scenario from the established norm was embarrassing to them, and they felt it set them "apart." Some feared they might be judged unfairly by others if their case "differed."

The discomfort of feeling as if they don't fit—either in their family and among coworkers because the incident even happened in the first place, or with fellow experiencers and those more knowledgeable of the phenomenon who might criticize them in some manner—is a strong factor that can influence how story components are positioned in a storyline. This is why I urge teenagers and adults to consider their episodes from various angles before they decide what they mean. There may be several perfectly valid ways to interpret both the imagery and its message.

Some child experiencers did the same thing as their older counterparts, but for different reasons. With those I interviewed, overly zealous or assertive family members and teachers were the biggest problem. The influence they had over the children became quite plain to me when I saw kids check for approval when they said anything, and in the way they would mimic their elders' words.

With youngsters, patience is crucial. Their stories need to be heard in a loving and nonjudgmental way, with lots of time given to them to play with the "idea" of what they experienced. That play is essential if they are ever going to make their episode scenario part of their daily life in a healthy manner, and find any meaning that is relevant to them as they mature.

A Wake-up Call for Researchers

After telling me about a long and involved interaction between her and angels, Jesus, and God, the little girl I was speaking with went on to proudly announce that everything she experienced during her near-death scenario was exactly what the nun had taught her in the Catholic school she attended, and wasn't it wonderful that she was "chosen" to prove that the nun was right. Her parents then uttered "Amen," and marched her away. This interview session was a wake-up call for me, and I promptly changed how I worked with kids because of it—no more adults present during interviews, and greater emphasis placed on nonverbal body language to inspire their response.

How We Can "Stage" Storylines

Language, emotions, and cultural and religious traditions and taboos are all tightly interwoven in the tapestry of near-death states and what we assign to them. This sets the stage for how scenario storylines are believed and expressed, as if the "telling of the tale" were on some level a type of "theater."

Words Won't Do

Experiencers insist that the power of their near-death event lies beyond the power of words to express. It is *ineffable.*

Experiencers need to talk about what happened to them, but often they can't. The struggle for words can lead to a frustrating exercise in wasted time and effort. What spills out is usually disconnected strings of images, sounds, and feelings that wind up with catchall kinds of labels that "make do." A figure robed in the brilliance of "ten thousand suns," for example, is called "God," a slightly lesser light-form is named "Jesus," and the bright realm itself is dubbed "heaven." The labels are picked from the language at hand and from the particular vocabulary that language consists of.

New Word

Ineffable refers to that which is incapable of being expressed or described. The term recognizes that some things are simply inexpressible, unspeakable, and unutterable. The further implication is that even to attempt description is somehow to defile or nullify the enormity of what was witnessed or experienced.

The words finally chosen to describe "that which cannot be described" will always match the experiencer's knowledge at the time, along with vocabulary

Guys Are Shy

Kenneth Ring, PhD, considered to be the "dean" of near-death researchers, has discovered an interesting oddity during his long career in the field. He found that 70 percent of the female experiencers he spoke with readily shared what happened to them, but only 30 percent of the males were as cooperative—even though both men and women have near-death experiences in almost equal numbers.

usage. Should that individual expand his or her command of language and available resources later on, descriptions of the phenomenon will alter accordingly, as if the storyline setting had magically enlarged. The need to communicate eventually overrides any frustration or fears the individual may have about feeling inadequate.

The Power of Emotions

What experiencers feel as they revive (i.e., their emotional state), plays a significant role in the way they verbally respond to the phenomenon. For instance, if an individual is frightened by what happened, negative terminology will be used—even if what was experienced was gloriously wonder-filled. But if the experiencer is somehow encouraged or uplifted by an episode, even one that was disheartening or distressing, positive terminology will prevail. Emotions, then, tend to drive speech.

"Emotional Speak"

The mere act of naming something confines it to a mode of thought. The struggle to find words beyond the familiar all too often gives way to the power of words to decide for us what something is. Yet, in attempting to describe the ineffable, emotions have a way of overtaking spoken language and becoming a vocabulary unto themselves.

You cannot listen for long to near-death experiencers without hearing a flood of "emotional speak." For these people, the heart, the gut, and all that we associate with them are flung wide open. Experiencers return consumed with new-found feelings that affect the description and interpretation of scenarios just as surely as words do, affecting how storylines are presented or "staged." This spills out in vivid facial expressions, excessive gesturing, fluid or jerky body movements, feet that can't hold still; tears, frowns, chortles, sighs, and laughter.

Afterward, how experiencers feel about what happened, how they feel about how others respond to them, how they feel about what their episode might mean, how they feel about the aftereffects and the fact that they seem to be changing from who they once were—all of this—overlays any description and any interpretation they give to their scenario. Accounts unburdened by emotional overlays come only from the very young. There is no sense of "theater" with kids. They are "straight arrows"—quick, direct, brief.

Thought Guards

Emotions are primary. Positive or negative, they color near-death scenarios and give each episode its depth. How storylines are staged illustrate this. Yet social and religious traditions and taboos tend to override how all of us think and feel about the prospect of direct revelation of spiritual truth. It would be a mistake to say that near-death experiences free the individual from all the influences or stigmas of their social order. As newly freed as experiencers claim to be, the fact is they are still tethered to the world they left.

How most of us are raised and what we come to believe because of that instruction has more to do with how we were "programmed" to fit our society's expectations of us than it does with how we might have been prepared to contribute. This programming or conditioning (imprinting) begins early and influences everything we are exposed to or experience. Because of this, people seldom become creative, abstract thinkers capable of independent thought until their middle years, if then. This programmed bias operates like "thought guards" that ensure the majority never stray too far from "that which is acceptable."

After a near-death episode, experiencers, literally overnight, become for the most part full-blown abstract, creative thinkers. They have been exposed to worlds more real than this one, truths more pertinent, ways of living more enlivened. This is both good and not so good. The good part is apparent. The not-so-good part involves that programming.

What is needed in today's modern societies is a language that accommodates the spiritual/religious experience of its citizenry in a way that honors the individual. To do less is to deny that sense of worthiness everyone deserves to have.

To the Point

"I saw Jesus. But he told me it wasn't my time and I need to go back and be with my daddy."

—Victoria, three years old, after being revived by a police officer. Her mother lost control of the car; it flipped over into a ditch. (Story on page 7 in the book *The New Children and Near-Death Experiences*—see appendix C.)

Can You Imagine That

I've had experiencers apologize to me for having been in the presence of God or for hearing Jesus speak to them, as if such wonders were forbidden—not only by society, but by the religious traditions that shape society. I've even noticed that experiencers will sometimes describe and interpret the elements in the storyline of their scenario according to whatever belief system feels the "safest."

Another Look at the Need Factor

The personal needs of the individual experiencer play out to some degree

How Language Has Changed

All early alphabets were actually a code language tied to a desire for Holy Revelation. Every one of them had as a central core the need to communicate a relationship with the Source of All Being. Thus, the names of God revealed the power of God through the forms God takes as the Logos—the sound of the Holy Word. Religion was life and life was religion. The written word was sacred; those who could read it, a priestly caste. This situation changed when growing populations demanded the practicality of record keeping and mass literacy. Currently, there is a worldwide trend toward reestablishing the importance of spiritual terminology and creating a "dictionary" for what seems to be ineffable.

in scenario storylines. Here's a synopsis of some of the things I've already pointed out to you that indicate this:

- Most episodes happen during major junctures or times of unusual stress in the individual's life, when guidance or direction would be most helpful.

- With young children, relatives and caregivers can be affected as well—to the degree that it's almost as if the child had the experience for them. Yet the extent to which the episode transformed the youngster becomes more apparent as he or she matures, and can be a quiet but powerful directive in the life path chosen.

- Causes and conditions of death can reflect, at least symbolically, the experiencer's past or current growth patterns.

- Greeters on death's threshold always match (accommodate to) whatever is necessary to alert or calm the experiencer.

- As the episode deepens, the scenario's message parallels almost exactly the subconscious needs of the individual at that moment in time.

- Life reviews and "lecture" sessions cover material either omitted, ignored, or not yet learned in life by the individual involved. Previews alert to what might be the future—for good or ill.

- Afterward, the experiencer's behavior tends to shift to whatever has been undeveloped or partially developed—*physically* in the sense of brain function/nerve sensitivity, and *psychologically* in the sense of personal growth/maturity—as if whatever traits are missing in the individual's maturing process are now being "filled in."

Doesn't Matter

"I wasn't even upset that I had a dirty house."

—anonymous experiencer, from the research base of Scott Taylor, EdD

I Got What I Needed

I never cease to be amazed at how forthcoming experiencers are when asked to evaluate what happened to them. Almost to a person they say, "I got what I needed." This blunt answer suggests that another agenda may be in force besides that of the personality self: perhaps that of a greater version of the self—the soul. Whatever the truth of this, and it may never be proved one way or the other, the need factor is plainly obvious as to the timing, storyline, and outcome of near-death states—not in the sense of predetermination or wish fulfillment, but rather, in terms of a subconscious "agenda" of a higher order.

What impresses me the most is how the scenario people experience always catches their attention in exactly the way and manner that is the most effective for them. Near-death scenarios hardly ever touch on what you or I might expect considering the gravity of that person's life choices and deeds.

For instance, murderers hardly ever wind up in dungeons where hellish demons can prick them to pieces with hot pokers. Such criminals usually experience those scenes that infuse them with life's true meaning and purpose—after they have been subjected to "living through" on every level what they did to others. They are subjected to trading places rather than being punished. Those I know who experienced scenarios like this were so utterly shaken by what they went through that they never returned to a life of crime. One Mafia hitman, for example, after such an episode, devoted the rest of his life to serving the impoverished by dishing up meals in a church soup kitchen. His explanation? "I want to make up for what I have done."

The tendency to "get what we need" can sometimes be rather bizarre, as in the case of young children being greeted by the familiar on the other side of death—classmates and teachers quite alive. Once they relax into their scenario and feel more comfortable, the living disappear and imagery more typical of near-death states emerge.

A particular case I discuss in both *Children of the New Millennium* and *The New Children and Near-Death Experiences* involves a four-year-old who drowned in a backyard swimming pool. After being resuscitated, he blurted out that he was met "over there" by his little brother who told the story about Mommy having him pulled out of her tummy when she was thirteen. This shocker upset everyone, since the four-year-old was an only child (there was no "little brother") and because Mommy's tearful admission afterward set the record straight (about her secret abortion).

God Loves You

Howard Storm admits to once being a confirmed atheist who lived a mediocre life of little meaning. During his scenario, he experienced the depths of demonic humiliation and defilement and was painfully tortured. Then a voice inside him said, "Pray to God." When he did, darkness turned to light and Jesus appeared. Howard is now an inspired minister who finds life richly rewarding.

New Word

As sometimes happens, the initial greeter or even the background imagery first encountered during a near-death scenario can be an **accommodation**, meant either to relax or to alert an experiencer—rather than inform or enlighten. For instance, if the initial greeter is asked, "Is that what you really look like?" invariably that image will either disappear or shape-shift (e.g., an angel morphing into a globe of light). I came to regard such temporary images as "accommodations," because their purpose seemed to hinge on "setting the stage" or perhaps introducing the experiencer to a deeper and more meaningful phase of the episode.

There are many reasons to study this case. One question to ask is this: Would the four-year-old have responded so favorably to his close brush with death had he not been met by someone appearing younger than he to put him at ease? Another question concerns the parents. Did their son have his experience for them? Both parents were driven and materialistic achievers who were forced to reevaluate their lives and their marriage because of what happened. A divorce ensued.

Let's Reconsider Experience Types

The subtle psychological profile I discovered that seems to support each of the four types of near-death experiences appears somehow to be "predictive" in the sense of who has what. This profile is consistent with the vast majority of people I interviewed regardless of their race, educational level, status, religious beliefs, or location.

Although much more research needs to be done to establish how universal this profile is, so far it has withstood the scrutiny of researchers and experiencers alike.

As a reminder, here again is the profile, which we first discussed in chapter 2:

- *Initial Experience.* Usually encountered by those who seem to need the least amount of evidence for proof of survival, or who need the least amount of shakeup in their lives at that point in time. Often, this becomes a "seed" experience or an introduction to other ways of perceiving and recognizing reality.

- *Unpleasant and/or Hell-Like Experience.* Usually experienced by those who seem to have deeply suppressed or repressed guilts, fears, and angers, and/or those who expect some kind of punishment or discomfort after death.

- *Pleasant and/or Heaven-Like Experience.* Usually experienced by those who most need to know how loved they are and how important life is and how every effort has a purpose in the overall scheme of things.

- *Transcendent Experience.* Usually experienced by those who are ready for a mind-stretching challenge and/or individuals who are more apt to use (to whatever degree) the truths that are revealed to them. Seldom personal in content.

You could shorten this to read:

- *Initial Experience.* Awakening to a greater reality.
- *Unpleasant Experience.* Untangling false perceptions.
- *Pleasant Experience.* Recognizing true values and priorities.
- *Transcendent Experience.* Embracing universal oneness.

When you shorten the profile in this manner, it illustrates stages of development in the growth of human consciousness, both personally and en masse, as it expands to embrace the responsibility we all share as members of same universal family.

Moody's Discovery

During the early days of Raymond Moody's work, his publisher, Mockingbird Press, expressed concern about his reports of people who had returned from death and told astonishing stories. They felt his material was "a little skimpy" and asked if he could add something more. At his wife's suggestion, he went to the Atlanta library and looked up what existed on the topic of death and dying. He happened upon the Tibetan and the Egyptian versions of the Book of the Dead, and a compendium of Emanuel Swedenborg's writings about the spiritual world, citing his best known work, *Heaven and Hell* (self-published in London in 1758). From this additional information, Dr. Moody completed his seminal book, *Life After Life.*

The Teachings of Swedenborg

Precedents exist in Western society for the idea of a need factor and how it might function. One in particular comes from the voluminous writings of a Swedish genius by the name of Emanuel Swedenborg (1688–1772), who mastered the ability to "see" beyond the veil of death.

The prolific Swedenborg was a psychologist, philosopher, mathematician, geologist, inventor, metallurgist, mineralogist, botanist, chemist, physicist, zoologist, aeronautical engineer, assayer, musician, author, traveler, crystallographer, instrument maker, machinist, cabinetmaker, legislator, mining engineer, economist, editor, cosmologist, theologian, lens grinder, clockmaker, poet, linguist, biographer, reformer, astronomer, and bookbinder, among other things. Not content to sit on these laurels, he also made the first sketch of a glider-type airplane, and invented a submarine, machine gun, ear trumpet, and airtight hot-air stove. He discovered the function of ductless glands, the brain-lungs connection, and wrote and published the first Swedish algebra. At age fifty-six, he gave up the worldly sciences and became a seer and revelator, devoted to giving the world a new religious philosophy, which later became the New Jerusalem Church.

Leon S. Rhodes of Bryn Athyn, Pennsylvania, a member of the Swedenborgian New Church and the author of *Tunnel to Eternity: Swedenborgians Look Beyond the Near-Death Experience,* was kind enough to interpret some of Swedenborg's observations about what an individual faces after he or she physically dies.

According to Leon: "Several places in his thirty-volume accounts, he follows [what happens to] 'newcomers' [the newly dead] who are allowed to experience exactly what they thought heaven or hell would be like. Someone who expects to flutter about with winged cherubs playing harps and singing *hallelujah* is allowed to do precisely that until he realizes that this is certainly not a real heaven. Others expect to spend all their time (eternity) in prayer and glorification—until it is clearly demonstrated to them that this is a phantasy-to-be-abandoned. Even those convinced by their religious leaders that they will be tormented in hell-fire are given an experience to learn that this is only true if they have hell-fire in their hearts. In brief, this first experience is transitory and a preparation for the real life for which we have been created."

Leon continues: "This is why so many Catholics see the Virgin Mary and others report that the 'Being of Light' was Jesus—or perhaps their grandfather [imagery that accommodates the familiar or acceptable]. Swedenborg gently introduces us into the 'world of spirits' as a preparation for the real life we will choose for ourselves after we have passed the 'immigrant' state [as a spirit after death].

"From Swedenborg's remarkable books, we are taught that we are not 'thrown into hell' or 'elevated into heaven.' We do—just as we do now—find we are attracted to those others and the setting which reflects our own temperaments. We spontaneously gather in 'societies' with others like ourselves. This is itself a process of 'judgment.' We would do well to think about the environments we presently seek out, reminding ourselves that this will still apply after our own final near-death experience."

A Back-Glance at Shared Experiences

Swedenborg's visionary insights appear to confirm my own observations from several decades of investigating near-death accounts. During the talks I give, when I mention the subtle psychological profile, I've noticed that someone in the audience invariably asks: "Does this mean we always meet our own beliefs after we die? Do we really determine our hells and our heavens by our attitudes? Is it us doing all this to ourselves?"

On one hand, the answer to these questions seems to be yes. And there is ample evidence to back up this assumption. Yet, on the other hand, I must say "not necessarily," and here's why: The notion that we alone decide our heavens and our hells based on our own personal beliefs begins to fall apart when you examine shared and group experiences. These events offer a major challenge to any pat conclusion we might make about storylines or how we may regard great seers like Swedenborg—or even some of the mystical traditions of other cultures.

Consider the following:

- *Shared near-death states.* There are cases in which several experiencers seem to share in each other's episode; that is they have the same or similar elements, scenario type, or basic storyline. Usually, you encounter most of these when two or three people are involved in the same accident at the same time or are in the same general section of the hospital at the same time. Sometimes these states are experienced singly (one individual is not aware of the other during the episode but learns later on that both apparently had the same scenario). Sometimes the people involved are aware of each other, and are able to confirm the extent of that awareness after they are able to compare their separate stories.

- *Group near-death states.* These are rare, but they do occur. With this kind, a whole group of people simultaneously seems to experience the same or similar episode (as per previous). What makes these so spectacular and challenging is that all or most of the experiencers see each other actually leave their bodies as their scenario begins, then dialogue with each other and share messages and observations while still experiencing the near-death state. Their separate reports afterward either match or nearly so. Reports like these emerge most often from events of a harrowing nature that involve a lot of people.

Shared and group near-death experiences imply that no matter how sure we are that near-death states mean this or that, and are the result of whatever, no single idea, theory, or pat answer can explain them. Even clues from the powerful patterning that researchers like myself have identified fail to explain all aspects of the phenomenon.

Just as in the field of anthropology—where treasured beliefs and traditions as well as meticulous and evidential scientific fieldwork were challenged, if not overturned, by findings from a broader base of inquiry—we in the near-death community of researchers and experiencers are now faced with the same situation.

> **New Word**
>
> The **bardos**, or stages an individual supposedly journeys through after death, are detailed in the Tibetan Book of the Dead (a chronicle of tales from prehistoric Tibet). Descriptions given dovetail the various types of near-death states I discovered and the scenario elements originally identified by Dr. Moody. The Egyptian Book of the Dead is similar. Instruction in both warns that a person's beliefs and spiritual maturity influence his or her journey into the "hereafter."

Other Cultures—A Major Challenge

Researchers are now probing ever deeper into near-death reports from non-Western cultures, some preliterate, and what they are finding causes us all

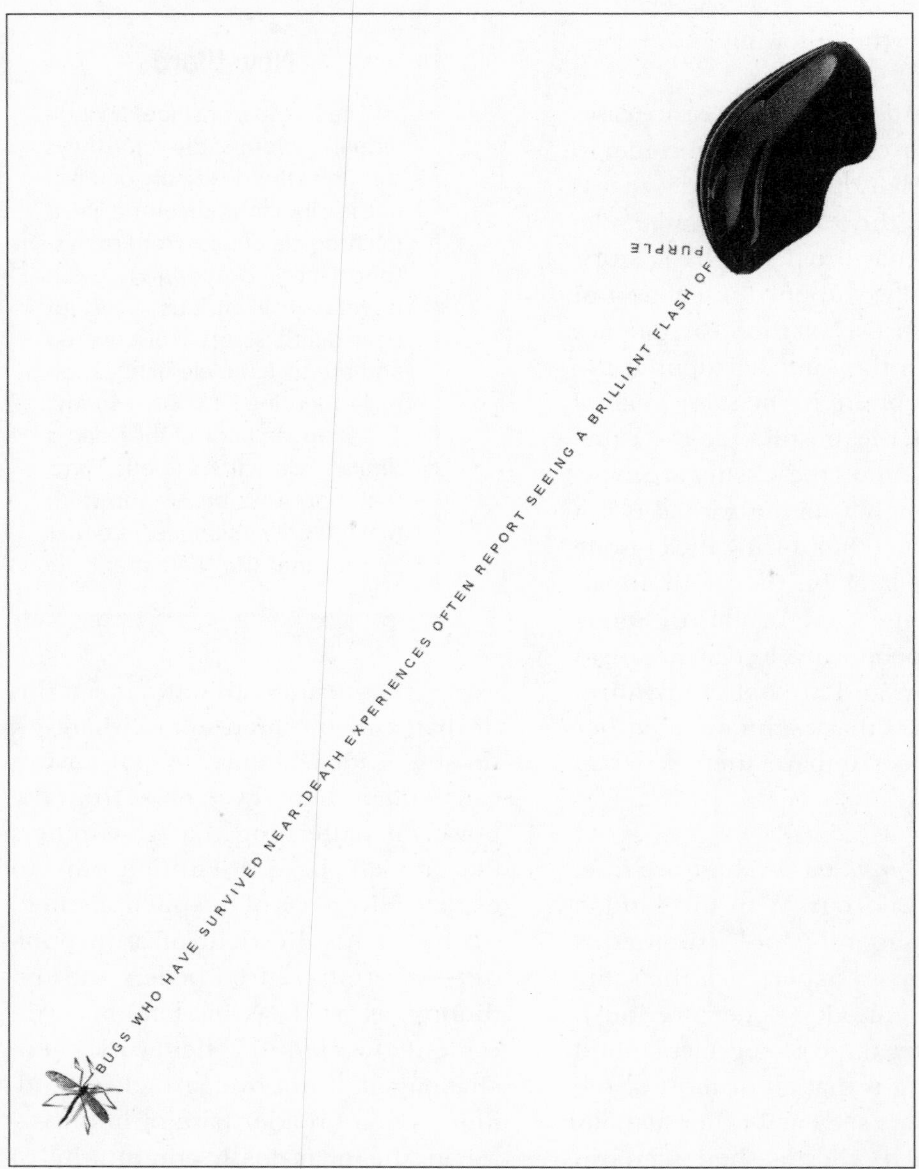

Giro, the maker of helmets and other accessories for bikers, ran this ad in one of their advertising campaigns (used with permission).

to pause. Just as what happened within the field of anthropology, we too are discovering some amazing differences and startling challenges to what we thought we knew about near-death states, as we enlarge the research base and look farther afield.

Chinese Earthquake Survivors

Feng Zhi-ying is a chief physician and Liu Jian-xun is a physician-in-charge, in the Department of Psychiatry at Anding Hospital, Tianjin, China. Together, they investigated stories from survivors of the 1976 Tangshan earth-

What Does This Really Mean?

An article published in a mainstream medical journal verified that near-death accounts reported to researchers prior to 1975 had essentially the same content as did accounts being reported today (*Journal of Nervous & Mental Disease,* G.K. Athappilly, Bruce Greyson, and Ian Stevenson, 2006, see appendix C). Another peer-reviewed journal published a similar article three years earlier (*Journal of Near-Death Studies,* Jeffrey Long and Jody Long). Both of these studies seem to establish that near-death scenarios are not influenced by individual cultures. Yet, since the bulk of research that has been done was conducted by Western researchers in Western societies, new work in the field that broadens the research base questions earlier views.

Severly Injured

Survivors of the Tangshan earthquake had been severely crushed when their homes were destroyed. Thirty-eight percent of them were housewives or educated youth who had followed Chairman Mao's instructions to settle down in the countryside and become the new class of peasants.

New Word

Yamatoots are messengers from Lord Yama, Lord of the Underworld, according to the Buddhist beliefs of Southeast Asia. In Thai society, these spirit beings pervade popular comics, advertisements, religious morality books and posters, and popular television shows. Religious tradition has it that Yamatoots are charged with escorting the newly dead to Lord Yama for judgment.

quake. All subjects in their study were patients at the Paraplegic Convalescent Hospital in Tangshan. Of the eighty-one survivors they interviewed, 40 percent had a near-death experience.

The typical patterning found in near-death states held up with those in China, but not the scenario elements commonplace to Western narratives. Differences were "sensations of the world being exterminated or ceasing to exist, a sense of weightlessness, a feeling of being pulled or squeezed, ambivalence about death, a feeling of being a different person or a different kind of person, and unusual scents." The predominant features encountered: "feeling estranged from the body as if it belonged to someone else, unusually vivid thoughts, loss of emotions, unusual bodily sensations, life seeming like a dream, a feeling of dying, a feeling of peace or euphoria, a life review or 'panoramic memory,' and thinking unusually fast."

Although some of these elements seem similar to Western cases, most deviate just enough to cause Zhi-ying

Asian Golden Rule

"The most popular expression of the laws of karma in Southeast Asia is the formula: 'Do good; receive good. Do bad; receive bad.'"

—Todd Murphy

and Jian-xun to speculate that race, religion, psychological, and cultural backgrounds might be what accounts for the difference. (Zhi-ying and Jian-xun, 1992; see appendix C.)

Yamatoots in Thailand

Todd Murphy, a Buddhist theologian interested in neurology, has done a study of near-death accounts in Thailand, especially of child experiencers. He believes Thai cases are indeed culture-bound and can be understood within the framework of beliefs and customs unique to Southeast Asia.

Murphy points out that Lord Yama is a wrathful being, believed to assign souls to appropriate rebirths after death. In so doing, a person could be reborn as a human with any social status and any degree of attractiveness, as any type of animal, into any one of fourteen hells, or into any of nine heavens. Near-death accounts from Thailand, then, often feature Yamatoots, the messengers of Lord Yama, instead of angels or light beings. Out-of-body experiences in these accounts are commonplace. Tunnels are virtually absent, as are panoramic life reviews, light, and profoundly positive affects. Facing one's karma usually predominates; often incidents from the individual's life are read from a book or declared during a kind of courtroom setting. Scenario elements tend to be both positive and negative and can involve stern lectures, criticisms, judgments, along with revelations of one's future if the individual is told to return.

"It may be," says Todd Murphy, "that NDEs of all cultures share common patterns, but that these patterns are obscured by the different cultural phenomena through which they manifest." (Refer to Murphy, 2001, in appendix C.)

Some Comparisons from Dr. Kellehear's Research

Typically Western: Experiencer moving through a tunnel or cylinder such as a pipe, being shot through a tailpipe.

Typically Non-Western: Walking through dark fields or subterranean caves, emerging through the throat of a lotus flower.

The Work of Allan Kellehear, PhD

With a broad background in death and dying, loss, health social sciences, and religious experience, Dr. Kellehear has specialized in non-Western near-death states. His work covers cases from Asia, the Pacific Region, Native Americans, and various preliterate hunter-gatherer peoples. Here are some comments on what he has discovered:

- Out-of-body experiences are common throughout, as are reports of supernatural beings and the existence of other worlds besides this one.

- Few experiencers report anything like a tunnel.

- People with nonlinear beliefs do *not* have life reviews (e.g., for Australian Aborigines, life is like a Mobius strip—you are born and born and born—an unending wraparound).

- Life reviews are a cultural function of individuality, reflecting one's interior self and linear concept of time. In many cultures, however, the "collective" or group consensus predominates.

- Experience descriptions cannot be separated from the language used to describe them. The culture itself provides the crucial components.

On the basis of his cross-cultural studies, Dr. Kellehear suspects that features such as tunnels and life reviews are actually signs of brain development. He points out, "You find them mostly in Western societies, but not in preliterate ones."

When we were reconsidering experience types earlier in this chapter, I illustrated how initial, unpleasant, pleasant, and transcendent experiences could be viewed as states of development in the growth of human consciousness. What Dr. Kellehear further suggests is that even the scenario components themselves may reflect evolutionary changes in the human brain and how it functions. I do not regard the absence of tunnels as being as significant as he regards it, since not that many people in any society report them, but the almost complete absence of life reviews in non-Western cultures and what that might imply about the individuation process is an important observation.

As we widen the lens of study and dig deeper into near-death accounts, new opportunities to explore the mysterious are revealed.

17

Some Striking Effects

> Man is a stream whose source is hidden—I am constrained every moment to acknowledge a higher origin for events than the will I call mine.
>
> —Ralph Waldo Emerson, *The Over-Soul*

Experiencer testimony cannot be ignored—from toddlers barely old enough to speak in sentences, kids trudging off to school, teens whispering to each other, adults scratching their heads. There are millions of them, these near-deathers, and their numbers are growing.

We need new vocabularies and new symbols to accommodate them. Religious teachings several thousand years old need to be brushed off and reread, this time in consideration of the phenomenon. And science, specifically medical science, needs to reevaluate the discoveries of leading-edge scientists and researchers of near-death states. A whole new world is emerging right under our noses, if we would but awaken to the view.

True, we can rationalize away a few of the findings in the field of near-death studies, but we can't even begin to explain the core drama, its clarity and consistency over time, and how lives are transformed—most of them

Hello, Down There

"Research in near-death experiences suggests that after death a person is still alive in some other form. British scientists report that many people who have been brought back to life in emergency rooms are able to recount in detail how their souls had exited their bodies and floated above the medical personnel."

—*Epoch Times*, New York City, Jan. 16, 2005

Vacating the Body

Michael Sabom, MD, interviewed more than a hundred cardiac-arrest survivors early in his career. Thirty-two of them claimed to have vacated their bodies and watched their own resuscitation. When he compared their descriptions with twenty-three patients who did not undergo a near-death state but guessed what one might have been like if they had, he found that none of the experiencers made a single error, but twenty of the twenty-three made serious mistakes. Experiencers even correctly detailed readings on medical machines that were not in their line of vision, and described other circumstances they should not otherwise have been able to know.

permanently. We are constrained to consider, as Emerson wrote, that perhaps another will besides that of individual experiencers must somehow be involved. There are too many coincidences, too many miracles, and too many manifestations of spirit for the impossible not to be possible—for "mystery" not to be real.

Poof! Go Limitations

Research of near-death and near-death-like states continuously "pushes the envelope" regarding what is believable and what is unbelievable. It's a fact that astonishing occurrences are now so commonplace, they're often "tossed off" as natural to the phenomenon. Our minds are stretched again and again because this is so. Whether you are a fundamentalist Christian, Moslem, Buddhist, Wiccan, New Ager, or neurologist, the near-death experience will challenge whatever beliefs you hold dear. Guaranteed!

The unerring accuracy of experiencers to give testimony about details they could not have known is striking. Let's look at some examples.

The Blue Tennis Shoe

In her book *After the Light,* Kimberly Clark Sharp talks about a Hispanic migrant laborer named Maria who had suffered a massive heart attack. While on duty as a social worker at Harborview Medical Center in Seattle, Washington, Kimberly was asked to check on Maria, as Maria seemed upset and was behaving strangely. After struggling with language differences, Kimberly managed to learn that the woman had been floating near the ceiling looking down on her body during her crisis. She was able to provide precise details of her resuscitation and about the people in the room—where they stood, what they did, what each said—as well as the placement of machinery and the movement of paper on the floor from the electrocardiogram. These details could be verified, and all of them were.

But that wasn't all. Maria mentioned how she had moved away from her lofty perch to a point outside her hospital room where she could look down at the emergency room entrance. She described the curvature of the driveway, vehicles driving in one direction, and the automatic doors. She remembered staring closely at an object on a window ledge about three stories above the ground. It was a man's dark blue tennis shoe, well-worn, scuffed on the left side where the little toe would go. The shoelace was caught under the heel. To satisfy Maria, Kimberly began to look for the shoe. She found nothing on the east side, nothing on the north. "I was four rooms into the west side of the building when I pressed my face against a window pane, peered down on yet another ledge, and felt my heart go thunk. There it was."

Carefully opening the window and reaching for the blue shoe, Kimberly's own near-death experience, which she had had years earlier and still could not quite accept, suddenly overlaid her present activity. At the moment she validated Maria's story, she realized that her own story was also true. When she presented the shoe to Maria, Maria gave it back—as a reminder that they both had once been visitors in the bright worlds on the other side of death. What happened to these two women became the talk of Harborview.

Countless people heard about the affair and marveled at the shoe.

Years later, long after Kimberly had lost the shoe during one too many moves, she realized that there was no way Maria could have seen the shoe as clearly as she did, especially the tucked-away shoelace and scuff mark, unless she was hovering midair directly in front of the shoe, three stories up. Kimberly's adventure with the shoe has been called into question, since no one of late has been able to locate Maria. But at the time, many people talked to Maria and saw the shoe. Because of this, I don't consider the case to be hearsay, as some researchers do.

Skeptics Backtrack

A team of scientific debunkers investigated the blue-shoe case. They took photographs to prove that Maria could have seen the shoe from the window. They could not explain, however, how she saw the scuff mark and the shoelace caught under the heel, especially since she was confined to bed at the time. Nor could they account for most of the other details she saw while out of body.

The White Boy Charred Black

In *Beyond the Light,* I wrote of Margaret Fields Kean, who nearly died in 1978 after being hospitalized for about three weeks with severe phlebitis. A blood clot had passed to her heart and lungs, and she became deathly ill. She was then given injections for nausea that, due to the blood thinners she had previously received, caused internal hemorrhaging. Pandemonium reigned as she slipped away. While absent from her body, she witnessed the scene below her, then heard and saw—right through the walls—people in the waiting room down the hall, as well as nurses at their station. She also knew their thoughts.

Margaret went on to have a transcendent near-death experience in which she instantly knew and understood many things, including her future,

Being a Healer: Gift or Curse?

The case of Margaret Fields Kean is similar to what happens to Ellen Burstyn's character, Edna, in the 1980 movie *Resurrection,* directed by Daniel Petrie. In the movie, Edna experiences clinical death as the result of a car accident, has a near-death episode, and returns to life with the amazing ability to heal. The resistance and difficulties she encounters not only touch upon some of what Margaret went through, but reflect what the larger number of near-death experiencers face as they seek both to integrate the phenomenon into their daily lives and to use their new abilities to help others (fulfill their mission).

and the fact that she would become a healer. This completely contradicted her vision of herself prior to that moment in her life, for she was content being a super-mom farmwife who rode horses, taught Bible classes, led 4-H and Girl Scout groups, gardened, canned, and baked bread. A healer? Ridiculous!

Yet when Margaret revived, she immediately began to heal other patients in the room around her by "reaching out" to them with her mind. Then she "projected" what seemed to be her body into the isolation room of a white boy charred black by severe burns. She "sat" next to him on the bed, introduced herself, and proceeded to counsel him about his purpose in life. She told him it was okay if he chose to die as God was loving and he had nothing to fear.

Months later, while continuing her recovery and still in great pain, Margaret was attending a horse show when a couple, hearing the loudspeaker announce her daughter's name as a winner, sought her out. They were the parents of the severely burned boy. Before he died, he had told them about meeting Margaret and relayed all the wonderful truths she had told him about God and about life.

The parents were thrilled to have finally located Margaret so they could say thanks for what she had done for their son. The dying boy had identified her by name—even though the two had never met or spoken in the physical world. Nor had any nurse seen Margaret in the boy's room. Nor had it been possible that Margaret could have known if the isolation room was even occupied, much less who might be there.

Faced with the task of "physician, heal thyself," Margaret Fields Kean successfully facilitated her own healing, and later that of thousands of others, before she moved to South Africa where she taught the native healers of Swaziland and Transkei her techniques. Margaret trained many people before she left the United States. Her numerous students have now become teachers and carry on in her stead since she retired. (To contact some of those she trained, see appendix E.)

Poof! Go Illnesses

Occasionally, individuals undergo miraculous remissions of their illnesses, sometimes complete healings, either as

Mindsight

In his book *Mindsight,* Kenneth Ring details his investigation of near-death states among the blind, with 80 percent claiming to have possessed sight during their episode. Since fourteen of these people were blind from birth, it's questionable exactly what they saw. Nonetheless, all of them did experience exceptional states of expanded sensory awareness that seemed to them like what sight might be.

Hold Everything!

One of the more unusual outcomes of near-death experiences is where previous symptoms of illness and affliction, both self-induced and natural, disappeared completely afterward. Jeffrey N. Howard, PhD, of Wichita State University, has been researching this anomaly, and he has discovered that near-death states not only facilitate sudden and spontaneous remission of physiological symptoms and physical affliction, but they also extend healing properties into the personal lives and private relationships of experiencers. Although his preliminary finding—a 72.7 percent spontaneous remission—has yet to be verified by other researchers, it is still a stunning discovery!

part of their near-death scenario or upon reviving from it. So far, medical science has been unable to explain why or how anything like this could occur.

Here are a few cases that have been confirmed through medical testing:

- A young man diagnosed with advanced AIDS had a sudden drop in his HIV readings (viral load) after his episode. One year later, he was nearly HIV-free.
- The brain tumor that "killed" Mellen-Thomas Benedict (see chapter 2) was absent from brain scans taken shortly after he revived—and never reappeared. It was there beforehand and throughout his illness, measurable, and getting larger.
- The damage done to her heart from rheumatic fever, along with a serious heart murmur, were instantly healed after Muriel Kelly's childhood near-death episode. Years later, when she enlisted in the U.S. Navy, she passed the physicals with flying colors—her heart showing no trace whatsoever of her early trauma.

Even though there aren't that many instantaneous cures or reversals of physical handicaps, there are enough of them to warrant asking the question: How could this happen?

Poof! Goes Death's Sting

Tom Harpur, an Anglican priest turned journalist, has done some investigating on his own regarding near-death experiences that has added immensely to his understanding about the prospect of an afterlife. His book *Life After Death* seems headed for

How We Rack Up Nationwide

According to a 2006 survey conducted by Baylor Institute for Studies of Religion, 20 percent of Americans believe that the living can communicate with the dead. In an online survey of 10,000 members of Beliefnet (www.Beliefnet.com), 77 percent said they had felt the presence of a spirit, angel, or dead soul.

"classic" status in the unique way it explores the phenomenon in comparison to religious and spiritual traditions.

In the Canadian magazine *Maclean's* (April 20, 1992, page 40), Tom wrote: "It is now my conviction that it is the phenomena related to near-death experiences that have convinced humans from earliest times that there is life beyond the grave, rather than the other way around. Instead of it being the product of an attempt to deal with the enigma of death by projecting one's wishes into another world, the near-universal belief in a hereafter is, in my view, the attempt to express what has already become known, at different times and in different places, through direct experience."

Of all the avenues employed to seek some shred of proof that life might extend beyond death's door, findings from research of the near-death experience come the closest to qualifying as persuasive evidence.

Teaser Tidbits about the Living Dead

Although the appearance in near-death scenarios of deceased relatives and friends as quite alive is rather typical, occasionally there are reports that take your breath away.

Here's a sampling of some of those that defy explanation:

- It's not possible that while he lay "dying" of a cardiac arrest, Lloyd Haymon could have known that his parakeet, Doolittle, suddenly died. It was only through the appearance of his dead brother—with Doolittle perched upon his shoulder—in Lloyd's near-death scenario that Lloyd learned this (refer to chapter 11).

- There's no way Lynn could have known about a particular uncle who was killed in World War II, as it was a family secret that he ever even existed. All records concerning his brief marriage to her aunt were destroyed; utterance of his name was forbidden. Yet Lynn was met by him when she "died" during open-heart surgery. After her recovery, she told her family about him, giving his correct name, a description of the uniform he wore, and the fact that the baby he had fathered with her aunt (who had miscarried) was with him and was okay. This news so traumatized her family that the man she had once thought was her aunt's only husband refused to ever speak to her again (refer to chapter 4).

- No one can explain how the young woman "killed" in a car-truck accident was met in death by her supposedly healthy and quite alive father. Yet, numerous phone calls later, it was discovered that her father had died five minutes before she did, and in the manner she had detailed to her unbelieving relatives (refer to chapter 11).

- The family of Carroll Gray is still stunned by the fact that at the age of two, while "dead" of hypothermia, she spoke with a grandfather who had died several years before she was born. Several months after recovering, not only did she accurately describe him, she relayed numerous and exact details about the two-bladed pocket knife he let her play with and his gold watch and chain, including the fact that the watch had stopped at 1:17, that the knife casing had a decoration on it of a little shield surrounded by a flower garland and was dated 1917, and that her grandfather said they all belonged to her.

Stunned as her family was, no one would give her the "shiny things" promised to her during her "death," until, when she was twenty years old, her mother, while sorting through papers, was flabbergasted to find the grandfather's missing will. In it, he had bequeathed his watch, chain, and gold pocket knife to his granddaughter and namesake. At the time of his death, he had no granddaughter or namesake. Nor did anyone have any inkling that he expected to have one, or that through perhaps an act of *precognition* he was privy to futuristic knowledge. Carroll was finally presented with the treasures her grandfather said she could have when she "died" at the age of two (refer to chapter 4).

New Word

Precognition is a research term that refers to knowledge of a futuristic event or situation that was obtained through extrasensory means, rather than through the normal channels of information gathering. Traditionally regarded as a psychic talent, the ability of "knowing in advance" can be and often is taught in classes on psychic development.

A Typical Encounter with the Dead

The year was 1994. Alice Roberts of Athens, Alabama, was driving to work. Commuter traffic was heavy. She stopped at a light, reached across the seat for her soda, and then found herself walking through an underground tunnel, having to move aside an abundance of branches and roots so she could proceed to a brightness ahead of her.

"As I entered the opening," Alice explained, "there was a bridge with water flowing underneath. The water was crystal clear and I could see straight to the bottom. Two benches were on the other side. Both my maternal and paternal grandparents were sitting there. I was awestruck by the beauty of this place.

"Purple flowers hung from the trees and the grass was greener than I had ever seen. I was thinking, what am I doing here? when I saw a tall man standing on the bridge. He was wearing a long robe and held out his hands for me to come to him. He never opened his mouth, but read my thoughts as I read his.

Alice seeing her grandparents sitting on parklike benches, and her father standing on the bridge. Drawing by Alice's daughter, Heather Dawn Roberts.

"'Do you know who I am?' he asked. Immediately, I knew he was the father I never had, as he died when I was only nine months old. I felt so many emotions: joy, happiness, confusion, and sadness. I knew my father died a long time ago. Did this mean I was dead, too? I couldn't be dead. I had a family to raise.

"He took my hand in his and said, 'Alice, you have two choices. You can walk across this bridge and stay, or you can go back. I must warn you, though, that right now you are feeling no pain. If you choose to return, there will be a lot of pain and suffering, and a lot more heartache.'"

Alice had already surmounted a lifetime of trouble, but she chose to return. Her father smiled at her decision. "Take good care of my grandchildren," he told her. Before leaving, she requested that he give her something to prove that she had really seen him. He pointed to a small red mark on his face and said, "Ask your mom about this mark. If no one else believes you, she will." When Alice opened her eyes, she was trapped beneath the dashboard of her car. A strange man was on the hood with a sheet. She moved, and he yelled, "She's alive!" He asked that she not move again until they could get her out. This stranger said that some guy came over the hill doing eighty, and he never hit his brakes. "Lady, you've been lying there stone cold for fifteen minutes. We called the coroner."

As soon as she was able, Alice called her mother. "Mom, I have to tell you something. I saw my father and I need to know about this red mark on the side of his face." Her mother's reply took her breath away. She told her that at a Fourth of July celebration, a firecracker he had been holding in his hand exploded, leaving a red pockmark on the side of his face. None of the photos she had seen of her father while growing up showed the mark, nor did anyone, including her mother, ever mention it. Alice feels that her mother's validation proves that she really did die and that at long last she was finally able to see and speak with her real father.

The Unexpected from Violence

I've mentioned several times before how those caught up in the violence of suicide attempts and barbaric crimes can change utterly after having a near-death experience. The story about the reformed Mafia hitman that I mentioned in chapter 16 is quite true. Experiencers previously engaged in a life of crime do not return to such a destructive lifestyle afterward—at least none on record have.

But there's another aspect of violence I have not discussed. Imagine if you will what it would be like to grow up living with your own "murderer."

Carroll Gray had to. During most of the near-death episodes she experienced as a child (she had five), she witnessed—while she was out of her body and invisible to him—her father's torturous acts as he tried to kill her. She saw every detail each time, but could never convince anyone of his villainy when she sought help, as no one believed he was capable of such things. As an adult, she was forced, on more than one occasion, to hire bodyguards to protect her from him. "The monster is gone" is all she would say when he died.

Laura of San Francisco, California, had to also. At the age of three and a half she was raped, sodomized, and beaten to "death" by her drunken and enraged father. It was the middle of the night, and she was fast asleep when it occurred. Laura well remembers how horrific it was to return to life afterward and how, for years, her father would cruelly mock her for talking about the angels who came to help her that fateful night. But Laura's assessment of her ordeal, now that she is an adult, is most unexpected. She has allowed me to share this with you.

"I learned how to live with my

Even in Cartoons

On a particular episode of the popular television show *The Simpsons,* Bart Simpson's dog, Santa's Little Helper, flatlined while in surgery to straighten out his twisted stomach and had a near-death experience. During his episode, Santa's Little Helper left his body and traveled through a long, dark tunnel. He heard a voice say, "Go to the light, boy, go to the light." The pinpoint of light opened to reveal a huge, shining, golden gate with a small dog door at its base. The door flopped open, then abruptly closed, and Santa's Little Helper was whisked back to his canine body, where he quickly recovered and bounded into the arms of his cartoon family.

A Better Way

Regardless of age, those who experience near-death states typically shift their concerns afterward to issues of moral upliftment, service, and spirituality. What is truly incredible, though, is how they handle violence. Almost to a person, they shy away from violent speech and acts, preferring to use innovative and responsible ways to deal with conflict.

murderer for another fifteen years by learning what I could from him and leaving the rest. I learned that the most important phenomena in the universe are love, truth, and the quest for knowledge. I received a clear sense of my purpose in life and how I must achieve it. I was given the gift of foreseeing things before they happen and the ability to visualize events, images, and forms, and then bring them into being. I learned how to interpret the world around me, how to make connections between things, and how to see the big picture. I learned that we are wounded, and heal from deep wounds, not so that we may somehow be safe forever, but so that we may be wounded again in a new way."

Because of their tender age, both Carroll and Laura were unable to remove themselves from their violent environments. Yet each credited their near-death experiences with giving them a strong sense of morality, vision, and the courage to retain their sanity.

The Unexpected from Death Dreams

Early in my career as a researcher, I noticed that some people had most unusual death dreams. Not the kind where you dream you are going to die or see yourself in a coffin or hover above your funeral. Rather, the individuals actually experienced what seemed to be the physical process of dying as if that's exactly what they were doing, and then suddenly awakened with the same traumatic response of an individual who had just been resuscitated in a hospital.

I know medical science claims that it's impossible for anyone to dream of their actual physical death as it occurs. Yet that is exactly what some of the people I interviewed feel that they did.

Although this peculiarity happens to adults, I've discovered more of these cases with children—especially of school age, but more specifically around the time of puberty and the early teen years. Of the child experiencers I spoke with, the majority never told their parents or teachers about the incident out of fear that they would either be made fun of or be sent to a hospital. All of them were physically stressed afterward, and had great difficulty for a while negotiating tasks expected of them—as if their bodies needed time to repair themselves. A few were already under a doctor's care for various reasons. (For instance, one had rheumatic fever, another was fighting a serious staph infection, and still another suffered a sudden, sharp abdominal pain.) But the rest seemed to be reasonably healthy before they "died" during their strange dream.

To give you an idea of how complex and involved these death-dream/near-death episodes can be, I offer two as examples, one from a teenage experiencer and the other from an adult. What is presented here are brief renditions of the original accounts.

An Odd Falling Dream

Tom Meeres of southern New Jersey was fourteen when, on a summer night, his peaceful sleep turned into a terrible fall through a spiral or tunnel. Falling dreams are quite common. Tom had had them before and had experienced a similar sensation under anesthesia, so the thought "Here I go again" was of some comfort. Yet this "dream" was to be unlike anything he'd experienced before or since. It seemed to him as if he were dying.

As he felt his physical body shut down, the "self" he identified with as himself fell through a noisy tunnel with ribbed walls so fast and for so long that he became nauseated and gripped with terror. The fall ended when he found himself in a soft, velvety dark void that, although comfortable at first, became too isolating. The moment he thought about being stuck there forever, he recognized that he was in a cave and to the right was a round opening to a beautiful light. Drawn to the light, he floated out of the cave, noticing that below him was the sheer drop of an immense cliff. Fear paralyzed him at first, but the light helped him to fly.

Tom described his experience: "I'm high above a strange landscape with a river valley that seems to stretch out forever. The light suffuses everything so that forms are discernible only in shades of gray. All fear is gone and there's just a wonderful lightness of being. I am myself yet there is no feeling of separateness from the light." While sensing a city and people beyond his view, Tom glanced around and saw no shadows anywhere, just this incredible light. Then his grandparents appeared in front of him and, while they conversed, they urged him to return. That proved to be quite a task, as he had forgotten what cliff opening he needed to reenter in order to go back. He started to panic, but at last found the right one and fell through.

"The euphoria upon awakening," said Tom, "was greater than anything I have ever felt. Was it a dream? No, it was too real. Were the people my grandparents? They said they were, but what's important is that they care about me and that I have a purpose in life. Who can I tell about this? No one."

Tom went through bouts of depression and confusion afterward. He was unable to understand why he had died, why he had come back to life, and why he was now so different from before. He displayed learning enhancements (increased intelligence, abstract and clustered thinking), future memory episodes (the ability to "prelive" the future), incredible psychic abilities (knowing things impossible for him to know, hearing people's thoughts, and so on), low blood pressure—in fact, all of the aftereffects typical of near-death states. It wasn't until Tom read books about the near-death phenomenon that he made the connection with his own experience. He feels he really did physically die that night, although he

Dying while Asleep

Contrary to what you might suppose, it is possible to experience a near-death episode during a dreamed "death event." What arises from situations like these can mimic or match all of the elements and patterns typical of near-death states, including the lifelong aftereffects. It has been surmised that such individuals really do die while asleep, but revive before medical intervention is deemed necessary.

No Joke!

Death dreams can be literal! One man I interviewed said he fell fast asleep after having sex with a beautiful woman. During his sleep, he dreamt that he had a heart attack and died, then experienced a full-blown near-death episode. He awoke in a hospital and learned, much to his surprise, that he really had had a heart attack. His lady friend had dialed 911 after repeated attempts to awaken him had failed to produce any response.

has no medical proof to back up his claim.

A Blessing and a Curse

At the age of forty-one, in a hotel room in San Francisco, Ishtan Natarajan (whose story I told in chapter 1) had his last good night's sleep. He reports that before he went to sleep that night, he had an awareness that he had fulfilled his purpose in life and was ready to "go home." He slept so soundly that it was as if his physical body had collapsed and ceased all functioning. The next morning he seemed to "emerge" rather than awaken. There were strange scars on his neck that he couldn't explain, and he felt very strange, as if he had suddenly moved in consciousness and energetic vibration to another, higher level of existence beyond his physical state.

Suddenly, Ishtan could move energy around a room with just his eyes, see and work with a person's energy fields, give bliss to another by a simple touch, be in many places at once and be seen by others while in those places (who later confirmed they had seen him), see and converse with deceased beings, and visit with "The Masters" like Jesus and Buddha and Mother Mary. He could accurately hear another's thoughts, see inside people's bodies, and read auras and past lives. Electrical equipment "froze up" around him; streetlights popped when he walked by. His breath often stopped for no particular reason, which would panic anyone around him, especially during the night when he appeared to die rather than sleep. He could walk in and out of various worlds, realms, dimensions, and time frames at will. People noted that his physical countenance had changed, and that there seemed to be a "glow" about him.

"I used to walk down the street," said Ishtan, "and see people whose character was good and I would go into a state of bliss and step aside and bless them. I am never diminished when I give away energy like this, for I am only allowing more space in my heart for more of that precious energy to come in and take me to even higher levels of awareness." He speaks of being able to "sit" in Buddha's body, "see" through the eyes of Christ, and be one with God.

The elevated state Ishtan awakened to after that last good night's sleep continues unabated to this day, many years later. He is now consciously aware and active while supposedly asleep, even when he stops breathing. His sensitivity to his surroundings is so acute it's as if he has no skin and no personal boundaries to separate him from his environment. Although he is a miracle worker for others, he has found it extremely difficult to negotiate the tasks of daily living. He went on disability for two years at first, as he couldn't handle the energy he encountered in crowds. Subject to accidents, he fell inside a bus once and injured his back. For five years, he lived with the pain of that injury and the terror of feeling overwhelmed by his situation. "How do I handle this?" he asked. "How do I live in the world?"

Ishtan, like Tom, is convinced he physically died on that night he felt like he was dying. But in Ishtan's case, he had previously experienced the near-death phenomenon, as a child, and had already dealt with the aftereffects. Even though he has no memory of any scenario per se during the San Francisco incident, when he awoke, he stepped into a full-blown, fully conscious, transcendent near-death state that has yet to end.

Ishtan is currently seeking ways to balance the challenges of Earth with the life of spirit, so he can function with more confidence and joy in the world around him. He has discovered—as many do—that transcendent states, regardless of what type or under what condition, don't guarantee a healthy or successful life. With the help of an open and receptive counselor, better eating habits, and a new career in which he can use many of his talents, he is moving closer to the balance he seeks, while discovering within himself even greater depths of wisdom and knowledge.

Gustave Doré's Painting

Of all the paintings done of death and the afterlife, past or present, one and only one is singled out by the vast

Painting of Dante and Beatrice as they experience the beatific vision. This particular painting is part of a series done by Gustave Doré (1832–1883) to illustrate the poem *The Divine Comedy,* by Dante Alighieri.

majority of child and adult near-death experiencers as the truest depiction ever of the near-death phenomenon. That painting was done in the mid 1860s by Gustave Doré, a popular French artist and illustrator, as part of a series of drawings to illustrate the work of Dante, especially of his epic poem *The Divine Comedy*. This particular piece is of Dante and his beloved Beatrice as they experience the beatific vision.

What fascinates me about this particular painting is that, not only do near-death experiencers relate to it intimately, but children who do not know they are about to die and do drawings before they die tend to mimic Doré's work in these drawings. Case in point is on pages 193–195 in my book *Beyond the Light*—the story of Katie Thronson of Moorhead, Minnesota. Katie, a healthy, happy six-and-a-half-year-old, surprised her mother one day with the question "Am I going to die?" and then busied herself creating a special drawing. Three days later, she was dead of a cerebral hernia. Months passed before her mother found Katie's drawing, of angels ringing the entry portal to the one true light, which Doré had depicted more than a century before. Whatever source Doré tapped for that drawing of his appears to exist in all of our psyches.

18

The Importance of Otherworldly Journeys

The real voyage of discovery lies not in seeking new lands but in seeing with new eyes.

—Marcel Proust, French novelist

Ronald Siegel, an associate research professor at the University of California at Los Angeles, thinks that scenario descriptions of near-death states are the same as the hallucinations that people who take hashish, opium, angel dust, and other psychedelic drugs report. He is quoted as saying: "Just as physiological shock helps the body survive, a near-death experience keeps potentially damaging emotions in check."

He states that the cities of light encountered on the Other Side resemble the geometric forms that dominate early hallucinogenic intoxication. Beautiful flowers, luminous clouds, visions of dead relatives, and so forth are but "retrieved-memory images." He further comments: "Visions of the afterlife are suspiciously like this world. We see subjects having so-called near-death experiences on almost a daily basis in the lab. They fly through tunnels, see lights, talk to God. Their lives are changed forever. It is a valid experience but takes place only in people's heads." He notes that such "visions" can also be triggered by anesthesia, fever, exhausting diseases, and certain injuries.

Ronald Siegel has a good point. What he's failed to consider, however, is the full range of components found with near-death experiences: details in them that could not possibly have been known before that are later verified; the clear, coherent, and lucid recall the majority of experiencers have of the event throughout their lives; and the amazing pattern of aftereffects that is in itself as universal as the experience.

Obviously, the notion of "hallucination" doesn't define the territory.

The Extraordinary

Louis E. LaGrand, PhD, reminds us that: "Mystical and extraordinary personal experiences have been occurring since the dawn of human history. Of all such unexplainable phenomena, arguably the least publicized although among the most influential in life, are the extraordinary experiences (EEs) of the bereaved. These events involve the belief by those mourning the death of a loved one that they have received a spontaneous sign or message from the deceased or a divine being. The key word is spontaneous: the experience is not invoked or a product of psychic intervention."

New Words

Exceptional human experiences (EHEs) are unusual, paranormal occurrences that somehow make a significant difference in a person's life. Some examples of EHEs include telepathic communication with other people or animals, a sudden uplifting revelation or vision, a "peak" experience (spiritual "at-one-ment"), seeing a ghost, spontaneous past-life recall, knowing things without any reason to, seeing the future, or any transformative state of consciousness.

Another does: that of myth and legend, and the exceptional ability people have to transcend what seems to limit them as they strive to reach greater truths and otherworldly realities. Get ready to stretch your mind as we explore these interesting issues in this chapter.

Exceptional Human Experiences

As we open our minds to the "impossible" and stretch ourselves, amazing things begin to happen. We discover how much more there is to life—to us. Ideas pop into our head. Visions occur. New strengths are revealed. Miracles take place. And it all began because we dared to think and feel differently.

Exceptional human experiences (EHEs) is the name given to subjective events such as these and one that recognizes their value and the life-changing impact they have on individuals. The term was first coined by Rhea A. White, a parapsychologist, who authored *Exceptional Human Experience: Background Papers,* and, with Michael Murphy, *Transcendent Experience in Sports.* Her dedication to exploring the entire venue of unusual subjective occurrences sprang from a near-death experience she once had.

Rhea offers as an example of exceptional human experiences what athletes refer to as "being in the zone." That special internal state occurs when, suddenly, there's no difference between you, your equipment, your goal, and the environment you're in—all merge or unify into a single focus of

360-degree awareness. Like meditation, "being in the zone" has a "feel" that is unmistakable. You know when you're there. Once in that state of mind, you're less likely to miss your goal or to be injured. Because it's as practical as it is euphoric, athletes regularly incorporate techniques for cultivating this mind state as part of their practice routines.

Such an awareness of "unitive consciousness" or "oneness," in which you converge with whatever you are focused on, applies not only to athletics and "the zone," but addresses a wide gamut of altered states of consciousness—from life-changing ("peak") spiritual experiences (and the near-death experience is such an event) to magical mystical moments when the puzzle pieces of your life suddenly fall into place and a reality greater than that of your own self-interest reveals itself.

Rhea now considers these experiences a "call" to change, grow, and transcend any self-imposed boundaries you might have. "If dreams are the royal road of the unconscious," she explained, "then possibly EHEs are the royal road to heightened consciousness—even to eventual enlightenment."

Tell Me One More Time

Just hearing the stories told by near-death experiencers, and those who have been touched by the extraordinary or exceptional states of consciousness, is enough to change lives. People tend to embrace visionary experiences with the same enthusiasm as the visionaries themselves do.

New Word

The realm of the **numinous** is a spiritual or supernatural domain wherein "The Mystery of Mysteries" resides. Considered timeless and eternal, it's a place beyond what words can describe. **Experiencing the numinous** refers to the arousal of spiritual ecstatic emotions that surpass anything previously felt. **Revelations of the numinous** are said to be life-changing.

The "Other Worlds" of Myth and Legend

Incidents of unitive consciousness (where we experience being one with everything else) include journeys into the "other worlds," in which the goal is to improve your life or learn a lesson rather than experience a fantasy that merely entertains. Otherworldly journeys can emerge from the imaginations of inspired storytellers, interweaving the social and religious fabric of a given people and time span (for example, stories of the hero's journey, in which great trials are risked to achieve a goal). They can also spring from ritualistic practices or phenomenal events that unexpectedly intrude on an individual's life as a direct personal experience of the *numinous*, a startling vision or visitation by a spirit being. Among the latter would be near-death states.

New Word

An **archetype** is the original or main pattern after which all else follows—the "first mold." Carl Gustav Jung, the famous psychotherapist, defined an archetype as an unconscious genetic image of a universal human experience expressed in myth; "racial memories" of universal, human experiences that are passed on in myths and genetically from generation to generation; for example, "a great flood," the creation of the world.

Although they can certainly take on the aura and feel of simple escapism (the tendency people have to daydream or "wish" themselves elsewhere), otherworldly journeys are closely aligned with myths and legends about heroes and how to transform from a selfish ego-bound personality (your little self) to an unselfish, caring individual who seeks to serve and help others (your higher or true self).

Let's explore otherworld journeys further, and the near-death state as a type of such an experience.

Universal Mind Plays

Otherworld journeys that arise from the imagination always center on the ultimate questions: Is there a realm other than Earth where justice and order abide? Can human beings survive the jaws of death? What is the purpose of life and death?

Most people never bother to confront their own mortality on a deep level, nor do they ponder life's verities. Stories of other worlds and our ability to visit them, then, become for many an impetus for self-improvement and self-education. Crisis or conflict is included in the narratives in a manner that forces characters to risk the "hero's quest" into the abyss where solutions await discovery. This enables the reader or listener to stretch beyond the boundaries of perception and belief. This type of story, myth, or legend is so compelling that, thanks to storytellers, it can span several thousand years of repeated use, and become the basic framework of *archetypes*.

The same or similar archetype for the same or similar item consistently emerges worldwide, irrespective of period or culture. The brief rendering that follows will give you a sense of how stories of other worlds have tended to grow and expand over time without losing their universal appeal or archetypal value.

- *Prehistory*. There is ample evidence in relics and cave paintings to suggest that even Cro-Magnon people created and participated in the storyline of journeys to worlds other than their own.

- *Hellenic*. Thanks to the genius of Plato and Homer, the ancient Greeks were treated to refinements of the earlier stories, and to tales of Odysseus and his underworld journey to the House of Hades and the realms of eternal damnation.

- *Roman*. The creation of European civilization was strongly influenced by

Spinal Lore

One example of an archetype is the World Tree. Said to fix the position in space and time of heaven and Earth and all created things, it is also used as a metaphor to depict the human spine—the nervous system, its branches. All things are said to proceed from its centering strength and wisdom.

Another example is the Sacred Umbilical Cord, which operates as the "Road to Sky." In Olmec and Mayan lore, we are each connected to this Road through our own luminous "silver cord," emanating in spirit form from our navel. The Sacred Umbilical Cord came to be represented as a serpent of power and knowledge that dwells within us—and is located in our spine.

World Tree, Sacred Umbilical Cord, and Serpent Energy are all reminiscent of the ancient Hindu/Vedic concept of Kundalini, the spiritual energy at the base of our spine that rises up through the spine as we develop in higher states of consciousness.

the long poems of Virgil. His narrations of Persephone (the death queen), the Golden Bough as tribute, and the heavenly Elysium Fields, which were a place of rest before the soul returned to Earth in another body, all expanded on previous storylines, while emphasizing the importance of spirit as the animating force within and behind everything.

Look These Up

For more information about the imagery and storyline of otherworld journeys, check out these books: *The Power of Myth,* by Joseph Campbell; *The Complete Idiot's Guide to Classical Mythology,* by Kevin Osborn and Dana L. Burgess; *Out of This World: Otherworldly Journeys from Gilgamesh to Albert Einstein,* by Ioan P. Couliano; *The Secret Teachings of All Ages,* by Manly P. Hall; *Memories and Visions of Paradise: Exploring the Universal Myth of a Lost Golden Age,* by Richard Heinberg; and *Man and His Symbols,* by Carl G. Jung.

- *Christian.* The belief in Christ replaced the classical stories with promises of hope and redemption. Biblical writers and visionaries like Dante (author of *The Divine Comedy* epic poem mentioned in the previous chapter) revamped the concept of "hero" (a daredevil who risked the impossible to prove himself worthy) to one of "pilgrim" (a seeker of wisdom and knowledge who sought to uplift and support others).

Numerous cultures from antiquity to the present owe their very survival to the power of otherworld journeys to teach, guide, and heal their people. These compelling stories that concerned the ultimate questions about life became the fodder of myths and legends. Every one of them, as well as the rituals they may be based on or inspired by, track back to what may be the ultimate archetype—

You Don't Need Drugs

Using drugs to create otherworld journeys is dangerous. Hallucinogens taken during rituals in native societies were never used alone, but as part of a ceremony that emphasized the intention and meaning behind the experience along with supportive interactions between participants and elders. The process tended to balance the drug's effect. Many times, drugs were considered unnecessary to achieve a desired effect, and not used.

the near-death experience as "proof" of life beyond death.

Ritualistic Practices

Most of the otherworld journeys described by people in various stages of drug intoxication lack the lucidity, coherence, and the long-term effectiveness of personal empowerment commonly found with near-death experiences. The imagery may sound similar (cities of light, luminous clouds, winged angels, devils and demons, the Almighty Presence), but the powerful patterning that cradles that imagery and gives it meaningful depth and direction are missing. Those who experiment with drugs seldom connect with anything of value that enhances or improves their life.

Rituals that honor and celebrate special moments as well as life's major turning points empower people, strengthen society, and invariably lead to a greater appreciation of the numinous. We moderns have forgotten the importance of rituals. In so doing, we have denied ourselves the power and passion of worlds internal to us.

Recreations of Near-Death States

The mystical underpinnings of the Judeo-Christian tradition encourage rituals that touch individuals in a unique way. An example of this comes from John White's *The Meeting of Science and Spirit.* He reminds us in his book that the original purpose behind full-body immersion when baptizing someone was to hold the individual under water long enough to induce what we today call a "near-death experience." This practice of "near-drowning" enabled many religious converts to "leave" their bodies long enough to have a direct, personal experience of resurrection: "the transcendence of death, the reality of metaphysical worlds, and the supremacy of Spirit."

We use movies today as a safe and pain-free method to attempt the same thing—experience the powerful lessons encoded into otherworld journeys (for example, the *Star Wars* series by George Lucas). Yet, more and more films are depicting what may be the progenitor, the near-death experience itself:

All That Jazz (1979)
Resurrection (1980)
Brainstorm (1983)
Return of the Jedi (1983)
Bliss (1985)
The Quiet Earth (1985)
Jo Jo Dancer (1986)
Ghost (1990)
Flatliners (1990)
Jacob's Ladder (1990)

Heart and Souls (1993)
Saved by the Light (1995)
What Dreams May Come (1998)
Dragonfly (2002)

A Transforming Event

Three days before director George Lucas was to graduate from high school, he almost died in a spectacular car crash. His father notes that he changed so dramatically afterward that it was as if he became another person. Although Lucas has never claimed to have experienced a near-death episode, he has displayed the pattern of aftereffects ever since and behaves as if he had one.

The Four Levels of Otherworldly Imagery

When you examine the descriptive imagery of near-death states and then compare that to the depictions of classical otherworld journeys, you get a match—on four distinct levels.

The four levels of near-death and otherworld imagery are:

1. *Personal.* Images from one's own life. Examples include landscapes and environments the same or similar to your own life; loved ones and pets that were once a part of your world; and conversations and dialogue that concern personal matters, family secrets, and intimate revelations. There is an awareness of physical occurrences during out-of-body states that are later verified as accurate.

2. *Mass mind.* Images of a cultural nature that reflect the human condition. Examples include landscapes and environments typical of what you could adjust to or expect from your culture;

Illustration from the book *Patriarchs and Prophets,* by Ellen G. White, published in 1890. Ellen was one of the first women in the United States to have a book of hers published.

Invisible Libraries

There is scientific precedence for the idea of "libraries of consciousness." Sigmund Freud labeled such a memory bank "racial memory"; Carl Jung called it "the collective unconscious." Rupert Sheldrake, an English plant biologist, uses the term "morphogenetic fields" or "M-fields" in his provocative book *A New Science of Life* to describe how these invisible "blueprints" could direct the shape, development, and basic behavior of living species and systems. He points out that DNA tells a cell what to do (such as form skin), but not what to be (for example, a hand). What supplies the necessary guidance, according to Dr. Sheldrake, are these "libraries" of memory.

an overriding sense of the familiar—even if particular sights seem somehow peculiar or different; interchange with beings about the human condition and how it has evolved and where it might be headed; and objective overviews about advancements in the human family. There is an awareness of a mission or a job yet to accomplish for the betterment of your fellows, and of how every effort counts.

3. *Memory fields.* Images as much archetypal as they are primordial. Examples include access to panoramic archetypal symbols of historical appeal such as God as a man, angels as humans with wings, religious figures as loving authorities, globes or cylinders of light as guardians, demons as elements of punishment, and satanic figures as the personification of evil. Also covers representative symbology such as a skull for fear, whirlpool for a threat, yin/yang circles for principles of ordered thinking, the tree of life for continuity, the river of no return as a warning, the book of life for accountability, and tribunals for judgment. There is an awareness of wisdom levels, life stages as stairways, and layers of thought-forms as differing realms of existence (such as the twelve heavens and twelve hells commonly reported by visionaries throughout time).

4. *Truth.* That consistent, stable reality that undergirds and transcends Creation and all created things. Examples include a sudden "knowing," a strong feeling or sense of higher knowledge and greater sources of that which is true from regions of The Absolute. Seldom is there much in the way of imagery except for vague or indefinite shapes and abstracts. Invariably, thought-form "overleafs" provide the kind of imagery that is familiar or helps you to feel secure, until such time as you can relax; then overleafs dissolve. Recognition of Truth level is accompanied by unbridled joy, complete and unconditional love, all-knowing intelligence, peace and compassion, ecstasy, and a communion with oneness. All relationships and interrelationships, connections, and interweavings of all

> Creation are instantly known or revealed. There is no sense of doubt with Truth. There is an awareness of having found one's true home and true identity; true purpose follows. Questions cease.

Components, levels, and interpretive styles describing the inner worlds of subjective experience have historically remained so consistent that it's as if a grand design or matrix exists to ensure their continuance. Personal and societal advancement seems to hinge on the ability of individual(s) to access these "libraries of consciousness" where, among other things, archetypal knowledge appears to reside.

Feeling Alien

Returning to earthly consciousness after an otherworldly experience is a shocker. You were transported "elsewhere" by the episode and it's hard to come back. No matter what triggered your trip, you're never quite the same again. As you learned a little earlier, otherworld journeys take us into the depths of various mind states, and they pluck at our heartstrings. For some, this is the only way they ever connect with their own soul.

It's natural to feel somewhat foreign or different afterward. Depending on the depth of involvement you achieved and what surfaced for you, the feeling that you are now "alien" could predominate. Most of us feel that way anyway from time to time, so sensing that you are an outsider, a stranger in a strange land, may not be of any particular importance. For others, though, such an identification strikes at the chord of memory in a peculiar fashion—specifically with near-death experiencers whose episode was especially intense. Some actually begin to identify with extraterrestrials.

> **Another Kind of Space**
>
> "I had a sense of being between time."
>
> —an anonymous near-death experiencer

Maybe It's a Question of Timing

Most of the child experiencers of near-death states in my research base were clustered around three age groupings: birth to fifteen months, three to five years old, and puberty. Of these three clusters, the largest number of experiencers I found was in the three-to-five age range. This struck me, for as a mother, I've been keeping an eye on kids for quite some time, noticing what they did at what age, observing other youngsters at play, then poring over data on child brain development. Some of what I learned from doing this concerned the fact that most children commonly exhibit paranormal activities such as out-of-body experiences, flying dreams, disembodied voices, spirit visitations, heightened intuition, and playtime in "the future"—where kids seem to "rehearse" the future as a way to prepare for demands soon to be made of them—between the ages of three and five. Most of the reports of childhood cases of extraterrestrial/alien abductions and alien sightings,

Pattern Holders

Research on childhood brain development suggests that the temporal lobes are the pattern holders—that place near our temples that adjusts to changing imagery as we learn and grow. They are thought to be where our original "templates" of shape, form, feeling, and sound are stored. Development of the temporal lobes in childhood is heralded by scientists as the birth of imagination and creativity.

You Can't Skip the Numinous

The more we moderns immerse ourselves in the pursuit of artificial imitations, the more we hunger for a taste of that which is truly authentic. Since we no longer seek the truly numinous, maybe the numinous is seeking us—perhaps at least partially accounting for the exceptional increase in the numbers of near-death experiences, alien abductions, and paranormal episodes, and the renaissance in storytelling occurring worldwide. What typically happens to us as children seems to be reasserting itself in our adult lives.

not to mention near-death states, cite the experiencers as being in this age group.

All of us—child behaviorists, alien abduction specialists, and myself as a near-death researcher—have zeroed in on the peculiarity of children's experiences *during the time when the temporal lobes in the brain develop.*

Children between the ages of three and five inhabit futuristic scenarios on a regular basis as a way to identify with and assert their egos in creative and inventive ways. Two examples might be acting out going to school long before they get there, or practicing what it would be like to play football. Memory formation piles images atop images as the young construct their version of the world around them, building social stereotypes that help them make sense of the larger archetypal patterns they seem to have been born with.

As we age, the real secrets to keeping young are to immerse ourselves in imaginative endeavors and keep stretching the limits of possibility as we develop our greater potential. Art does this for us; so, too, do music and dance and the thrill of invention and discovery. Creative activities, enhanced by the revelatory guidance we gain from otherworld journeys—how they inspire us—ensures healthy temporal lobe function and the continuation of the imaginative process.

Maybe It's a Question of Personality

Kenneth Ring, with the help of Christopher J. Rosing, did an empirical study of people who experienced near-death states to see if there might be common traits among them—perhaps links to personality that might address who is more prone to fantasy. Their findings were published in the *Journal of Near-Death Studies* (Volume 8, Number 4, Summer 1990).

Although they found that experiencers measured significantly higher than nonexperiencers in *psychological absorption,* they could find no evidence to suggest that experiencers were fantasy-prone. What they did find, however, is that the experiencers reported being quite sensitive to alternate realities as children; the majority suffered the pain of child abuse. To escape the pain, they mentally "went elsewhere."

> **New Words**
>
> **Psychological absorption** refers to the tendency some people have to become deeply involved in sensory and imaginative experiences. The trait often takes on the characteristic of a "mind merge" or becoming "one with" whatever is focused on. Although absorption abilities vary among people, an individual can identify so much with the point of focus that anything else ceases to exist for a time.

Other studies, including my own, seem to refute the child-abuse connection. For example, research done on mystical and visionary states demonstrates that the main predictor of having such an experience is the ability of the individual to access nonordinary realities and become fully immersed in them—psychological absorption. Some people acquired this ability through positive means, others because of a need to escape painful situations, but most were simply born that way.

Regardless of what may actually be the cause, a highly developed absorption ability did indeed set near-death experiencers apart from nonexperiencers in Ring and Rosing's control group. I also found it to be one of the typical aftereffects most experiencers of near-death states reported. Yet Dr. Ring went on to observe the predominance of this same characteristic in many of those who report alien abductions and alien sightings, electrical sensitivity, and a host of various paranormal activities, prompting him to suggest that there may well exist an "encounter-prone" type of personality.

Kenneth Ring has spoken at length about this, and he calls such individuals "the omega prototype." He claims that these omega "edgelings" (those closer to a higher development of human potential) are more typically found among near-death experiencers than any other group. He posits that the crucible of the near-death phenomenon itself is responsible, fashioning, if not a new leap in the evolution of our species, then a new order of spiritually adept and more creative and intelligent people.

Exceptional human experiences, whether directly or indirectly experienced because of unique abilities, visitations to other worlds, or awareness of other realities, have not only transformed individuals, but have also guided and directed the development of entire societies and religions throughout history. Each new opportunity a person has to experience a higher order takes him or her from a sense of separateness to one of unity. We all benefit when this happens, because of the creativity and innovation that is unleashed.

19

The Possibility of Alternate Realities

If you don't know where you're going, you will wind up somewhere else.
—Yogi Berra, baseball superstar

During a radio interview in Canada, Kenneth Ring, PhD, spoke about the unique sensitivity some people have to nonordinary realms outside everyday reality. "I call it an imaginal realm—that's not my term. And I don't mean to imply that it's imaginary. I mean to imply that there is a special alternate reality in which these experiences can be said to have their origin. And there are lots of them. I mean the similarity of reports among people who have UFO abductions or near-death experiences is so striking that one almost has to conclude that these experiences have a kind of reality of their own. I suggest that that reality derives from this imaginal realm."

Dr. Ring invites us to consider that imaginal realms consist of a type of substance or energy that gives them the same "feel" as physical reality. You can't photograph either the places or their inhabitants to prove they exist, although some people say you can (refer to the ghost photos in chapter 4). Yet these worlds are perceived as solid and real by those able to access them.

In this chapter we'll explore the prospect of living worlds parallel to, within, or existent beyond our own to see what the concept has to do with the reality of life and death and what near-death experiencers report.

Is There an Afterlife?

From the dying, from those who *channel* the dead, and from near-death experiencers, there are as many stories as stars in the sky—all claiming that

New Word

Channeling refers to the ability certain people have to go into a trancelike state and allow their vocal chords to be used by spirit beings, serving as a channel (passageway) for messages from other planes of existence.

See Me? I'm Right Here

James L. Hallenbeck, MD, in his book, *Palliative Care Perspectives,* said: "In normal wakefulness, we function and interact on a relatively narrow and shared frequency that allows both transmission and reception of shared experiences. When patients at the end of life experience altered states, it is as if their radio frequency, their wavelength, has shifted. That small shift allows the patient to experience both the 'normal' wavelength on which we coexist and yet receive signals on a wavelength that we cannot perceive. Such a patient might be perfectly aware of being in a hospital bed and of dying but be able to see and hear a deceased relative sitting in a chair next to the bed."

there are planes of existence beyond, within, and interpenetrating the physical earth world. And that once we leave this plane, once we die, we continue—elsewhere.

And these stories are as extraordinary as they are persuasive. You've already been exposed to many from near-death experiencers. Here are a few others that challenge what is thought to be death's finality:

- As he lay dying on the ground near his mangled car, comedian Sam Kinison was heard talking softly with an unseen presence. An individual at the scene later told reporters from the *Las Vegas Sun* what he had said as he conversed with "somebody upstairs." Sam pleaded, "I don't want to die," then he paused as if listening to a voice speak to him. "But why?" he countered. Then he replied, "Okay, okay, okay," with the last "okay" so soft, so peaceful, and so sweet, it was as if Sam's concerns were put to rest by someone he loved and fully trusted. He then relaxed, and died.

- Frank Tribbe of Penn Laird, Virginia, had this to say about the death of his wife Audre: "Frequently throughout 1992, as she sensed the imminent threat to her mortality, she mentioned the names of long-dead friends and relatives and smilingly commented on the pleasure of seeing them again. She looked forward to the pleasures of [life after] death, but complained of the pain and the interminable time it took to die, as well as her reluctance to leave me and her many wonderful friends. During much of September in the hospital, she lay with eyes open and conversed with interesting spirits—and told me of them."

- Seven people died in a terrible car accident, but one survived—a six-year-

Shiners

Occasionally, when the dead are seen by the living, they are said to look like foggy apparitions or projections from a motion picture show. Most accounts, though, claim that the dead are 100-percent real-looking, and as lively as when they last breathed a puff of air. Notable differences include: They always look younger than when last seen; they're cured of any illness, handicap, or injury they may have had; and they're aglow with a special light that seems to emanate from within them. In other words, the dead that return generally look better than before—and they "shine."

Visitations

Cross-cultural accounts of the dead's "visitations" agree that the dead come back to either comfort or harass the living. Sometimes they impart advice or give instructions, but mostly they talk about the afterlife. "You go where you belong after you die," is the most common phrase given, indicating that our thoughts, attitudes, and deeds make some type of difference in determining what becomes of us.

old child named Ashley. In an article carried in the *Wisconsin State Journal,* Madison, Wisconsin therapist Karen Moore, who worked with the girl afterward, said Ashley would often point to the hospital ceiling where she saw her dead mother and father. "Don't you see them?" she'd ask. "No," Karen replied, "what are they doing?" "Oh, they're laughing and eating." "It was eerie," the therapist stated later. "There was nothing to indicate she was hallucinating. This went on for several weeks, and then they moved her to Rusk Rehabilitation Center, and I remember her saying, 'They're gone. I can't find them anymore.'"

Is It Really Just in Our Minds?

Reports like these imply that life after death is the true "norm," and that any claims to the contrary are false. Sometimes these stories include details a person can check for verification, but this fact alone doesn't necessarily prove anything other than the mind's capacity to invent creative alternatives to the finality of death. Yet, when you consider the large volume of cases that have proved to be accurate, with details impossible to fake or invent, you simply cannot avoid coming to this conclusion: An afterlife of some type does exist.

Words spoken by the dead—whether in historical or contemporary accounts, in dreams, through telepathy, or what seems like oral dialogue—describe the afterlife as consisting of layer upon layer of realm after realm, with each "world" separated from the other according to its vibratory frequency. Regardless of how dated or new the description, similarities are truly amazing. Although interpretations differ, the consistency in patterning is globally significant.

New Word

After-death communication (ADC) is defined as a unique or spiritual experience that takes place when a person is contacted directly or spontaneously by a family member or friend who has died. "Directly" means there is no third party, such as a psychic.

Reaching Over

James A. Houck, PhD, of Neumann College (Aston, Pennsylvania), as part of a larger study on grief reactions and religious or spiritual coping methods in bereavement, asked about after-death communications. Of the 162 bereft people he interviewed, 75 percent said they had experienced at least one type of ADC since their loved one had died.

Is There Research on After-Death Communication?

In 1982, Bill Guggenheim heard a voice that sounded like his deceased father. It told him to check the swimming pool. He did, and found his twenty-one-month-old son floating in the water. Had he not heard that particular voice, his son would have drowned. Since then, he and his former wife, Judy, have conducted the largest study yet done on *after-death communication,* and, in so doing, they initiated the research field now termed "ADC."

Judy and Bill Guggenheim's study of ADC is contained in their landmark book *Hello from Heaven: A New Field of Research Confirms That Life and Love Are Eternal* (refer to appendix C). In the seven years it took them to complete the study, the two interviewed 2,000 people and collected more than 3,300 firsthand accounts of after-death communication. They conservatively estimate that 20 percent of the U.S. population has had one or more ADCs.

The 12 types they identified:

1. *Sensing a presence*—the sense of knowing a deceased loved one is nearby.

2. *Hearing a voice*—often telepathic, can be a voice heard inside one's head.

3. *Feeling a touch*—a tap, caress, kiss, or nudge from a deceased loved one.

4. *Smelling a fragrance*—the smell of something that isn't there, like roses in wintertime.

5. *Partial appearances*—only part of the deceased appears, or the figure is translucent.

6. *Full appearances*—seeing the deceased whole, healed, and smiling.

7. *Visions*—can feel as if looking through a window or picture into another dimension where loved one is.

8. *Twilight experiences*—communications that occur when individual is falling asleep or waking up.

9. *While asleep*—unusual, memorable, and vivid dreams that feel like actual visits with the deceased.

10. *When out of body*—some people have spontaneous out-of-body experiences that are similar to NDEs.

11. *Telephone calls*—receiving a phone call from the deceased, even having a two-way conversation.

12. *Involving physical phenomena*—communications from the deceased can involve light, window shades, photographs, songs on the radio, TVs turning on and off. Things can be moved.

ADCs Are Old Hat

Serious research on after-death communications actually began over a century ago. Ambitious studies done in Britain and France collected thousands of such accounts. Many of them evidential. Subsequent studies done here and abroad, including the work of Bill and Judy Guggenheim, have documented that it is commonplace for normal, healthy people to have such experiences.

Bill and Judy Guggenheim found that symbolic after-death communications can occur when an individual asks for or desires a sign that his or her loved one still exists. Common signs given were butterflies, flowers, animals, birds and feathers, or inanimate items such as coins, pictures, and rainbows. These signs tend to have symbolic and special meaning for the loved one.

The Knowledge of Your Own Death

In my life, I've often been close on the heels of unexpected deaths: first as a policeman's daughter, later when my former husband became a crop-duster pilot specializing in night jobs, flying barely inches above the ground of tree-lined farm fields, and finally when I served in healing prayer for those ill or about to die. Whenever appropriate during my visits to the bereaved, I asked questions about the deceased and what they were like before they died: Were there any changes in their behavior? Over the years, a peculiar pattern emerged: People who died suddenly or accidentally, subconsciously communicated their "knowingness" about what was to come through a specific pattern of behavioral clues:

- Usually, about three months to three weeks before their deaths, individuals begin to change behavior normal for them.

- Subtle at first, this behavioral change begins as a need to reassess affairs and life goals—a shift from material concerns toward philosophical ones.

- This is followed by a need to see everyone who means anything special to them. If visits are not possible, they begin writing letters or calling on the phone.

- As time draws near, the people become more serious about straightening out their affairs and/or training or instructing a loved one or a friend to take over in their stead. This instruction can be quite specific, sometimes

Fetus Fun

In my research of 277 child experiencers, half could remember their birth; one-third had prebirth memories. What's intriguing, though, is that some remembered not only choosing their parents before conception, but selecting what genes—and even physical handicaps—they might need to accomplish their life's goal. They spoke as if they were a soul leaving one home to go to another. Most of the prebirth memories I was able to trace began at around seven months in utero, a time when it is known medically that the fetus can respond to pain.

involving details such as what is owed and what is not; what insurance policies exist and how to handle them; how possessions should be dispersed; and what goals, programs, or projects are yet undone and how to finish them. Financial matters seem quite important, as is the management of personal and private affairs.

- There is a need, almost a compulsion, to reveal secret feelings and deeper thoughts, to say what has not been said, especially to loved ones. There is usually also a need for one last "fling" or to visit special places and do what is most enjoyed.

- The need to settle affairs and wind up life's details can become so obsessive that it appears "spooky" or weird to others. Many times, there's a need to talk over the possibility of "what if I die," as if the individual had a dream or premonition. The person may on occasion seem morbid or unusually serious.

- Usually, about twenty-four to thirty-six hours before death, the individuals relax and are at peace. They often appear "high" on something because of their unusual alertness, confidence, and sense of joy. They exude a peculiar strength and positive demeanor as if they were now ready for something important to happen.

I've noticed this pattern in people from the age of four on up, regardless of their expressed beliefs or intelligence level. I have also observed it in some people who were later murdered. It is somewhat similar to the behavior of people, such as cancer patients, who have been directly advised that they are about to die. Certainly, not everyone displays advance knowledge about their coming death, but all of those in my investigation did. I rather suspect the reason some do and others don't has more to do with sensitivity to inner promptings than any real knowing.

Because what I saw and heard was so compelling, as a young woman I came to accept the reality of an afterlife. But that's not all. To have a sense of your future—through dreams, feelings, or subconscious behavioral clues—brings up the topic of a "life plan," a purpose for living. This curiosity fueled the next round of my research, and led me to "knock" on different doors. You'll get a gist of what I discovered throughout the chapters in part 4. Remember, as a researcher, it's my job to present you with my findings, but it's your job to decide what this material means to you.

I Came, I Saw, I Was Born

Investigations into the extent of before-birth awareness have legitimized the growing field of research aimed at the prebirth experience, or PBE (mentioned in chapter 4).

There are some startling findings along this line that back up claims of life before birth (the research of each passed considerable scrutiny). For example, David Chamberlain, PhD, author of *Babies Remember Birth,* clinically hypnotized young children and discovered that they possessed prebirth awareness as newborns and were fully cognizant of their inherent selfhood at birth, despite the lack of anatomical maturity and psychological development. This refutes the notion that birth memories are fabrications or guesswork.

David B. Cheek, MD, a retired obstetrician, wrote a paper published in the *Journal of Pre- & Peri-Natal Psychology* (Vol. 7, Issue 2, Winter 1992) that details his quest to determine at what age a baby is aware. He found evidence to suggest that by the time a woman realizes she is pregnant, the embryo is already aware of her and her surroundings—indicating that awareness may begin at conception.

To give you a sense of how curious this can be, let's look at two cases from my study of near-death experiencers: One addresses aborted babies, and the other, a soul's sudden awareness of existing as a baby.

No to Abortions

When I queried near-death experiencers about their thoughts on abortion, I found that three-fourths of them flatly disapproved. They respected a woman's right to choose, but felt that through proper counseling and appropriate alternatives, a woman could find ways to respect and honor God's gift of life—whether the child was kept or given up for adoption.

- Ned Dougherty of the Hamptons, New York, is a former nightclub owner and self-professed former hedonist and womanizer, who "died" following a violent fight. During his near-death scenario, he found himself in the presence of a number of beautiful children. Upon asking the angel who accompanied him who they were, he learned to his horror that each one was a child intended for him while he was on Earth. But because he didn't want to be inconvenienced by fatherhood, none of them were able to be born and they now existed as "spirit children." This experience so transformed Ned that not only did he reprioritize his life, he also became an active supporter of the "Right to Life" movement and has since testified against abortion at a congressional hearing. His entire account, including revelations given to him, is detailed in his book *Fast Lane to Heaven* (see appendix C).

Kids Remember the Past

Child experiencers of near-death states are more apt than adult experiencers to relive segments from previous existences as part of their scenario. Many children even remember people and places they knew before. Most, however, eventually lose interest or encounter so much opposition they forget about it.

New Word

The **earthplane** denotes the vibratory frequency of the physical earth world we can see, feel, hear, and touch. The term owes its usage to the mystical idea that the soul has numerous planes of existence to experience and traverse in a journey that, traditionally, is said to spiral back to the Source of Creation.

New Words

Reincarnation as a theory posits that we are each born into a series of lives, one after another. Reincarnation as a belief addresses the larger issue of a soul's evolution or devolution. Part of this belief involves **karma**, a principle based on the law of cause and effect, which states that we reap our rewards and suffer our punishments from one life into the next.

- Vivid in Dorothy Bernstein's mind when she remembers her infancy is a tiny person who one day perched at the head of her crib. After studying her quizzically, the being said, "You're a baby." This inspired her to glance up at a nearby mirror. Catching her reflection, that of a baby lying in a crib, she grabbed a foot and stuck it in her mouth and bit down. "Yup, this is me," she recalls saying to herself. "This is real. I really am a baby. Wow, isn't this something!" Dorothy was born with prebirth awareness and went on to have several near-death episodes as a young child. This discovery of hers that she was now a baby alive in the *earthplane* is so similar to the many stories I hear from other child experiencers (including the presence of an informative spirit being) that I consider it typical. Although in her case, she's now an older woman looking back, the degree of objectivity she offers is actually quite common, even with the young.

Why Do I Feel Like I've Been Here Before?

The majority of near-death experiencers—children and adults—become enamored afterward with the idea of *reincarnation*. Some even experience reincarnational themes and past lives as part of their near-death episodes.

The researcher who has done the most credible work investigating cases of reincarnational memories is Ian Stevenson, MD. A retired professor of psychiatry and former director of the Division of Personality Studies at the

Two cartoons from the pen of Chuck Vadun. Both appeared in his book *In My Next Life I'm Gonna Be a Princess* (Valley of the Sun, 1984), a compilation of Vadun's work. Reprinted with permission.

University of Virginia, Dr. Stevenson has written two books that are both trailblazers: *Twenty Cases Suggestive of Reincarnation* and *Where Reincarnation and Biology Intersect* (see appendix C).

Although he has built a detailed base of 2,600 cases from people who recall having lived before their present life, his current work specifically addresses 225 individuals who show fantastic correlations between their birthmarks and birth defects and the way they were killed "last time around." For instance, some have birthmarks at the entry and exit points of the bullet that killed them in their previous incarnation; others have digits or limbs missing as a result of being murdered and having certain body parts chopped off.

> **New Word**
>
> An alternate explanation of reincarnation is **cryptomnesia**, the spontaneous surfacing of deeply buried memories from the subconscious. The subconscious mind, as a vast storehouse of everything we have been exposed to, is capable of clustering bits and pieces of information to form storylines suggestive of previous lives. This explanation, however, does not account for all reincarnational memories, especially those of small children with vivid, detailed recall that was later verified.

In my research, I've come across a number of cases like Dr. Stevenson's. A remarkable one concerns a little boy clinically dead from a breech birth who was resuscitated. As soon as he was old enough to speak, he not only described the near-death experience he had while dead, but told of numerous visits he made to his real-life sister while he was still in spirit form. The reason he gave for his prebirth forays was to see New York City through her eyes while the family still lived there. He said he had lived there before and he wanted to know how much the city had since changed. He was so miffed at what he

> **Treatment Based on Past-Life Memory**
>
> Reincarnational treatment, where trained hypnotherapists regress an individual into past lives, has proved helpful in treating not only psychological problems, but some physical disorders and illnesses, as well. This method has, on occasion, been more effective than medical CT scans, MRIs, and blood tests in arriving at an accurate physical diagnosis.

saw that he "refused" to be conceived until the family moved to Canada. His detailed comparison between what he saw via his big sister and what he remembered from his prior life was so precise, it could be checked and was. It turned out to be totally accurate, which dumbfounded his parents.

Taking Dr. Stevenson's place at the Division of Personality Studies, as relates to reincarnational research, is Jim Tucker, MD. He specializes in cases involving children, and works like a police detective, not only interviewing parents, family members, friends, but checking medical files, reports from coroners and police, eyewitness accounts, and other documentation. His book *Life Before Life: A Scientific Investigation of Children's Memories* (refer to appendix C) is a show stopper!

An Altered View of Reality

While researching the near-death phenomenon, I routinely encountered both child and adults experiencers who would say things like "I feel like an alien" (or "a misfit" or "a foreigner"). And they'd admit to being homesick for what they had to leave behind in order to come to Earth. Persuasive as these stories are, and there are many of them, I question whether the claims signify extraterrestrial origination, or if, just maybe, something else is being remembered. I took an in-depth look at this in *Children of the New Millennium* and *The New Children and Near-Death Experiences*. Here is an overview.

Numbers from my research are revealed in the chart on the following page.

While not as many adult experiencers as child experiencers said they

www.sacredcowsonline.com www.cafepress.com/sacredcows

Adult Near-Death Experiencers (based on 3,000 cases)	
Identified with being from another planet	20 percent
Claimed to have been abducted by a UFO	9 percent

Child Near-Death Experiencers (based on 277 cases)	
Identified with being from another planet	9 percent
Identified with being from another dimension	39 percent
Claimed to have been abducted by a UFO	14 percent

had been abducted by a UFO, a number of adults stated that they now occasionally dream of seeing spaceships. The most surprising difference I found between the two groups concerned "place of origin." As we've just seen, adult experiencers remembered, either during or right after their episode, that they had come to this planet from another. Youngsters recalled not so much coming from other planets as from multidimensional realms. No adult I interviewed ever expressed his or her origin in terms of multidimensionality. Only the kids said this.

Other Kinds of Lives

Many child experiencers related more to life in other dimensions of existence than here on Earth. Two distinctive expressions of this awareness were evident to me back in the 1960s, when I was investigating children's accounts of wee folk (like fairies and gnomes), invisible friends, spirit beings, and so on. The same pattern emerged again in my near-death research, irrespective of the experiencer's culture or country. What follows is based on my current studies of the near-death phenomenon.

Following are two distinctive expressions of multidimensionality:

1. *Oriented to the life continuum—concerned with life embodiments and the progression of souls.* The majority of child experiencers who identify with multidimensionality—about three-fourths of the 39 percent—expressed this viewpoint. They had memories of prebirth and after-death realms as "exit" and "entrance" points to a single life stream or life continuum inhabited by the type of spirits they once were and would be again. These realms, they said, were their true home.

2. *Oriented to the cosmos—concerned with the universe's inner workings and the progression of Creation.* In my studies, only about one-fourth of the 39 percent had this viewpoint. These are the ones who speak of identifying with formlessness—like a gas, or waves, or energy pulses, or particles of sparks. They talk as though the substance of their being and their place of origin were one and the same, that their beingness is part of the very mechanism and structure that holds together and maintains Creation itself.

Those who relate the most to a life continuum are adamant that life goes

Massive Changes on Every Level

The multidimensional kids who related most to the cosmos made it quite clear to me that they were here to help "for the changes." When I asked what they meant by that, all said that Earth, its countries and people, would have to deal with "big troubles." And they described this time of massive change as happening when they were grown and had children of their own, or when they were grandparents (this differed according to the child's age at the time). By projecting ahead from the date of their episode to when they could be parents or grandparents, I came up with the time frame of 2013 to 2029. This matches predictions from both statistical analysts and professional astrologers as to a time when the United States will face the greatest challenge in its history. Predictions of Earth changes worldwide, along with a possible pole shift, are mounting ever year as global warming becomes more of an issue.

on and on, and that birth into a body does not begin life nor does death end it. And they speak of their true origination in hearty giggles, as if adults were stupid to have ever forgotten something so important. Home to them is the luminous life stream, a place of varied life forms—some even more alien than the extraterrestrials of movie fame.

Are these memories just a child's vivid imagination at play? Those I interviewed of this expression displayed a higher level of spirituality than the other child experiencers with whom I had sessions, and truth was more important to them than parental authority. I noticed that they were unusually tolerant, drawn to service and philanthropic endeavors, and were totally unconcerned about either societal standards or role-playing.

Children who identified more with the cosmos than the life stream, though, were decidedly different. They were so abstract they seemed to be wholly mind, as if their body and body functions were insignificant and merely tolerated. The ones I met spouted advanced concepts about wave forms, energy sources, and power grids in much the same manner as the average child might quote football scores. And they were certain about their origins: "Not bodies, [but] bits and pieces of things" (referring to their sense of being part of Creations's inner workings). Occasionally they did mention other planets but not in the sense of familiarity. "Home" for them was the universe at large.

These cosmically oriented kids, although aware of the life stream and soul progression, were determined to "save the Earth" and "make repairs." Their physical body and emotional nature seemed of little use to them, as if they existed mostly in their heads. Ecological sustainability fascinated them, as well as alternate power sources, leading-edge science, photonics, and large-scale economic and medical reforms. They regarded themselves as "keepers" of the matrix or fabric of the universe.

Other Kinds of Living

Multidimensional youngsters challenge our concept of life's ordering. Adult experiencers also bring into question our conventional world view when they describe the alternate realities they faced during the drama of their near-death episode. Here are two examples:

- Brian, from California, was driving his camper home from an outing in the desert when his brakes failed. He remembers seeing blood-soaked clothes and his head split open in two places, before he was engulfed by many colors and a blinding white tunnel. "I visited different types of worlds," he told me, "many with different colored skies. I was shown many varied life forms and civilizations in this universe; some appeared frightening and some wondrously beautiful. My understanding of my previous life was so different from what I was experiencing. The only thoughts that kept repeating to me were 'If I had only known of the beauty I was seeing. I must stop being so fearful and egotistical in the assumption that I was the only intelligence in the Universe.'" Brian was met by what he calls a highly evolved spirit who told him about his past lives. This was his first exposure to the subject of reincarnation, and it rendered him speechless.

- May Eulitt, from Oklahoma, experienced the near-death phenomenon three times; the most recent via a lightning strike. During her third episode, she "lived" in another lifetime with people other than those she knew. "I had a family [there] that I loved," she related. "I had friends and foes. At first I searched for a way to go back to what I considered my real world and [my real] family, but soon I began to accept this new life I was building outside the pale. When I grew old and died, I suddenly was back at the scene [where I was hit by lightning]. I was overwhelmed with joy to be back, but at the same time I was devastated by the loss of the ones I had grown so much to love in the other world." Readjustment took a while, as she dealt with the same stress as those who suffer trauma shock. The present seemed like the "distant past" to her. "When you are forced to accept the reality of another realm, sometimes you begin to question the validity of both worlds and also your own sanity. If you accept one and not the other, even though both are equally solid and substantiated, how can you ever know what is real again? I feel I have no recourse but to accept the reality of both, though my psyche balks at the idea. We do not want to let ourselves slip into some other consciousness because we fear losing who we are. We are afraid that other realities will make this life less tangible. In fearing the loss of who we are, we cannot see the potential of who we may become." (May was referred to me by Steven Hoyer, Ph.D., a clinical psychologist in Pittsburg, KS.)

A Vast View

William A. Tiller, physicist at Stanford University, presented a paper that was published in the *Journal of Scientific Exploration* (Issue 13, 1999). He began by saying, "Humans see only a small fraction of the electromagnetic spectrum and hear only a small fraction of the sound spectrum. Perhaps we similarly perceive only a small fraction of a greater reality spectrum."

A Spectrum of Realities

F. Gordon Greene, an investigator of alternate states of consciousness whose research papers are often published in the *Journal of Near-Death Studies,* reminds us that "[o]ur own three-dimensional world, in ways that we may find extremely difficult if not impossible to visualize, may actually be surrounded by a space extended in four dimensions. One view of Albert Einstein's theory of general relativity is that our own three-dimensional space does actually curve back in upon itself by extending through such a fourth dimension."

Forever and Ever

Those who undergo near-death states are witnesses to this truth: that beyond the familiar are worlds and realities without number.

Dropping the Bohm on Our Current Worldview

What we call "real" is what we can measure. But that measurement confines what we think reality is to the instruments used and the conditions employed to measure it. A new breed of physicists have challenged this fundamental thinking by demonstrating that what is true is only true at the level it was measured. The term "reality," then, is largely governed by mutual opinion, not "bottom-line" evidence.

While a professor of physics at Birbeck College in England, David Bohm declared that reality consists of an "implicate order" where every relatively independent element contains within it the sum of all elements (each part reflects the whole). Everything and everyone is part of the same energy continuum (interconnected and intertwined).

David Bohm's concept of the implicate order is based on twenty years of test results from both mathematical theories and laboratory experiments. These tests showed how subatomic particles are able to respond and relate to one another in ways not explainable by the law of cause and effect. In other words, he found that on the subatomic level, Newtonian fundamentals are no longer reliable. At this level, all things are interrelated, intertwined, and intimately connected, because physical reality is threaded together in a seamless web of responsive, conscious intelligence—a continuum.

He defines this in terms of an "unbroken wholeness" which cannot be analyzed into separate and independent parts because no such separation actually exists. It only seems so.

The notion that reality is a continuum agrees with much of the imagery, 360-degree vision, and heightened abilities of individuals undergoing out-of-body and near-death episodes. It also explains the descriptions they give of a single luminous life stream we exit and enter as our awareness alters and our form changes. Experiencers may be right after all when they indicate that a universal *matrix* of adjustable "fabric" (a web of intelligence "threads") cradles Creation.

> **New Word**
>
> A **matrix** is that which gives origin or form to a thing, or that which serves to enclose it.

Death, Like Life, Is a Journey

Sukie Miller, PhD, a psychotherapist, has drawn together the various stories, myths, and visions of an afterlife and produced a "road map" for the pathway to and through the Other Side. Her book *After Death: How People Around the World Map the Journey After Life,* identifies the four adjustment phases she discovered that, historically, people claim we must negotiate once our bodies have sloughed away and we exist in spirit form. These phases are:

1. *Waiting Place*—where the deceased is transformed from a physical to a spiritual being.
2. *Judgment Phase*—where the "traveler's" life is reviewed and evaluated.
3. *Realm of Possibilities*—either a time of enjoyment or something to be endured, as determined by the previous judgment.
4. *The Return (Rebirth)*—where the "traveler" is reintroduced to the physical world via a new body and a new identity.

Where Dr. Miller focused primarily on the journey we go through once we enter the "other worlds," George W. Meek went one step further: He decided to map the "other worlds" themselves. George retired from a successful career in industrial research and development to devote the rest of his life to investigating the possible survival of consciousness after death. His book, *After We Die, What Then?* is both an overview of research on the subject as of 1980 and a primer on his own projects. He's the first person to develop electronic equipment that could achieve dialogue with purported beings from the worlds of spirit.

> **Spirit Faces**
>
> Since 1999, Mark Macy has also been taking spirit face photographs. What makes these faces appear? They seem to be facilitated by the presence of a subtle energy device that changes the vibrations in a room. Macy's purpose in doing this is to prove the existence of other realms, as well as aid the grieving. His latest research and his views on the spiritual destiny of humankind are described in his book *Spirit Faces: Truth About the Afterlife* (refer to appendix C).

Interpenetrating Levels of Life and Consciousness

(adapted from the research of George W. Meek)

Planes	Brief Description
1. Physical Earth Plane	You exist here in a physical body, and at the same time in both an interpenetrating, nonphysical etheric body, and an astral body. The etheric is the energy "blueprint" that supports the physical and dies when the physical body does. The astral holds "the real you" and can travel to other planes.
2. Lowest Astral Plane	This plane is the equivalent of emotional excesses, demonic possession, and hell.
3. Intermediate Astral Plane	Rest and rehabilitation await you here. Similar to Earth, except lovelier, with many opportunities to learn.
4. Highest Astral Plane	Here you find the "summerland" of heaven, with angelic assistance and unconditional love. Wider perspectives about life are gained, and greater vistas to creation are revealed.
5/6. Mental and Causal Planes	These planes offer you unlimited development of mind and soul. You have access to all accumulated wisdom, and have your final opportunity for rebirth into the Earth plane before you ascend into the celestial.
7. Celestial Plane	Biblically referred to as "the third heaven," here you have contact with the Godhead and learn the secrets of miracles and of all Creation.
8. First Cosmic Plane	The last plane in our solar system and the one where you can reach "at-one-ment" with the Godhead.
9. Second Cosmic Plane	The end of manifest, vibratory creation.
10. Third Cosmic Plane	The Void, nonvibratory or pure consciousness.
11. Fourth Cosmic Plane	Full "at-one-ment" and entry into states of consciousness beyond human comprehension.

His careful and detailed analysis of the communications that followed revealed an array of planes said to exist beyond that of Earth. Now that George has passed on, Mark Macy continues his work, through an organization called Continuing Life Research in Boulder, Colorado, and in the new field of study called Instrumental Trans-Communication (see appendix E for details as well as contacts for American Association of Electronic Voice Phenomena, Tom and Lisa Butler, who do research along the same lines).

A brief version of the chart George Meek created that summarizes the communications he received about the various planes of reality and existence is on the previous page. It reflects what millions of near-death experiencers across the globe report. In reading about these planes of existence, keep in mind that Meek was quick to say that, although after death we appear to go to whatever level we resonate with vibrationally, we are not trapped at any level, nor is any of them an endpoint (even though his chart stops at level 11).

The Aramaic word for death translates as "not here, present elsewhere." This ancient concept of death best describes the near-death experience and what happens to those who go through it. These people were present *elsewhere!*

20

Transformations of Consciousness

> Waking up is not some mystical exercise in spiritual fantasy. It is a deeply human and practical necessity if our lives are to have meaning, quality, and integrity in this rapid-fire information age.
>
> —Diane Kennedy Pike, author, consciousness coach, and personal growth facilitator

Many mistakenly point to Acts 26:2–29 in the Christian Bible as evidence that Paul had a near-death experience on the way to Damascus. This passage recounts Paul's description of what happened to him: He saw a light from heaven shining on him, greater than the sun; he heard the voice of Jesus, admonishing him for his past deeds and saying he must become a minister of Christ's New Gospel; he was overwhelmed by the event and temporarily blinded. Paul's experience has some elements in common with near-death states; but, as we'll see in this chapter, it is in fact part of a larger type of experience—as is the near-death phenomenon.

In the previous chapter I introduced researcher George W. Meek and his eleven Interpenetrating Levels of Life and Consciousness. There are many passages in the Bible in which Paul goes on to speak of spiritual bodies and the third heaven in words almost identical to that of George and his discovery of how we, in bodies of spirit, seem to pass through these eleven levels (or more) in our journey back to our Source. George was not researching near-death states per se when he produced his chart of how we may progress in spirit form after death. He was investigating something far more encompassing.

George W. Meek focused on people in general as he sought to determine what our fate might be after we die. Although his work seems somewhat old-fashioned compared to the tools of today's scientists, he nevertheless covered his subject matter in a disciplined

www.sacredcowsonline.com www.cafepress.com/sacredcows © 2006 SpiritPainter

and rigorous manner. His conclusion that each of us, as a soul, inhabits a spiritual body that changes form and function as we ascend or descend in our growth toward a reunion with God, seems like an addendum to Paul's "knowings" after he was shown "Truth."

Incidents like the one that happened to Paul parallel the transcendent aspect of near-death states, but you could classify such episodes otherwise—as part of a larger genre. Read on.

A Larger Genre

When you keep everything in context—the experiencer, the experience, and the aftereffects—you encounter a universal pattern so large and sweeping in its implications that you can't help but wonder, "Why didn't I recognize that before?" This pattern, this larger *genre*, is that of a transformation of consciousness.

Perhaps because of my previous experience researching altered states of consciousness and spiritual transformations back in the 1960s, I quickly came to notice that near-death states didn't have the necessary characteristics to be considered a uniquely separate or exotic phenomenon. The more people I interviewed, the more I observed and studied, the more it seemed to me that this state was but another version of a larger genre. What made it seem unique were the hi-tech trappings that went with it—mangled steel, rushing ambulances, sterile surgical rooms, beeping monitors, skilled surgeons and support staff, code blue, and the speedy last-ditch effort to bring back the dead.

This scientific, by-the-book drama was paving the way for spiritual, by-the-heart breakthroughs. I came to realize that I wasn't so much investigating strange occurrences at the edge of

> **New Word**
>
> **Genre** refers to a class or category (a genus) having a particular identifiable form, content, style, or the like, that distinguishes it from anything else.

death as I was momentous awakenings to life's fullness at the doorway to a greater reality—akin to Paul's experience.

Higher Consciousness

What spiritual or religious seekers undergo to reach enlightenment is similar to what experiencers of near-death states often confront. That's why it's appropriate and reasonable to use the near-death phenomenon as a neutral model to explore transformations of consciousness—neutral because most experiencers are everyday people engaged in ordinary pursuits, whereas most seekers have made a commitment to grow spiritually, some fervent in their desire to experience enlightenment.

The Controversy over Viewpoints

An ongoing debate regarding the transformative experience itself revolves around the issue of whether the shift in consciousness that takes place should be labeled a spiritual awakening or a religious conversion. What's the difference?

A *spiritual awakening* inspires an individual to take on a personal, intimate relationship with God. Spirituality honors intuitive knowing and direct revelation, with an emphasis on the power of the heart to heal through love and forgiveness.

A *religious conversion* connects an individual with the strength of God's word as revealed in Holy Writ or Commandments. Religion, through set standards or dogmas, provides for the spiritual and secular education of its adherents with an emphasis on the power of guidance to establish morality and salvation.

It's possible for a person to be both spiritual and religious, or support one viewpoint over the other.

Much has been written about this controversy, and it has been discussed endlessly. But as near as I can tell, the issue is not so much a problem of

> **The Big One**
>
> Traditionally, a transformation of consciousness is said to differ from an alteration of consciousness in the fundamental and lasting changes that can result. While altered states are known to be short-term, shifting with a person's mood and mind state, transformations are long-term in the way they turn people's lives around and bring about greater wisdom, compassion, and spirituality.

> **Lost and Found**
>
> Although nothing can prepare anyone for that actual moment of "breakthrough" into higher states of consciousness, there are, in religious and spiritual traditions, teachings and precedents to guide seekers along the way and help minimize struggles or confusion. Nothing like that exists with near-death experiencers, who are left to fend for themselves. Some figure out what's going on; others don't.

Viewpoints

Basic Element	Religious Conversion	Spiritual Awakening
The experience	Baptism by the Holy Spirit	Light of God
What it represented	A new covenant, born again	Enlightenment, illumination, or awakening
What it was	Heaven	Home
A life force	Angel	Light being
Words spoken	Message from God	Conversations
Words felt	A Gift from God	Telepathy
Opinion of self	Chosen of God	Children of God or Light Workers
The return	A mission to fulfill as God's Chosen Messenger	Unfinished business to complete or a job yet to do

identifying what happened as it is a challenge of dealing with *other people's opinions about what happened.* It seems to me that the biggest difference is simply one of semantics.

Using the near-death experience as an example, here's a list of descriptive words experiencers use to support their interpretation of what they encountered during their scenario. The elements are the same. All that differs is the language the various people used to describe them.

I have come to realize that we color the meaning of our transformations either by a need for attention, a desire to satisfy others, or by making a commitment to remain true to what really happened no matter what that means. We have found "home," and we wish somehow to acknowledge that.

Egocide

Central to transforming consciousness is undergoing an "ego death." This catches near-death experiencers totally without warning, accounting in large part for the confusing personality switches afterward. Most spiritual seekers are prepared for such an occurrence, as prior teachings they receive from their mentors (or gurus) are explicit regarding the subject of "dying unto the world of flesh and materiality" so the brilliance of spirit "can shine through."

The spiritual path dissolves the ego as sure as day follows night. Taitetsu Unno speaks of this in his book *River of Fire, River of Water*: "Awakening is dynamic, constantly evolving in accordance with life's realities—unfolding from ego-self to compassionate self, from enclosed self to open self, from foolish self to enlightened self." We die unto the world of self-centeredness and vanity, and are reborn into a world of joy, laughter, and "at-one-ment" with our fellows and our environment. It's the change in one's focus that runs so deep, and this change can transfigure even the individual's physical appearance. You don't just feel differently after a transformational experience, you look different, too. (Before and after photos can vary.)

Turbulent Transformations

A transformation of consciousness can occur so suddenly it may seem like a bolt out of the blue. Such an event can be "invited" to the degree that individuals already involved in religious or spiritual pursuits are prime candidates. Still, the actual moment of "breakthrough" is always unexpected regardless of how prepared a person is. In fact, "the real thing" occurs more frequently to those who expect it the least than to those who think they're ready.

Occurrences that intrude upon a person's life for no apparent reason are the ones that tend to be the most overwhelming, sometimes even violent. They come in various forms: baptism of the Holy Spirit, near-death episodes, Kundalini breakthroughs (which I'll discuss in a moment), shamanic vision quests (if unexpectedly intense), sudden accidents, a lightning strike, or certain types of head or spinal trauma.

Transformations that emerge from turbulent incidents are the hardest to take and require the greatest struggle to understand and cope with. Powerful forces beyond our control, which may take years of adjustment to integrate, are central to the experience. It's no wonder that some people are unable to deal with the phenomenon, and wind up either committed to a mental institution for treatment or become so spacey and detached that others avoid them.

Symbolic Death

D. H. Rosen, a therapist who specializes in suicide and life-threatening behavior, coined the term "egocide" to describe the sacrifice of conflicted parts of the personality when an individual chooses to heal. Grief and suffering are replaced by broader, more flexible insights. In transformations of consciousness, the ego takes a back seat: A "symbolic suicide" takes place as conflicts inherent in the individual's personality give way to a need to improve and refine the self, serve others, practice forgiveness, and seek spiritual wholeness.

This is vastly different from "The Near-Death Experiment" proposed by Greg Kasarik, and discussed at the close of chapter 5. His plan to have subjects commit medically supervised suicides to see if near-death experiences can be caused completely overlooks the reality of egocide, and that the experience itself has more to do with breakthroughs into the psyche than it does with anomalous phenomena that further the attainment of "magical gifts."

The Shaman's Journey

Putting it succinctly, *shamanism* is a 30,000-to-40,000-year-old spiritual worldview and way of living that awakens and enlivens the neglected potentials of the human heart, mind, and spirit. There

New Word

According to anthropologist Michael J. Harner, PhD, author of *The Way of the Shaman,* "**Shamanism** is simply a method of awakening to one's fuller nature in a disciplined way." Shamans are known to "enter into" or merge with the spirits of things: obtaining guidance from worlds within and around them. They "ride" energy in the sense of knowing how to respond to subtle changes in vibration and feeling.

are no priests; it is not a religion. Shamans often obtain their "office" by proclamation from a social group, tribe, or community. Other times they acquire their positions as a result of otherworld journeys in which they learn healing and helping, and then become self-appointed practitioners or healers.

Shamanic rituals vary according to culture and country, but invariably, drumming, dreaming, dancing, singing, and using rattles evoke the shift from ordinary consciousness to a 360-degree awareness of both visible and invisible worlds. Although some traditions sanction the use of psychedelic drugs to reach this state, drugs are not necessary and sometimes impede the process. There is a difference between shamanic journeys and shamanic vision quests:

Shamanic journeys are subjective "flights" to other planes of existence, undertaken as a service for others, either to assist in healing someone, to find what is lost, or for some specific project that will benefit another.

Shamanic vision quests are done for self-knowledge and self-development, and are times of fasting, prayer, and solitude as the individual prepares to receive a new vision (spiritual guidance).

The states induced by initiation rites into the world of shamanism bear a remarkable resemblance to near-death states. Numerous researchers now suspect that the ancient practice could have evolved as an extension of the near-death experience. A master shaman (an individual in control of self and spirit) is often called a "medicine man" or a "medicine woman"—a "soul doctor" adept at moving between existence and nonexistence at will. Although many modern-day practitioners actually had a near-death episode as a child or in young adulthood and exhibit the typical aftereffects, having a near-death experience is not a prerequisite for being a shaman. Shamanic training can be a reliable way for the average person to develop higher and more expanded states of consciousness. One note of caution concerning vision quests: They are not for the untrained, as a "death" is demanded—the death of the ego.

Close Link

"NDEs seem more closely linked to shamanic, visionary processes than to the physiology of dying."

—James McClenon, PhD,
Elizabeth City State University,
North Carolina

High Stress

"Dying unto the self" is the initiatory experience that awaits those who seek the core of shamanic vision quests and other similar rituals. This point of symbolic or ego death is reached through the "high stress" (excessively intense stress) that results from the fear one encounters at the edge of death. The panic button is pushed on purpose in these rituals. If the individual successfully moves beyond the fear/stress threshold, a transformation of consciousness can occur.

There is a correlation to this in an announcement made several years ago by Dr. Bruce Greyson, when he revealed through careful research that the stress of dealing with intense trauma can push people into dissociative states that become or are like near-death episodes. "The study shows that near-death experiences are normal responses to intense trauma, not a sign of psychiatric illness," he explained. "I don't think [this] takes away from the mystical interpretation. I think it just takes away from the pathological interpretation."

Kundalini Breakthroughs

From Meso-America, Asia, India, and the steppes of Mongolia to Old Europe and later the Celtic nations, comes a diversity of myth and legend about a "serpent power" said to be latent within the individual. (Briefly discussed in chapter 18, the sidebar "Spinal Lore" notes that the World Tree and the Sacred Umblical Cord are both symbolic representations of the Serpent Power said to reside at the base of one's spine.) Once called forth, this transformative power is thought to be able to turn ordinary men into "invincible warriors and mighty priests" (later in history, women's extraordinary changes were recorded, too). Commonly, this power is referred to as *Kundalini*, or *Ku*.

This serpent power is said to ignite or activate seven whirling vortices of energy that are located in or near certain areas of our bodies on the trunk, neck, and head. These whirling vortices, called *chakras* (a Sanskrit word meaning "wheels") or flowers (Meso-American for that which opens and "blooms"), are described as spinning energy generators. They are associated with each of the seven major glandular centers (endocrine glands), located at or near:

1. The base of the spine
2. The genital area
3. The solar plexus

New Word

Kundalini is a Sanskrit word meaning "coiled serpent." It derives from the older Meso-American word **Ku**, which translates as "the spirit force of God awaits within each person." Both words refer to the "serpent power" said to be coiled at the base of a person's spine, that, once stimulated, uncoils and rises up the spine to the brain, transforming the individual.

The Medical Version

The medical caduceus symbolizes the nature of serpent power once activated to elevate the art of healing as it frees the mind. It's associated most often with Greek mythology and fables about Mercury, the messenger of the Gods. The caduceus consists of two entwined snakes (one representing the negative aspect of the energy, said to be located on the left side of the body; the other depicting the positive aspect, to the right), the messenger's staff (the spine as the conduit of the two aspects of this rising power), the ball atop the staff (the higher functions of the brain/mind), and duo wings (the release of attained knowledge to heal and help others).

4. The heart
5. The throat
6. The brow (between the eyebrows—called "the third eye")
7. The crown of the head

Humans are said to have a channel within their bodies for spiritual energy to travel (i.e., the spine) and the powers (i.e., the endocrine glands) to speed it along its way. Details of how this works depend on which tradition you study.

It is claimed that once Kundalini/Ku rises full length, after stimulating, activating, expanding, and enhancing each of the seven major chakras/flowers and bursting out through the head, enlightenment occurs and reunion with God is possible. In truth, this bursting forth is but a signal that an individual's awareness is shifting from one mode to another—a shift, if you will, to the spiritual path (an enlightening experience but not *full* enlightenment).

Just as everyday life goes through various phases of development in order to spiritualize, the spiritualized life is also said to go through various phases of development before "attainment" is reached. A Kundalini/Ku breakthrough does not guarantee complete or lasting enlightenment, and is considered dangerous to undertake unless the individual has a good teacher or is prepared. Difficulties arise if people are frivolous, power-hungry, or overly zealous when trying to raise their own Kundalini.

Results can be unpredictable.

Baptism of the Holy Spirit

Baptism of the Holy Spirit is not to be confused with the baptismal ritual prac-

The higher aspects of serpent power (Kundalini/Ku) are symbolized by the medical caduceus.

ticed by most religious denominations. Christian in concept, the event describes a particular phenomenon in which a powerful force (termed "the Holy Spirit") suddenly and unexpectedly descends on and overwhelms an experiencer, leaving him or her forever changed by the encounter. Many Charismatics and Evangelicals refer to the effect of this awe-inspiring energy surge as feeling as if you were "slain in the spirit."

The entrance or activation of this energy surge initiates a "Christ-like" state of consciousness in the sense of how spiritual and divinely led an experiencer can become afterward. The phenomenon itself is characterized as being:

- Struck as if by lightning or a blinding flash
- Consumed as if by fire or great heat
- Torn as if by an explosion or great wind
- Immersed as if by heavy rain or flood swells

The spiritual force of this "Baptism" enters the individual's body from outside the self, from "heaven," God On High, or through some saintly emissary or angel. This experience of a powerful, intense force is said to come only when the recipient is truly ready (as opposed to when a person thinks he or she is ready). The power itself usually enters through the top of the head or through the heart and fills the entire body. This activation of divine spirit energizes and illuminates, transforming the individual's concerns from the everyday to the spiritual. Many religious teachings on the subject indicate that this event is not the culminating union with God but rather a beginning, a step toward that goal. Various stages or initiations are necessary after illumination before true divinity can be attained.

Triggering the Energy

Yvonne Kason, MD, a near-death experiencer (the result of a dramatic plane crash into the frigid waters of a Canadian lake) and coauthor of *A Farther Shore: How Near-Death and Other Extraordinary Experiences Can Change Ordinary Lives,* believes that near-death experiences trigger the rise of Kundalini energy. She has done extensive research on the tie-in, especially positive and negative issues concerning the physical changes that occur because of such experiences, and how to handle them.

New Word

Baptism of the Holy Spirit is considered by most Christian faiths to be that moment when the "worthy" are recognized by God and showered or struck by an energy "not of this earth" that transforms them utterly. "Gifts of the Spirit" supposedly result: the ability to prophesy, heal, speak in diverse tongues, work miracles, discern spirits, recognize truth, and become one within the Body of Spirit.

No Real Difference

The traditions of shamanic vision quests and Kundalini/Ku breakthroughs are virtually the same as Christianized accounts. They differ only by the general direction powerful energy is said to take once activated, as it fills one's body, mind, and soul. Said to be spiritual in nature, the results of the transformative energy being released or received are readily noticeable.

New Words

Being **mindful** is the act of being fully conscious, alert to and focused on, individual sensations, moments, interactions, and activities. For example: when eating an orange, pay attention to its sweetness and texture, the total experience of eating it. **Mindfulness**, in traditional Buddhism, is considered an essential component to liberation. By being mindful of the distortions in our lives and in our personalities, we can free ourselves of them. Our deep connection with others is then revealed.

Tranquil Transformations

Most people pursue more tranquil routes to spiritual development and eventual transformation, and do so in a manner that honors the three sacred paths of mystical and religious tradition. These paths take longer to traverse, but involve less trauma and struggle along the way. The three sacred paths are:

1. *Silence*—meditation, contemplation, prayer, *mindfulness*

2. *Imagery*—guided visualizations, mandalas (symbolic circles), spiritual art, spiritual architecture (sacred geometry), imagination, dreams/visions, storytelling

3. *Movement*—rituals, singing, mantras/chants (repeated phrases), dancing, graceful body movements, music, service to help others, pilgrimage, celebration, festivals

All spiritual/religious disciplines, rituals, festivals, and techniques are anchored by the first of these three sacred paths: silence. True power, it is said, begins and ends in silence—listening, communing, aligning, and becoming one with a force greater than you.

Spiritual practices like meditation are known to bring about emotional releases. Unfinished business and repressed emotions—for example, anger, resentment, and jealousy—can become exaggerated and wash over you, as well as joy. Spiritual moments open us up and release whatever is potential within us. As Elizabeth Lesser (author, meditation teacher, and cofounder of the famous Omega Institute) says, "A deep meditation can often make me cry."

If a spiritual or religious discipline becomes a habit, it's no longer regarded as a discipline. Conscious intent and sincere desire are necessary if we are to stretch beyond our capacity. We will never grow in spirit or improve ourselves as individuals, it is said, if we are unwilling to put into daily practice the teachings we most need to learn. According to mystical tradition, the path of a spiritual seeker is the path to wisdom and service.

Prayer Power

Prayer is when you talk to God; meditation is when God talks to you. One without the other is considered incomplete, like a one-sided conversation. Although consulting various books and teachers for guidance is helpful, there's no substitute for just "doing it." Consistency is the key. Payoffs include stress reduction, improved health and memory, and becoming more patient, relaxed, loving, perceptive, and knowing.

The Crown Jewel of Enlightenment

Mystics from all ages have told us that we are transformed by the "renewing of our mind," by that transformation possible once we shift in consciousness toward the spiritual. The initial enlightenment we receive from this does indeed change our priorities, values, and behavior—and very much for the better.

But that initial encounter is nothing like "the full blast." The greater state is godlike in how the individual involved becomes all-knowing, all-loving, and all-giving. Those who attain this state are referred to as avatars (great teachers), messiahs (anointed of God), buddhas (awakened ones), or similar titles. Full enlightenment is the goal of any true seeker; it is the "crown jewel" of spiritual attainment, achieved by only the few.

Weak/Strong

"About 30 percent of the population will have weak transcendent experiences, and about 10 percent strong transcendent experiences, very similar to NDEs, in which they see through into the structure of the universe."

—Peter Fenwick, MD, FRCPsych

Never has any step in the transformational process, whether turbulent or tranquil, been an easy ride or devoid of struggle, however, for anyone. *Sacrifices* are many, as those who "walk the path" of spiritual development, or are flung into it, begin to withdraw from lives based on the self-centered interests of their ego personality in favor of a more simplistic lifestyle devoted to learning and helping others. The idea of "cheap grace," of attaining wisdom without earning it, doesn't exist except as a gimmick to sell books or make someone famous. No credible teacher ever taught shortcuts to the process. Even though turbulent experiences are often dramatic in their suddenness and display of force, they are not more desirable than the slower methods and can require years of adjustment time afterward.

New Word

Sacrifice comes from two words meaning "to make sacred." Viewed in that light, whatever seems oppressive or difficult as we begin our spiritual journey toward enlightenment can be embraced as a sanctified step on the upward path.

All the Way Back

James McClenon, PhD, from Elizabeth City State University, North Carolina, tells us that: "Throughout history NDEs have creatively shaped religious beliefs in a manner contributing to psychological health, sometimes providing images preceding formal changes in theology."

The Sounds of The One

Few realize the extent to which early languages were patterned after spiritual revelation and a belief in deity. Sanskrit and Hebrew are examples of this, and so is every other ancient language from Icelandic to Indo-European. It is said that The One extends Itself through the Logos (the sound of the first word and the first principle that governs and develops the universe). Because attempts "to name God reveal God," the oldest records we have state that deity cannot be named—because to name is to contain—and deity is beyond containment, description, or comprehension. Eventually, First Cause, The One True Source Of All, was commonly given the name "God."

Religion's Beginnings

Even during the early days of investigation into the near-death phenomenon, various researchers have surmised that most of the world's great religions were either started by or gained their inspiration from an individual who had experienced a near-death state. Dr. Raymond A. Moody has been the most vocal regarding this provocative theory, going so far as to suggest that codes of ethics and morals, including the pursuit of higher knowledge that sprang from the Golden Age of Greece, owe their origins to revelations from near-death experiences.

Arguments that challenge Dr. Moody's theory address such achievements as the Code of Hammurabi, which far predated what happened in Greece, yet profoundly influenced Western ethics. There are links, though, that can be made between messages received from those who miraculously survived death's grasp and what came to be the mystical underpinnings of religious faith.

There is no way to prove, one way or the other, the actual source of what inspired the enlightened—those whose teachings led to the religious orders we know today. Still, it's reasonable to assume that near-death episodes played a role. You need only examine how language changes for modern-day experiencers afterward, how their beliefs turn to knowing, how deeply their lives are affected, how they inspire and uplift others—and then compare all of this to the spiritual passion each historical period has evidenced once the multitudes responded to "a spiritual messenger." They match.

People who undergo transformations of consciousness, and especially near-death experiencers who survived death's finality, are explicit about saying that they no longer "believe" in God, for belief implies doubt. They have no more doubts. They now "know" God. And because this shift from believing to knowing has occurred, many seek other ways to name and regard God. Popular names are: The One, The Force, The One Mind, Source, All, Isness, and Universal One. Some still use the title "God," but their conceptual understanding has shifted to that of a "Father/Mother God" (all-inclusive) or simply "It" (beyond human identifiers as to gender).

The shift in consciousness from nonreligious or religious concepts of deity to the mystical goes like this:

Atheist	There is no God.
Polytheist	There are many gods.
Monotheist	There is one God.
Pantheist	There is only God.
Mystic	There is only one interconnected whole.

Although it is believed in most parts of the world that any given religion must remain true to its original vision, experiencers of transformative states often lead others by taking on the role of challenger. They point out, and rightly so, that the process of transformation is an ongoing dynamic, ever fresh, and charged with revelatory vigor. But theirs is not so much the idea of casting former beliefs aside as it is reinterpreting and reenlivening the old myths.

So True

A lighthearted definition bandied about at meetings of near-death experiencers is "*Spirituality* = Questions that may never be answered; *Religion* = Answers that may never be questioned."

Transformative states return the experience of God to the individual in an intimately personal way. People who have been so changed can no longer be governed or controlled, for they follow a higher law and quite literally "walk to the beat of a different drummer." They may still maintain church and religious affiliations afterward, but usually as reformers or challengers rather than obedient parishioners. Many become ministers themselves; some are "guided" to create their own church, even their own seminary (which is what Carol Parrish did with the founding of Sancta Sophia Seminary, discussed in chapter 6).

The Bucke Stops Here: A Test for Genuineness

One individual who sought to better understand enlightenment and recognize "the truly changed" from a

Cosmic Consciousness

Dr. Bucke narrowed his study of the enlightened to fifty cases he believed were genuine: people who seemed to possess another type of consciousness and operated on a higher, more spiritual level of mind. In 1894, he presented a research paper on what he termed "cosmic consciousness" at the annual meeting of the American Medico-Psychological Association. He later authored a book by the same name, first published in 1901. While admiring the stars on a winter's night in 1902, he slipped on the ice and died instantly. His book, however, became the seminal reference work on the enlightenment process and its universal pattern of aftereffects, and remains so today.

Translucents

Arjuna Ardagh authored *The Translucent Revolution: How People Just Like You are Waking Up and Changing the World* (see appendix C). In the book, he identifies "translucents" as people who reflect a state of consciousness in which the ego no longer blocks the higher consciousness from shining through. According to Ardagh, when we experience ourselves as connected with others rather than separate, our ego becomes servant, not a director. His book is based on a survey of hundreds of people who have gone beyond worshiping spiritual standards and ideals to now living them and making a difference in the world as a result.

phony was Canadian psychiatrist Richard Maurice Bucke. He met poet Walt Whitman in 1877 and became his personal physician. A close friendship ensued, inspiring Dr. Bucke to investigate illumined states of awareness.

Dr. Bucke considered the illumined mind not a mystical or religious phenomenon, but a psychological one—a potential state of the human mind that, although rarely found in human history, was beginning to occur more often and would eventually be the consciousness that would lift humans above their fears, ignorances, and into a more loving, wiser nature. (In this sense, Dr. Bucke was a foreteller of the future, as we're seeing the very thing he predicted coming true in the latter half of the twentieth century and into the twenty-first. Trends such as the human potential movement, the New Thought movement, the holistic health movement, what has come to be called the Translucent Revolution, along with the awareness of altered and transformational states like the near-death experience all indicate growth or evolution in human consciousness.)

The pattern of enlightenment he discovered, both the process and the aftereffects, resembles what you've already read in this book concerning near-death experiences. Compare for yourself how he identifies "the real thing" in this brief rendition of his work:

- *The subjective light.* A brilliant blinding flash is seen. The individual's surroundings take on colors of unearthly hues and brilliance. Everything expands in size and brightness.

- *The moral elevation.* Afterward, the individual becomes moral and upright, shunning the temptation to judge or criticize another, or be less than honest and fair. A greater duty and service to God and humankind becomes a life priority.

- *The intellectual illumination.* All things are made known, all knowledge is given, all secrets of the universe are revealed. The individual feels no weight as he or she is overwhelmed by total and complete love. Glowing beings give instructions, as the "Word of God" is seen or felt; the oneness of all things shown. A sense of having been "reborn" prevails.

- *The sense of immortality.* Thinking is replaced by knowing. The individual realizes his or her divine identity and the fact that there is only life, which varies by degree of vibration and ascension. This illumination brings the knowledge that salvation is not necessary, that we are all immortal and divine from "The Beginning."

- *The loss of the fear of death.* Death loses all meaning and relevance. The individual now knows death does not end anything; it's simply a change of awareness.

- *The loss of the sense of sin.* Evil is understood as good misused, and all things are good in God's eyes.

- *The suddenness, instantaneousness of the awakening.* Whether a person is actively seeking an Eastern type of enlightenment or what is known in the West as "Baptism of The Holy Spirit," the actual moment of illumination is always unexpected, sudden, and blinding. It can last minutes, hours, or even days.

- *The previous character of the person.* Most people who experience enlightenment are morally upright and intelligent to begin with, and have strong bodies and strong wills. These resident characteristics are expanded and enhanced even further. Latent abilities surface, including genius. Even if the individual is sickly and soon to die, the desire to learn and excel is strong.

- *The age of illumination.* This usually happens when one is more mature and in the middle years, especially around springtime, early summer, or in the first few months of the year.

- *The added charm of the personality.* The individual becomes so magnetic that people and animals are drawn to him or her. The individual seems divinely protected and guided. Other people are affected right away, and animals become more docile around the person.

- *The transfiguration.* There is a marked change in appearance. The individual seems to glow and have a light around him or her. There are physical changes. The face looks different, and the individual behaves like a "new" person—as if suddenly "more" or greater than before.

Born of the Spirit

"The wind bloweth where it will, and thou hearest its voice, but knowest not whence it cometh or whither it goeth; so is everyone that is born of the spirit." (John 3:8)

Yup

Consider this truism: *Psychic abilities* (in and of themselves) = Build the ego. *Spiritual gifts* (regardless of what type) = Dissolve the ego.

According to Dr. Bucke: "The reports of those who have had cosmic consciousness correspond in all essentials, though in detail they doubtless more or less diverge (but these divergences are fully as much in our misunderstanding of the reports as in the reports themselves). . . . The person, suddenly, without warning, has a sense of being immersed in a flame, or rose-colored cloud, or perhaps rather a sense that the mind is itself filled with such a cloud of haze. . . . At the same instant, he is, as it were, bathed in an emotion of joy, assurance, triumph, 'salvation.' . . . Simultaneously . . . there comes to the person an intellectual illumination quite impossible to describe. Like a flash there is presented to his consciousness a clear conception (a vision) in outline of the meaning and drift of the universe. He does not come to believe merely; but he sees and knows that the cosmos . . . is in very truth a living presence. . . . That the foundational principle of the world is what we call love."

The precedent established by the work of Dr. Bucke provides us with a useful guide in recognizing the kind of aftereffects that indicate that something far greater and far more transforming than a change in attitude or a renewed appreciation of life has taken place in the lives of experiencers. He cautioned that there are no guarantees during or after a transformative episode. A person can backslide if ego or greed are allowed to overshadow the illumination.

21

The Lights of Enlightenment

Nothing real can be threatened. Nothing unreal exists. Herein lies the peace of God.

—*A Course In Miracles,* Introduction

The oldest English account of a near-death experience was recorded by the Venerable Bede in the eighth century. It concerns a Northumbrian by the name of Drythelm who suddenly arose from his deathbed and said: "I was guided by a handsome man in a shining robe. When we reached the top of a wall, there was a wide and pleasant meadow, with light flooding in that seemed brighter than daylight or the midday sun. I was reluctant to leave, for I was enraptured by the place's pleasantness and beauty and by the company I saw there. From now on I must live in a completely different way." Afterward, Drythelm gave up all his worldly involvements and joined a monastery. His story, and many others equally light-filled—a light brighter than the sun—are recorded in Carol Zaleski's *Otherworld Journeys: Accounts of Near-Death Experience in Medieval and Modern Times* (see appendix C).

Ancient Gnostic texts found hidden in a jar and buried in the Nag Hammadi area of Upper Egypt in 1945 are also of special interest, because they show the extent to which the Gnostic Christians believed that God the Father is Light:

> "Father of everything is pure light into which no eye can look—Father as the infinite light—Light dwelling in the heights . . . Father is the light of the world."

J. M. Robinson's compendium *The Nag Hammadi Library in English* continues this link to light: "Enlighten your mind with the light of heaven," and "Light the light within you."

Is God Light?

T. Lee Baumann, MD, asks the questions: "Are God and Light the same? Or are they just intimately related?" His answer, in article form, was written for the newsletter *Personal Spirituality* (January 2006), a publication of the Association for Research and Enlightenment (ARE). His article has the same title as his book, *The Akashic Light* (quotes with the permission of John Van Auken, editor; refer to appendix C for information about his book and appendix E for how to contact ARE).

"The relationship [between God and Light] is extraordinary when you study the scientific nature of Light and examine its role in each of the world's sacred texts. Not only do each of these books describe its God (or gods) in terms of Light, but Einstein and the newly found field of quantum physics specifically define Light in terms of supernatural and god-like qualities: omnipresence (being everywhere), omniscience (being all-knowing), omnipotence (being all-powerful), and, lastly, possessing that singular human trait that some physicists refer to as 'consciousness.' The . . . term *akasa* (or *akasha*) helps to depict the essence of this ubiquitous, luminous, and eternal energy force.

"From the onset of recorded history, people have worshiped the Sun and its related Light . . . The contemporary major religions are teeming with comparisons of God and Light. At the time of Muhammad's birth (according to Islam), Light radiated from his mother's womb. In Hinduism, the Buddha is identified repeatedly as the 'Enlightened One.' Buddhism identifies 'enlightenment' as an energy force . . . Sikhs describe one's individual Light as being derived from God's 'Supreme Light.' The *Kabbalah* identi-

Death Light

"Light at death is very common. A mother in one of our studies whose son was age seven and dying of leukemia in the hospital told us that, as he became more seriously ill, the curtains were drawn around his bed. She told us that, in the twenty minutes before he finally stopped breathing, the whole area around his bed was flooded with light—the same light that you talk about in the near-death experience: the light of love and compassion. And as he died, the light slowly faded."

—from Peter Fenwick, MD, FRCPsych

New Words

Akasha (Akashic) comes from the Sanskrit word for "ether," "radiant space," or "sky." It is also said to mean "primary substance." In many religious and spiritual traditions, **Akashic Records** is used synonymously with the term "Book of Life," to depict that record of everything that has ever happened said to exist forever "upon the skeins of time" (see chapter 2, sidebar "The Book of Life").

Information Fields

Hungarian systems philosopher Ervin Laszlo believes that the Akashic is another name for what is known in science as the quantum or zero-point field (morphic field). All the experiences of living beings in the universe are supposedly stored there. Laszlo theorizes that people and animals might be capable of tuning into the information from this universal data bank. (Ervin Laszlo is the author of *Science and the Akashic Field: An Integral Theory of Everything*; see appendix C.)

This universal data bank (Akashic Records/ Book of Life) is what many near-death researchers postulate as the "source place" experiencers tap into for their life reviews and previews.

Satan as a Ploy

The Bible identifies Satan (or Lucifer) as "the morning star" who uses light to trick people. In her book *The Origin of Satan,* Elaine Pagels seeks to clarify this situation by pointing out that it was the life of Jesus that suddenly brought the idea of a "devil" or Satan into prominence. She argues that the authors of the Gospels had to find a way to justify why the Messiah was rejected by the Jewish majority, abandoned by his followers, and executed as a common criminal. The dilemma was resolved, Pagels claims, by framing the events of Jesus' life as a cosmic battle between God and Satan, Good and Evil, Light and Darkness.

fies God as 'a mirror from which shines a brilliant light.' Indeed, the sixth sephirot of Kabbalism, known as the Tiphareth, represents the Sun itself. Even in Christianity, Jesus is associated symbolically with the Sun and Light.

"Scientific research implies that Light, like God, is omnipresent, omniscient, and omnipotent and exhibits an awareness or consciousness of its surroundings. My research implies that Light and God are intimately related, if not the same. The preponderance of the world's major religions offers the same conclusion—the intrinsic relationship between Light and God may well be literal."

The Light of God/ The Devil's Dark

There is no question about the importance of light in transformations of consciousness, near-death experiences, religion, and mysticism. What isn't commonly recognized is that darkness is important, too. Down through the ages, light and dark have become closely associated with certain concepts, attitudes, and objects.

Light day, right, masculine, father, objective, strength, intelligence, domination, good, joy, sun, white, gold, angels, life, heaven, God

Dark night, left, feminine, mother, subjective, weakness, instinct, cooperation, bad, sorrow, moon, black, silver, devils, death, hell, Satan

Cross-Cultural Studies Needed

Most research findings in the near-death field are based on limited samples. Larger, international studies are needed to explore the extent to which experiencers might add interpretive "extras" to what they encountered during their episode, based on whatever belief system is predominant in their region.

Nice Dark

Some of the kids who had dark experiences said they found themselves inside the deeper reaches of "The Darkness That Knows." Their attempts to describe what this was like involved such phrases as: "It was alive and it slurped me Up"; "It had a soft voice and it told me things, lots of things"; and "I just suddenly knew everything 'cause that dark-dark is really smart."

The problem is these associations are now engrained in the universal archetypes of light and dark, and archetypes can mislead as well as instruct. For instance, associating darkness, suffering, and devilry with females has for several thousand years led to women being persecuted. Conversely, males, seen as the essence of strength, intelligence, and light, have been given blanket authority—deserved or not.

Place Mother on the same pedestal as Father, Goddess with God, Light with Dark, and you have partners instead of adversaries, complements in "the dance of life" rather than combatants in the "battle between good and evil." You'd think we'd be too smart as a society today for the "medieval" mindset that spawned this situation. But the truth is, we moderns respond to many of the same patterns as did our ancestors. Light still means God; darkness, Satan.

The Devil Made Them Do It

The historical idea of a Satan or Devil tragically devolved into an excuse to demonize anyone or anything seen as different. This tendency to identify good or acceptable events with God, and bad or unacceptable events with the Devil, is unfortunately most clearly seen when near-death experiencers tell their stories in places of worship. Members of the clergy and congregants who believe the stories attribute the experience to God; those who disbelieve call the experience the work of the Devil, which can result in the experiencer being shunned.

Hear What I Mean, Not What I Say

There are individuals, child and adult, who claim they saw God; others say they saw the Devil. If you compare the descriptions and drawings they offer, however, there is reason to question some of their claims—not about what they saw, but about how they label it.

Depictions of the Devil can indeed be gruesome, whereas God is almost always portrayed as a benevolent father figure. Still, the majority don't make

www.sacredcowsonline.com www.cafepress.com/sacredcows

such clear-cut distinctions between the two. For instance, with youngsters who haven't been to church yet, whose only meaningful teachings involve warm tummies, clean panties, lots of toys, and love, you discover a type of image patterning that deviates from the two-dimensional approach we as a society have virtually institutionalized. And it centers around—you guessed it, darkness and light.

Three Types of Subjective Light

Of the four kinds of near-death states I identified in chapter 2—initial, unpleasant and/or hell-like, pleasant and/or heaven-like, and transcendent—76 percent of the child and 20 percent of the adult experiencers in my study had the Initial type of episode. Typically, this experience consists of one to three elements—things like a loving nothingness, the living dark, a friendly voice, a short visitation of some kind, or perhaps a quick out-of-body experience.

I also found that experiencers can sometimes be bathed in "dark light" as opposed to brilliant light. The majority of those I investigated—whether adult or child—who reported "darkness," "dark light," or the "living darkness" described the experience as being in a safe haven, a place of comfort, peace, and healing. They spoke of this place with the same love and affection as they talked about their real Home (the place where God is), where they were before they had a body and where they will return once their body falls away. Dark light experiences, especially to youngsters, equate love with safety.

The majority who reacted negatively to any darkness they encountered were usually those who went on to report fearful or hellish scenarios. Others enveloped by "the living dark" simply expressed confusion and questioned the whole affair.

By reexamining the research I've done since 1978, I concluded that there are clearly three very different types of subjective inner light that near-death experiencers describe—regardless of how old they were when their episode occurred.

The Three Types of Subjective Light

Type	**Color**	**Function**
Primary Light	Colorless	A pulsating presence or luminosity usually perceived as frighteningly awesome, a piercing power, raw essence; the origin of all origins.
Dark Light	Pure black, often with velvety tinges of dark purple	A shimmering peaceful depth perceived as "The Darkness That Knows," a source of strength and knowing, sanctuary; the womb of creation.
Bright Light	The range of yellow-gold-white hues	A brilliant radiance usually perceived as an almost blinding glow that emanates unconditional love, a warm inviting intelligence, union; the activity of Truth.

Each of these three lights is consistently referred to, regardless of person, age, or background, as more real than manifest light on Earth and more powerful than any source humankind could harness—including the sun's rays and "zero-point" energy (the "stuff" of the universe; untapped electromagnetic energy). Symbolically, Primary Light is considered by most near-death experiencers to be God Light; Dark Light is Mother Light, and Bright Light is Father Light.

- *Primary Light* fosters exceptionally deep mystical knowingness in people afterward, and engenders more radical shifts in their sense of reality and life's purpose than do the other lights.

- *Dark Light* gently reassures and heals those it touches and leaves them with a sense of being nurtured and supported, while at the same time being linked to larger systems of learning and growth within the human family.

- *Bright Light* energizes and enlivens, as it triggers displays of a broad range of latent talents and abilities, as well as an unusual sensitivity to sound, sunshine, bright lights, pharmaceuticals, and anything electrically based.

"The Darkness That Knows"

Children in my research project often gave me details of being cradled in a womb-like darkness so purple-black that it shimmered, so deep that it knew all things, so peaceful, wonderful, bliss-filled, and perfect that we adults would call it "heaven"—yet it was devoid of what is commonly termed "light."

Joe Ann Van Gelder, one of my research participants, had nine near-death experiences as a child, the first occurring because of a drowning when she was fifteen months old. She had eight more by the time she was ten, precipitated by such conditions as malaria, automobile accidents, a burst appendix, electrical shock, surgeries, polio, and additional bouts with drowning. It was the first one, though, that impacted her the most. It involved the deeper reaches of a living darkness. She displayed an unusually high intelligence immediately afterward, which surprised everyone, including her parents.

Of interest is a letter I received from her not long ago in which she questioned just what that special dark place she encountered as an infant might have been. She offered the idea that perhaps it was some formless mode of pure consciousness, as no thoughts or feelings were present in her experience of it—only the existence of awareness, the bliss of knowingness. She asked, "When death comes near the young, do they in fact merge back into the Oneness we call by various names God, from which they've so recently come?" Even though Joe Ann has no explanation for the deep dark that once cradled her, she's convinced that it has something to do with a type of consciousness that interacts with Creation and created matter.

Intensity Matters

The aftereffect of electrical sensitivity is determined not by the length of exposure to the brightness of inner light in a near-death episode, but by the intensity of that light. In other words, it doesn't seem to matter how much light fills an individual's scenario, what type of light, or even if the person merges with the light. It's how powerfully and deeply felt the light is, even if only experienced for a brief period of time.

IQs Can Soar

Of the 277 child experiencers in my study, the ones most apt to display high IQs afterward were enveloped by "dark" light. Child experiencers between birth and fifteen months, who had exceptionally vivid encounters with what they called "The Darkness That Knows," grew up to have IQs registering 184 and higher, far exceeding the standard rating for genius of 134 to 136.

A Scary Dark

Kathie Younker of Saint Cloud, Minnesota, fell out of a moving car when she was three years old. Her father told her that the doctor said her heart had stopped while she was being treated. "My most severe struggle," she recalls, "has been with the memory of the darkness. What I interpret as the moment of death was so traumatic that I am still, in my early fifties, unable to remember it without trauma. My mind

Drawing done by Douglas M. King of the dark light that healed him.

simply will not allow itself to bring back what came immediately after this moment of death. I know it was darkness because I recall what I can only describe as a 'porthole of vision' closing. When this porthole closed, the feeling I had was of being trapped in a dark well. Because this feeling was so horrible, my whole being tells me that the darkness was horrible, too. I know that when I went to the light, I had no memory or feelings of trauma. What I felt as I went toward the light was curiosity.

"To the best of my recollection," she says, "that light was colorless and pulsating. Yet it was a warm, inviting, loving intelligence. The desire to go forward to meet the source of the light was so compelling that I cannot recall it without being moved to tears, and being consumed by a terrible loss because I was not allowed to go there."

After reading more about research on near-death states, Kathie found new meaning in her experience: "I feel as though I have reached a new threshold in my recollection of the darkness. I realize that I don't have to mix the memory of the darkness with my traumatic death struggle. If I remember it, rather, as a precursor to the light, it takes on a totally different perspective. It's like remembering backward from the light to the darkness that came before it."

A Healing Dark

At the age of fifty-two, Douglas M. King of Chicago was admitted to Grant Hospital with a mysterious lung infection. He nearly died. One night, just after the lights went out and while he was still close to death, a strange dark "blob" suddenly manifested in midair. This oval object, consisting of a light source that was "perfect black," floated over to him and stayed there until he was feeling better, then it disappeared.

After a second biopsy, no trace of Douglas's lung infection or its effects remained. What was a life-or-death crisis had become a miracle. The medical staff was left scratching their heads. Douglas's "greeter" while he lay on the edge of death turned out to be a mass of dark light that healed him.

A Purple Dark, Then White

Kathi Beasley, a middle-aged adult, was diagnosed with a brain tumor in April 2004. It was localized behind her left eye and was slowly causing her to lose her vision as it wrapped itself around vital brain structures. Just before the surgery that was to remove the tumor, the sleep disturbances that had plagued her for years grew suddenly worse.

"I struggled to stay calm, but the darkness became darker than I had ever known. I walked toward my bathroom and flipped on the light switch as if an external source of light would make the darkness that slowly engulfed me disappear. This time, though, the laws of nature were ignored. Light did not dispel darkness.

"As the room grew ever darker around me, I began to slowly accept the fact that I was going to leave this life. Slowly, very slowly, the acceptance of death came. But much to my surprise, I continued to have all my awareness even as I stood in total darkness, with heightened senses as to what would come next. I noticed something faint and dim circling and swirling above me in the form of a small golden form. I became aware of not one but of many small golden, oblong, disc-like lights swirling above my head. Fear was almost instantly replaced with a mixture of wonder, relief, and curiosity. I was not alone. The golden lights illuminated the dark places where they skimmed. And by doing so, they revealed that the place in which I was standing was not black, but instead a deep, royal, beautiful rich purple."

Kathi went on to experience a burst of raw brilliant energy as a Light began filling her, almost electrocuting her, with an unbelievable unconditional love. This was followed by a life review, along with an explanation from the Light about how these events in her review shaped her life for better or worse. Then, "I was engulfed in a pure whiter than white Light that scrubbed me in a celestial bath of newness. It purified and purged me inwardly from all my previous burden and pain in life. It gave me new eyes for the world without losing much of the wisdom I had gained. It gave me new levels of peace and new ways of thinking."

Walter Russell's Illumination about Light and Dark

The life of Walter Russell, a famous artist, genius, and mystic, was radically altered by numerous transcendental states, the first an unusual "awakening" to light at age seven. This prepared him in advance for the financial disaster his family would soon suffer. By 1881, when only ten years old, Russell was pulled from school and sent to work. Within a few years, he was entirely self-supporting

The Real McCoy

Walter Russell excelled at whatever he did, and won lasting friendships and lucrative art commissions. He had a studio in Carnegie Hall in New York City, became a commissioned sculptor for President and Mrs. Franklin Delano Roosevelt, was a longtime friend of Mark Twain, and painted and sculpted Thomas Edison. His motto was this: "Mediocrity is self-inflicted. Genius is self-bestowed." (Refer to appendix E.)

Unbelievably Detailed Revelations

Once he regained use of his faculties after being immersed in light for thirty-nine days, Walter Russell penned *The Divine Iliad,* the story of his illumination and the source for his book *The Secret of Light.* He then spent the next six years producing *The Universal One,* a text containing the drawings and revelations given to him during his lengthy experience, about the universe and how it worked, and covering such subjects as chemistry, physics, and electromagnetics. A correspondence with Albert Einstein advanced his own theory that this is a "thought-wave" universe created for the transmission of thought.

and self-educated, earning his way through five years of art school.

He experienced a full Transcendent type of near-death scenario when he succumbed to "black diphtheria" at the age of fourteen, and claimed to have discovered the secret of healing as a result. He described what happened to him as having entered into "at-one-ment" with God. These two experiences while still a youngster set the stage for dramatic periods of illumination that would occur every seven years throughout the rest of his life.

When he was forty-nine, Russell was suddenly enveloped in the fullness of what he called "Cosmic Consciousness." This state lasted for thirty-nine days and nights without abating. Afterward, Walter recorded that: "My personal reaction to this great happening left me wholly Mind [conscious of little else but mind], with but slight awareness of my electric body. During practically all of the time, I felt that my body was not a part of me but attached to my Consciousness by electric threads of light. When I had to use my body in such acts as writing in words the essence of God's Message, it was extremely difficult to bring my body back under control."

Walter experienced Light as being the One Mind and substance of the universe, and human consciousness as mind aware of itself. His illumination revealed that visible light is but an effect of that which is primary, all-knowing and all-powerful. He saw dark light as the manifestation of electricity's negative charge, functioning in the creative role of "Mother Light," and bright light as the presence of the positive charge that to him was directive in the sense of a "Father Light." He came to know that all things proceed from the Primary Light's reflection of Itself in dark and bright waves of motion.

The three main aspects of light's function revealed in Walter Russell's illumination, along with the symbolic imagery he associated each with, match the reports I have consistently received from near-death experiencers—child or adult—who describe the particular type of light they encountered during their episode.

Flame Letters

The mystical branch of Judaism called kabbalism regards the flame-shaped letters of the Hebrew alphabet as a sacred language, the medium of divine communication. Each of the Hebrew letters reveals some aspect of heavenly truth or revelation. Studying them one at a time is said to aid in meditation and with inner development.

More of Light's Mysteries

In 1 John 1:5, it says: "This then is the message which we have heard of him, and declare unto you, that God is light, and in him is no darkness at all."

Edward Hoffman challenges this biblical passage in his book *The Hebrew Alphabet*. In it, he notes how Hebrew scholars have warned that in order to understand God's message, we must overcome our tendency to think in dualities. They say, "The difference by means of which light is distinguished from darkness is by degree only; both are one in kind, as there is no light without darkness and no darkness without light."

Sharon Begley continued this line of thought in her article "Science Finds God," published in *Newsweek* (July 20, 1998), then she made a surprising statement:

"Take the difficult Christian concept of Jesus as both fully divine and fully human. It turns out that this duality has a parallel in quantum physics. In the early years of this century, physicists discovered that entities thought of as particles, like electrons, can also act as waves. And light, considered a wave, can in some experiments act like a barrage of particles. The orthodox interpretation of this strange situation is that light is, simultaneously, wave and particle. Electrons are simultaneously waves and particles. Which aspect of light one sees, which face an electron turns to a human observer, varies with the circumstances."

Physical light, then, as science has discovered, is both wave and particle. What form or type of light an individual actually sees alters relative to the situation and angle of view.

If radically slowed during scientific experiments, physical light changes its movement and behavior, appearing to bend and refract in a unique fashion. If consciousness is radically accelerated during near-death and other transformative states, inner light duplicates the slowing of physical light in that it is reported to bend, refract, distort, or alter. Inner light behaves as if it were quite alive when this occurs, with its own expressive intelligence that feels like love and appears in whatever form is most appropriate at the moment.

Considering the strange properties of physical light and how these properties can parallel those of inner light, what makes us think that the light in powerful subjective experiences was solely a product of our imagination?

The Ecstasy of Light

"I took the feelings of this love into every fiber of my being. It vibrated and massaged every essence of my being. I felt as if I would explode into a million pieces or shatter from the experience of this ineffable, unspeakable ecstasy. The Light knew me and understood everything about me. The Light affirmed me over and over."

—Kathi Beasley,
near-death experiencer

New Word

Enlightenment, by dictionary definition, is the act of giving or imparting intellectual or spiritual information; to instruct, teach, inform. The roots of the word actually come from *en* ("to provide with" or "cause to be") and *light* ("to illumine" or "bring out of the dark and make clear"). Enlightenment, then, means "provided with illumination"—the inference being to the transforming power of God's Light.

The Energy Charge of Enlightenment

Being immersed in The Light on the other side of death's curtain is ecstatically overwhelming. That light cradles your soul in the heart of its pulse-beat and fills you with loveshine. The "you" you think you are melts away, reforming as the "YOU" you really are, and you are reborn because at last you remember your true identity as a living soul. I know. And the majority of near-death experiencers agree with me. We feel as though we were given a glimpse of or a shove toward *enlightenment.*

East versus West

There has always been a steady procession of revelators and avatars (great teachers or messiahs) who have claimed divine authority to reveal Higher Truth. These great ones have often exhibited unusual powers. They have healed, taught, preached, and performed "miracles" for the benefit of those in need. They have assured the multitudes that anyone can do as they have done and have offered to teach how. What they have offered is invariably a course in self-development that involves discipline, sacrifice, virtue, and a lifetime of commitment in service to humankind. Although all have been products of their prevailing culture, their messages and methods have been similar in principle and can be condensed into two general teachings—what I call "Eastern" and "Western."

Eastern and Western versions of awakening to an experience of illumination are alike in the goal they strive for—oneness with The Holy—but are, for the most part, opposite in the paths they offer to reach that goal (like reflections in the same mirror). This is what I believe to be their essence:

- **Top Down (outside in).** *The Western version emphasizes descending force,* originating from outside a person's body, passing down through the top of the head, or through the chest area, and spreading throughout the body. It's an outward-directed process that seeks outside guidance and looks for The Divine On High. It receives outside energy in. The most familiar teaching of this version is Christos, or Christ Consciousness (Descent of The Logos).

- **Bottom Up (inside out).** *The Eastern version emphasizes ascending force,* originating from within a person's body, usually from the base of the spine, rising up until it bursts through the top of a person's head. It's an inner process that seeks inner guidance and looks for The Divine deep within. It projects energy from inside out. The most familiar teaching of this version is Kundalini, or Ku (Ascension into The Godhead; refer to chapter 20).

Let's stop for a moment. Be as objective as you possibly can. Doesn't what you have just read remind you of a formula for accessing strong doses of high-powered energy?

Move past "isms" and schisms, traditions and dogmas, legends and standards, symbols and revelations. Just look at the process of enlightenment itself and how it operates. Could it be that the path to God (transcendence) revolves around the issue of how an individual handles intense power, how he or she deals with The Force? If we are honest here, the only real difference between Eastern and Western versions of spiritual development is the directional path of the energy currents that facilitate the process. That's it.

> **Feeling the Force**
>
> It's the "punch" of power that triggers near-death and other transformative states that catches the experiencer's attention. You know something extraordinary just happened. You feel it. Imagery and spirit visitations take a backseat to that initial, intense "blow." Some individuals liken the feeling to being "hit by a two-by-four" or "clobbered by a heavenly sledgehammer." Those who did not feel such force still commented on the suddenness of an unusual lifting or tingling sensation that preceded what came next.

When we're talking about spiritual development and religious conversions, I believe what we are really talking about is energy itself, differing by degree and type of voltage, and how it can be accessed, maintained, and utilized.

Power Punch

During the sessions I had with near-death experiencers, rarely was I able to isolate what would show me that a singular path of energy was responsible for either the experience or its impact. Certainly, indicators of Kundalini/Ku or Christos directional currents were present, but they seemed secondary to me rather than causal. What caught my attention in the majority of cases was an indication of both power flows converging together into a single "power punch" that created a "light flash" (an unusual burst of light and/or that moment of enlightenment).

My theory concerning this convergence of power flows is too lengthy to discuss in this book, but I touch on the subject further in the next chapter. After the research I have done, I am confident enough of what I have observed to call the near-death phenomenon a "power punch" rather than an "experience." A force is involved, of this I have no doubt, and it triggers what comes next.

Power Rush

That initial power punch leaves its mark in how the brain and nervous system are affected. But the fuller import of its effect can be delayed or repressed by the experiencer, sometimes for decades. Although most of the pattern of aftereffects will be apparent in the individual's life, whether he or she acknowledges it or not, it takes willingness on the part of the experiencer or at least an openness to change or heal for the full "blow" to be felt. When that breakthrough "blow" arrives, it's most often described as a "power rush" or "energy overload."

To help you envision what I'm talking about, let's consider the case of Tina Sweeney, of Laval, Quebec. At the age of four, she received a terrible beating from her father, which almost killed her. "I turned around to see my father's face," she recalled, "and everything went completely black—The Void!" She described this void, this blackness, as "absolute silence, very secure, warm, and so peaceful, where there is a current of waves vibrating softly and gently. Although I can feel its power, it's like feeling the breath of creation breathing."

As her scenario progressed, Tina encountered both the dark light and the bright light. She remembers that the dark light was like being in a womb—not her mother's, but the womb of creation, which she considers to be The Void. Like many child experiencers (children are six times more likely to repress their near-death state than adults are), she blocked the fullness of her episode and the impact of its aftereffects, until, in her forties, she had to seek out a psychiatrist for treatment. During therapy, both her near-death scenario and

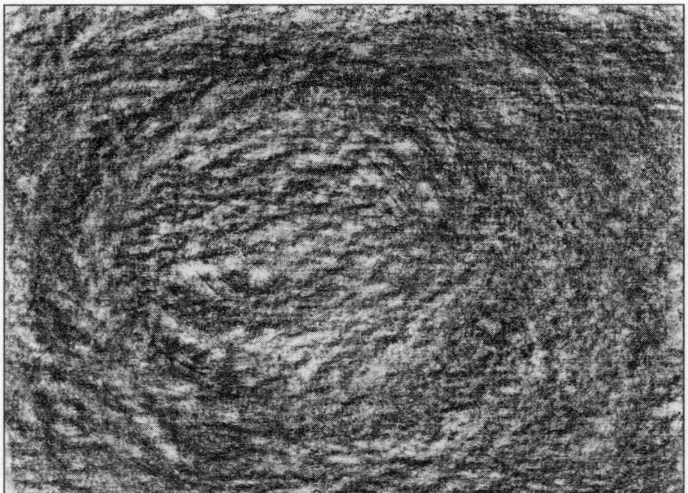

Drawing of the warm, wonderful dark light—The Void, by Tina Sweeney.

the aftereffects' intensity broke through in one immense rush of memory and physical sensations.

Tina continued: "I saw myself at the age of four standing in front of a wall of light. You know, it's really funny to say this, but I was dead yet here's this incredible light. And I remained in that light for a full three weeks after the therapy session. I couldn't sleep very much because of all this energy rushing through my body like information being poured into me. I could understand life, not the intellectual way, but I could 'feel' the sense of life as if I were part of the knowledge of the universe. After a while, I got scared of not knowing where this tremendous high voltage energy was taking me, so I asked it to stop. And it did. The therapy session helped me to make links between what happened to me at four and the changes that are happening to me now."

Her final drawing illustrates the breakthrough realization she made that she exists (the tree) as a fusion of dark negatively charged light (the lower part of the picture) and bright positively charged light (the upper part), so that Primary Light or Source (the sun) may ever shine from the center of her being.

When just a child, Tina Sweeney had to deal with a near-death episode and its aftereffects, coupled with family violence. Conditions made it necessary that she repress what she could. The rush of energy that "exploded" from her that day in her psychiatrist's office utterly transformed her, releasing with it a lifetime of grief and confusion. As difficult as her youth had been, Tina points to her near-death experience as being more powerful in its effect on her—reliving the memory of it, like a sudden energy overload.

The average experiencer moves past concepts of duality in his or her thinking,

Tina Sweeney's version of standing in front of a wall of light that had no end, when she "died" at the age of four.

Tina Sweeney's breakthrough realization when she finally embraced the fullness of her childhood near-death experience and its aftereffects.

and begins to embrace triune (three-sided) principles in the living of life. See the chart below.

Dualistic thinking is oppositional—sides opposing or competing with each other (like being confined to a box). Triune thinking is mutually supportive—sides interconnected and entwined with each other (like with a triangle, strength comes from linking equally each point with each of the other points).

Experiencers begin to act in mutually supportive ways with other people. Most of them think "outside the box." They tend to defy how society expects people to behave or what role they should have in life. Because of this, experiencers often become creative problem solvers, healers, who no longer fit the old stereotypes.

Duality Concepts		**Triune Principle**
Male	Female	Soul
Intellect	Imagination	Knowing
Bright	Dark	Luminous
Positively charged light	Negatively charged light	Unified-primary light

Part 5

Back Down to Earth

We're learning that the near-death experience may not only profoundly affect experiencers spiritually, but also physiologically. The very neurological patterns of their brains may undergo a startling change—a change that holds incredible promise for us all. We've much more to learn about near-death experiences. Flush with early media attention, many near-death experiencers are now finding that perhaps they were too easily tempted by promises of fame and fortune, and they momentarily lost sight of a higher purpose to their experience. Many researchers are also finding that financial support, like popularity, can be fickle.

Still, the story of the near-death experience is a fascinating one. Whether you're an experiencer, a friend or loved one of an experiencer, or someone intrigued by near-death experiences, you'll find something of special interest in these chapters—plus a "message for the twenty-first century."

22

Brain-Biology Link

Research is the highest form of adoration.

—Pierre Teilhard de Chardin, French Jesuit, paleontologist, theologian, and philosopher

Never was it the imagery alone in anyone's near-death episode (heavenly or hellish, initial or transcendent) that made the biggest difference. Always, it was the intensity of that imagery. Even with those who challenged the appearance of angels, God, or religious-type figures by asking, "Is that what you really look like?" then witnessing the entity dissolve into brilliant light or burst into a massive, sunlike sphere—still, it was the intensity of the experience that mattered most. And the spread of almost all aftereffects can be traced to the impact of that intensity.

The aftereffects, as profiled in chapter 7, suggest that near-death states may bring about a "brain shift"—a structural, chemical, and functional change in the brain. I examined this possibility in my research report titled "Brain Shift/Spirit Shift: A Theoretical Model Using Research on Near-Death States to Explore the Transformation of Consciousness." (For information on obtaining a copy, see appendix C.)

Because of the many connections that can be made between the aftereffects and the intensity of what occurs in near-death states, and what that seems to imply, I have come to regard the experience's impact (how it feels) as more significant than the imagery (who or what the individual saw or met) on the other side of death's curtain. You'll soon see why I would make that statement.

Brain Shift

Thanks to modern technology, we now know things about the brain that we never knew before:

Lasting Neurological Changes

One of my findings is that synesthesia is an aftereffect of near-death states. Considered a rare anomaly in sensory perception, synesthesia is linked to the limbic system in the brain and consists of sensations being registered in multiples, rather than as a single report. Examples: hearing a painting (not just seeing it), smelling colors (not just responding to them emotionally), or seeing images when touching something.

Richard J. Bonenfant, PhD, did a clinical study of the physiological aftereffects of near-death experiences. According to Dr. Bonenfant: "The overwhelming majority—90 percent—of the NDErs expressed the opinion that their NDE-related effects had either remained constant or increased over time, whereas only 5 percent felt that such changes had decreased. NDErs differed significantly from non-NDErs in this regard. These findings indicate that NDEs may provoke enduring neurophysiological states in addition to transformational changes in personality." How did synesthesia figure in his studies? Two-thirds had it. This alone is a major neurological finding! (See appendix C for reference to his study.)

Thought Power

Clinical trials conducted by New York State Health Department scientists show that thought alone can move a computer cursor around a display screen! They attached electrodes to the scalp of volunteers and asked them to concentrate on what they wanted the cursor to do. Thought commands in the form of brain-wave emissions were picked up by an amplifier, which signaled the computer to respond.

- Research on identical twins reveals substantial differences within the folds of each one's brain. We have long known that brain size is genetic, but these new tests show that learning *physically alters the structure of the brain itself.*
- PET (positron emission tomography) scans establish that not only is original thinking processed differently from regular thinking, but unusual, exciting, or creative thoughts can actually *change brain structure*—in a matter of minutes.
- Using EEG (electroencephalograph) machines, it was discovered that certain images, words, and timed pauses can *shift the brain into multiple and simultaneous ranges of brain-wave frequencies* identical to those achieved by experienced meditators and "wise ones."

Brain structure, chemistry, and function, then, can change faster and in more remarkable ways than previously believed.

Clusters and Spurts

In his book *Creating Minds,* Howard Gardner profiles the great minds of the twentieth century in an attempt to characterize genius. He discovered that letting go of your beliefs about what is possible makes it easier to take new ideas seriously, connecting things ordinarily not connected leads to insight, and a tolerance for ambiguity is crucial to creativity. He points out that the word "intelligence" means "to select among," a reference to individuals who are smart in recognizing details. But genius "shakes together" or "clusters" information, almost as a child would, so data can be rearranged to form different or larger wholes.

Gardner speaks of Einstein seeing a light ray in his mind and knowing its function and purpose, of the French composer Olivier Messiaen seeing the color different tones have, and of Picasso seeing numbers as patterns of contour and shape. This ability to see what others can't typifies the "shaking together" and "clustering" of data common to geniuses, and it raises the possibility that sensing in multiples (synesthesia) may also be involved. Both these traits, clustering information (taking in an array of data at once) and multiple sensing (seeing what others can't), are aftereffects general to near-death states and transformations of consciousness—whether the experiencer becomes a genius or not.

Growth Spurts

In my research, I discovered that the average near-death experiencer, whether child or adult, knows more after his or her episode than before. The experiencer is often able to detach from previous norms, abstract freely, envision broader perspectives, access latent talents, and in some cases display signs of genius. Could the increase in intelligence and the hunger for learning that is so much a part of the aftereffects be a sign that the neural pathways in experiencer brains have

Hello Brain

I was inspired to take up the ancient art of rune casting after having three near-death episodes in 1977. Unlike other divinatory systems, this particular artform necessitates right- and left-brain hemispheres to work together simultaneously for good results. Developing this skill enabled me to retrain how I used my own brain. I wrote the book *Runes of the Goddess* as a way of saying thank you, and passing the gift on to others. (Refer to appendix C.)

Watch That Wiring

Scientists now think that intelligence has more to do with how neurons (brain cells) are wired than with the neurons themselves. Neuroscientist Arnold Scheibel of the University of California at Los Angeles is quoted as saying: "Smart people have more complex, more efficient neural highways for transmitting information."

Brain Balancing

The near-death phenomenon appears to stimulate the brain hemisphere that was not previously dominant. There's also an observable change in the brain, functionally, toward data clustering and creative invention, as if the experiencer were developing a more balanced/cooperative type of processing network. This advances the potential for whole-brain responses (less dependence on hemispheric dominance, greater flexibility and utilization of the brain itself).

Who Dies?

Dr. Pim van Lommel has stated that near-death experiencers during loss of brain function still have out-of-body states, clear enhanced consciousness, self-identity with emotions, cognition with associative thought perception, use of faculties, and intact memories. "How," he asks, "can a brain produce all of this when it isn't working?"

somehow been rewired or reconfigured? Or that neural sprouting (the "branching" out of cellular connectors) has accelerated due to a possible growth spurt in brain capacity?

Impossible, you say? Child experiencers of near-death states evidence unusual growth spurts in brain capacity, at a time when their brain is about one-fifth the size of an adult brain and lacking in the billions of connections necessary for higher brain function and conceptual thought.

Other near-death researchers claim that experiencers become more right-brained afterward. At first glance, this seems to be so. Yet, of those I interviewed, switches in brain hemisphere dominance varied: If analytical (left-brained) before, then they tended to be more creative/intuitive (right-brained) after—but the reverse also happened. Many came back more left-brained.

Getting Zapped

Based on my research, a sudden charge of energy or voltage current is present in intense states of consciousness transformations. We've already discussed in the previous chapter how Eastern and Western methods for "awakening" involve at their most basic level pathways that energy travels: outside in (descending force), and inside out (ascending force). Sudden energy surges and floods of emotions are sure signs of altered brain chemistry, indicating a neural-biological component to the transformative process (whether the turbulent type or from slower methods).

What causes us to awaken to the greater potential within us is a transformative state of some kind. Most people experience an initial or partial one, enough to inspire and uplift and strengthen in them a desire for change. But the deeper states are more intense and can be traumatic, with complex and long-lasting aftereffects. A powerful force unleashes these states. In some cases, this energy is felt as a singular voltage—ascending (from the lower part of the body up to the head) or descending (from outside the body, entering at the head or chest area, and traveling down)—but in the more involved and dramatic experiences, it's like being zapped by both flows at the same time. How experiencers described this reminded me of how lightning operates.

It's Like Lightning

Compare what happens with lightning with what I suspect may be at the core of major transformational events such as the near-death experience:

- *In the natural world,* descending bolts of electricity (from the clouds) and ascending bolts of electricity (from the earth) meet to create a huge light flash (lightning) during a thunderstorm. This equalizes pressure differences between the clouds and the energy field of the earth, so environmental stability can be maintained. It also stimulates plant growth through the creation of nitrogen compounds.

- *In human consciousness,* descending currents of force (possibly from the soul level, Higher Self, God) and ascending currents of force (perhaps from the ego, lower self, personality level) meet to create a powerful light flash (illumination) during a transformation of consciousness. This equalizes pressure differences between latent spiritual potentiality and ordinary personality development, so mind-body stability can be maintained. It also stimulates human growth through the expansion and enhancement of consciousness.

Guess Who's a Universe?

We human beings are electromagnetic by nature, stuffed full of water and chemicals with a few added minerals. Any change in electrical or magnetic energy around or within us, or with whatever we ingest or absorb, subtly or significantly alters our behavior, emotions, coordination, and ability to think and reason coherently. We are like self-contained universes symbiotically connected to and dependent on the universe at large. We operate more as "nerve cells" or "half-asleep" until we "wake up" and take charge of our lives and our environment.

Watch Out

Also like lightning, light flashes can harm as well as help. For instance, fire can result when lightning bolts are too close to the ground; people and animals can be killed. Similarly, individuals can be hospitalized or committed to an institution if "shaki bolts" (Sanskrit for "active spiritual power") are out of control.

The Limbic System and Emotions

The *limbic system* is our emotional center, our "gut" or third brain, and the seat of our survival instinct. The limbic also controls our immune system, has a direct neural connection to

New Word

The **limbic system** is located in a semicircle in the middle of the brain, capping off the topmost extension of the brain stem. It consists of various parts and sections that together twist around the brain stem like "limbs" or "vines"—hence its name, "limbic." This small but extremely efficient system has been around for fifty thousand years or more in the evolution of brain development.

Body Changes

"In a true near-death experience, large changes in physiology are involved; the typical near-death experience which then occurs has many features that will allow its classification also as a true transcendent experience."
—Peter Fenwick, MD, FRCPsych

the heart, and acts as an "executive office" in the way it determines what information goes to what area of the brain—including the neocortex ("new brain")—for further processing. Stimulating the limbic system activates the imagination and the basic patterns for imagery and sound stored in the temporal lobes.

Note the connections in the limbic system with the heart, emotions, immune system, temporal lobes, and survival. If we were to view each of these connections at their next highest level of performance, here's what we would have:

- The heart—love
- The emotions—ecstasy
- Immune system—upliftment
- Temporal lobes—otherworld realities
- Survival—awareness of life as ongoing

Near-death states enhance and enlarge whatever already exists within the individual, including potential. This spread of enhanced performance—all the areas directly linked to limbic system involvement—exactly matches the core components of a near-death experience. Also, nearly all the aftereffects from near-death and other transformative episodes can be traced to limbic system enhancement and acceleration. This is why we need to know as much as we can about the limbic system.

When the limbic is stimulated, it leaves "prints" in the manner of how we respond. With a little bit of stimulation (such as from music, rituals, and celebrations), we get excited, perk up, emotions flow, and our receptivity to ideas and relationships is enhanced. Our feelings of passion and compassion turn on with more stimulation, along with displays of psychic/intuitive abilities and the inspiration to take action.

Charismatic speakers and shocking news headlines often trigger this response in us (for instance, listening to the speeches of Martin Luther King

Jr., or hearing of the tragic death of Princess Diana). Overwhelming surges of love and light, faculty changes, panoramic visions, and the emergence of wisdom and knowing occur when the limbic is deeply impacted by a sudden intense experience that flips it into a different "gear."

Once the limbic system is "spun around" or "flipped" by such a "blow," it's as if the temporal lobes, nervous system, and heart are signaled to do one of two things: Shut down or speed up. Shutting down means damage or death. Speeding up means healing or enhancement. What we refer to as the aftereffects in cases of near-death and near-death-like states may well be the "cascade effect"—a series of aspects coming on the heels of each other, similar to how water tends to tumble downhill if a lot is released at once. The extent of the cascade effect—what various bodily systems exhibit as they react to limbic enhancement/enlargement/acceleration—appears to indicate the degree to which the limbic system was affected.

Guardian at the Gate

Far from being just a handy-dandy survival center, the limbic system jump-starts emotional expression and the learning process. Once accelerated in function, it appears to be the gateway of initiation for such conditions as multiple sensing (synesthesia), clustered thinking (a marker for creative genius), parallel processing/simultaneous brain-wave function ("the awakened mind"), and mind over matter (psychokinesis). By reexamining the aftereffects of near-death states through this very different "lens," we can see how potent the impact of limbic acceleration can be on the brain organ, and how this might engender a brain shift.

The Theories of Melvin Morse, MD

As you learned in previous chapters, Dr. Melvin Morse is an outspoken near-death researcher and pediatrician based in Renton, Washington. After many years of research and hearing thousands of stories, Dr. Morse claims that he's never heard a single account that made him think someone actually "left their body" during an episode. Instead, he feels that as we lose our ordinary senses in dying, we acquire senses we never used before. "We are capable of remote viewing, telepathy, the ability to perceive other realities, and the ability to communicate with, well, something that most people call God," he says. "This is totally astonishing. It is a completely unexpected finding, given modern neuroscientific theory of brain function. For one thing, it strongly implies that the storage and retrieval of memory is not dependent on a functioning brain."

Right Temporal Lobe

"Human beings have a sixth sensory ability located within our right *temporal lobe, hippocampus,* and related limbic lobe structures," states Dr. Morse. "This

Spooky Action at a Distance

The experiments with telepathy done by Rupert Sheldrake, PhD, a biologist and author of *The Sense of Being Stared At, and Other Aspects of the Extended Mind,* are challenging the entire scientific world. *Telepathy* means "distant feeling" and involves the ability to sense communications, activities, thoughts, and states of being nonlocal. Pets as well as people have reacted when someone they are bonded to has an accident or is dying, even if many miles away.

"There is an analogy for this process in quantum physics," says Dr. Sheldrake. "If two particles have been part of the same quantum system and are separated in space, they retain a mysterious connectedness. When Einstein first realized this implication of quantum theory, he thought it must be wrong because it implied what he called 'spooky action at a distance.' Experiments have shown that quantum theory is right and Einstein wrong. A change in one separated part of a system can affect another instantaneously. This phenomenon is known as quantum nonlocality or non-separability."

Yes, our minds are centered in our bodies and in our brains in particular, but Dr. Sheldrake's work demonstrates that our minds are not confined to our brains but extend beyond them—through the fields of the mind, or mental fields, that exist both within and beyond our brains. (Refer to appendix C for information on Dr. Sheldrake's book.)

New Words

There are two **temporal lobe** regions of the brain in our head. One is located on the right side near the temple and upper part of the ear, the other in the same spot on the left side. Both are situated on the temporal bones that form the sides and base of our skull. The **hippocampus** is a section of the brain stem that looks like the cross section of a sea horse and is involved with emotions and memory.

area interprets information obtained through communication with an interactive universe. It allows communications with other human beings through their right temporal lobes. It involves perceptions of other realities. The classic function of the right temporal lobe is to interpret memory. This model adds the function of storing and retrieving memories from a storage site outside the human brain."

According to Dr. Morse: "Modern humans perceive the function of this area of the brain as 'intuition,' the 'inner voice' or 'gut feelings.' This area becomes activated in a variety of clinical situations, including dying, 'fear death' events, childbirth, severe physical or sexual abuse, religious prayer, extreme physiological stress such as starvation, or sometimes they just happen.

"The theory about the right temporal lobe can be tested by science and there is already a large mainstream [body of] scientific literature supporting it. It is a useful theory in that it explains a wide variety of previously ignored or dismissed pieces of scientific data which do not fit into our current scientific *paradigm.* Past-life memories, false memory syndromes, mind-body healing issues, ghosts, after-death communications, religious and spiritual encounters, near-death experiences, premonitions of death, UFOs, alien abductions, telekinesis, remote viewing, and telepathy can be studied as right temporal lobe functions."

Dr. Morse described a case that seemed typical of near-death scenarios: The person had an out-of-body experience, went through a tunnel, saw a heavenly place with bright flowers, was given a choice to come back, fell backward through tunnel, and felt healed. This happened to a twelve-year-old girl with migraine headaches who was having a right temporal lobe seizure. "Such cases may indicate that there is an underlying neurological mechanism which allows us to have the experience, which can be inadvertently triggered by a seizure. . . . The absence of a 'god' or spiritual aspect to this experience may indicate that the real thing, the near-death experience, involves both the neurological machinery and the interaction with another spiritual reality."

New Words

A **paradigm** is a set of ideas and conditions in a society that forms an overall theme or pattern. A **paradigm shift** occurs when deeply entrenched patterns of thought undergo a change, often with unsettling or threatening consequences to the established social order.

The God Spot

Two reference sources of material regarding what may be the brain's role in spiritual experiences are the article "Toward a Psychobiology of Transcendence: God in the Brain" by Arnold J. Mandell and the book *Neuropsychological Bases of God Beliefs* by Michael A. Persinger, PhD (see appendix C for details).

Image Patterning for Heaven and Hell

Scientifically, we know that the left temporal lobe specializes in negative emotions and images (fear-based things such as paranoia and sorrow), whereas the right temporal lobe is associated with positive emotions and images (love-based things such as joy and peace).

Michael A. Persinger, PhD, induced what seemed to be pleasant, heaven-like near-death experiences in subjects by stimulating the sylvian fissure in the right temporal lobe. He used magnetic signals of the same strength as those produced by the earth's magnetic field to accomplish this feat. Because his results are similar to those of Wilder Penfield, MD (author of *The Mystery of the Mind*), many researchers are now convinced that unpleasant or hellish near-death states are a product of exciting the left temporal lobe, and pleasant/ heavenly ones, the right.

Dr. Persinger's experiments and

Mirror, Mirror, on the Wall

The fact that the so-called "classical" near-death scenario is easily reproduced or "caused" was undoubtedly an impetus behind Raymond Moody's exploration of "mirror gazing." By resurrecting this centuries-old technique, he had hoped to see if volunteers could contact a spirit being or deceased loved one by staring into an angled mirror while background music played. His book *Reunions: Visionary Encounters with Departed Loved Ones* caused quite a stir, to say the least, but did result in a few claims of success.

those of physicians such as Dr. Penfield, however, have consistently failed to produce anything other than a general series of image patterns (a basic "blueprint"). With cases of temporal lobe seizure (as with the twelve-year-old girl Dr. Morse spoke of), centrifuge pilot training, and excessive stress, the same results occurred: The otherworldly episodes people had were generalized, fragmentary, and lacked the details, intensity, and aftereffects of genuine near-death states.

The idea of a "God spot" and of the singular importance of the right temporal lobe have both been undermined by Swedish and American researchers in a series of experiments. Anahad O'Connor, writing in the *New York Times* article "Following a Bright Light to a Calmer Tomorrow" (April 13, 2004), reported that "The scientists assumed that the near-death group [in their research] would show patterns of brain activity similar to those seen in temporal lobe epileptics, who often describe undergoing spiritual out-of-body events during seizures. The abnormal activity, however, did not spring up in the right temporal lobe, as is sometimes the case with epilepsy. Instead, the activity appeared almost exclusively in the left temporal lobe."

In reality, the temporal lobes are the location in the brain where basic patterns for shape, form, and feeling appear to be stored. As such, they function as some sort of "resource center" or "data comparison device" we have tapped into since childhood for learning how to distinguish and discern differences. As we age, engaging in creative imagination and invention ensures that both lobes not only remain active but can continuously expand and update the image-patterns available for our use. Knowing this, we can more readily accept the growing consensus in research that near-death experiences activate a number of regions in the brain, not only the right temporal lobe.

Mediator between Worlds

If mind states alter significantly, as in what appears to happen during a brain shift, the temporal lobes seem to assume more of a role of "mediator between worlds." This "mediator within" role is strongly in evidence in near-death cases. Initial imagery, sometimes called "overleafs," always matches what is appropriate for the experiencer's most urgent need at that

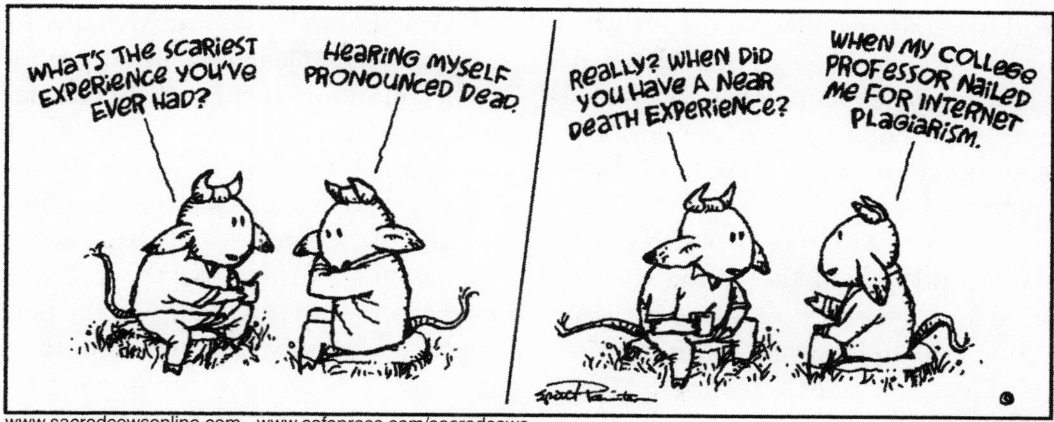

moment and/or what will have an impact on those around him or her.

No one knows for certain how this works, but the temporal lobes seem able to produce "accommodation" patterning and temporary "overlays" at the onset of near-death experiences. Two examples are the child who saw his older, aborted brother as a younger brother so he wouldn't be frightened by the encounter, and experiencers who are greeted by the living until they calm down, then imagery more typical of near-death states emerges. The temporal lobes as our patterning center obviously has more functions than that of a "library."

This leads me to believe that the initial imagery that appears in otherworld journeys is first and foremost either to relax the experiencer (put the person at ease—pleasant, heavenly experience) or to tense the experiencer (put the person on alert—unpleasant, hellish experience), so whatever needs to be accomplished by the episode will have an opportunity to be addressed. What seems to be the "primary directive" of the temporal lobes can, and often does, alter once the scenario is fully under way (for example, loving angels dissolve into a brilliant ball of light once challenged as to their real appearance). Experiencers, once so relaxed or alerted, tend to have deeper, more involved scenarios.

The Importance of "Future"

Because near-death experiencers come to have an extraordinary relationship with things "future" (most

Future Memory

Brain shift experiencers, adult or child, develop a relationship with anything "future." Many claim to "live" the future in advance to such a degree that it becomes like a memory of something already done (future memory episodes). What happens to these experiencers mimics what happens to ordinary kids aged three to five, and with the same impetus—the need to "rehearse" an event before it occurs.

readily know, see, hear, sense, or prelive the future), I searched for what might be an explanation and discovered studies done on early childhood brain development that might provide a clue.

Infants and toddlers have no sense of time and space. Between the ages of three and five, they gain this by projecting into and engaging with futuristic ideas, images, feelings, and sensations. But the future does not appear as "future" to children. To them it is simply another aspect of now (that which is immediate), and remains so until they are able to establish the validity of continuous scenery (for example, what is seen as a tree today will remain as the same tree tomorrow) and connected wholes (for example, families consist of people who are related to each other and live together). Once they accomplish this, they have the perspective and the sense of continuity they need to adapt to ever-changing environments and the meaningfulness of cause and effect (consequences). In other words, the imaginal adventures of

Brain Development Comparison Between Three-to-Five-Year-Olds and Brain Shift Experiencers

Three-to-Five-Year-Olds	**Brain Shift Experiencers**
Temporal Lobe Development	*Temporal Lobe Expansion*
Emerging Consciousness	*Enlarging Consciousness*
Prelive the future on a regular basis; spend more time in future than in the present.	Prelive the future on a regular basis through dream states; visions; future memory episodes.
Play with futuristic possibilities as a way of "getting ready"; rehearse in advance demands soon to be made on them.	Experience life's challenges and opportunities before they occur as a way of preparing for demands they will soon face.
No natural understanding of time-space states; consider "future" an aspect of "now." Gain perspective and continuity by establishing the validity of action/reaction or "future" (continuous scenery and connected wholes).	No longer restricted by a sense of time-space states; an awareness of simultaneity and the important of "now." Embrace broader dimensions of experience beyond that of "future" (unlimited perspectives validated by the continuity of stable reference points).
Progress from archetypal mental models to stereotypical ones in a process of self-discovery.	Progress from stereotypical mental models to individuation processes in a journey of soul discovery.
The Birth of Imagination	*The Rebirth of Imagination*

childhood are necessary for the development of healthy minds.

The similarities between what three-to-five-year-olds go through and what brain shift experiencers begin to engage in, regardless of their age, is uncanny. Consider the striking comparisons in the table on page 344.

Emphasized by this chart I put together is how reliable engaging in futuristic awareness and future memory episodes can be as a signal that an experiencer's brain is in the process of shifting in structure, chemistry, and function: a growth spurt. And that, as part of the shift, experiencers tend to revert back to the same brain-development stage of three-to-five-year-olds, and I believe for the same reason: to reestablish continuity and order through "futuristic rehearsals" so they can ready themselves for the greater challenge of higher mind states and spiritual maturity. If I'm right, this means that accessing the future to the extent that experiencers do is not a display of psychic ability, but a natural brain-development stage as we accelerate in brain function and capacity.

Throughout my research, I've observed that being able to live the future in advance and remember that you did alleviates much of the stress and fear that worrying about unknown variables can cause. This advanced preparation enables the human psyche to negotiate the demands of sudden change more smoothly. The ability imparts an immense sense of confidence and peace and often leads to frequent incidences of synchronicity (meaningful "coincidences"), as if your life was caught up in some type of "flow."

Adaptation or Evolution?

All species of life on this planet either adapt to changing environments or die. Accordingly and intriguingly, today, at this exact moment in history, when we need people who can increase their flexibility, thrive on change, have brains that can reason and intuit with equal skill, have bodies that can adjust to fickle climates, and have energy levels that can mix and merge efficiently with technological equipment without much in the way of training—what happens? Tens of millions worldwide are going through a transformation of consciousness that is preparing them physically as well as psychologically to adapt successfully to the

The Future Now

One evening, while watching television, Patreesa King, a near-death experiencer, flipped the channel to a movie entitled *Bounce,* starring Ben Affleck and Gwyneth Paltrow. Several days later she was watching *The Oprah Winfrey Show,* which featured interviews with Ben Affleck and Gwyneth Paltrow. They had starring roles in a soon-to-be-released movie, entitled *Bounce.* Patreesa immediately called the television station and confirmed that the show was not a rerun *and* that the film had, in fact, not yet been released. Episodes like this, of futuristic occurrences happening in the present, are typical of Patreesa's NDE aftereffects, and of the thousands of near-death experiencers I've had sessions with.

DNA Hop

Barbara McClintock won a Nobel Prize in 1983 for showing that certain genetic sequences constantly jump from one chromosomal location to another. She established that our DNA is not a static structure but is always changing.

God Breathing

"Light is what happens when God breathes."

—Pam Reynolds, near-death experiencer

demands of our new global society. Yet maybe, something even greater than adaptation is involved.

Jumping Genes of Light

In an issue of Dr. Melvin Morse's newsletter *Into the Light* (Volume 1, Number 6), he mentions some fascinating facts. Among them is that "Colm Kelleher, of the National Institute of Discovery Science, has proposed a mechanism by which spiritual experiences of a godlike Light can alter our DNA. Kelleher points out that throughout history there have been descriptions of the body dramatically bursting into a radiance of white light. Usually this happens at the point of death, but [it] also occurs as part of religious ecstasy."

Dr. Morse, in continuing to discuss Colm Kelleher's theory, acknowledges that many well-documented cases are on file in the Catholic Church of physical transformations that occurred once individuals reached a point of religious ecstasy that caused them to glow. Other similar records exist, such as one about a Tibetan monk by the name of Tsong Khapa who emitted bright rays of light when he died in 1419. "Kelleher states," says Dr. Morse, "that the physical human body is only encoded by 3 percent of the genetic information in each cell. Much of the remaining 97 percent evolved through 'retrotransposition.' This is defined as the movement of tiny pieces of our DNA to different locations on our chromosomes."

Dr. Morse believes that the subjective, inner light of ecstatic states is powerful enough to be visibly seen outside a person's body, and to alter his or her DNA. Since this idea is testable, he is determined to raise enough money from subscriptions to his newsletter to fund such research.

Junk DNA

The 97 percent of three million DNA base pairs whose function science has yet to determine is termed "junk DNA." Since nature never gives more than is needed to any organism for functioning in its environment, this massive amount of unidentifiable potential exists as a "sore spot" in the scientific world.

Current knowledge tells us that genes and DNA do not control our biology. DNA is controlled by signals outside the cell, including the energetic messages emanating from our positive and negative thoughts. Russian scientists, testing this discovery about thought and its affect on DNA, compared the rules of syntax (the way words are put together to form phrases and sentences), semantics (the study of meaning in language forms), and the basic rules of grammar. What they found is that the alkaloids of our DNA follow a regular grammar, just as languages do. Junk DNA, then, is exceptionally malleable, perhaps explaining why affirmations and hypnosis are so effective. Add to this discovery scientists such as Colm Kelleher who are finding more links between the so-called "junk DNA" and clairvoyance, intuition, spontaneous and remote acts of healing, self-healing, age reversal, levitation—even transfiguration and spiritual ascension.

We are standing at the edge of what may well be the greatest discoveries of all time—who we are, what we are, and what we're capable of. Research on the near-death phenomenon makes up the vanguard of this interest, directly challenging how consciousness is defined and how we regard the human body.

Evolution's Nod

It does not take much of a leap in thought to recognize evolutionary signs in what happens to people who undergo near-death experiences. Initially, though, the brain shift for adults from near-death and other similar transformative states is more like a growth event—a sudden, unexpected twist in life that operates like a washing machine, motivating us to clean up our habits, flush out our minds, and overhaul our lifestyles. Such brain shifts are powerful and far-reaching occurrences that bring about movement toward the spiritual and that challenge individuals to adjust and adapt to significant internal and external changes.

Among child experiencers, however, the brain shift from transformations of consciousness is more clearly an evolutionary event. The "second birth" children undergo as a result of a transformative experience reorders or "seeds" them in ways that are uniquely different from regular behavioral development. Children's brains are also affected to a greater degree by these occurrences than are adults, propelling them into abstract thinking and enhanced learning, as creative expression soars. This marks them as different from their agemates and at variance with family and societal expectations.

Once grown, these child experiencers attempt to enter the traditional workforce with a nontraditional mindset, ever pushing for change and new, or even exotic, options and alternatives. The "second born" continuously challenge every aspect of society on every level. They inspire the kind of cultural

The Search for Meaning

Dr. Pim van Lommel explains: "Consciousness is not rooted in the body. Consciousness continues in a dimension beyond our normal concept of time and space. Waking consciousness is only part of Higher, Divine, or Cosmic consciousness. The world as we see it, also during near-death states, derives its subjective reality from our consciousness. *I have my body. I am consciousness.* Science should be searching for the meaning of these new mysteries, rather than sticking with old concepts."

Brain Shifts/Spirit Shifts

After decades of research and sessions with thousands of people, I am convinced that once we understand the import of brain shifts (structural, chemical, and functional changes that are visibly apparent and can be clinically tested and measured), and spirit shifts (in-depth spiritual changes that are felt, not seen, and signify the movement of spirit forces and the development of true faith), we will solve the secret of how the human family and mind itself evolve and for what purpose.

growth that fuels social revolution. And they possess the necessary traits to indicate that they may indeed be part of the next "quantum leap" in the evolution of the human species—where aspects of the higher mind are said to become commonplace, rather than exceptional. (This is covered at length in my book *Beyond the Indigo Children*. See appendix C.)

Discussions about a neural-biological component to near-death and other transformative states are useful, but such findings don't cover or account for the entire range of the experience and its aftereffects. Nor do they address the initial mechanism that triggers the phenomenon. Not even what is known about Kundalini/Ku and the force that energy is said to release, even as a rushing "bolt," fully explains it. All attempts to identify *cause* fall short. The origin of that power remains elusive. We are left to conclude, then, that these experiences are spiritual in nature and beyond science to prove or disprove.

23

But Are All the Claims True?

All have their own personal ways of acting according to their visions. We must learn to be different, to feel and taste the manifold things that are us.

—Lame Deer, Native American medicine man

Transformative states, like the near-death experience, are slips in between ordinary time and space. They are moments when history and schedules and goals and obligations evaporate into a nothingness "flicker" that straddles new light. When the experience ends, it doesn't end. Suddenly, without choice or intention on anyone's part, you have been introduced to another way of living quite apart from anything you've known before. Do you just enjoy the "afterglow" for a while, then tuck what happened away into some type of mental closet as you scurry about to resume life as always? As if nothing unusual ever occurred? Or do you incorporate the experience into your daily life and embrace the challenges that brings?

Questions come a mile a minute. The reality check of "What do I do now?" is as frightening as it is wonder-filled. All of us mean well at first. All of us want to tell the world that there's no such thing as death, that we are each more important and loved than we could imagine, and that we have purpose—a job only we can fill in a larger "plan." But, being the humans that we are, the message we seek to deliver all too often gets lost in the translation. What we claim, and the way we communicate our claims, tends to confuse as many as it informs.

Researchers, too, have their struggles—sometimes with each other, sometimes in academia, and sometimes within themselves. In this chapter, we'll look at the varied cross-purposes experiencers and researchers have faced and still deal with, and how this tends

'Tis True

"We human beings invent reality as much as we discover it."

—Lawrence LeShan, psychology professor, author, and consciousness researcher

My First Was Hell

The very first near-death experiences I was exposed to were of the hellish type. Back in the 1960s, I was at Saint Alphonsus Hospital in Boise, Idaho, visiting a woman who had suffered a heart attack. While clinically dead, she had experienced being in a colorless world filled with nude, zombie-like people, all standing elbow to elbow, staring at her. She was resuscitated screaming from the horror of it. While I was talking with her, two other people hobbled in using canes and said the same thing had happened to them. A nurse whispered about a fourth, but I was not allowed to speak with him.

to influence the claims most of them make about near-death episodes. We begin with researchers.

Don't Rock the Boat

In the late 1980s, I encountered more people who had experienced hellish episodes than heavenly. When I sought out advice from other researchers as to how best to handle this, I was told to "forget about it." Later on, I found out why.

Some researchers had simply never encountered experiencers who had unpleasant or distressing episodes. But the majority refused to believe such cases could even happen, considering the fact that substantial numbers of accounts already on record covered only uplifting descriptions of heavenly scenes. Their minds closed to further discussion. Published research reports also sidestepped anything "negative," whether relating to scenarios or experiencer response to the aftereffects. My insistence that claims about the phenomenon were misleading and incomplete without this additional material fell on deaf ears. Since then, so many experiencers of the not-so-pleasant variety have come forward that today the field of research is far more balanced and informative than it was previously.

Perhaps the larger issue of whether anyone took my findings seriously has to do with credentials. In the research community, credentials refer to degrees such as PhD and MD and to the years spent establishing a reputation of expertise. The study of the near-death phenomenon is so new that those who wished to pursue the subject during the early years found themselves in an awkward position. With or without "proper" degrees, any precedent used to measure findings was hotly debated; in addition, research done over a century ago was paid little if any heed.

Who had the right to do such work? Who had the research expertise necessary for a field that would straddle religion and mysticism, science and biology, consciousness and the supernatural? It was never the credentials I lacked that was the real question, but the credentials almost all of us lacked. Our struggle for the recognition of our findings ran counter to how modern science regards the practice of research.

The Mighty Sword of Scientism

Researchers who are convinced ahead of time that something isn't true will be drawn to those facts and claims that seem to substantiate their beliefs. This isn't true science. Yet it's the way most scientists operate today, as demonstrated, for example, by the preponderance of those who refuse to consider any explanation other than oxygen deprivation to account for all near-death experiences. A closed mind closes the doors to discovery and innovation. How do you know if your mind is closed? When you reject alternate viewpoints without giving them a fair hearing. When this is done in the name of "science," it is called *scientism.*

A true skeptic is an open-minded seeker who avoids coming to any final conclusion about anything. This individual constantly searches and questions, knowing full well that yesterday's "snake oil" remedy might become today's miracle drug. Should the skeptic turn toward scientism, however, the opposite behavior holds sway. His or her mind closes to any variables discovered, protocols (methods used) become disproportionately rigid, and claims take on the status of "absolute." This attitude serves no one.

The "Other Kind" of Experiencer

I'll never forget the fellow I met in Las Vegas, Nevada, in the late eighties, who walked up to me as I was signing books in the open space of a busy mall. He had rigid body language, his face stern and serious. He stretched out his right arm, then pointed at me, glaring as he did, and yelled: "You got to tell people there's a hell. All them pretty stories about heaven and love aren't true. There's a hell and I've been there and it isn't pretty at all. Them love and light people are liars. That's not the way it is."

We had quite a talk afterward. I listened intently and what I heard was fear. He just couldn't accept what happened to him during his near-death scenario as compared to the other stories experiencers were telling. He seemed empowered by the terror he experienced and he clung to his fear as if he had earned the right to do so. His mind was completely closed to interpreting his scenario in any other manner than literally. I noticed that he seemed to need the power his fear gave him—the power to be different, to hurt deep inside without having to face why or what he could do to heal. It was as if his fear protected him from taking responsibility for his life.

New Word

Scientism refers to an attitude that demands scientific methods be used as the only way to determine truth. Science itself actually evolved from philosophy. If it weren't for the principles of matter, truth, and reason laid out by the philosophers of old, science as we presently understand it would not exist. Methods such as clinical trials are rather new historically, dating back about a hundred years or so. (Refer to chapter 13, and the sidebar entitled "The Scientific Method.")

A Stacked Deck

James McClenon, PhD, is quoted as saying: "IANDS members may have reported a higher incidence of core features because their experiences were sufficiently compelling to motivate them to join an organization dedicated to NDE research."

No Money, Honey

There's no doubt in my mind that near-death research falls short of its goal to describe and define the many factors present in the phenomenon. Still, as a researcher myself, I can affirm that we have all done remarkable work and accomplished a great deal. Frankly, though, it's not been enough. Looking back, some of the snags in the claims we have made involve:

- Studies based on too small a sample group
- Study after study confined to the same religious or cultural order or region
- Studies slanted by the researcher's personal beliefs and preferences
- Studies relying on the same procedures even after it's pointed out that the questions used are biased and "leading"
- Studies tied to a set protocol (scientific method) to the exclusion of other methods just as credible
- Studies centered around little more than a literature search and a few interviews
- Studies dependent on volunteers attending experiencer meetings rather than a true sample base from the public at large

Some of the challenges we've had to face in doing our work include:

- *Passion.* Finding a way to remain objective while being overwhelmed by the lure of unconditional love expressed by experiencers. (Some researchers have left their families to pursue love trysts with experiencers.)
- *Jealousy.* Finding a way to deal with the pressures of one-upmanship. (Com-

petition sometimes wins out over discovery.)

- *Prestige.* Finding a way to meet the pressures of publishing in the "right" journals. (Academic recognition depends on this.)

- *Power.* Finding a way to handle the immense attention that follows speaking engagements and book tours. (The "superstar" complex can overshadow common sense.)

- *Anger.* Finding a way to cope with losing tenure and status just because of an association with near-death research. (This has happened to some of our finest researchers.)

- *Sacrifice.* Finding a way to have a life while still doing necessary research and remaining employed. (The countless hours research demands is hard on marriages and a social life.)

- *Commitment.* Finding a way to raise funds and pay bills without becoming cynical. (Very few have financial support for their work or receive much money from book sales.)

Only the findings of a handful of researchers ever came from in-depth fieldwork (one-on-one sessions with a cross-section of experiencers). Even less came from observational analysis (behavior and body language study) or from interviews with "significant others" for their opinions. Seldom were attempts made to learn much about an experiencer's life before he or she had the experience. Rather, the majority of researchers relied almost exclusively on either questionnaire mailings or anecdotes. Some used control groups.

The reason research methods have been so lopsided in favor of mailings and anecdotes is not because that way of doing things is more scientific, but because it costs less to do and takes less time.

The various snags and challenges researchers have had to juggle against personal feelings and beliefs have been compounded by recent decisions made in the world of academia. Universities across the nation are now taking steps to phase out departments and professors who pursue the "embarrassing" activity of near-death research—because it delves into "questionable" phenomena. Grant monies have dried up. Endowments so far have proved useless, as the controls they demand bias any findings in favor of purposes that have little to do with the project at hand. I experienced an example of this: A well-funded institute offered to give me $10,000 if, as part of my near-death research, I took the time to design a protocol to test whether any

Changes That Impress

Although it's true that most near-death researchers become as transformed as their subjects after being around them, it's also true that some researchers are more interested in impressing the media than in turning their lives around. Near-death experiencers are no different.

Credibility at Last

Television talk shows and a spate of sensationalistic books on the near-death experience in the nineties trivialized the field so much that it was difficult for research to be taken seriously by legitimate scientific concerns. This situation has now reversed because of supportive clinical prospective studies that were published in the most respected medical journals.

person could heal another through simple touch. As much as I needed the money, I turned the offer down.

The Second Generation

Regardless of the past criticisms of near-death research and the researchers who did the work, most of the research findings have held up to scrutiny. For example: Strict scientific protocols were employed by near-death researchers in Europe who worked independently from their U.S. counterparts. Their results confirmed what was accomplished here. The same is holding true with preliminary work being done in China and in a number of very different cultures/countries.

First-generation research is now over. That scruffy band of pioneers, of which I am a part, launched and established the near-death field of study. And we did a good job, all things considered. Yet, as far as I am concerned, we have barely uncovered the tip of a giant iceberg. New researchers are proving this to be true.

The second generation active today is more focused on the aftereffects, the brain, and biology, and on inviting specialists in other and related fields to share their expertise and participate in joint projects (people such as microbiologists, bioengineers, theologians, shamans, and experts on consciousness and physics). This new group of researchers has the vigor and the vision to carry near-death studies to the next level of discovery and into the schools of medicine and academia. And they do so proudly. Whereas us old-timers had to "fly by the seat of our pants" and dig deep into our own pockets just to keep things going, the next bunch will fare better, it is hoped.

No Saints or Angels Here

Being both an experiencer and a researcher has given me equal access to both groups of people and their differing points of view. I have "sipped the wine in both tents," as the Arabic saying goes. But as an experiencer, I'm not always proud of what I've seen of fellow experiencers. The truth is that none of us has always lived up to the grandiose claims made about how transformed we were by the experience.

For instance, at annual conferences held by the International Association for Near-Death Studies, a recurring complaint (and the only one, I hasten to add) made about experiencers is that they are rude, arrogant, and discourteous. I was so shocked at this allegation that, at various conferences for several years running, I quietly sat behind hotel decorations in lobby areas and just watched and waited for an hour or so. In doing this, I discovered that the complaint was valid. But I also saw the opposite: Experiencers so kind and so humble they went out of their way, again and again, to help anyone and everyone—even anticipating needs and providing for those needs before a request was made. I've seen experiencers make incredible sacrifices for another's good and then disappear, expecting nothing in return. And I've seen them be the instigator of miracles—because of the strength of their faith.

Experiencers have a personal stake in how the near-death phenomenon is portrayed and by whom. That's why I've learned to be tolerant of their behavior, and mine, as well. Any claims of our sainthood are grossly overstated.

Not So With Everyone

Hypertension among African-Americans is about twice that of whites, as are panic and anxiety disorders and sleep paralysis. In a study comparing rural African-American near-death accounts with Caucasian experiences previously published in the U.S. and Britain, James McClenon, PhD, found a greater incidence of negative emotions in the scenarios of the black people. He suspects this is the result of "survival fatigue" from the higher stress levels they suffer from (refer to appendix C).

Twenty percent of the adult experiencers in my research were of the black race; 12 percent with children. Even though most of them were city or suburbia dwellers, I did not encounter the same prevalence of emotional negativity in their episodes that Dr. McClenon did in his study. My hope is that a concerted effort be made to investigate African-American cases more thoroughly. Far too much of our data base is Caucasian.

The Love That Backfires

It's true that the majority of near-death experiencers have positive, uplifting episodes. Theirs is both the opportunity and the thrill of being totally engulfed by overwhelming sweeps of love, a love beyond precedent, beyond description—so forgiving, so immense, that nothing else is quite like it. This unconditional love makes any kind of earthly love dim by comparison. You float in the wonder of it and, when you return, you want everyone else to know about it. You want to spread the good news about love.

A good share of the charisma that exudes from most experiencers comes from their ability to project and express loving kindness. Initially, the average person may interpret this as a flirtatious overture when nothing of the sort is meant. Also, experiencers tend to be spontaneous in their responses, motivated more by their heart than by their head. These traits are misunderstood—by both parties—as experiencers seldom recognize how others see them.

This has caused numerous divorces and all manner of hardships among blacks *and* whites, as well as other people of color. It can seem like the more loving experiencers become, the more trouble they have and the more complex their lives are. Yet the biggest stickler

Relief at Last

Why at near-death conferences are experiencers seen as rude, arrogant, and discourteous, and as generous and pleasant-tempered—both at the same time? Perhaps it's because near-death experiencers are so relieved to discover others like themselves and be privy to the acclaim of a noncritical audience that they tend to let go of "all stops." This relief is no small thing. Most learn early on to hold back. Few are ever able to share what happened to them, or how they feel about it, or explore any questions they may have.

The Love That Hurts

An experiencer in Southern California contacted me and said, "I love my wife and children more than I ever thought I could. I love everyone. My experience taught me real love, unconditional love!" Yet his wife and children did not feel the kind of love he described, and a gap developed between what he felt and what they felt. Within three years, his wife would leave the room when he entered, his children would not speak to him, and he was losing customers at work. Confused by this and deeply hurt, he decided to leave town and drift for a while until he could figure out what went wrong. I haven't heard from him since.

New Word

Unconditional love can be compared to agape (a term used in the New Testament for the love of God or Christ). More specifically, it denotes a brotherly/sisterly type of love, a universal platonic love. To near-death experiencers, unconditional love means an unselfish, open-ended caring that is given without thought of conditions or gain, embracing all as members of the same family created by God.

may be unconditional love itself and how it's felt or not felt.

A Broader Definition of Love

We misinterpret, because we don't understand, that unconditional love is a state of being, not an emotion of sentiment or attachment or possession. *Unconditional love* takes some getting used to if you've never experienced it before. The desire to express it is automatic. The knowledge of how best to do that is not.

Exaggerated Claims

Experiencers have a mixed record of living in accordance with their claims. Some have truly represented the higher calling they speak of and displayed a greater wisdom in the way they have conducted their affairs. Others have become like demigods in how they preach the gospel of their own self-importance.

Experiencers sometimes get caught up in the bias of what I would call "rightness" ("I'm right, you're wrong"). This can lead to self-deception—that certain blindness that can occur when you start believing your own press releases.

Occasionally, experiencers exaggerate, making their stories and claims sound grander than at first telling. In all fairness, I want to suggest some reasons as to why this sometimes occurs:

- Many book publishers won't touch an experiencer's story unless he or she promises to allow them to sensationalize it.
- Some talk show hosts will not invite experiencers on as guests unless they agree in advance to "keep things lively."
- No experiencer comes back with a set of instructions on how to handle the aftermath of what happened to him or her. Because of this, he or she can mislead instead of inform, frighten instead of enlighten—when none of this was intentionally meant.

There are no guarantees with the phenomenon, no brownie points given for glimpsing the bright realms beyond the earthplane. Although higher levels of mind and spirit do indeed arise afterward, the pressure to be perfect now, to fit the *myth of amazing grace,* can and does push some experiencers into making outlandish claims that they can't possibly fulfill.

Overall, though, when compared with those who never underwent a near-death episode, experiencers shine. They do become better people than they were before. They do make positive changes in their lives that benefit many.

There Is No "Best"

No single researcher is privy to everyone else's cases, and not all accounts have been published. Therefore, it cannot be said that any particular near-death experiencer's case is longer or more complete, powerful, or unique than another's.

New Words

The **myth of amazing grace** goes like this: After undergoing a near-death episode, experiencers are supposed to return as selfless servants of God, devoted to the spiritual path and to serving others.

"I Was God. God Was Me"

Joe Geraci, an experiencer from New Britain, Connecticut, once told me: "This total love and sometimes incredible sadness, on the surface, they don't go together. I am unable to adequately express the love I experienced. I have been told by some people they can feel the love when I am with them. That makes me very happy, because then I know that I have shared the love even if it was nonverbal."

As Joe told me more of what he went through, he explained that, "I was

The Shadow Side

"There is an absolute conviction that firsthand experience creates religious experience. What occurs is so real it feels like truth. Unfortunately, the step from higher wisdom to violence is all too common."

—Stanley Krippner, PhD

God. God was me." That kind of experience, that kind of bond, is beyond comprehension for most people. How do you bring that kind of love and knowing back to Earth, back to everyday living, without appearing to be some kind of Messiah? Or a joke?

God's New Messengers

Many researchers suspect that the near-death phenomenon has played a prominent role historically in the development of spiritual and religious thought. Revelations that emerge from the scenarios are powerful in the way entire populations can be affected. That's why, as we saw in chapter 15, so many religious authorities around the world have concerns about the reports of near-death episodes. The messages that experiencers are receiving are somewhat different from what has become holy writ.

The so-called "religion of the resuscitated" that has emerged from experiencer accounts of the near-death phenomenon exists simply because so many millions of people have said essentially the same thing when sharing their story:

- Death is not fearsome.
- Life exists beyond death.
- Service is more important than material gain.
- Forgiveness is possible for anyone.
- Men and women are equal in God's Light.
- Unconditional love is inclusive, not exclusive.
- Each person has a purpose in life.
- Everything happens for a reason.
- We each possess a soul and can communicate with our soul.
- Revelation is ongoing.
- Prayer works when the aid requested is surrendered to the Will of God.

What Happened in China

Imagine what it might be like to return from death's finality filled to overflowing with message after message of great import. How do you communicate what you feel driven to share? This quandary applies as much to the general public as it does to near-death experiencers. What happened in China in 1837 is an example of why.

In 1837, when he was twenty-three years old, Hung Hsiu-ch'uan, a peasant farmer's son, failed in his third attempt to pass the official state examination held in Canton that would determine his future. He later fell into a prolonged delirium, his body wasting away as he lay near death for forty days. He revived after having a miraculous vision that portrayed him and an "elder brother" searching out and slaying legions of evil demons in accordance with God's will. When six years had passed, Hung came across a Christian missionary pamphlet. He used what he read in the pamphlet to substantiate his conviction that his vision was real, and that he, as the younger brother of Jesus Christ and God's Divine Representative, was ready and willing to overthrow the forces of evil (which he saw as the Manchus and Confucianism).

With the help of converts to his cause, he established the God Worshippers Society, a puritanical and absolutist group that quickly swelled to the ranks of a revolutionary army. Numerous power struggles later, Hung joined forces with the Taiping Rebellion of 1850 to help lead a massive civil uprising—the bloodiest in all history—that lasted fourteen years and cost twenty million lives. When the wholesale carnage was over, he changed his name to Tien Wang, the Heavenly King, and forged the "Heavenly Dynasty" that ripped asunder the very fabric of China.

Hung believed that real truth had been revealed to him during his near-death experience, and that it was his sacred and solemn duty to save the populace in accordance with what he believed himself directed to do. His scenario was of the transcendent type (see chapter 2). Yet the bitterness he felt from flunking those three tests (they alone determined what he could do with his life) and from the treatment he received at the hands of the government (the citizenry had little or no choice in how they were treated) is evident in the way he chose to interpret his otherworldly experience (Christ telling him to kill the evil ruling class—mass murder in the name of God).

> **His Grandson**
>
> *The Last Emperor* (1987) is a movie about Tien Wang's grandson, the last emperor to rule China.

What Happened in Africa

It was late November 2001. Pastor Daniel Ekechukwu was driving his old Mercedes along the steep road home when the brakes failed. The smashup left him near death from a brain injury and internal hemorrhaging. A rescue team arrived, did what they could, then took him to a hospital where he was pronounced dead. His body was moved to a mortuary of limited means where the mortician administered chemicals to prevent decay until the body could be embalmed the next day. Around midnight, the mortician was awakened, so the story goes, by "church singing" coming from the building where the body lay. Three times, the man tried to find the source of the music, but could not, so, in panic, he sped to the home of the dead man's father. The father said the music occurred because his son was a man of God.

The following day, Daniel's wife insisted that her husband's body be taken to the church where a visiting evangelist would be holding a dedication ceremony. She was convinced that God would bring her husband back to life. The body was put in a coffin and the lid shut. After much hassle among relatives and church elders, the body arrived at the church only to be turned away by security guards. Eventually, permission was granted for the coffin to be taken into the lower hall, directly beneath where the evangelist stood preaching and praying in the sanctuary. The coffin lid was removed.

Soon the corpse began to twitch and breathe in short bursts. This excited the crowd that had gathered. His burial clothes were removed and his body massaged head to toe. It was recorded that the body was "stiff as an iron rod." Once the news reached the sanctuary of what was occurring in the room below, hysterical pandemonium broke out. Camera crews covering the dedication ceremony rushed downstairs. A man dead for two days now alive is big news! The cameras captured the whole scene. A DVD of this is now available. (Yes, I have one.)

Whether it can ever be proved that Pastor Daniel Ekechukwu was an actual corpse for two days or just a victim of poor medical care, his description of being escorted by angels through heaven and hell is vivid and very moving. In his memory of the journey he took, he is aware of "recording everything he saw in files" while still on the Other Side. His first words when he revived were, "Where are my files?" Of course, they were nowhere to be found, as they were of spirit.

I have no doubt this man had a transcendent near-death experience while dead or nearly so, which continued as he revived. There are many resurrection stories on the order of Pastor Daniel's in near-death literature. I have investigated a number of them myself. What is disturbing here, though, is that the evangelist involved is using this affair as proof of his "power" and as a recruitment tool. Pastor Daniel's original testimony has since grown in details and "biblical religious zeal" to the point where millions of people have become followers, praising his name. Articles and websites about this are numerous. (See appendix D for a short list of websites if you wish to pursue further information.)

Testing the Spirits

The same driving passion Hung had—allowing personal feelings and preferences to override the interpretation of scenario revelations—is evident in the story of Pastor Daniel Ekechukwu, as well as in those of some other near-death experiencers. It's a human thing to expand on one's story and, to be fair, details of a scenario can and do continue to be revealed as time passes. But what concerns me is how "slanted" interpretations are sometimes used to sway the masses. As the motto "Buyer Beware" cautions us before we make a purchase, why not adopt the motto "Test the Spirits" before we believe someone else's vision?

Years of experiencing multiple realities, coupled with the research I have done, have shown me that it's not the experience that matters as much as the power unleashed by having had the experience. The Christian Bible says, "By their fruits ye shall know them." I can't think of a better measuring rod for assessing the true spiritual effect of a transformative experience. As for "testing the spirits," on page 361 there's a guide I developed—and first wrote about in *Goddess Runes* (available today as *Runes of the Goddess*)—to help you see the difference between that which is spiritual and that which isn't.

Just because something appears to be right on doesn't mean it is. We have a brain equally capable of intuition and intellect. To use only half of it not only cheats us, but also misleads others. There's an old Russian proverb that teaches us how to handle this situation: "Trust, but verify."

What about the Ceiling?

Researchers have noted for decades that individuals, once out of body, claim to see their physical form from a position above looking down, from the foot of the bed, or from a ceiling corner. F. Gordon Greene tackled this subject, concluding that: "From the corner ceiling, more of the room's surface is available for viewing in a single glance than from anywhere else in the room. Of all possible views in the room the corner ceiling is the most comprehensive." (Refer to appendix C.)

What is missing from his study and from all other researcher reports, except mine, is the importance of *left.* Three-fourths of my accounts (adults and children) went either to the left ceiling corner or hovered to the left of what seemed to be their "vacated" body. Nurses in critical care units have noted that between 80 and 90 percent of their patients see spirit visitors manifesting to the left. Hospice volunteers and medical staff have made the same observation.

Subjective Voices/Visitors:
Discerning Their True Source

Lesser Mind	**Greater Mind**
The Voice of Ego	*The Voice of Spirit*
Personality Level	*Soul Level*
Flatters	Informs
Demands	Guides
Chooses for you	Leaves choice to you
Imprisons	Empowers
Promotes dependency	Promotes independence
Intrudes	Respects
Pushes	Supports
Excludes	Includes
Is status-oriented	Is free and open
Insists on obedience	Encourages growth and development
Often claims ultimate authority	Recognizes a greater power or God
Offers shortcuts	Offers integration
Seeks personal gratification	Affirms Divine Order along with the good of the whole

I Spy

Researchers trying to stage experiments in hospitals to test what near-death experiencers can see when out of body that can be verified by doctors, nurses, and relatives have repeatedly struck out. Elaborate experiments have been tried using moving digital sign-strips, special lights, and so forth. Nothing works. Until it is recognized that the near-death experience is an emotional one, which centers around the emotional perception of what occurs, I believe success will continue to elude us.

If we want to catch their attention, we need to see through the "eyes" of the experiencer and place targets where they look—like on top of surgical lights, medical caps, emergency vehicles, around resuscitation equipment, and the like.

Anything *left*—left hand or left side—was associated as early as prehistoric times with magic and demonology (visible in cave drawings). There are still taboos in various cultures against *left* as being evil or unclean. In the psychological study of symbols, signs, and archetypes, however, things *left* have come to be understood as representative of the unknown and the mysterious, having to do with the abstract or the creative. In esoteric traditions left of one's natural sight line is said to be where one can locate entry or exit portals to "other worlds." For instance, death is said to hover near one's left shoulder.

Is the symbology of *left* literal? Is this what experiencers of out-of-body, near-death, and deathbed visions are trying to show us? Things *left* relate to the right hemisphere of the brain—the intuitive, creative, abstract, spiritual region of brain function that ever seeks a broader lens with which to view and consider. And our heart is located on the left side of our chest. When we die, it's our heart that guides us, not our head.

Think about that . . .

24

Integrating the Near-Death Experience

To him that waits, all things reveal themselves, provided that he has the courage not to deny in the darkness what he has seen in the light.

—Howard Thurman, first African-American dean of Boston's University Chapel and spiritual advisor to Martin Luther King Jr.

May Eulitt of Oklahoma had a near-death experience and then wrote to me of problems she was having living with the aftereffects: "I am writing this time to ask if there is any research being done on the possibility of reversing some of the worst aspects of the aftereffects.

"I didn't finish my studies at Pitt State," she went on to explain, "because I can't use a computer. I can't drive a computerized car, either. I can't wear a watch. It is frustrating to a writer to no longer be able to spell well enough to write a letter."

Then she asked the pertinent and poignant question: "If, as you say, the brain chemistry changes, is there any research to change it back? I would gladly give up all the 'gifts' and 'strange powers' my experiences have given me if I could sit down at my daughter's computer without crashing it. I have a very expensive red yard ornament in place of my little red car. [That's because] I drove it home and wiped the computer out."

Unfortunately, I had to write May back and tell her, "No, there's no such research, nor are there any plans for any."

For most experiencers, near-death states elicit more than a simple change in attitude or a desire to alter relationships and lifestyles. The impact from them is deeply personal and intimate, and challenges the very basics of body, mind, and spirit. There's no avoiding what comes next after you've had one, but you can adjust—and quite successfully! In this chapter, I give some suggestions for doing just that.

Electrical Sensitivity

Of the 3,000 adult experiencers with whom I had sessions, 73 percent reported having electrical sensitivity. With child experiencers, it was lower—52 percent—but still the majority. The novelty of being able to make electrical equipment (in some cases, even light bulbs) do strange things in your presence without physically touching them can be fun at first, but the novelty factor wears off quickly. I've found that controlling the ability has a lot to do with how successfully you can control your own attitudes and emotions. The more respectful and poised you become—at peace—the fewer problems you have from electrical sensitivity.

For Adult Experiencers

Many individuals feel as May Eulitt does. After my three experiences, I railed against the heavens when the cost to repair and replace electronic equipment started to exceed my income. Additionally, the challenge to retrain my brain so I could use it efficiently was a real biggie for me, necessitating numerous classes and more work than I care to mention.

I know well how exasperating the aftereffects can be. I also know what a blessing they can become.

To illustrate what I mean, here's what I finally learned to do in dealing with my own electrical sensitivity:

- Before I use technological equipment, I enter into a state of prayer.
- In that state, I envision the item I am about to use.
- I imagine it filled and surrounded by beautiful light.
- Then I merge (join) with the equipment in that light.
- While together, I converse with it as if it is a person I just met and we are getting better acquainted.
- I affirm the mutual benefit that will come from our association and how wonderful it is that we can work together.
- In closing, I thank both the equipment and God for blessing my life with the opportunity I am about to enjoy and the help I will soon be given.

As long as I remember to do this, I experience few problems with electrical sensitivity, and electronic equipment works just fine for me.

Readjusting your life in the aftermath of a near-death experience requires a lot of effort, regardless of the extent to which you were transformed. I know of only a few who were able to glide right through the integration process without having to negotiate bumps in the road. What makes the biggest difference in the process? How others treat you, initially.

Starting Off on the Right Foot

The reaction other people, especially medical personnel, have to your near-death experience immediately after you share it carries great weight and sets the stage for what comes next. To start the coming-back process in the best possible manner, I recommend this five-point plan:

1. Empathetic listeners who exhibit interest instead of scorn. Plenty of time for talking is essential.

2. Absence of pressure to resume everyday routines. Ease back. For a while, don't expect to be the same person you once were, and don't be too surprised if you find yourself wanting to make sudden or unusual changes in your life.

3. Freedom to explore new ideas and ask all kinds of questions. A thirst for knowledge afterward is typical. You may feel smarter somehow or more knowing. Take classes, study, experiment. Allow yourself to be adventurous.

4. Supportive therapy of some kind. Even just a family rap session is great. Group sessions with fellow near-death experiencers are ideal, but only if professional or caring strangers are also present. That's to ensure that you get a range of other viewpoints without being overwhelmed.

5. Exposure to as much information about the near-death phenomenon and its aftereffects as possible. Track down scientific findings, personal accounts, books, videos, and articles. Your local library is a good place to start. So are the appendices in this book.

> **A Tough One**
>
> Although unpleasant experiences can be instructive and positive in the illuminations and healings that may result, not everyone can deal with them. The same is true with the more uplifting, pleasant kind. These also can be traumatic to handle. For example: a woman with whom I once had a session was consumed with anger for having to come back from the splendor of where she had been, yet she was also assailed with guilt that she'd rather be on the Other Side of death than with her earthly children.

The sooner you realize how normal and typical your feelings and concerns are for what you've gone through, the easier it will be to stabilize your aftereffects and integrate your experience into your daily life.

The Darkness Light Can Bring

While making the adjustment, much of what you formerly thought of as life's challenges and paradoxes may disappear, as new outlooks and goals replace the old. Personality (the lesser you—your ego) takes a backseat to soul (the greater you—or higher self). A preference for the spiritual puts you at variance to those around you. Whether

New Word

Mysticism is the practice of intuitively knowing spiritual truths that transcend ordinary understanding. It's considered a direct, intimate union of the soul with its Source through contemplation and love. A mystic is someone who through either formal training or personal dedication pursues "The Holy."

Shadow Sourcebooks

Two excellent sources of advice on how to handle the darkness light can bring are *The Near-Death Experience: Mysticism or Madness,* by Rev. Judith Cressy; and *Romancing the Shadow: Illuminating the Dark Side of the Soul,* by Connie Zweig, PhD, and Steve Wolf, PhD (see appendix C).

your death resulted from a physical cause, a close call, or was "unexplained," you must still grapple with the fact that the world is the same—only you have changed. Realizing this can be depressing.

No one can prepare you for "the darkness light can bring," for the disappointment that often follows an "awakening." And this disappointment specifically revolves around the realization that visiting heaven did not make you perfect. Nor must you be perfect to prove you were there.

When things don't go right, when disagreements with family, friends, and employers arise, most of us tend to blame it on our own failure to measure up to the higher standards we now feel we should have. Few of us have prior knowledge of the "journey within" and the years it takes to "know thyself." The near-death phenomenon does not shortcut this process; it quickens the desire to begin. This path is heart-based, and can lead to the development of various spiritual practices—including *mysticism.*

It's normal for us to feel as if we're going crazy when overcome by the inconsistencies that must be dealt with afterward. Carl Jung, the famous Swiss psychotherapist, had a name for this type of situation. He said we are meeting our "shadow"—not a negative energy per se, but a force with enough power to push the raw, hidden parts of ourselves into view so we can understand them better. Meeting our "dark side" means facing the fears we can no longer keep hidden.

New Order from the Chaos of Change

Validation of your experience—that it was real—becomes an overriding issue after you have shifted in consciousness. Yet the truth is that the only person who can do this for you is you. No one else can. Once you realize that, questions like "Was it real?" become "What am I going to do about this?"

In dealing with the latter question, consider this mystical insight: Order is heaven's first law. I have found this to be true, that whatever is lost because of a near-death experience is replaced—

order reorders itself—but always at a different level than before. The way we change can surprise us—not to mention others.

I've observed that the phenomenon seems to enhance, enlarge, accelerate, and expand whatever was present or existed as potential within the individual at the time the experience occurred. Keep this observation in mind as I list the most common negative and positive changes experiencers make afterward.

Don't Be Fooled

The near-death experience detaches you from your life, your body, your relationships, and your beliefs. As reality seems less so, your senses and your mind sharpen considerably. Time slows as buried memories surface. Professional counselors are usually quick to label such behavior as "dissociation" (considered to be a maladaptive disorder in troubled people). Just the opposite is true with experiencers. What seems characteristic of withdrawal from one's life is actually an opportunity the experiencer has to reassess and reorder what is important and what isn't, to heal in remarkable ways, and to develop spiritually.

The most common negative changes after the near-death experience are:

- *Confused and disoriented.* Feeling lost or disconnected. Unable to trust your own instincts or believe your own insights. Scattered thinking.
- *Disappointed with the unresponsive or uncaring attitudes of others.* Resentful, perhaps easily angered. Tend to relocate often and drift from one teacher and group to another. Seldom satisfied in your search.
- *Depressed, unable to integrate the experience into daily life.* Uncommunicative about your feelings and inner thoughts. Low energy levels can make it difficult for you to accomplish anything, enjoy what you have, or fend off illness.
- *Behavior threatening to others.* Becoming an isolationist or at least uncooperative in mannerisms. Extremist views to the degree that you appear to be antisocial.
- *Seen as arrogant and unloving.* So absorbed in whatever interests you that you seem uncaring, even selfish. Rude sometimes, and rather superficial in how you relate to others.
- *The know-it-all syndrome.* Wanting to take charge and run things without consulting others. Occasionally feel as if driven to interrupt or intercede because of a vision or dream that extols how special you are.

The most common positive changes after the near-death experience are:

- *More loving and generous.* Still capable of intimacy but no longer as needful of the kind of ego-driven role-playing

An Additional Birth

Before many child experiencers have had the opportunity to truly understand their place in this world, their near-death experience flips them into a different dimension of existence. When they're resuscitated, they undergo what could be described as "a second birth." And as second born, these children are truly unique. Unfortunately, though, parents are usually not prepared for the fact that child experiencers have aftereffects just like adult experiencers do; nor do they realize that aftereffects are not something you heal from, but adjust to.

that society expects in relationships. Volunteerism becomes an important part of your life.

- *Open-minded and childlike.* Adjustable and flexible in your dealings with others. Happier. Spontaneous activity that is often playful in nature.

- *A heightened sense of the present moment.* Knowing what is really important in life and what is not. A shift in priorities and values.

- *Enhanced sensitivities and a greater awareness of others' needs.* Sensitive to subtle impressions, energy vibrations, and the power of suggestion. More intuitive and creative.

- *Expanded worldview, fewer worries and fears.* No longer afraid of death. More tolerant of different people and cultures. Change is not as upsetting as it once was.

- *Knowledgeable of spiritual identity.* Aware and responsive to the sacredness of life and the importance of personal responsibility.

- *Accepting of a greater reality and the existence of a Higher Power.* Convinced of Deity, your true identity as a soul, and that you have a role to fulfill in a Larger Plan.

For Child Experiencers and Their Parents

You don't get back the child you "lost" to a near-death experience. Usually, the child you get back is a remodeled, rewired, reconfigured version of the original. Most exhibit a decided interest shift toward moral integrity and social justice.

This can be a tremendous blessing if the family is willing to explore the ramifications of what happened. Such a family environment allows the young to chatter away without embarrassment or censure and act out their episode via a puppet show, children's theater, or family fun night. Everyone benefits when this occurs. Greater family intimacy, interactions, and reverence for life invariably result.

Supportive parents, although essential, are not enough. Child experiencers need more than that; they need freedom "with a fence around it" (loving guidance) so they can safely test the multiple realities they now know exist. Some suggestions for parents follow:

- Sleep patterns for the young abruptly change afterward: less nap time, increased flow states, even restlessness about going to sleep. Some may fear sleep and suffer nightmares; others may seem exhausted on waking, as if they'd been very busy "elsewhere." Reliving their episode while dreaming is common. If your child does dream about his or her experience, encourage the child to share this. Listen without interrupting.

- Child experiencers often change the way they express love. It's normal for them to detach from the parent-child bond. This doesn't mean they cease to be loving and thoughtful, but it does mean they tend to act more distant than before—as if there was another source of guidance they listened to. The child switches gears and begins to mature faster. He or she becomes independent and his or her interests change.

- After their experience, most kids have a marked decrease in their ability to express themselves and socialize. Since being able to communicate is one of our most precious abilities, stimulate the child's speech with your own. Promote dialogue with question/answer games, group storytelling, reading out loud, or speaking on "pretend" microphones. Encourage the child to participate in community projects as a volunteer. They're naturally service-oriented. Also encourage them to participate in the arts, such as orchestra, choral singing, and the music of nature.

Denial Hurts

There can be lifelong repercussions for child experiencers if family members refuse to admit what happened to the child, or deny or ignore the aftereffects. What the family suppresses, the child represses. This can lead to a sense of alienation in the child as well as behavioral problems at home and school.

- Writing and drawing about their experience is just as important as speaking about it. Help the child make a special book about his or her near-death episode. This book can include the youngster's drawings of each aspect of the incident, a newspaper account of the death event (if any), his or her written description of what happened, dreams, sketches of any "beings" that continue to appear, poems—whatever the child and parent can think of. Choose a title and bind the book with cord or ribbon. The parent should keep a journal of the experience, too. This helps to restimulate parent-child bonding, and can serve as an invaluable resource once the child matures. "Making your book" can be life changing in and of itself. Even if now an adult, encourage child experiencers (no matter how many years have passed) to make their book.

- Child experiencers tend to withdraw; they may even reject hugs and cuddles.

With the Very Young

The tiny ones, via their expressions and language, show signs that suggest they may have identified with the otherworldly imagery and behaviors they were once exposed to, rather than, or in addition to, those of Earth and their earthy human family. Their temporal lobes, as they form, seem to build "libraries" of shape, size, sound, smell, color, movement, and taste *to accommodate the otherworldly models provided by the near-death experience.* This imprinting is augmented by sensory patterns and intuitive knowing to the extent that the child can seem wise beyond his or her years when, in all probability, the youngster may simply be responding to what now feels perfectly natural.

Recenter them in their bodies through touch: Pat their shoulders when you pass by, touch their hands when you speak to them, nudge a knee from time to time, rub their backs. Smile. Teach them to pat and touch you as you do for them. Pets are wonderful for touch therapy, as are plants and gardening. So is cooking, especially making cookies. Pick a recipe the child can help prepare, then let him or her shape the cookies by hand into imaginative designs. Create food sculptures. You'll find inspiration in books such as *Play With Your Food,* by Joost Elffers (see appendix C).

- Watch sugar levels. Child experiencers are more sensitive than the average child to chemicals and excessive sweets, particularly refined sugars and the preservatives in prepackaged meals. Practice good nutrition. Serve veggies and fruit for snacks, along with honey or fruit-sweetened cookies.

- Full-spectrum lights are preferable to fluorescent. Avoid overexposure to electrical items (especially electric blankets); cottons usually work best for clothes and bedding. At meals, have a burning candle for a centerpiece, and say the type of grace where each person in turn can offer his or her own prayer. Flowers put children at ease. Let them pick and arrange them.

- Ideally, child and adult experiencers should get together once in a while, for each can help the other. Adults can provide the opportunity to talk about the experience and socialize with older experiencers. Children can inspire confidence and stability in adults, as kids are often more understanding and open than their elders. Above all, parents who were child experiencers themselves should speak of their episode and what they went through in front of their child experiencer. Such a sharing has a "ripple effect" for years afterward.

How a Family Transformed

Denise Mendenhall (mentioned in chapter 4) died at the age of ten from diabetes and a stroke. No one knew she had diabetes, not even a diabetic nurse and a medical doctor, who were consulted by her parents for advice about the child's sudden craving for water, extreme weight loss, and reversal of personality—going from a happy ten-year-old who loved school to a girl who hated just about everything. By the time she was hospitalized, it was almost too late. The stroke she suffered was on the left side of her brain in the main artery. Two-thirds of her left brain was destroyed (you'd never know it today); blood vessels and capillaries fragmented like tissue paper. With all her organs shutting down, doctors gave her twenty-four hours to live, fully expecting her to become a vegetable if she survived at all.

"She stayed in the coma for three days and never quit breathing," said her dad, Doug Mendenhall. "At the end of the third, she woke up, looked at her mother, Dianne, and me, and said she was hungry." The nurse couldn't believe it. Doctors descended on the child. It was a miracle! Twenty-five days later, Denise went home. "We figured that life would go on as normal," continued Doug, "except that we did have a miracle child with us. Though we now had to give her two injections of insulin each day for her diabetes."

Forget normal.

"One day I was trying to give her a shot of insulin," explained Doug, "and she kept fighting me. After forty-five minutes I was upset with her, and let her know it. She yelled, pointing her finger above my head that I 'was mad and I was red.' I asked what in the world she was talking about. 'You're mad, you're red,' she said again. I had read enough that I knew about the energy field around our body, called the aura. 'You can see auras?' I asked. 'What's that?' she responded. I told her it was the energy around our body. She said that she could see them since she woke up from her coma. This was the start of our family entering a world we did not know existed. The many psychic and spiritual gifts she displayed after that were incredible."

According to Doug: "She is able to see 'spirits' as we call them, or people that have passed on (died). She sees Christ and her Heavenly Father. She can tell what kind of person you are; she sees into your heart. The most fascinating thing she told us was that while she was in the coma for three days, she had spent that time with Jesus. She told me about His birth, life, His suffering in the garden, the cross. It was in detail, all the colors, smells, and sounds. She told me things that I knew a little ten-year-old could not know.

The First (It Is Hoped) of Many

Denise Mendenhall is the first child experiencer, *while still a child,* to write about her near-death experience. With her dad's help, *In His Arms* was created, a book that speaks volumes about how differently a child accepts and interprets his or her experience, and then deals with the aftereffects. Her views show overlays from her family's religion; her aftereffects include an active and continuous relationship with the beings she met on the Other side, as well as with Jesus.

Over or Under 18

Experiencers older than 18 have a wonderful opportunity to meet and share their accounts in a supportive environment provided by the International Association for Near-Death Studies (IANDS), or at any of its local Friends of IANDS groups. If an experiencer is younger than 18, he or she must have parental permission to participate. Refer to appendix B for contact information.

"All of this changed our lives significantly. My wife and I have six living children, five were at home during this time. The events polarized our family somewhat. I knew in my heart that Denise was telling me the truth of what she had experienced. Yet it was hard for others to understand and accept. We learned many 'lessons' from our little ten-year-old daughter."

For Significant Others

Significant others—be they loved ones, neighbors, or coworkers—are often challenged the most by the near-death phenomenon. They didn't have the experience, and they don't know what's going on. Especially in families, as with the Mendenhalls, this can become an issue. Instead of transforming a family, it can lead to anger, distrust, misunderstandings, and divorce.

Such a situation can be improved greatly if the people involved do one thing—make a commitment to read and discuss research on the near-death experience *together*! Then talk to other experiencers and find out what they went through. Read their stories. Talk to their families. Attend IANDS meetings and conferences, preferably together.

With the countless people I have spoken with since 1978, that's all it ever took—information, dialogue, and the willingness to listen with an open heart and an open mind. If this is done, the near-death experience becomes a shared event in which everyone can benefit if they choose to.

Integration's Four Phases

My research has shown that it takes the average child or adult experiencer a minimum of seven years to successfully adjust to what happened to them. Those seven years are actually part of a four-phase integration process, true not only for near-death experiencers, but for many of those who have undergone a transformation of consciousness, no matter how it was caused.

Remember, aftereffects are ongoing. Dealing with the significance of the

Seven Years It Is

My finding that it takes a minimum of seven years for an experiencer to integrate a near-death experience was verified by Pim van Lommel, MD, and his associates, in the Dutch Study published in the *Lancet* medical journal. (Refer to appendix C.)

scenario is one thing, but learning how to cope with both psychological and physiological aftereffects is quite another.

The four phases that most experiencers "grow" through are:

- *Phase One: First three years.* Impersonal, detached from ego identity/personality traits. Caught up in desire to express unconditional love and oneness with all life. Fearless, knowing, vivid psychic displays, substantially more (or less) sexual, spontaneous surges of energy, a hunger to learn more and do more. Childlike mannerisms with adult experiencers; adult-like behavior from child experiencers. A heightened sense of curiosity and wonder, IQ enhancements, much confusion.

- *Phase Two:* Next four years.* Rediscovery of and concern with relationships, family, and community. Service- and healing-oriented. Interested in project development and work environment. Tend to realign or alter life roles; seek to reconnect with one's fellows, especially in a moral or spiritual manner. Unusually more (or less) active/contemplative. Can resume former lifestyle, but more desirous of carrying out "mission"—even if not clear about details.

- *Phase Three: After the seventh year.* More practical and discerning, often back to work, but with a broader worldview and a confident attitude. Aware of self-worth and of "real" identity. Tend toward self-governance and self-responsibility. Spiritual development an ongoing priority, along with sharing one's story and its meaning. Dedicated; strong sense of spiritual values.

- *Phase Four:** Somewhere between twelfth and fifteenth year.* Immense fluctuations in mood and hormonal levels. Often discouraged or depressed while going through a period of "grieving"—reassessing gains and losses from the experience while fearful that effects are fading. Many problems with relationships, money, and debts. A crisis of "self." If the person can negotiate "the darkness light can

With Kids, It's Longer

With some child experiencers, it can take longer. Children tend to compensate, not integrate. It is not unusual to find child experiencers who took twenty to thirty years to "connect the dots" and embrace their aftereffects. Even with those who experienced no delay with integration, the sense of being "different" from their agemates is noticeable during the growing years.

---

* Child experiencers in my study who turned to alcohol for solace began drinking during this phase (one-third out of a research base of 277). Refer to my book *Children of the New Millennium* and its reissue *The New Children and Near-Death Experiences* (see appendix C for both books).

** Child experiencers who attempted suicide afterward (21 percent) did so during this phase.

bring," a depth of maturity and confidence emerges that is unique to the long-term effects of a transformation of consciousness. Some people don't undergo this "second drop" and "second shift" until about twenty years after the experience.

Just When You Think You've Got It

At the seventh year, or close to it, there is a marker—a first birthday, if you will—that celebrates the experiencer's ability to "bring to earth the gifts of heaven" in practical and meaningful ways. However, somewhere between the twelfth and fifteenth year, maybe extending to the twentieth, there is another marker—a second birthday—that catches the majority unaware (for child experiencers, this phase may be delayed). This "second drop" is like a second death in that it often heralds a time of life reversals and the need to ask some tough questions:

- Were the sacrifices I made since my experience worth it?
- Am I capable of carrying out my mission? Is it possible to live a spiritual life in the earthplane?
- Have I been honest with myself?
- Are my aftereffects fading?

If the experiencer can successfully negotiate the challenges of this second drop, a "second shift" is possible—a major advancement toward "the peace that passeth all understanding."

What Catches Child Experiencers

All the child experiencers in my study who ever had a serious problem with alcohol started drinking during Phase Two—a period when relationships of varied types become primary and the pressures of job and school versus "mission" tend to overwhelm. As to why they drank, most said it was to ease the pain they felt in not being able to communicate or socialize easily. For others, it was a way to escape the ridicule of family and friends.

Of those child experiencers I studied who attempted suicide after their near-death scenario, every one of them did so during Phase Four, when the second

www.sacredcowsonline.com www.cafepress.com/sacredcows © 2006 SpiritPainter

drop occurs (usually within ten years of their episode). The majority of those who had another near-death experience in adulthood had it in Phase Four, as well. For example: A young boy drowned at the age of five, miraculously revived fifteen minutes later, and immediately began to see "through" people's actions as if their real thoughts and attitudes could be seen and heard. He was also considered "odd" in the sense that he could speak to plants and animals telepathically and they would respond accordingly. As he matured, what interested his agemates bored him. Behavioral problems resulted when he was made fun of. Once eighteen, he joined the Army, hoping he would die. He did, in an accident. He had another near-death episode during resuscitation that explained his earlier one and gave him the courage he needed to turn his life around.

This young man's second drop was an actual death event that had all the earmarks of a suicide, except that he had not physically caused it. The second shift that followed was dramatic in how it revealed to him what he needed to know.

Take Charge

There are no shortcuts in the integration process, despite what some people claim. You can make the process easier, however, by informing yourself, using techniques others suggest are appropriate for you, and making the conscious decision to bring spirituality into your daily life and affairs. The most common result of such effort is peace of mind; for many, there is also boundless joy.

Second Drop/Second Shift

The second drop is seldom as perilous as it was for the young man I just mentioned. But unlike the first birthday, this is the *second time* that experiencers are faced with the challenge of *reckoning* and *reassessment* and the need to make major decisions that require new commitments. The first shift can be linked to the original episode. The second shift seems more dependent on the experiencer's willingness to surrender to a Plan greater than his or her choices and self-interests.

Irrespective of how integrated and spiritual an experiencer may appear to be after the seventh year, the challenges of spiritual growth up to that time pale in comparison with the power unleashed *if* the second shift occurs. Not everyone undergoes that second shift. When we refuse to grow and change, decline begins.

What the Effects of a Transformation Imply

Here's how I regard the difference in meaning between child and adult near-death states:

Effects of a Transformation of Consciousness (Brain Shift/Spirit Shift)			
With Adults:	Renewal	New life	A growth event
With Children:	Rebirth	New race	An evolutionary event

New Words

Transpersonal psychology studies human experiences that occur beyond the realm of ordinary ego and personality. These include such states as unitive consciousness, cosmic awareness, mystical experiences, and maximum sensory awareness.

Creative Approaches to Therapy

Some type of therapy that helps develop clarity and discernment makes a positive difference during the integration process. Those professionals who usually have the best record working with adult near-death experiencers are the ones trained in *transpersonal psychology.*

Therapies that work best for child experiencers are touch-based: things like creating scenes in sand trays and boxes (analyzed by professional practitioners), or shaping pottery on a potter's wheel or finger painting (monitored by art therapists). The actual method or medium doesn't really matter; the idea is to provide a way for the child to use his or her hands and feet to express and receive *feelings.*

Variations on the Theme

Here are some other therapeutic methods other experiencers, adult or child, have tried and found helpful (contact information for any professionals mentioned can be found in appendix E):

Healthcare Professionals Have NDEs Too

Karen Herrick, a mental health clinician, was transformed by a spiritual experience. She noticed that other mental health and allied healing professionals and their clients were having such experiences too, including near-death states, yet no one knew what to do about what had happened to them. Karen went on to obtain her PhD in Spiritual Psychology, and is now dedicated to teaching the professional community how to recognize a spiritual experience, deal with their own, and do a better job assisting clients/ patients with theirs. Refer to appendix E, "Getting in Touch," for how to contact Dr. Herrick.

- *Hypnosis.* Good for recovering details about the scenario and for being objective about the impact of the experience. Caution: Make certain the hypnotist is a licensed professional and has a solid background in working with transpersonal states.

- *Philosophical Counseling.* A new approach for helping people to reexamine their lives from the broader perspective of satisfaction and meaning. Utilizes a procedure of thoughtful and probing questions. Many ministers and philosophy professors, as well as therapists, are doing this.

- *Consciousness Coaching.* An experienced individual, usually a specialist in teaching personal-growth techniques, inspires clients to identify and realize their fullest potential. Features the type of "pep-talks" any coach is noted for, except that the emphasis is on personal insight. One such duo with a successful coaching track record is the team of Diane Kennedy Pike and Arleen Lorrance of the Teleos Institute.

- *Inner Life Mentoring.* A unique counseling style developed by G. Scott Sparrow, EdD, LPC, a psychotherapist who once lived in Virginia Beach, Virginia. This style recognizes the relationship between therapist and client as being one of mentor (teacher) and initiate (student) who work together to create a learning environment that benefits them both. Any professional wanting to incorporate this method into his or her practice may do so through a certification process.

- *Healing Music.* Music therapy is now widely practiced. Styles and practitioners vary. Among them is Ruth Rousseau, a near-death experiencer originally from Casper, Wyoming. She was shown during her episode how to take the keys of sound and create healing pathways of vibration through which anyone can connect with inner wisdom. Her cassettes, compact disc, and instructions are available by mail.

- *Creative Inner Space Explorations.* Developed by Michael Brown, EdS, of Richmond, Virginia, this therapy uses the mediums of mandala art, music, role playing, ritualistic games, and vision quests to effect an inner growth program based on transpersonal psychology. Michael presents his programs and gives lectures all over the country. His goal is to show other therapists how to turn the process of counseling into an exciting art form.

> **Good Advice**
>
> "You cannot depend on your eyes when your imagination is out of focus."
>
> —Mark Twain

The Power of a Group

Among the new opportunities for exploring thoughts and feelings within the dynamics of group work is one developed specifically for near-death experiencers by fellow experiencer Robert Stefani of Merced, California, as part of earning his master's degree in counseling from California State University, Fresno. This Eclectic Group Intervention program covers ten sessions. According to Robert, "Group participants need not be limited exclusively to near-death experiencers. Family members and close friends of experiencers may need support, too, as well as people who are losing (or have lost) a loved one, who have questions about death, or who are themselves dying."

Briefly, the goals of Robert Stefani's intervention program are:

1. Educate the experiencer to understand that the intrapersonal changes

that may have taken place in their attitudes and beliefs are not signs of mental instability or psychotic disorder. Redefine normality.

2. Help the experiencer to integrate changes in attitudes, beliefs, values, and interests with expectations of family and friends.

3. Alleviate interpersonal fears of separation and rejection by assisting the experiencer in learning to communicate with significant others who have not shared the experience.

4. Reconcile the new spiritual transformation based on universality, oneness, and unconditional love with prior religious beliefs.

5. Overcome the difficulty in maintaining former life rules that no longer seem significant, and reconstruct a purposeful life balanced between the aftereffects and the demands of everyday living.

6. Address the dissolution of major relationships or careers, if the experiencer finds it impossible to reconcile them with the changes he or she has undergone.

7. Accept the limitations of others in human relationships, in spite of the person's feelings of unconditional love gained through the near-death experience.

8. Use the gifts and insights gained from the near-death experience to help comfort those who are dying, grieving the loss of a loved one, or learning to accept their own near-death experience.

This procedure is a model other groups can use to design their own programs of openness and sharing for mutual growth.

Prayer and Meditation

It's been said that prayer is when you talk to God, and meditation is when God talks to you. Like two halves of the same whole, one is not complete without the other. Although not everyone on the path to becoming more spiritual embraces the concept of Deity, few will argue that these two practices complement each other.

Relaxing into "the silence" might be a good way to describe meditation. There are many schools of thought on how best to do this, but I have yet to find one that applies to everyone. Some people meditate best while active—like

> **Kids, Too**
>
> Children can be taught to meditate by learning how to slow their breathing and relax. Teach them how to visualize their favorite place in nature, experience peace and thankfulness in that place, and return to waking consciousness feeling refreshed and happy. Although sessions need to be brief, meditation can become a valued skill—helpful to use if the child is hurt (pain relief) or in need of additional guidance (clarity).

A Prayer

One of the prayers I often say whenever I hear an ambulance siren is "I now affirm that Divine Order is in charge of this situation for the highest good of all concerned. Thank you, God, for this truth, and the truth of our value in your eyes. Amen."

in a "Zen" state where you become "one with" whatever you're doing and totally merge or enter into "at-one-ment" with the environment. Others do it best while quietly sitting with their spines straight, facing forward with their eyes closed. Still others lie down on the floor to relax and flow with the rhythm of their own breath, or follow along with the sweeps and pauses of any music that is being played. Your local bookstore has many good books on the subject, so get one and experiment. You might start with *The Complete Idiot's Guide to Meditation* (Alpha Books, 1999). Find what works best for you by giving the various methods a try.

Likewise, there are many ways to pray, and you needn't be in a church to do so—you can pray while walking in the woods or even dusting the furniture! Affirmative prayer is the type preferred by most experiencers (as opposed to pleading or beseeching prayer), where the biblical teaching "It is done unto you in accordance with your belief" is the proper prayerful attitude. Prayer is a practical life skill that is powerful in its use. Just ask child experiencers: So many of them actually "saw" prayer beams of bright or rainbow light arc over from the one saying the prayer to help, comfort, or heal another. Many of them were recipients of prayer as well, and described how warm and good they felt after the prayer beam touched them. I, for one, can't imagine starting my day without time spent in prayer.

What also appeals to a lot of experiencers is some form of movement prayer. For instance, walking along the enfolding passageways of a labyrinth as you pray for guidance and healing, or the old tradition of "trance dancing" or "sweating your prayers," when you lose yourself in the sacredness of the moment and allow your body to speak for you in the grace and fluidity of the movements you make. This type of prayer in motion is said to cast aside negativity as it purifies body and soul. Used the world over for spiritual expression, movement prayers are passionate offerings to the Divine (for example, the Whirling Dervish Order of Sufism, founded by the poet Rumi).

Good Sources

The best source for information about the sacred use of labyrinths is the organization Veriditas, founded by Rev. Dr. Lauren Artress and based at Grace Cathedral, San Francisco, California (appendix E). A reference for prayers in motion is *Sweat Your Prayers: Movement as Spiritual Practice,* by Gabrielle Roth; for prayerful techniques, refer to *Prayer and the Five Stages of Healing,* by Ron Roth, PhD (see appendix C for details).

You Bet!

Old mystical axiom: "Wherever you have once been in consciousness, you can return to."

Revisiting the Near-Death Experience

You can revisit your near-death episode at will—go back there—regardless of how young or old you were when the experience occurred. The basic steps are:

- Find a quiet place where you can be alone for a while without interruption. Relax.
- Gently state your goal; affirm God's protection. Close your eyes.
- Visualize being back where you once were during your near-death experience. Embrace all aspects—see, feel, hear, sense, smell. Experience every detail, every emotion, fully and completely. Involve all your sensory faculties and your imagination. Surrender. Allow. Be there.
- Do not set limits, only direction.
- Adopt an attitude of gratitude. Be thankful for the opportunity to revisit your near-death episode. Recall it clearly, knowing that it is alright for you to do so.
- Relax again as you affirm that you are now back to full consciousness in your body at the present time. You are alert and awake, healed and whole.
- Open your eyes and stretch your limbs. Drink some water. Breathe in fresh air.

Be honest about your intentions in doing this exercise. "Going back" shouldn't become an excuse to escape your present life condition, but, rather, an opportunity to uplift and enrich it. I honestly feel if children were taught to do this simple exercise, there would be a marked decreased in any regrets they might harbor about what happened to them, and virtually eliminate any desire they might have to stop their breathing as a way to return to the bright worlds where they once were. These worlds are accessible. You don't have to die to visit them.

25

Redefining How Life Is Viewed

Life is the childhood of our immortality.

—Johann Wolfgang von Goethe,
German poet, dramatist, and novelist

You cannot ignore more than thirteen million people whose stories at the edge of death are remarkably consistent, and whose changes afterward follow a universal pattern.

If you look at the research on near-death states, all of it, and are completely honest with yourself, however, you'll recognize what I have: The near-death experience speaks more to life than it does death.

Admitting this invites people everywhere to take a second look at how they regard their life. Of the thousands I have interviewed, the most frequent comment experiencers made was, "Always there is life." If that's true—and I believe it is—then how can there be an afterlife? Maybe it isn't death we need to redefine, but life—how we view it, how vast it is, and what it actually encompasses. In seeking to enhance our understanding of death, I suspect what we are really seeking to enlarge is our concept of life itself.

Implications from Near-Death States

We know that experiencer attitudes and viewpoints change after their near-death episode. But when you study how

> **Where's the Key?**
>
> "The bad news is: There is no key to the universe. The good news is: It's been left unlocked."
>
> —Swami Beyondananda
> (Steve Bhaerman)

Explain This

Isn't it true that you need eyes to see, ears to hear, a nose to smell, a mouth to talk, a nervous system to register stimuli, and a brain to think? The presence of faculties outside and beyond the physical body, and irrespective of the distance in between, begs for an explanation.

Where Are My Teeth?

In his study published in the *Lancet,* Dutch cardiologist Pim van Lommel described the near-death experience of a clinically dead, forty-four-year-old cardiac-arrest victim. Doctors restarted his heart with defibrillators. A nurse removed his dentures so a breathing tube could be inserted in his throat.

A week later, the man saw the nurse who had removed his false teeth. He recognized her instantly, even though their previous encounter had occurred when his condition ranged from coma to clinical death.

"You took my dentures out of my mouth," he told her. He then accurately described where she put them, and other such details that he could not possibly have either seen or known.

they change, you begin to sense a paradigm shift—that at a level deeper than ordinary perception, a new order is indeed rising from what had once seemed confusing or chaotic. The implications of this concern our very concept of who we are, what we think, and why and how we live. As a result, the definition of life, as we currently understand it, is subject to challenge.

To explore the basis for these implications, let's take that second look.

The Range of Our Faculties

Individuals who undergo an out-of-body component to their near-death episode say that they can still see, hear, smell, think, move, question, and tell jokes if they want to, no matter how far away they are from their physical body. And the majority of their reports have been independently verified.

Not only are our faculties fully functional when we are out of our bodies and "dead," they acquire heightened characteristics. It's as if once released from their connection to our bodies, they expand. When experiencers revive or are resuscitated, some of that expansion remains—labeled as "psychic" or "intuitive" abilities.

By seeking to understand the greater capacity of our faculties and the varied conditions under which they can operate, we can develop the reliable use of this source as a healthy adjunct to a normal life.

The Range of Our Consciousness

Not only our faculties expand once we leave our bodies in what appears to be death, so do our consciousness, our mind, and our sense of self. Suddenly, we are larger and more powerful; we know more and are not limited by the restrictions of "wearing" a fragile, physical form. And that knowing, that intelligence, is quite startling. I have yet to talk to a single experiencer who was not absolutely amazed at how much smarter they were outside than inside their body.

What is truly amazing, though, is that the majority, once they return to their bodies, retain some of that mental expansion. And their consciousness, just as with their other faculties, continues to become bigger and better than before. This state of an expanding consciousness—as shown in chapter 20—is possible for anyone to attain, anyone who is willing to engage actively in the spiritual practices that facilitate such a shift. That this can be done implies that higher consciousness might be the next step in the growth and development of the human species as a whole.

Sources on Intuition

The Edgar Cayce Institute for Intuitive Studies, now part of the Association for Research and Enlightenment (ARE), offers a course curriculum on the practicality of intuitive abilities. Their program features three certification levels: (1) Personal Competency, (2) Trainer, and (3) Professional. *Shift* magazine, an outreach of the Institute of Noetic Sciences, covers a wide range of subjects related to intuition, as well as the inner workings of the human mind. Intuition Networking Group (formerly Global Intuition Network) enables individuals interested in cultivating and applying intuition, to contact each other via electronic means and in small gatherings. Business leaders and athletes are especially active in this area, since numerous research studies have demonstrated the effectiveness of using intuitive abilities not only as a career tool but also to enhance life satisfaction and meaning. (See appendix E for contact information about these organizations.)

The Range of Our Choices and What We Focus On

Experiencers, adult as well as child, return to life bowled over by the discovery that they now have and have always had the power to make choices independent of what had seemed expected of them. The realization really hits home that none of us is as much a victim of circumstance as we are guilty of ignoring the responsibility that goes with making a decision. Even little kids come back aware of this; many were shown the results of their choices, sometimes even of their parent's choices, during their scenario.

Free will exists. Even though we can't always control the circumstances of our lives (what happens to us), we can control how we respond to those circumstances. What is revealed to most experiencers is that they have a broader range of choices than they had thought and more power to change the conditions in their life than they had realized.

Interestingly, this new awareness that "choice is the life process" goes hand in hand with the discovery of how significant our attention is—what we focus on.

We empower whatever we focus on. We make an issue or item more

Wise Words

An old mystical axiom says: "Wherever you put your attention is where you put your power. To remove the power, remove your attention."

important than it would have been otherwise if we dwell on our notice of it. Recognizing this has inspired most experiencers to be more careful of the movies they see, the television programs they watch, what they read, listen to, purchase, or concentrate on. They become more selective and make wiser choices. Discovering the range of what can be affected through choices made and attention given, powerfully drives home the point that what holds most of us back in life is how we see ourselves. Once we shift our self-image to reflect the higher truth we have come to know about our spiritual identity, our world and everything in it transforms right before our eyes.

The Range of Our Emotions

Life reviews emphasize the consequences of our choices and emotional responses. Once we gain a greater realization of what this means and of our power to choose, "appropriateness" takes the place of "have-to's," "shoulds," and "musts." Emotions take on different meanings as well. Fear, for example, is seen as an asset once its ability to signal caution is recognized and respected. The same is true with anger when it's used as a motivator.

Of all our emotions, though, near-death experiencers declare that love is primary. Not the kind of love that possesses, expects, or seeks domination. The love as defined by experiencers is an unconditional energy that unifies, heals, and uplifts. Most of them think of it as the "glue" that links the created with the Creator. This love is considered heart-based and compassionate yet never sentimental in the sense of attachments or exclusivity. Love, real love, they say, is felt as if the human heart has the power to encompass eternity. (See chapters 7 and 23 for more on agape and unconditional love, respectively.)

To the best of their ability, experiencers strive to replace competition with loving kindness, and come to use appropriateness as their measurement for assessing behavior and taking action.

The Animating Force That Drives Us

Almost to a person experiencers speak of the soul as being their true identity. The soul is said to be the energy mass that animates us, whose essence is light and whose power is that spark of divinity infused by "the fire of its creation" (God's creative force). I've mentioned the soul on numerous occasions in this book. Now it's time to take a closer look at the subject.

Soul Existence

How do you prove that the soul exists? Maybe no one ever can, but some researchers did try—by measuring weight loss at the point of death.

George W. Meek made some interesting comments about the soul in his book *After We Die, What Then?* (see appendix C). "There have been a few serious attempts to measure the loss of weight which takes place at the instant of death," he explains. "One piece of research stands out. While this work was done a long time ago [in the early 1900s], there has never been serious question of the methodology, the integrity of the scientist who did the research, or the quality of the findings. Dr. McDougall [the scientist] found that the instantaneous weight loss at death varied between one-half and three-quarters ounce."

> **Heart Power**
>
> Researchers at the Institute of HeartMath have discovered that the heart generates the strongest electromagnetic field produced by the body, and that this field becomes measurably more coherent as the individual shifts to a sincerely loving or caring state. This field contributes to the energy exchange between people in close proximity or who touch, and between healer and patient. Researchers Linda G. Russek and Gary E. Swartz, as quoted by Paul Pearsall, PhD, in his book *The Heart's Code* (see appendix C), report that although the brain may contain more cellular connections than there are stars in the Milky Way, the heart has been measured at *five thousand times* more powerful electromagnetically than the brain.

Meek continues: "The research of McDougall seems to have been replicated in the work of five physicians at a Massachusetts hospital. These men built a large and very delicate balance. On one platform they would lay a person who was at the very point of death, while on the other platform they placed counterweights so as to bring the large pointer into a balanced condition. At the moment the heart stopped beating the doctors said, 'With startling suddenness the pointer moved, indicating a weight loss from the now dead patient's body. The amount of the weight loss which we encountered over

Guess Who?

British scholar Anthony Peake, after studying quantum physics, neurophysiology, clinical psychiatry, and various mystical traditions, states that the encounter with the "being of light" in near-death experiences is actually an encounter between the normal, everyday "I" and the higher self. He explains that the life review shows how death is an impossibility, because at the point of death, the individual must necessarily choose an alternate universe in which he or she still lives.

New Words

The notion of **right timing** is found in every spiritual and religious tradition, and refers to that sense of "rightness" concerning the time for action. In some traditions, astrologers are consulted or perhaps a diviner (for example, a shaman or medicine man or woman) gifted in spirit communication. In other traditions, right timing is only thought to be revealed after a period of "humbleness" (fasting and prayer).

such tests in a six-year period averaged at about one ounce.'"

Meek wondered how such a small amount of energy could possibly encompass the vast amount of power attributed to the soul, until he stopped to realize how much information a tiny computer chip can carry and how, with each passing year, we are successfully miniaturizing many of our modern marvels. "So it no longer seems so preposterous," he mused, "that our Creator has devised an infinitely more compact and efficient method of 'packaging' the individual human mind, personality, and soul."

Soul Plans

Near-death experiencers accept the soul's existence as fact; its brilliance, a spark of divine fire. And it becomes clear to most of them that the soul has plans of its own. No matter what our choices are as an ego personality, they say we are still subject to the intervention of a force greater than we are. Yes, the range of our choices as the personality we are is truly remarkable, even more than we think. But there is a higher level—they call it the soul level—and a greater power beyond that: deity.

The majority of those I interviewed chalked up the entire genre of transformations of consciousness, especially near-death states, to this type of intervention. Their common lament after undergoing the near-death phenomenon—"I needed what happened to me"—admits that there exists some form of what is commonly called *right timing.*

The kick in the pants we occasionally get by some type of life reversal, be it a time of hardship or an event that tests our faith, not to mention the fuller import of transformative experiences—what I have always called a "growth event"—is referred to by many experiencers as a "soul event." They claim

The Higher Self

Various spiritual traditions link the soul directly with deity, especially as per the fulfillment of our life's purpose. But these same traditions caution that "promptings" from the soul can be blocked, turned off, or ignored—because we have free will, the choice to cooperate with or reject "the voice of the soul," that guidance more commonly labeled our "conscience" or "higher self."

that soul events put us back on track, doing what is truly "right" for us to do, when we've been living our lives by not listening to the deeper wisdom of our souls, when we've been making our choices without regard to our equal need to develop spiritually.

Soul Cycles

The majority of near-death experiencers refer to broad, sweeping cycles the soul seems to take in its own growth. Many either were told or it was revealed to them that the soul matures in ways that parallel what we do as a personality. Whatever progress our egos make, then, enriches us on a soul level as well as on the personality level.

In other words, growth events are said to help us as embodied human beings change in ways that bring about more balance in our lives—personal maturity. But soul cycles cover the full range of our life as a whole, and whether other incarnations of various types would be necessary for the mastery of such attributes as patience or courage, for instance, before reunion with Source is possible. The soul, they say, matures in the sense that its desire is to fulfill The Greater Plan. We advance as a personality, yet we also advance as a soul.

Different Aspects to the Soul

The experiencers' understanding that we are immortal beings born into a human body extends to embrace different aspects of what the soul might be capable of and the different forms it may inhabit. For instance, many were met on the Other Side by animals of various kinds—deceased pets as well as animals unknown to them who acted as "guides." Children occasionally speak of an "animal heaven" they must visit before they can reach the heaven where people are. Ask these experiencers if an animal has a soul and they reply with an unequivocal yes.

Greater Cycles of Learning

The mystical understanding of the principle "As above, so below" tells us that whatever applies in heaven, applies on Earth. This is also true for the soul, which might explain reincarnation—that it's not necessarily a progression of "life after life" so much as cycles of greater learning and expression that ensure the reunion of the created with the Creator.

Group Souls

There are numerous spiritual teachings that refer to "group souls," where members of a given species are guided by the same overlighting intelligence. An example of this would be the varied types of insects, birds, fish, and wild animals—each possessing its own degree of intelligence but following the guidance of a supportive and directive source common to its kind. Also taught is that any creature can develop individuality, grow beyond the awareness of its order, when in close association with humans. This is a gift we can give: "helping the lesser awaken to the greater."

New Words

Spirit translates as "breath," the inference being "The Breath of God" or "that energy that infuses all Creation." **Spirituality**, in the strictest sense, then, means "The Breath of God Breathing." **Holy Spirit**, as part of the Christian Trinity, is considered that aspect of God that serves as a "messenger" or "the carrier wave of divine energy that carries out God's Will."

Some experiencers described powerful oversouls whose job it was to assist in the advancement of many others—a hierarchy of brilliance—encompassing levels and levels of different aspects of what the soul is capable of, what it becomes.

The Reality of Spirit

As well as describing the animating force that drives us, the majority of near-death experiencers I studied were adamant about a special type of energy that they felt permeates life itself—*spirit.*

The Vividness of Spirit

Some experiencers claim they are now able to see spirit. They describe it as a luminosity that sparkles, shimmers, and glows with a radiance all its own. "It's what you see shining through any substance or flesh," an experiencer told me. "Especially with food. If I don't see that glow in it, then I know the food has no spirit. The vitality is gone."

For the rest of them, though, spirit seems to be more of an energy that can be felt—a liveliness that has its own special vibration. They equate spirit with upliftment or enthusiasm. Even our language denotes this: "They are a spirited bunch" or "The team has a lot of spirit." In this sense, spirit can flow through us like a revitalizing breath of fresh air.

Manifestations of Spirit Visions

Mystics and shamans of old spoke of spirit in terms of what shapes and forms it can take to deliver its messages of aid and advice. What survives of their teachings matches the claims of modern-day experiencers, especially about spirit visions and spirit beings.

Spirit visions that featured spiritual truths occurred often to Walter Kupchik, the fellow you met in chapter 9. Walter displayed unusual abilities ever since he had scarlet fever at the age of eight. With no one to talk to about this, he sought out medical advice and was told that his spirit visions were *eidetic images,* although no one could tell him why or how he had them.

Unlike eidetic imagery, Walter's "visions" did not always conform to anything he had seen before. They often manifested as fully dimensional, panoramic realities that were completely alive and lifelike. He was wide awake when he had one. Although what Walter experienced could be considered a higher component of sight, it could also be regarded as spirit itself imparting what he needed to know for his spiritual development.

> **New Words**
>
> **Eidetic images** are defined as visual imagery from a person's memory that can be readily reproduced with accuracy and in detail (such as an image of a person that exactly duplicates the real person in every manner).

Manifestations of Spirit Beings

Spirit beings generally appear as some form of messenger. They can show up in near-death scenarios, but they most often manifest in the experiencer's life afterward. Many experiencers develop lifelong relationships with these spirit friends and come to consider the world of spirit every bit as real, accessible, and useful as the earth

Drawing of a spirit vision that manifested for Walter Kupchik when he was at Natural Bridge in Kentucky, showing him the biblical version of creation.

Tonya's depiction of the angelic being she first met in "death" who has since become a protective spirit that manifests when needed.

world. Some experiencers, however, are only visited by spirit beings during times of need.

Richard Bonenfant, the researcher who told me about Scott (the youngster we discussed in chapter 2 who met the devil in his near-death state) also told me about Tonya, a woman who drowned in a backyard swimming pool when a young adult and experienced a near-death episode. In her scenario, she encountered a beautiful woman framed in light with her hands outstretched in welcome. Once revived, Tonya described the angelic being as having long dark-blond hair, blue eyes, and wearing a white dress. The being radiated motherly love.

Fifteen years later, after Tonya's daughter was attacked by a dog and required facial surgery, the angelic being appeared again to reassure Tonya that her daughter would recover and be all right. She now considers the beautiful woman her very own guardian angel, a spirit being who watches over her and protects her.

The Big Picture

The tremendous range of the life we have, the power of our soul, and the outworking of an energy many call Holy Spirit present us with a picture of reality far greater than what ordinary perception depicts. Near-death experiencers are infused with this: a bigger picture of what constitutes life.

In his book *Beside Still Waters: Searching for Meaning in an Age of Doubt* (see appendix C), Gregg Easterbrook tells us: "The ratio of matter and energy to the volume of space at the Big Bang must have been within about one quadrillionth of one percent ideal." Translation: Our world could not have been an accident; the universe seems to have desired a place where life could manifest in material form, not as a randomness of births and deaths, but

Everything Is Alive

The more sophisticated science becomes, the more evidential are the findings that indicate an underlying intelligence that exists throughout the universe. Every cell displays a form of consciousness. Every molecule and atom, quark and pulsar, seem to know about each other and can respond to situations in ways not explainable by science. As near-death experiencers make plain: All of Creation is alive!

And indeed so—photos from the Hubble telescope in space reveal star nurseries and what looks like umbilical cords sending nutrition into wombs/embryos.

Spiritual Get-Togethers

In April 2006, the very first Spiritual Retreat for Near-Death Experiencers was held in Saint Louis, Missouri, sponsored by IANDS. The turnout exceeded all expectations. "We're hungry for this," an attendee exclaimed. Linda Jacquin, an experiencer herself and former editor of IANDS' newsletter *Vital Signs,* had a vision that the retreat needed to happen, and she was right. From this emerged "The Clan of the Fireflies"—a kind of spiritual bonding among participants—that has resulted in the website www.neardeathexperiencers.org. Many uplifting messages and sharings are located there. Another such retreat was held at the same place in 2007. IANDS now plans to hold these retreats annually. (Contact IANDS for details; see appendix B.)

with purpose and reason. We are here because we were meant to be.

Cruising the Life Stream

The majority of near-death experiencers, when they return, are faced with redefining what life is. Very few are as much impressed with the notion of an afterlife as they are with the idea of a life continuum consisting of waves and pulsations of intelligence. And they tend to view Creation as what the Creator uses to develop the Created, the souls we are. Hence, through the gifts of time, space, and matter, we, the ensouled, have a way to awaken to our potential. This process of awakening refines and strengthens us.

A lofty concept, certainly, but one that is ever so real to an experiencer. Most consider earthly life a rite of passage, one of the levels and planes they must traverse as they grow in consciousness and mature as a soul. Almost uniformly, they come to regard themselves as spiritual beings having a human experience, rather than the other way around.

Breathing In/Breathing Out

I never cease to be amazed at how many experiencers sense an overall pulse or movement within the world that seems to them as if all of Creation is breathing. They describe this as an unmistakable pattern of inhalation and exhalation.

Listen

"To know the road ahead, listen to those coming back."
—Yang Li An

We need to realize in hearing accounts like this how dynamic life is to experiencers and how absolutely vibrant spiritual reality is regarded. Our human lives, say the average experiencer, don't begin at birth or end at death; neither do they encompass the activities of what is construed as a "lifetime." Life is akin to an immortal consciousness that grows and develops in myriad and unlimited ways.

An example of this unique viewpoint would be the computer simulation Richard Borutta of Hopewell, New Jersey, made of what he saw when he "died" at age forty-two. As a consequence of acute alcoholism, Richard's liver had stopped working. To save him, physicians did a risky procedure that involved abdominal surgery to drain fluid. A near-death experience ensued but abruptly ended when he was "pulled back" by the actions of his doctor. Angry about what he had missed yet still feeling "connected," he, by choice, returned to the Other Side.

An entity there challenged Richard to show major lesson he had learned which would account for his life. Defiant about doing that, he says: "I met with an all-understanding, all-knowing entity that I couldn't offend. I was still left with a choice of how I would participate in the ongoing process of creation, but I decided it would be better if I could straighten things out before I went on to some other form of existence." Feathery spirits then guided him into the light where he says he was cured of alcoholism and his liver was restored. Amazingly, once revived, his liver was indeed found to be miraculously healed and his addiction gone. As Richard explained, "Months after, all my doctor would say when I asked him about it was, 'You are a very lucky man, and there's no brain damage.'"

Regarding the feathery spirits that guided him into the light where he was cured, Richard says: "The central light was an attraction to the individual lights or feathers. They seemed to represent some spiritual form that responded to the warm flow from the central light and the natural interaction with each other. Some lights were alone, individual, and hung like stars in the blackness. Some feathers paired and helped each other.

"I needed help from specific entities that were already down nearer the center. As I was guided by one of the feathery [spirits], I drew closer to the source, and the special entities were able to contact me. It was some sort of transference of these vibrations that gave me the understanding I needed, and would need in my future life. You see, it involved not only a union of spirits but a communication of ideas and values at a pure instinctive level—thus the term *communion.*

"Another aspect of this communion is the realization that it's what we have in COMMON that is important, not our differences. It's when we give and share, rather than separate and take, that makes things get better."

Richard feels that what happened to him is possible for anyone to attain, without having to die to do it. "Being part of life and participating fully, not withdrawing like I was prone to do, is part of it. Giving of yourself and your specific talents without expecting a reward is a quality that can liberate you. I never seem too disappointed anymore. Truly worthwhile things have become apparent and attainable. It is a reward in itself."

The Book of Life

Some near-death experiencers have talked about having seen The Book of Life during their episode. A few described it as a single large book, emblazoned in gold, that contains the full history of everyone. Most, however, claim there is a volume for each soul and you are only permitted to read what applies to you. Regardless of how described, the notion that such a book exists is an old one, found in many stories and legends.

What intrigues me is that experiencers occasionally "remember" years later what they saw in The Book. And sometimes that memory emerges as a "future memory episode" of what is about to happen but hasn't yet, at least not in the earthplane. Apparently, The Book of Life encompasses the future as well as the present and past, and contains a Big Picture of what life is for and where we are headed as evolving souls.

The reality of accounts such as this can be debated, but there are times

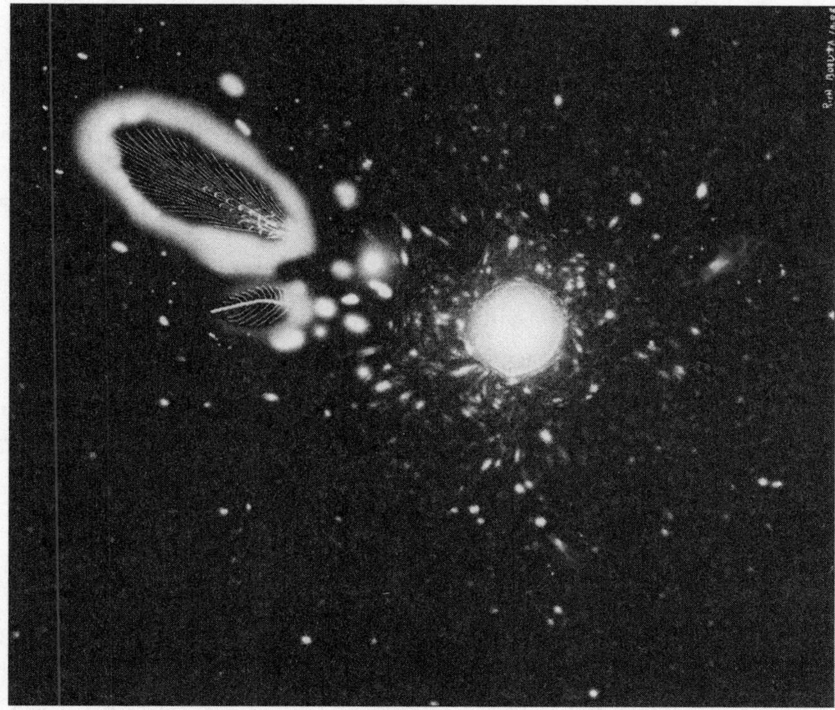

Photo of Richard Borutta's computer simulation, entitled "Communion," depicting the feathery spirits that accompanied him into the light during his near-death episode.

Records of the Soul

Edgar Cayce, one of the most accurate psychics ever known, credited most of the information he gave during his readings to what he read in The Book of Life while in a trance state. Although he described it as an actual book, he clarified what he meant by saying our every thought, word, and deed is "recorded upon the skeins of time and space." This record, he said, was God's Book of Remembrance, or the "Akashic" records. According to Cayce, each soul is imprinted with its own record and carries that imprint into the physical body as an energy pattern upon birth. Anyone can access these records if he or she is spiritually ready.

when I'm confronted by a case that makes me wonder. Not long ago, I received a communication from Kimberly Scheurer of East Rochester, New York, that was about her grandmother. Although The Book of Life is not mentioned per se, the brief story that follows is identical to how such reports are told and what they contain.

Kimberly begins: "My grandmother was twice pronounced dead within a year's time. She described a near-death experience to me, and she seemed to have acquired psychic abilities that she was not aware of before. BUT, the difference is—approximately six months before her death, she telephoned me and told me detail by detail of everything that would happen after her death; her funeral services, particular conversations people would have, clothing people would wear, just as if she had lived it [already]. She even proceeded to tell me of events that would happen months after her death, that were not related to her directly, but to me.

"After she told me these things, it was almost as if I had an amnesia of what she said. I didn't remember her words until the things she was telling me were happening. MAN, did that knock me off my feet!"

The Law of Grace

As life is redefined by each experiencer, a strong moral compass surfaces. The average person trusts that a Higher Order exists, but an experiencer *knows* that it does. And therein lies an incredibly amazing difference—what some call *grace.*

Mystical tradition teaches that grace is one of the laws that governs Creation. And, as a law, it is that step we take *in* love that frees us to experience more *of* love. It is said that in grace we

New Word

Grace is most commonly regarded in spiritual and religious terms as an awareness of God's generosity; a sense of being blessed. This awareness is experienced as a great truth. To live in grace is to transcend human pettiness and freely give that which is already given: forgiveness, compassion, loving kindness, and joy.

awaken to the power of our soul and the truth that life is immortal. We give only that which is already given, because that's what we are.

The Return to Things Spiritual

Because of what happens to people who undergo near-death experiences and other consciousness-transforming episodes, science and the professional community are taking note—and what they're finding is transforming them.

Dr. Bruce Greyson, for instance, when researching mystical experiences, discovered that all nine of the major features that identify these states *exactly match* how the near-death phenomenon affects people. Compare these features for yourself:

1. Sense of cosmic unity or oneness
2. Transcendence of time and space
3. Deeply felt positive mood
4. Sense of sacredness
5. Noetic quality or intuitive illumination
6. Paradoxical (examples: I'm dead and yet I'm alive; I'm one with everything and yet I'm myself; "I'm overcome with love and yet I'm beyond all emotion")
7. Ineffable (incapable of being expressed)
8. Transient (lasting only a short time)
9. Persistent positive aftereffects

This consistency, irrespective of the type of consciousness transformation an individual had or in what country or at what age, has excited the scientific world in ways no one could have imagined.

God Leads in Polls

A FOX News poll done in 2006 found that 91 percent of the people in the United States profess a belief in God, 87 percent believe in Heaven, 84 percent in miracles, and 79 percent in angels. Hell was affirmed by 74 percent, and the devil by 67 percent.

A survey done that same year in China revealed that 56.7 percent of the people claimed to have had a religious experience. In a country where atheism is taught as an official government position, this is remarkable!

In England a similar survey showed that 80 percent reported having had a "nonreligious" or spiritual transformation of consciousness.

New Studies, New Fields

We learn from Dr. Peter Fenwick that in England, more than one thousand psychiatrists are now practicing *spiritual psychiatry*. They have discovered that the spiritual, taking on a personal relationship with God/Deity, heals and uplifts better and faster than many of the procedures they once used. "There is an upwelling of spiritual interest," notes Dr. Fenwick.

To back up his claim, he revealed that in 1995 only three U. S. medical schools had courses on "Spirituality in Medicine." In 1998, there were forty, and by 2001, one hundred medical schools had formal classes on medical spirituality. "There is a new breed of doctors," explains Dr. Fenwick, "who

Genome Pioneer Discovers God

The scientist who led the way to crack the human genome code, discovered something else as well—he discovered God. Francis Collins, MD, PhD, director of the U. S. National Human Genome Research Institute, has written a revealing book called *The Language of God: A Scientist Presents Evidence for Belief* (refer to appendix C). Dr. Collins believes the sequencing of the human genome is the most remarkable of all "texts," and that it gives a detailed view of the mind of the Creator at work. "Science is not threatened by God," he said, "it is enhanced."

are increasingly open to the role of spirituality in medicine. They are part of a huge impulse globally toward spiritual development."

Mario Beauregard, a neuroscientist working at the University of Montreal, is part of that new breed of doctors to which Dr. Fenwick refers. He peeks inside the minds of nuns using the latest in technological wizardry, to identify and track what happens when they achieve union with God during prayer. In chapter 22, I discussed work similar to this, but scientists like Dr. Beauregard are actually going a step further, they are building a database in the new field of study called *neurotheology*.

Science is now proving that we are "hardwired" for God. Spiritual psychiatry is recognizing that spirituality brings one a sense of purpose and a reason for living. It uplifts and heals where no drug can. Near-death experiences, even more particularly than other transformative states, reveal not only the continuity of consciousness, but also its existence in field arrays beyond that of the brain.

Just hearing about this—how science is embracing things spiritual—is very encouraging. As more people share their stories and tell of how they live now and what they have come to know, even near-death experiencers themselves are healed. We help each other by sharing life's surprises and what they mean to us.

What happened to Joe Ann Van Gelder is a case in point (we first met her in chapter 21). She had nine near-death experiences as a child, caused by multiple illnesses and accidents. Her story is in my books *Children of the New Millennium* and *The New Children and Near-Death Experiences* (see appendix C). She sent me a letter describing a trip she took to India to see Sai Baba, a holy

New Word

A growing number of scientists using the latest technology are researching **neurotheology**, the physiological basis of religious and spiritual experience. They are finding that more of the brain is involved in these experiences than previously supposed. Contrary to claims of a "God spot," they are discovering that the religious or spiritual experience is encoded into our very makeup and brain structure.

man. She made an important connection while there that she described for me. The unconditional love she felt when he looked at her *was the same love she was bathed in as a toddler when she had a dark-light near-death experience.* This overwhelmed her. Here's an excerpt from her letter:

"There were thousands seated in large blocks of people, so that there would be aisles in which he could walk among them. We all watched him intently. At that time he was at least 150 feet away from me. At the very moment he turned in my direction, I experienced the very same experience I had in my childhood NDEs—the dark womb-like void that was not frightening but filled with unconditional Love. Since I was 'there' [reliving my near-death experience], I was not aware of what was happening around me until a lady seated next to me poked me with her elbow and said in a stage whisper, 'He said how are you.' Knowing that he probably knew my situation, I simply gasped, 'I'm fine, Baba, I'm fine.'"

26

Message for the Twenty-first Century

> Each person's experience of great unity and beauty is a new chapter in a living personal Bible. And we are all living a Bible whether we write it down, whether we look at anything formal or not.
>
> —Steve Straight, founding editor of *Vital Signs* newsletter (IANDS) and coeditor of *Anabiosis–The Journal for Near-Death Studies*

In the book accompanying his audiotape program "The Transpersonal Vision: The Healing Potential of Nonordinary States of Consciousness," psychiatrist, psychiatric researcher, professor, and author Stanislav Grof writes: "The many strange characteristics of transpersonal experiences shatter the most fundamental metaphysical assumptions of the Newtonian-Cartesian paradigm and the materialistic world view." He also noted that any attempt to dismiss transpersonal experiences as irrelevant products of human fantasy or hallucinations was naive and inadequate—for they represent "a critical challenge, not only for psychiatry and psychology, but for the entire philosophy of Western Science."

That's quite a claim! But as I hope I've shown in this book, in the twenty-first century, a transpersonal experience such as the near-death phenomenon has, indeed, challenged "not only . . . psychiatry and psychology, but . . . the entire philosophy of Western Science."

That challenge has laid the groundwork for a whole new way of looking at the future of human existence and consciousness.

Remember This

"The intuitive mind is a sacred gift, and the rational mind is a faithful servant. We have created a society that honors the servant and has forgotten the gift."

—Albert Einstein

What Changed Buddhism

Previous near-death research has uncovered a link between near-death states and the transformation of first-century Buddhism in China and Japan. Mahayana Buddhism suddenly emerged at that time, a reflection of near-death "visions" that depicted caring and enlightened individuals reaching back to help others less fortunate. Before then, only Hinayana Buddhism existed—a singular path that encouraged the severance of all earthly ties.

An Agency of Change

Let's come back to the writing of Dr. Grof, which accompanied his audiotape program "The Transpersonal Vision": "Materialistic science holds that any memory requires a material substrate, such as the neuronal network in the brain or the DNA molecules of genes. However, it is impossible to imagine any material medium for the information conveyed by various forms of transpersonal experiences. This information has clearly not been acquired by conventional means—that is, by sensory perception—during the individual's lifetime. It seems to exist independently of matter, and to be contained in the field of consciousness itself or in some types of fields undetectable by scientific instruments."

In other words, transpersonal experiences suggest that there's a field of consciousness—a source of knowledge—that exists independent of any one person's mind and is accessible to us beyond our ordinary sensory and mind-body ways of receiving information.

The Fields of Hyperspace

Scientifically, it is now recognized that three-dimensional space is embedded within a hierarchy of higher dimensions. These higher fields are referred to as *hyperspace.*

F. Gordon Greene, while studying the issue of "corners" and why people who leave their bodies in near-death experiences usually wind up viewing the scene below from a ceiling corner (see chapter 23), advances the idea that consciousness fields exist in hyperspace. He stated that: "Hyperspace theory . . . is large enough and flexible enough to provide possible answers."

Dr. Pim van Lommel, in tackling the issue of fields of consciousness, explains that "phase-space" is an invisible, nonlocal hyperspace that consists of probability fields—where every past and future event is available as a possibility. "Within this phase-space no matter is present, everything belongs to uncertainty, and neither measurements nor observations are possible by physi-

New Word

Hyperspace consists of four or more dimensions. Most of the useful notions about our experience in three-dimensional reality have exact counterparts in hyperspace, even beyond the fourth dimension where time and space are said to merge.

cists. The act of observation instantly changes a probability into an actuality by collapse of the wave function . . . The phase-space in this invisible and non-measurable phase-space varies from the speed of light to infinity . . . At the speed of light, the speed of a particle and the speed of a wave are identical.

"Our whole and undivided consciousness with declarative memories finds its origin in, and is stored in this phase-space, and the [brain] cortex only serves as a relay station for parts of our consciousness and parts of our memories to be received into our waking consciousness. In this concept consciousness is not physically rooted. This could be compared with the Internet, which does not originate from the computer itself, but is only received by it." (See paper entitled "About the Continuity of Our Consciousness," full citation in appendix C.)

Research with experiencers of near-death states underscores the idea of fields of consciousness existing in dimensions beyond three-dimensional reality. During a cardiac arrest, for example, or with people in coma, there can still exist the full consciousness, full memory, and full faculty engagement *even when the brain has flat-lined or is nonresponsive.* "Based on recent scientific research on NDEs, we should consider the possibility that there is a continuity of our consciousness," stated Dr. van Lommel, "and that death, like birth, may well be a mere passing from one state of consciousness to another."

Are there fields of consciousness? Yes. Personal fields, group fields, mass mind—all of them, it seems, are located in some dimension of hyperspace, and they are completely accessible by anyone.

> **Who's in My Organ?**
>
> DNA has been compared to the bar code that identifies a part with its whole. It seems to work as a receptor mechanism that attunes people to their specific field of consciousness. This observation has become an issue with organ transplants. The DNA of any organ belongs to the consciousness field of the donor, not the recipient. There are numerous cases of record now where an organ recipient developed radically different desires and lifestyles after the transplant—which *exactly matched* those of the donor.

The Global Mind

The closest modern science has come to evidencing that mass mind, a universal field of consciousness common to us all, exists, is what happened on September 11, 2001, when the World Trade Center in New York City was attacked. The evidence emerged via the Global Mind Project.

Roger D. Nelson and a team of fellow scientists set up the Global Mind Project in 1998, headquartered in the Princeton Engineering Anomalies Research Lab. The project consists of random event generators scattered across the world in sixty-five host sites, which measure subtle correlations in random data that appear to reflect the presence and the activity of consciousness globally. And they have found

Consciousness Is Interconnected

Dean I. Radin, PhD, a participant in the Global Mind Project, wrote *Entangled Minds: Extrasensory Experiences in a Quantum Reality* (see appendix C). Throughout his many years as a scientist, he has repeatedly observed that the universe is an interconnected whole, and that the fabric of reality is woven together from strange "holistic" threads that cannot be located in three-dimensional time and space. He further advances the notion that a hierarchy of consciousness exists and that we can access this in nonordinary mind states.

exactly that when readouts from all the machines cohere around major events. What shocked everyone is that *the day before* the attack on the World Trade Center, worldwide data merged, then, *four hours before* the attack, there was a spike in global consciousness that continued rising almost off the charts and for several days afterward. It is almost as if the entire world knew on some level what was about to happen and responded with a emotional shock wave that even today confounds statistical explanation. (For website addresses, refer to appendix D.)

Hints from the Past

In his book *The Last Laugh: A New Philosophy of Near-Death Experiences, Apparitions, and the Paranormal* (see appendix C), Dr. Raymond A. Moody offers numerous stories about historical figures who made significant contributions to society after entering into nonordinary states of consciousness through dreams, visions, and near-death experiences.

Among those he mentions is French philosopher and mathematician René Descartes, who shut himself in a room for a day and night and had a "mindquake." New information poured into his mind providing him with the basis for his theories of analytic geometry and the mathematical principles used in quantifying all the sciences.

More specifically, in both *Children of the New Millennium* (also *The New Children and Near-Death Experiences*) and *Future Memory,* I devote extended sections to discussing history makers who "died" as children, revived, and immediately afterward began to exhibit the typical aftereffects of a near-death experiencer. Most of their names will be familiar to you: Abraham Lincoln, Black Elk (a Lakota Sioux who became

Brain Jump

While researching historical figures, I discovered that many of the most creative mathematicians, scientists (especially physicists), musicians, artists, inventors, computer geniuses, and psychics, both past and present, displayed a jump in brain development after having had something like a near-death experience—and usually as a child. Major advancements in their chosen field were achieved by each.

a famous medicine man), Albert Einstein, Mozart, Edward de Vere (the Seventeenth Earl of Oxford, believed by many to be the real author of Shakespeare's work), and Walter Russell (a well-known artist and visionary).

Visions for Everybody

In *The Last Laugh,* as in his previous books, Dr. Moody makes a pitch for *apparition chambers.* He is convinced that the average person needs to have some kind of safe, reliable way to replicate nonordinary states of consciousness like near-death experiences. This option, he contends, is worth trying.

Dr. Moody's design of an apparition chamber consists of the following:

- An enclosed, lightproof, soundproof, closet-sized room, with walls painted completely black
- A mirror both four feet high and wide on one wall, its bottom edge three feet from the floor
- An easy chair, without legs, sitting on the floor about three feet in front of the mirror, with headrest tilted slightly back for greater comfort
- A small lamp with a four-and-a-half-watt bulb directly behind the chair, which diffuses light so no mirror reflection can be seen when the door is shut and the lamp is on

Bright, curious people who are emotionally stable make the best subjects, Dr. Moody found. He asked each of those he worked with to choose a deceased loved one to contact. Participants brought along personal objects once owned by that person to make the session more poignant. Preparation consisted of general, open-ended questions and a discussion about what could happen. Then individuals were escorted into a chamber and left to relax in the chair as they gazed at the mirror. About an hour and a half later, they were led back to the central area where they talked about what, if anything, had happened.

The results? "About half felt they were reunited with lost loved ones during the process," explained Dr. Moody. "Many saw lifelike, three-dimensional visions of departed dear ones. Sometimes, they saw apparitions in the mirror, and sometimes the apparitions emerged from it. In about a third of the cases, subjects heard the voices of their lost loved ones. In almost all the other cases, subjects felt they were in mind-to-mind or soul-to-soul communion with their departed. Sometimes, there were lengthy conversational interchanges."

New Words

The **apparition chambers** of ancient Greece provided anyone interested with an opportunity to experience "otherworldly spirits" and receive "guidance." The site of the chambers was called a **psychomanteion,** and included space for preparatory sessions and purification rituals with trained mentors, the sacred chambers, and meetings afterward to talk over what happened. Lately, creating psychomanteions has undergone a revival.

Other Ways to Do It

Using psychomanteions to experience nonordinary states of consciousness is beneficial for some, but not for others. Guided visualizations are an excellent alternative, and incorporate skills anyone can learn. An instruction book made to order for the subject is *Anyone Can See the Light: The Seven Keys to a Guided Out-of-Body Experience,* by Dianne Morrissey, PhD (see appendix C). Says Dr. Melvin Morse, "I tried these techniques and they work!" No method yet discovered, however, can top prayer and meditation for effectively setting the stage for miracles and laying the groundwork for an intimate, ongoing dialogue with the spiritual.

Induced After-Death Communication

Allan L. Botkin, PsyD, discovered quite by accident, while working with psychologically traumatized combat veterans, that in using standard eye movement techniques his patients could experience in essence what Dr. Moody was trying to accomplish with his psychomanteions. The technique of eye movement desensitization and reprocessing (EMDR) not only enabled a patient to relax into a deep focus that aided in moving the individual's brain into higher processing modes, it did even more.

Patients who were "locked" into reliving the horrors of war were sometimes able to move past that and actually converse with the deceased. In a number of cases, the deceased person related information previously unknown to the patient that later proved to be true. This experience produced a healing and a recovery that was long-lasting. When Dr. Botkin expanded his therapy sessions to include people who needed help relieving grief over a loved one's death, the same thing happened with a significant number of them. He now teaches others his technique, and coauthored the book *Induced After-Death Communication: A New Therapy for Healing Grief and Trauma.* (Refer to appendix C for more information on his book and appendix D for his website address.)

Thanks to professionals like Dr. Botkin, the door to other worlds and nonordinary states of consciousness are no longer the province of fantasy.

Evolution's Next Step

As agencies of change, near-death and other transformational states of consciousness represent more than direct-access routes to a higher source of universal knowledge. They also func-

But Be Open

"I am convinced at this point that people who have strong beliefs about the experience have a more difficult time achieving an induced after-death communication (IADC), because their expectations interfere with the receptive mode."

—Allan L. Botkin, PsyD

tion as stimulants in molding what Dr. Kenneth Ring calls a new "prototype" for the human species. He feels that those who undergo these experiences become the vanguard of evolution's next quantum leap.

Nonverbal Intelligence

The curiosity about recent IQ test scores worldwide concerns nonverbal intelligence, or creative problem solving. Nearly all of the child experiencers of near-death states in my study exhibited this trait (genius or not)! This is the ability to abstract—to think "outside the box."

Skyrocketing Intelligence

There is no question that the human race is evolving. The Millennial Generation, defined by William Strauss and Neil Howe (authors of *Generations: The History of America's Future, 1584 to 2069;* see appendix C) as those born between 1982 and about 2003, are already the smartest in history. A surprising percentage of their IQ scores show a jump of about twenty-four to twenty-six points over previous ratings. This affects the marker for genius, which has stood at around 134 to 136. All other countries administering the tests reported the same phenomenon.

The gene pool cannot change fast enough to account for this jump. So it has been supposed that better nutrition and more efficient schools are the cause. Yet neither explanation accounts for a fascinating curiosity that appears in the IQ scores: "Acquired intelligence" (that which comes from rote schooling) improved only slightly, while "nonverbal intelligence" (that which is based on creative problem solving) soared!

Trying to make sense of the situation, experts have surmised that either kids are getting better at taking tests, or something in their environment accounts for this astonishing difference. Some top educators feel that the spread of "image-intense" technologies such as video games are partially responsible, as they train a child to concentrate and respond (unlike television, which demands nothing of viewers). Others suggest that it is permissive or relaxed parenting—the child leading the parent, rather than the other way around—that can promote vocabulary building, a critical skill.

In the near-death research I have conducted since 1978, however, roughly half of the children who experienced such episodes fall within the same IQ score range as the Millennials, upward of 150/160 and higher. Yet their change was sudden and could be traced to that moment when death seemed their only option, not to playing with video games or trying to outwit parents. Nor were they born with exceptional IQs. Additionally, few of those I spoke with ever used image-intense technologies to any extent, and the majority described their parental relationships as "strained."

The Second Born

Commonalities between the Millennial Generation and child experiencers of near-death states are numerous (nonverbal intelligence

The Best Books about This

The best book in my opinion for covering the switch in brain processing these children have is *Upside-Down Brilliance: The Visual-Spatial Learner,* by Linda Kreger Silverman, PhD (Denver, CO: DeLeon, 2002).

The best one for making the point that, with these children philosophy must be part of standard curriculum in grade school, is *Little Big Minds: Sharing Philosophy with Kids,* by Marietta McCarty (New York: Penguin Group, 2006).

And by far the best book ever written on the active spiritual life these kids have is: *The Secret Spiritual World of Children: The Breakthrough Discovery that Profoundly Alters Our Conventional View of Children's Mystical Experiences,* by Tobin Hart, PhD (Makawao, HI: Inner Ocean, 2003).

being just one). You could easily use the latter as a model to understand what might be happening with the new crop of young people. But if you do, something else emerges—descriptive evidence suggestive of a second birth.

What I refer to concerns near-death kids who exhibit certain telltale characteristics that make them appear as if they were "rewired and reconfigured" by the phenomenon—as if they were "reborn." Consider these observations I made while conducting my research:

- Temporal lobe expansion in the brain begins to precede or accelerate natural brain development.
- The learning curve starts to reverse itself, placing abstract conceptualizing before foundational understanding.
- IQ and sensory enhancement accompany heightened spatial/nonverbal/sensory-dynamic thinking, giving rise to unique problem-solving skills.
- Future awareness becomes commonplace, along with the ability to rehearse life demands before they occur.
- The ability to sense in multiples enables whole new worlds of possibility to surface.
- A drive toward social justice and moral integrity becomes primary, complemented by a tolerance for ambiguity and paradox.

These characteristics imply that the brains of child near-death experiencers may have changed in structure, chemistry, and function (how much and to what extent has yet to be measured clinically), owing to, as I suggested in chapter 24, their near-death states occurring at critical junctures in their childhood brain development.

A New Race

When you continue to question what is happening with the Millennial Generation and the near-death kids, aside from unexplained jumps in intelligence, you begin to notice that they display almost the same physiological differences, suggesting a change in the root stock or genetic core of the human family.

Many psychics today say that fifth root race types can best be recognized by differences in their eyes (greater field depth with pupils not as reflective), digestive systems (less tolerant of "rich" diets), and DNA structure (unique immunities). Also, they supposedly have noticeable sensitivities to electromagnetic fields, certain foods, excessive light and sound, and industrial chemicals/pharmaceuticals, and they are creative intuitives, with abstraction one of their greatest talents.

These are basically the same characteristics that appear as the aftereffects of near-death and other transformative states, and that are present in the Millennial Generation and those "new ones" making up the next phase in generational advancement, the "9/11s."

Root Races

Various mystical traditions refer to times when the life stream alters, enabling the "root race" to advance. No reference is made to "race" in the sense of genetic subgroups, but rather, to evolutionary mutations in the "root stock" or gene pool of the human species. Seven evolutionary advancements have been predicted before humankind is said to reach its full potential. The first four are scientifically termed *Homo habilis, Homo erectus, Homo sapiens,* and *Homo sapiens sapiens.* What was foreseen for our current period is the emergence of the "fifth root race," those "quickened" in spiritual awareness and genetic makeup—what consciousness researcher John White calls *Homo noeticus.* I discuss this at length in my book *Beyond the Indigo Children: The New Children and the Coming of the Fifth World* (refer to appendix C).

The Global Village

Political pundits have noted that the governments of the future will be influenced more by bankers than by elections. Yet a shared economy, the unhindered flow of goods and services across borders, cannot take place without shared values. Unknown to most politicians is that the foundation for those shared values is steadily being laid by individuals committed to spirituality and consciousness transformations.

This movement toward a more authentic way of living gained real momentum after the publishing spree that resulted from revelations about the near-death experience and how it seemed to validate Eastern and Western religious traditions as mirror reflections of the same basic truth. By networking with each other, all manner of people have discovered that the way to circumvent mainstream bias concerning the mutually supportive and respectful way they wanted to live was to create a subculture of their own. In the United States, this growing faction has come to be called *cultural creatives.*

New Words

Sociologist Paul Ray, vice president of the San Francisco–based market research firm American Lives, coined the term **cultural creatives** to describe an "integral culture" that he estimates now numbers fifty million Americans, or roughly one-fourth of the population. These people merge and integrate modernism with traditionalism, East with West, to create a renaissance mindset that is so powerful it has become a political presence in society.

Social Evolution

Computerization has made it possible for any individual to co-participate in dissolving the borders of countries in the sense of how he or she can now outmaneuver governments. Populace insistence that moral integrity and social justice should matter more than global power relations and religious fundamentalism is gaining majority strength thanks to the technological revolution engulfing the world. Because this is happening, nothing less than the evolution of society itself is at hand; the subculture is poised to become the dominant culture.

Curiosity about the near-death experience, by itself, is creating a common international language of shared concepts and mutual beliefs that informs social change. That's because the phenomenon addresses the deepest desire of people everywhere: the desire to know why we exist—our purpose.

A Timely Source

Ode, the magazine for "intelligent optimists," covers these issues and many more in the most exciting and timely format I have yet discovered. (Refer to appendix E for information on how to contact them should you be interested.)

The Real Global Village

When near-death experiencers talk about what they learned from their episodes, you can't help but notice that their stories express a larger agenda, that of the human family seeking to awaken. The real global village, the sum of who we are and where we really live, can be found in the collective nature of the human heart. And this the near-death experience speaks to directly.

As an example of what I mean, consider what happened to J. R. Mondie of Russell Springs, Kentucky, a three-time near-death experiencer, as he lay dying in an ambulance as it raced to a hospital in Lexington:

"The realization I received [of where I was] was combined with the sudden awareness of every living soul around me, beginning at my immediate center and flowing outward/inward. I was part of a larger picture. I sensed the three souls in the ambulance with me, not only their presence, but their love, their hearts, their emotions, feelings, senses—both physical and mental. I heard their thoughts. I felt their caring hands. I looked through each of their eyes, and saw not only their immediate physical future, but their past, as well.

"I also noted [the presence] of animals and other souls around me, such as: an angry bus driver in Seattle, Washington; a lady killing an annoying spider in Ripley, West Virginia; a bug hitting a train [as it traveled through] Oklahoma. All of these feelings were felt in a split second, and seemed like eternity. I felt love, hate, famine, awe, destruction, revolution, caring, hope, and a barrage of other feelings. What was so funny is: I realized the purpose of it all. Why doesn't God stop the violence? Because God didn't start it in the first place."

The realization of the human family as a collective whole (irrespective of our individual natures and shortcomings), of our oneness with Source, of the opportunities we hold and the responsibilities we are charged with, underscores the revelatory aspects of the entire genre of consciousness transformation.

The Greatest Ethical Potential

Kazimierz Dabrowski, a Polish psychologist and psychiatrist, found that children who displayed the greatest potential for an ethical, compassionate adulthood were those creatively gifted individuals who displayed more pronounced responses to various types of stimuli. The characteristics of this "overexcitable" bunch matched those of child experiencers of near-death states almost exactly: abundant physical energy, heightened faculties, vivid inner life, intellectual curiosity, and a deep capacity for caring.

Social Justice and Human Rights

The role of justice is becoming an imperative. But what is justice without the right of each person to live in dignity? Announced over a radio news program recently were these shocking statistics: "Ninety percent of the world's people have no control over their lives. Of the billions who inhabit this planet, one out of every 200 is a refugee from political violence."

Numbers like these threaten global economics. For this reason, governments and corporations are finally paying more attention to issues such as social justice and human rights. Yet it is the individual who always has and always will make the biggest difference. Awakening in consciousness means awakening to the power of a Higher Order—and striving to live in accordance with that revelation. There are many who have, more who will. As our numbers increase, the louder will be our voice.

You Begin with Yourself

Living in accordance with a Higher Order is the stumbling block that trips up most people, and near-death experiencers are no exception.

Consider the case of Jeffrey Spender Wickstrom of Park City, Utah.

At the age of ten, he was hit by lightning and had a near-death episode. That single event colored everything in his life from then on, marking him as different and setting him on a path to develop what some might call sacred or spiritual creativity. Jeffrey tells us of an event that intervened, though, while he was seeking to achieve this goal:

"I am an award-winning, independent filmmaker who relocated to Utah. I came to develop, cast, scout locations, and shoot five feature-length science fiction films about the Native American prophecies concerning our environment and our nuclear and nerve gas weapon systems. Coming from southern California, I felt as if Utah was untouched by the serious problems facing the more populated areas of the USA—I was wrong.

"In January of 1990, on my way to the Sundance U.S. Film Festival from my home in Salt Lake City, I was mugged and severely beaten, enough so to require twenty-eight months of medical/rehabilitative treatment. As an aspiring filmmaker, having just completed my apprenticeship, I had no insurance."

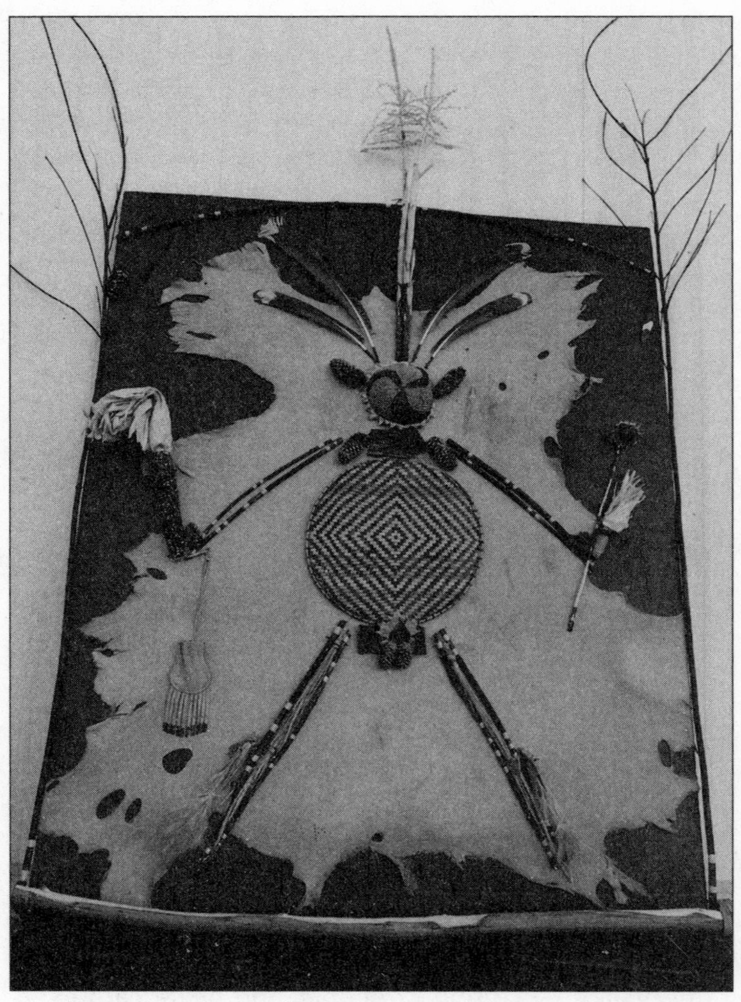
"Sunflower Man with Corn" is the ceremonial mixed-media earth sculpture created by Jeffrey Spender Wickstrom during his recovery from being mugged and beaten. This piece began his true adventure into the sacredness of creativity as he explored the power of forgiveness.

The prognosis was bad: Reconstructive surgery would, in all probability, leave him paralyzed; during initial attempts at holistic healing, he contracted a life-threatening intestinal infection. Jeffrey wasted a whole year reliving his attack and being consumed with anger, hatred, and fear, as he sought ways he could fight back, hurt "them." At long last, the spirit guide he met in death as a boy got through to him. "Build a circle garden," he was told.

"The garden, and garlic I ate from it, slowly but surely sweated out [the infection]. Sweating, planting, weeding, watering, being encircled by Devas [angels], Nature Spirits [fairies], and my own spirit-voice guidance [from his near-death experience]—all this inspired the artwork and the celebration of forgiveness that then helped the healing process. The spirits in the garden, high altitude, sunlight, thirty-six varieties of wildflowers when I only planted twenty-four different seeds—all of it spoke to me in a language of love, vibrancy, harmony, balance, and the constant renewal of life.

"You can get stuck in a nightmare," cautioned Jeffrey. "So I forgave them, and forgiveness, for me, was the key to recovery."

Jeffrey discovered the hard way that experiencing a near-death state does not exempt an individual from life's harshness. But it can establish a sound spiritual base from which to build future behavior. Although it took him a while to work the anger out of his system, once he did, his spiritual guidance returned as a steady presence in his life and his progress accelerated. Today, Jeffrey's anger and hatred are gone, and he shows no signs of having ever been crippled.

Then, You Include Others

The phenomenon of near-death speaks first to the experiencer, then to others—from the one to the many.

Jeffrey went on to use what happened to him to help others. So did Linda Redford of Santa Monica, California. In 1982, Linda went into anaphylactic shock after taking a pain pill she had safely taken before. Her "death" was immediate and violent; her near-death experience, transcendent. She revived in time to refuse all drugs the ambulance medical crew offered. She opted instead for prayer. This irritated the specialists at the University of California–Los Angeles Medical Center where she was rushed, and they tried to have her labeled "crazy."

Being looked upon as irrational by her doctors further complicated and confused Linda, as did the voice she heard during her near-death experience that asked her, "Are you willing to help create a way to return honor to Mother Earth and the human race?" When she said yes, the voice replied, "Good, for unless this is accomplished, the human race will not survive." Now, labeled "crazy" by her doctors, she wondered how she was supposed to be able to assist in creating a way to help the planet and humankind.

An Original Screenplay

Jeffrey Spender Wickstrom created an original screenplay about his near-death experience when he was ten. Entitled "Child in the Man," it is in the form of an interactive CD-ROM made especially for children and the "child" in all of us. While watching it on your home computer, you can experience the power of a near-death state, explore the "heavens" of other cultural traditions, and change the ending if you wish. For more information, contact Jeffrey's company, Electric Northern Light Films (see appendix E).

"At that moment," Linda says of her near-death scenario, "I was rapidly shown images of my life from a different perspective. It was uncomfortable. No matter how much I struggled, I could not escape this way of seeing. The truth was very loud. I was responsible for every decision, every action, and every consequence to myself and others. When I had harmed another, I

IMAGINE AND CREATE YOUR OWN WORLD

HONOR PLEDGE

I honor myself;

I live by principles that benefit future generations;

I communicate in a peaceful manner;

I respect all cultures and honor our differences;

I acknowledge that males and females are equal in their importance;

I understand what I believe about myself and others creates my world;

I feel in my heart that I am connected with all creation.

Adawee Tribe

The Honor Pledge from the Adawee Teachings, a program created by Linda Redford for children.

New Word

Adawee is Cherokee for "Guardian of Wisdom."

wounded my own soul. I felt like my brain was a computer and God was downloading vital information that I would be responsible to pass on. Matters such as accountability, responsibility, the power of words, sarcasm, the imprint of behavior passed on through generations, internalized spiritual maladies that are creating physical and emotional disease, and the destruction of Mother Earth were summoned.

"Then, suddenly, the images changed from my life to a vision of a world in harmony. It was breathtaking. An overwhelming feeling of love engulfed my being, for at the time, I had no body. What I had was a connection, a bond, between my spirit and some form of Higher Intelligence. Here, each individual was honored for their uniqueness, for it was understood we were all manifestations of the Creator's Imagination. I was in awe of the magnitude of what I was experiencing. The brilliance of the Great Mystery was overwhelming. When I was shown this world, I thought GREAT, I WANNA GO THERE! What I didn't realize was that I was being asked to mentor this vision into the world."

It took Linda many years to fulfill the mission she was given in her near-death experience, but, eventually, with the help of her daughter, Anne Vorburger, Linda produced the *Adawee* Teachings, named in honor of her Cherokee heritage.

Honor Kids International

The Honor Project is a school-based program aimed at preventing abuse and violence. It is produced through Linda's non-profit company, Honor Kids International. The program consists of a journal Linda and her daughter, Anne Vorburger, cowrote, entitled "My Right of Passage: An Adventure in Self-Discovery," plus the Honor Code, the Honor Pledge, and a T-shirt that says, "I am important to the world. The world is important to me [us]." More and more schools are incorporating this program into the curriculum they offer, especially in light of recent school shootings. For website and contact information, refer to appendix E.

The Adawee Teachings are part of "The Honor Project," a learning program she created for today's children. It's designed to discipline their minds as it helps them restore a sense of honor and value to their world. The program has been tested already in a number of schools. One teacher said, "I have never experienced such unity in a classroom since this pilot project ended."

The Honor Pledge, which follows, is a sample of the values system taught in the Adawee Teachings.

Making a Difference

The list of near-death experiencers who are making a demonstrable difference for the better in our world is mushrooming. Here are a few more examples (see appendix E for how to contact them):

- *Ken Prather*—who was brutally beaten, suffered total organ failure, and a broken back, beat the odds after being utterly transformed by his near-death experience. Today he is a hospice and near-death counselor in Fort Wayne, Indiana, and is the founder of the outreach program Reaching for Joy. What he does for children and adults in need and for those at the end of life is truly remarkable—considering that no doctor gave him any chance to live, much less walk again.

- *Caroline Sutherland, PhD*—who survived a serious automobile accident and had a near-death experience, now has the ability to "see" the underlying causes of illnesses, and recommends "corrections." She has worked with more than seventy thousand people since 1995 in both clinical settings and private consultations. She also developed a line of cuddly angel dolls and audiocassettes that help children sleep better, build self-esteem, adjust to family difficulties, handle mistreatment, and face hospital stays.

- *Gary Simmons*—in his near-death experience was told by a voice, "You are the one to bring peace to the world." He took the voice seriously, and to the best of his ability immersed himself in what it might take to become a peacemaker. He is now the director of Peacemaking Services for the Association of Unity Churches International and wrote the book *The I of the Storm: Embracing Conflict, Creating Peace.* He is sought after by many church denominations for his advice and the workshops he offers on integral leadership and peacemaking.

- *Lynnclaire Dennis*—"died" in a hot-air balloon that flew too high. Her near-death experience consisted of living geometric patterns that inspired her to develop what are now called Mereon Principles as a model of ethical social architecture. TeamPlay is an outgrowth of the Mereon Principles and is designed to help businesses and corporations increase the flow of benefits, productivity, and sustainability in an organization. Workshops and classes in TeamPlay are held worldwide. In 2006, Lynnclaire was nominated to receive a special Danish award for her work.

What's the Near-Death Experience All About?

In terms of research, consider the decree of physicist Wolfgang Pauli that a new science is needed to explore the objective side of human consciousness and the subjective side of matter. Not mysticism, but a science willing to incorporate objective and subjective avenues to discovery while recognizing the legitimacy of personal experience. He realized that intimate encounters can give shape and quality to scientific models, enabling multiple layers of information to surface.

The new science Dr. Pauli called for is exactly what is needed to explore near-death states, as the scientific method presently in use falls short; there are too many variables for it to work properly. What I've done is part of this new wave, and so is the research of many others. Yet, as we change, and we revamp our protocols and update our strategies, a central question remains: What is the near-death experience really all about?

Some Say It's Entertainment

On the forefront of the entertainment angle is Dr. Raymond A. Moody, the one who started the interest in the near-death experience in the first place. Because language utterly fails us in trying to communicate and interpret near-death and otherworldly states of consciousness, Dr. Moody sees no solution to achieving a point of consensus about the so-called "paranormal"—except through humor. Thus he brands himself a "playful paranormalist," explaining that the real subject at hand is entertainment. To his way of thinking, the "alluringly unknown" thrills us, tantalizes us, entertains us, and keeps us coming back for more—whether to hear stories of others or to learn how to experience "the paranormal" for ourselves.

He urges that special techniques be used to help anyone plumb the depths of self and reopen natural pathways to the "unknown." To this end, he extols the use of apparition chambers, guided visualizations, and shared and empathic experiences with the dying. After all, he says, "The paranormal is a game of rule-breaking—new truth out of old knowledge," a source of extraordinary entertainment and extraordinary revelation.

Moody Sets the Record Straight

In his book *The Last Laugh,* Dr. Raymond A. Moody refutes much of what has been attributed to him in the past about the near-death experience, saying, in essence, that it's his publisher's fault for leaving out the backmatter to *Life After Life.* That missing appendix is where he claims to have explained in detail how the phenomenon cannot be used as scientific rationale for life after death.

He adds: "For two decades now, the world has been enchanted by the words of those who returned from the brink of death with messages of hope and inspiration from a luminous realm of love and peace. It is time that we follow in their footsteps, because additional, real understanding of the near-death experience depends on our being able to recreate those sublime spiritual visions safely and reliably."

Others Say It's All about Love

Dr. Moody's call for a reconsideration of what we think we know about near-death states matches my own, although we advocate different approaches. While investigating the phenomenon, I have always been impressed that, once you peel away the research data and everyone's opinion about the stories, what remains is really all about *love.*

To sum up the truth about near-death states and what they're all about,

The Impact of NDE Stories

Betty Eadie electrified the world with her best-seller *Embraced by the Light.* Little known is the impact this book has had on people's lives. One older lady, an experiencer herself, propped the book up in the crook of her elbow and with calm intent, looked at it, smiled, and then died. Her daughter, finding her mother's body with the book face up in her arm, was so moved by what her mother had done that not only was she able to celebrate her mother's passing, but she also finally accepted the validity of her own near-death experience at the age of three (an event she had never shared with anyone).

I'll pass the baton to Brian, a near-death experiencer living in California:

"I spent the first forty years of my life as an 'equal opportunity hater.' I was filled with an underlying anger at everyone, including myself. My life had no real direction or purpose except for the gathering of possessions.

"I managed to destroy two marriages by sleeping around with anyone I could find. In the privacy of my own home I was extremely verbally abusive to my wives. I felt that women were very weak because they believed in something called love; and it was easy to manipulate them just by lying, and telling them what they wanted to hear. I don't honestly know why I married them, for I had never felt this emotion called love. I considered it a waste of time to even think about it, for we are all going to die someday, so why bother. I never showed any affection toward them because that was not a manly thing to do. Women were necessary for only a few things: sex, cooking, and cleaning up the messes I left all over the house.

"Men were a lot easier to understand. I felt that they were the only ones that I could have an intelligent conversation with. Besides, it was very easy to enter a room full of men and size them up, to weed out the weaker ones, and have my conversations and arguments with the stronger ones. I was usually quite polite with those who could help me in my career before I used some of them up, and then 'stabbed them in the back.' It was not very hard for me to take what I wanted from them (i.e., sex with their wives, or manipulation of their jobs).

"I did not feel powerful in doing any of these things. I just felt that this was what a man was supposed to do. I was addicted to watching the proliferation of violence on television and in the movies, and listening to angry conversations on the radio. I was never able to enjoy life, yet I refused to look at my own misery.

"Approximately eleven years ago, I was driving my camper home from an outing in the desert. Approaching a busy red-lighted intersection at about sixty miles per hour, I started to depress the brake pedal. It felt kind of mushy as the pedal went straight to the floor. I managed to swerve around the first car in view but was deeply broadsided by another vehicle. As I was slipping in and out of consciousness in the paramedic's van, I remember seeing my clothes soaked in my own blood, for my head had been split open in two places."

Brian had a long, transcendent, near-death experience, wherein he visited many different worlds with different-colored skies and was shown the varied life forms and civilizations in this universe. The beauty of it overwhelmed him. A highly evolved being filled with love and peace spoke of the many past lives Brian had lived in anger, aggression, and hate, and that in this life he could at last learn the lesson of unconditional love.

The being told him: "Wars and suffering were not created by God, but were the creation of the human race out of fear and hatred. God had created the human form to look different from each other, so that we would learn to increase our love for all kinds of forms. Death is the creator's greatest gift, used for the transition of your spirit into higher realms."

The doctor's verdict of no permanent brain damage was welcome news, but healing took a long time. Brian returned to his wife a changed man, but he was unable to understand or integrate his experience. Moreover, now his wife became the abuser: The nicer he was, the more hateful she became. Through spirit guidance, he was directed to refrain from judgment, leave her, and become a homeless person. "Begging and living in the streets," he said, "totally killed my ego." When he went back to his wife, he was unable to convey to her all that he had been learning from the experiences he had had. They divorced, and he went on to devote his life to God—eventually marrying a woman who could share his spiritual path.

"The universe was created out of love," Brian says, "and we are all a part of that creation. The unconditional love that I felt during my near-death experience was very powerful. Instinctively, we fear this kind of love by layering it with many conditions. The greatest fear we face is, will this love I give be returned? It's as if we all think that we only have so much to give, that it might run out. Somehow we have forgotten that the giving of love is the blessing—it returns to the sender an abundance of even more to give. Once we learn this lesson, we shall all be transformed and have even greater gifts to share."

A Special Thought

The Hopi word for "family" translates "to breathe together." Think about that.

Wrap-up: Thirty Years and Growing

Pamela M. Kircher, MD, director of integrative medicine at Mercy Medical Center in Durango, Colorado, and long active in near-death matters, paints a stark picture of what it was like for near-death experiencers more than thirty years ago:

- Health-care professionals wouldn't listen to patients talk about their episodes.

A Nonverbal Boy

David, an eight-year-old with cystic fibrosis, suffered brain trauma that left him quadriplegic and nonverbal. Social worker Rick Enright at Thames Valley Children's Centre in London, Ontario, discovered quite by chance that the boy had a near-death experience when the brain trauma occurred.

"Most people, myself included," admitted Enright, "made the quick assumption based on his appearance and his functional limitations that David was helpless and totally dependent, and that his cognitive abilities were as damaged as his body. We were wrong. Ironically, David's NDE eventually gave him back control over his life, and ultimately, his death. David also changed my life profoundly . . . I will never again look upon any of my severely impaired, nonverbal patients without wondering what they may want to tell me if they only had the means; and I will try to find the means."

(For the full citation of Enright's article on the subject, refer to appendix C.)

- Patients were told their experience was a hallucination.
- They were often given tranquilizers.
- They were often psychiatrically labeled for life.
- If they insisted on their near-death experience, they might have a psychiatric hospitalization.

What were the factors leading to the river of change evident today? Dr. Kircher answers:

- Increased absolute numbers of near-death experiences through improved resuscitative techniques
- Increasing awareness of these experiences in the lay public
- Increasing permission to speak about them and the insistence of experiencers to tell their stories
- Improved education about near-death experiences
- Increased research about near-death experiences

The climate of acceptance we presently enjoy didn't exist even ten years ago, let alone thirty. We have come that far, that fast. Hospice care has, too, as it also began in the mid-seventies thanks to Elisabeth Kübler-Ross, MD, the one who made it possible for Dr. Moody's best-seller to be published in the first place. Her support of his work made the difference.

In the twenty-first century, we face an unprecedented challenge that has never occurred before in recorded history: People are still living, active, and healthy *beyond the requirements of raising their children*. This is allowing large segments of the population to search for meaning in life—to seek the spiritual. The near-death phenomenon speaks to this hunger in a way no other transformative state can: through the doorway of death and the rediscovery of life and the power of love.

Appendix A

Glossary of New Words

accommodation Sometimes the initial greeter or even the background imagery first encountered during a near-death scenario can be an "accommodation," meant to relax or alert an experiencer instead of informing or enlightening. For instance, if the initial greeter is asked, "Is that what you really look like?", invariably that image will either disappear or shape-shift (e.g., an angel morphing into a globe of light). I came to regard such temporary images as accommodations, not because they weren't real, rather, because their purpose seemed to hinge on "setting the stage" or perhaps introducing the experiencer to a deeper and more meaningful phase.

Adawee Cherokee for "Guardian of Wisdom."

after-death communication (ADC) A unique or spiritual experience that takes place when a person is contacted directly or spontaneously by a family member or friend who has died. Directly means there is no third party, such as a psychic. ADCs are now a recognized field of research study.

agape The Greek word for "the love of God or Christ for mankind." The term was once used to describe the "brotherly/sisterly" or spiritual love one Christian had for another, but eventually came to mean an unselfish, more detached or unconditional type of love—a love that is freely given and without expectations. See also *unconditional love.*

Akasha (Akashic) A Sanskrit word for "ether," "radiant space," or "sky." It is also said to mean "primary substance." In many religious and spiritual traditions, Akashic Records is used synonymously with the term "Book of Life" to refer to that record of everything that has ever happened said to exist forever "upon the skeins of time."

anecdote The dictionary meaning of anecdote is "short entertaining tale." This has now been discarded in near-death research as a term to use when referring to near-death experiences. In its place, "narrative" is favored, as the latter term recognizes that near-death experiences are stories (narratives) from a person's life that have deep and profound meaning and are intimate to the experiencer.

anomaly That which deviates from consensual reality. Someone or something that is strange or out of place is considered an anomaly until accepted by society or proven to be true.

apparition chamber A structure in ancient Greece that provided anyone interested with an opportunity to experience "otherworldly spirits" and receive "guidance."

archetype The original or main pattern after which all else follows—the "first mold." Carl Gustav Jung, the famous psychotherapist, defined an archetype as an unconscious genetic image of a universal human experience expressed in myth; "racial memories" of universal, human experiences that are passed on in myths and genetically from generation to generation, for example, "a great flood," the creation of the world.

Baptism of the Holy Spirit Considered by most Christian faiths to be that moment when the "worthy" are recognized by God and showered or struck by an energy "not of this Earth" that transforms them utterly. "Gifts of the Spirit" supposedly result: the ability to prophesy, heal, speak in diverse tongues, work miracles, discern spirits, recognize truth, and become one within The Body of Spirit.

bardo A Sanskrit word meaning "intermediate" or "in-between state." In Tibetan Buddhism, it refers to the forty-nine-day period between death and rebirth, during which time the individual exists as an ever-changing continuum of consciousness experiencing either enhancement or confusion, while separated from the body. (The concept of an unchanging soul does not exist in Buddhism.)

channeling The ability certain people have to go into a trancelike state and allow their vocal cords to be used by spirit beings, serving as a "channel" (passageway) for messages from other planes of existence.

code blue A term used in the medical community to signal a cardiopulmonary arrest, that is, a life-threatening heart rhythm that may or may not involve the cessation of breath. The key here is speed. By calling a code blue, a medical team rushes to deliver the type of intervention that might prevent a full-blown heart attack from occurring.

complementary medicine Health care that embraces various modalities—naturopathy, homeopathy, acupuncture, and the like, as well as allopathy. This approach weds natural healing practices with technological advances, resulting in an ideal model of illness prevention and wellness care.

cryptomnesia The spontaneous surfacing of deeply buried memories from the subconscious. The subconscious mind, as a vast storehouse of everything we have been exposed to is capable of clustering bits and pieces of information to form storylines suggestive of previous lives. This alternate explanation of reincarnation, however, does not account for all reincarnational memories, especially those of small children with vival detailed recall that was later verified.

cultural creatives A term coined by Paul Ray, vice president of the San Francisco–based market research firm American Lives, to describe an "integral culture," which he estimates now numbers fifty million Americans, or roughly one-fourth of the population. These people merge and integrate modernism with traditionalism, East with West, to create a renaissance mindset that is so powerful it has become a political presence in society.

delayed integration A situation in which an individual, for whatever reason, is unable to process fully a given event until years after it happened. Although adult experiencers are able to integrate their near-death states within about seven years, it can take child experiencers twice to three times that long, depending on family circumstances after their episodes and the child's response to how he or she was treated.

depersonal occurrences This term refers to when individuals experience a separation from their bodies and the emotions associated with them.

dissociation Formerly used in the field of psychiatry as a label to describe individuals who "withdrew" or "severed from" any association with their body and/or environment. It was considered an aberrant mental state, unhealthy. New research, however, indicates that dissociation may not be unhealthy or unusual, after all.

earthplane Denotes the vibratory frequency of the physical Earth world we can see, feel, hear, and touch. The term owes its usage to the mystical idea that the soul has numerous planes of existence to experience and traverse in a journey that, traditionally, is said to spiral back to the Source of Creation.

eidetic images Visual imagery from a person's memory that can be readily reproduced with accuracy and in detail (such as the image of a person that exactly duplicates the real person in every manner).

electromagnetic fields (EMFs) An array of electrical currents and magnetic radiation that surrounds any given object or being. These field arrays are representative of the larger spectrum of electromagnetic waves, which includes radio waves, light, X rays, and gamma rays. Only about one-tenth of the spectrum is visible to the human eye.

enlightenment By dictionary definition, the act of giving or imparting intellectual or spiritual information; to instruct, teach, inform. The roots of the word actually come from *en* ("to provide with" or "cause to be"), and *light* ("to illumine" or "bring out of the dark and make clear"). Enlightenment, then, means "provided with illumination"—the inference being to the transforming power of God's Light.

Exceptional human experiences (EHEs) A term that describes unusual, paranormal occurrences that somehow make a significant difference in a person's life. Some examples of EHEs: telepathic communication with other people or animals, a sudden uplifting revelation or vision, a "peak" experience (spiritual at-one-ment), seeing a ghost, spontaneous past-life recall, knowing things without any reason to, seeing the future, any transformative state of consciousness.

experiencing the numinous The arousal of elevated or spiritual emotions that surpass previous comprehension. See also *numinous.*

fear-death experience A unique mental state usually associated with traffic and mountaineering accidents. The terror of imminent death—the type of fear that sees no hope, no other alternative but death itself—is sometimes enough to push people into a near-death-like episode, with the same pattern of aftereffects as a near-death state. Today, researchers term this a fear-death experience.

future memory The ability to live fully and subjectively a given event or sequence of events before physically living the same incident. The experience is then usually, but not always, forgotten, to be remembered later when some "signal" triggers its memory. Sensory-rich, future memory is so detailed and thorough that it is indistinguishable from everyday reality while occurring.

genre A class or category (a genus) having a particular identifiable form, content, style, or the like that distinguishes it from anything else.

grace Commonly regarded in spiritual and religious terms as an awareness of God's generosity; a sense of being blessed. This awareness is experienced as a great truth.

growth event Any kind of sudden twist in life that twirls you around and changes your attitudes and stretches your mind. It can be positive, negative, or both.

hippocampus A section of the brain stem that looks like the cross section of a sea horse, this area controls emotions and memory.

Holy Spirit As part of the Christian Trinity, the Holy Spirit is considered that aspect of God that serves as a "messenger" or "the carrier wave of divine energy that carries out God's Will."

hyperalertness When a person's sensory faculties become sharper and awareness more vivid than what is considered "normal."

hypercarbia An increased amount of carbon dioxide in the blood.

hyperspace Consists of four or more dimensions. Most of the useful notions about our experience in three-dimensional reality have exact counterparts in hyperspace, even beyond the fourth dimension, where time and space are said to merge.

ineffable That which is incapable of being expressed or described. The term recognizes that some things are simply inexpressible, unspeakable, and unutterable. The further implication is that even to attempt description is somehow to defile or nullify the enormity of what was witnessed or experienced.

karma A principle based on the law of cause and effect, which states that we reap our rewards and suffer our punishments from one life into the next. See also *reincarnation.*

Kundalini A Sanskrit word meaning "coiled serpent." It derives from the older Meso-American word **Ku,** which translates as "the spirit force of God awaits within each person." Both words refer to the "serpent power" said to be coiled in a ball at the base of a person's spine, which, once stimulated, uncoils, and rises up the spine to the brain, transforming the individual.

limbic system The limbic system is located in a semicircle in the middle of the brain, capping off the topmost extension of the brain stem. It consists of various parts and sections that together twist around the brain stem like "limbs" or "vines," hence the name "limbic." This small but extremely efficient system has been around for fifty thousand years or more in the evolution of brain development.

live in grace To transcend human pettiness and freely give that which is given: forgiveness, compassion, loving kindness, and joy.

matrix That which gives origin or form to a thing, or that which serves to enclose it.

metempsychosis The belief that at death, the soul passes into another body.

mindful Being mindful is the act of being fully conscious, alert to and focused on individual sensations, moments, interactions, and activities. For example:

when eating an orange, pay attention to its sweetness and texture, the total experience of eating it.

mindfulness Traditional Buddhism considers mindfulness an essential component of liberation. By being mindful of the distortions in our lives and in our personalities, we can free ourselves of them. Our deep connection with others is then revealed.

mindsight A state of transcendental awareness that enables an individual, sighted or blind, to access a realm of knowledge not available in a normal waking state. This awareness is described as omnidirectional—360 degrees of spherical vision—the ability to see with whole consciousness rather than depending on physical eyes.

mission Word used by most near-death experiencers, regardless of their age, for why they returned from death. The majority came back "knowing" that each and every person at birth was given a specific job to do, a purpose for their life on Earth (that is, a "mission"). And that, if unfulfilled, a "reminder" will set them straight. Most considered their near-death state that reminder.

mystic Someone who through either formal training or personal dedication pursues "The Holy."

mysticism The practice of intuitively knowing spiritual truths that transcend ordinary understanding. It's considered a direct, intimate union of the soul with its Source through contemplation and love.

myth of amazing grace The exaggerated notion that after undergoing a near-death episode, experiencers are supposed to return as selfless servants of God, devoted to the spiritual path, and to serving others.

narrative The term "anecdote" (dictionary meaning: a short, entertaining tale) is being discarded in near-death research as a reference to near-death experiences. In its place, "narrative" is favored, as the term recognizes that near-death experiences are stories (narratives) from a person's life that have deep and profound meaning and are intimate to the experiencer.

near-death experience (NDE) An intense awareness, sense, or experience of "otherworldliness," whether pleasant or unpleasant, that happens to people who are at the edge of death. It is of such magnitude that most experiencers are deeply affected, many to the point of making significant changes in their lives afterward because of what they went through.

near-death-like experience It's possible to experience the near-death phenomenon without being physically challenged by the onset of death. An individual may be terrified by what seems to be imminent death, only to be rescued or saved before the worst happens. Or experiencers can be engaged in everyday life routines when one suddenly occurs. These episodes are considered near-death-like experiences.

necrolatry Worship of or excessive reverence for the dead.

necromancy Communing with or conjuring up the dead in order to learn about or influence the outcome of forthcoming events in this life.

neurotheology A new field of science that explores the physiological basis of religious and spiritual experience, using the latest in technology and computer imaging.

nonexperience experiencers The term used by many individuals I have interviewed who fit the pattern of altered character traits soon after a childhood health crisis, yet have no memory of a near-death scenario. I now use this term as a separate category in my research.

nonlocal Not bound or restricted to any particular place, location, function, or event. The term is used mostly in references to prayer, healing states, and mind/consciousnss not being held synonymous with the brain organ. A scientific term in physics.

numinous A spiritual or supernatural domain wherein "The Mystery of Mysteries" resides. Considered timeless and eternal, it is a place beyond what words can describe. See also *experiencing the numinous* and *revelations of the numinous.*

omega Means "great." As the final letter in the Greek alphabet, it has come to represent "the end," "the last in a series," or "death." Kenneth Ring explains that as "the end," omega has a second meaning: that of an "ultimate outcome," or, as he used it, "the destination toward which humanity is inexorably bound."

otherworldly journey The general phrase applied to those subjective experiences that seem to propel the experiencer to realms or places beyond that of the physical here and now. They usually feature a "storyline" in the sense that there is an orderly progression of imagery, actions, sounds, or odors that greatly impress the individual. Most storylines are oriented toward revelation or are somehow instructive.

paradigm A set of ideas and conditions in a society that forms an overall theme or pattern.

paradigm shift The occurrence of deeply entrenched patterns of thought undergoing a change, often with unsettling or threatening consequences to the established social order.

prebirth experience (PBE) An occurrence in which an individual has clear memories of existence before birth, memories that, in most cases, are later verified by the mother.

precognition The research term that refers to knowledge of a futuristic event or situation that was obtained through extrasensory means, rather than through the normal channels of information gathering. Traditionally regarded as a psychic talent, the ability of "knowing in advance" can be and often is taught in classes on psychic development.

psychological absorption The tendency some people have to become deeply involved in sensory and imaginative experiences. The trait often takes on the characteristic of a "mind merge" or "becoming one with" whatever is focused on. Although absorption abilities vary among people, an individual can identify so much with the point of focus that everything else ceases to exist for a time.

psychomanteion Site of ancient Greek apparition chambers. It included space for preparatory sessions and purification rituals with trained mentors, the sacred chambers, and meetings afterward to discuss what happened. Lately, creating psychomanteions has undergone a revival.

reincarnation As a theory, the term posits that we are each born into a series of lives, one after another. As a belief, it addresses the larger issue of a soul's evolution or devolution. Part of this belief involves karma. See also *karma.*

religion A systemized approach to spiritual development that is based on set standards or dogmas that provide community support while establishing moral upliftment and behavior.

remote viewer A person who is trained through rigorous instruction to use his or her psychic ability to view certain people or places at a distance and in detail.

repress The act of rejecting something from consciousness that is too painful, disagreeable, or uncomfortable to remember.

revelations of the numinous Life-changing experiences of the numinous. See also *numinous.*

right timing A notion found in every spiritual and religious tradition. The sense of "rightness" concerning the time for action. In some traditions, astrologers are consulted or perhaps a diviner (for example, a shaman or medicine man or woman) gifted in spirit communication. In other traditions, right timing is only thought to be revealed after a period of "humbleness" (fasting and prayer).

sacerdotalism The teaching of and belief in the divine authority of the priesthood as being the essential mediators between humans and God.

sacrifice From the Latin for "to make sacred." Viewed in that light, whatever seems oppressive or difficult as we begin our spiritual journey toward enlightenment can be embraced as a sanctified step on the upward path.

scenario The content of the near-death experience: imagery, feeling-tones, sensations, landscapes, events, sounds, colors, beings, messages, light or darkness.

scientism An attitude that demands scientific methods be used as the only way to determine truth. Science itself actually evolved from philosophy. If it weren't for the principles of matter, truth, and reason laid out by the philosophers of old, science as we presently understand it would not exist. Methods such as clinical trials are rather new historically, dating back about one hundred years.

shamanism The animistic religion of northern Asia, embracing a belief in powerful spirits who can be influenced only by shamans. Shamans are known to "enter into" or merge with the spirit of things: obtaining guidance from worlds within and around them. They "ride" energy in the sense of knowing how to respond to subtle changes in vibration and feeling.

signature features Those components of a near-death scenario that are present in the majority of cases. They include out-of-body experiences, a light that shines brighter than the sun, a "voiceless" voice that speaks telepathically, calming feelings of total acceptance and unconditional love, a sudden knowingness, and feeling the need or being told to return. (Tunnels are not signature features.)

soul The principle of life that animates human form, yet exists apart from the physical body as a distinct entity. Most religions maintain that the soul survives death and is eternal. Some traditions teach that everything is ensouled. Others state that only humankind has a direct connection with God through the soul.

spirit Literally, "breath"—the inference being "The Breath of God" or "that energy that infuses all Creation."

spirituality In the strictest sense, this means "The Breath of God Breathing." Commonly defined as a personal relationship with God that can involve direct revelation, while recognizing and honoring the sacredness of all created things.

spontaneous recall The emergence of memories long hidden or locked away in an individual's mind. These memories or memory fragments can surface in unusual ways or be triggered by casual and unexpected associations. In the case of forgotten near-death experiences, the most frequent point of recall occurs after reading or hearing about someone else's episode that "feels" familiar.

standstill The nickname given to an operation called hypothermic cardiac arrest. It renders a patient "dead" by all known clinical standards. During the surgery, body temperature is lowered 60 degrees, heartbeat and breathing are stopped, brain waves are flattened, and blood is drained from the head. The procedure is only performed when other medical techniques cannot be used.

supernatural rescues Reported by many near-death experiencers, these are occurrences in which the person benefits physically from "heavenly" intervention, as in having tumors disappear or a "physical" detached hand that suddenly appears out of nowhere to pull the person to safety.

surrogate A substitute, a stand-in, one who acts in place of another.

synchronicity As used by the Swiss psychiatrist Carl Jung (and in this book), this term describes the phenomenon of seemingly unrelated events occurring in unexpected relation to each other, not connected by cause and effect but by simultaneity and meaning. Simply defined as "meaningful coincidence," this phenomenon is unpredictable and seemingly random in occurrence, yet it happens more often than might be supposed.

syncope Loss of consciousness from blood loss in the brain. It's most often caused by such things as a heart block, sudden lowering of blood pressure, or fainting. What's interesting about syncope is that it fosters imagery and sounds that appear to mimic near-death states.

temporal lobes There are two temporal lobe regions of the brain. One is located on the right side near the temple and upper part of the ear; the other is in the same spot on the left side. Both are situated on the temporal bones that form the sides and base of the skull.

transpersonal psychology A branch of psychology that studies human experiences that occur beyond the realm of ordinary ego and personality. These include such states as unitive consciousness, cosmic awareness, mystical experiences, and maximum sensory awareness.

unconditional love A brotherly/sisterly type of love, a universal platonic love. To near-death experiencers, unconditional love means an unselfish, open-ended caring that is given without thought of conditions or gain—embracing all as members of the same family created by God. See also *agape.*

unitive experiences Episodes in which an individual suddenly and unexpectedly becomes "one with all things." They are hyperstates of a radiant, luminous consciousness that unify or bring together in "oneness" the Creator with the Created. Ego boundaries and physical borders vanish; the sense of "separateness" is replaced by an identification with spiritual totality. Religious writings are filled with such accounts.

Yamatoots Messengers from Lord Yama, Lord of the Underworld, found throughout Thailand and Southeast Asia. In Thai society, belief in these spirit beings pervades popular comics, advertisements, religious morality books and posters, and popular television shows. Religious tradition has it that Yamatoots are charged with escorting the newly dead to Lord Yama for judgment.

Appendix B

International Association for Near-Death Studies (IANDS)

The International Association for Near-Death Studies (IANDS) exists to impart knowledge concerning near-death experiences and their implications, to encourage and support research dealing with the experience and related phenomena, and to aid people in starting local groups that wish to explore the subject. They have numerous publications, among them the scholarly *Journal of Near-Death Studies,* a general-interest newsletter entitled *Vital Signs,* various brochures and materials, a CD-ROM that indexes all journal articles, and CEU courses for medical, mental, and spiritual health-care providers. More such programs are in the offing. Membership in this nonprofit organization is open to anyone; dues are annual and include various benefits.

Donations to cover operating expenses are always needed and always welcome, especially for the NDE Research Fund. CDs and some DVDs of IANDS conference speakers are available. Ask for their list of national and international chapters (Friends of IANDS) if you're interested in visiting any of them. Individual reports about near-death episodes are solicited for the archives; you will need to fill out a form, so please ask for one.

Memberships, back issues of their publications, conference recordings, and other materials can now be ordered directly from the IANDS website. Check out their section on actual experiencer episodes; it is growing as more people are willing to share their story. Do start an IANDS group in your area, if there isn't one already, and invite "Compassionate Friends" to come, as those who have lost a child find great comfort when exposed to near-death experiencers and materials.

For information about the International Association for Near-Death Studies, contact:

International Association for Near-Death Studies
(or simply use their initials, IANDS)
P.O. Box 502
East Windsor Hill, CT 06028-0502
Phone: 860-882-1211
fax: 860-882-1212
E-mail: office@iands.org
Website: www.iands.org

Appendix C

Further Reading

Books and Publications Concerning the Near-Death Experience, Plus Related Material Mentioned in This Book

A Course in Miracles: Combined Volume. Mill Valley, CA: Foundation for Inner Peace, 1975.

Amatuzio, Janis. *Beyond Knowing: Mysteries and Messages of Death and Life from a Forensic Pathologist.* Novato, CA: New World Library, 2006.

———. *Forever Ours: Real Stories of Immortality and Living from a Forensic Pathologist.* Novato, CA: New World Library, 2004.

Arcangel, Dianne. *Afterlife Encounters: Ordinary People, Extraordinary Experiences.* Charlottesville, VA: Hampton Road, 2005.

Ardagh, Arjuna. *The Translucent Revolution: How People Just Like You Are Waking Up and Changing the World.* Novato, CA: New World Library, 2005.

Athappilly, G. K., Bruce Greyson, and Ian Stevenson. "Do prevailing societal models influence reports of near-death experiences? A comparison of accounts reported before and after 1975. *Journal of Nervous & Mental Disease* 194(2006):218–222.

Atwater, P.M.H. *Beyond the Indigo Children: The New Children and the Coming of the Fifth World.* Rochester, VT: Bear & Co., 2005.

———. *Beyond the Light: What Isn't Being Said about Near-Death Experiences,* 1994). Now available from Transpersonal Publishing, P.O. Box 7220, Kill Devil Hills, NC 27948; website www.holistictree.com; e-mail AllenChips@holistictree.com

———. *Brain Shift/Spirit Shift: Using the Near-Death Experience as a Theoretical Model to Explore the Transformation of Consciousness.* Self-published, 1998. Available at website www.pmhatwater.com.

———. *Children of the New Millennium: Children's Near-Death Experiences and the Evolution of Humankind.* New York: Three Rivers Press, 1999. This book was reissued as *The New Children and Near-Death Experiences.* Rochester, VT: Bear & Co., 2003.

———. *Coming Back to Life: The After-Effects of the Near-Death Experience*

(1988). Now available from Transpersonal Publishing, P.O. Box 7220, Kill Devil Hills, NC 27948; website www.holistictree.com; e-mail AllenChips@holistictree.com.

———. *Future Memory*. Charlottesville, VA: Hampton Roads, 1999.

———. *I Died Three Times in 1977*. Self-published, 1980. Available over website www.pmhatwater.com.

———. *Runes of the Goddess* (book and runes). Lakeville, MN: Galde Press, 2007. Contact Galde Press, P.O. Box 460, Lakeville, MN 55044-0460; e-mail Phyllis@galdepress.com.

———. *The Complete Idiot's Guide to Near-Death Experiences*. Indianapolis, IN; Alpha/Pearson, 2000.

———. *We Live Forever: The Real Truth about Death*. Virginia Beach, VA; A.R.E. Press, 2004.

Baumann, T. Lee. *The Akashic Light: Religion's Common Thread*. Virginia Beach, VA: A.R.E. Press, 2006.

Billi, Anita. *Afterlifefromabove: Healings of a Paranormal Nature*. Kill Devil Hills, NC: Transpersonal Publishing, 2006. Transpersonal Publishing, P.O. Box 7220, Kill Devil Hills, NC 27948; website www.holistic tree.com; e-mail AllenChips@ holistictree.com.

Blackmore, Susan. *Dying to Live: Science and Near-Death Experiences*. Buffalo, NY: Prometheus Books, 1993.

Bonenfant, Richard J. "A comparative study of near-death experience and non-near-death experience outcomes in 56 survivors of clinical death." *Journal of Near-Death Studies* 22:3(Spring 2004):155–177.

Botkin, Allan L., with R. Craig Hogan. *Induced After-Death Communication: A New Therapy for Healing Grief and Trauma*. Charlottesville, VA: Hampton Roads, 2005.

Brinkley, Dannion, and Kathryn Peters-Brinkley. *The Secrets of the Light: Spiritual Strategies to Empower Your Life . . . Here and in the Hereafter*. Henderson, NV: Heartland Productions, 2004.

Brinkley, Dannion, with Paul Perry. *Saved by the Light: The True Story of a Man Who Died Twice and the Profound Revelations He Received*. New York: Villard Books, 1994.

Britton, Willoughby B., and Richard R. Bootzin. "Near-death experiences and the temporal lobe." *Psychological Science Journal* 15:4(April 2004):254–258.

Bucke, Richard Maurice. *Cosmic Consciousness*. Philadelphia, PA: Innes & Sons, 1901. Continuous printings through Citadel Press, New York.

Callanan, Maggie, and Patricia Kelley. *Final Gifts: Understanding the Special Awareness, Needs and Communications of the Dying*. New York: Poseidon Press, 1992.

Campbell, Joseph, with Bill Moyers. *The Power of Myth*. New York: Doubleday, 1988.

Chamberlain, David B. *Babies Remember Birth*. Los Angeles, CA: Jeremy Tarcher, 1988.

Cheek, David B. "Are telepathy, clairvoyance and 'hearing' possible in utero?: Suggestive evidence as revealed during hypnotic age-regression." *Journal of Pre- & Peri-Natal Psychology* 7:2(Winter 1992):125–137.

Childre, Doc Lew, and Howard Martin, with Donna Beech. *The Heart-Math Solution.* San Francisco, CA: HarperSanFrancisco, 1999.

Cobbe, Frances Power. *The Peak in Darien.* London: Williams and Norgate, 1882.

Collins, Francis S. *The Language of God: A Scientist Presents Evidence for Belief.* New York: Free Press, 2006.

Couliano, Ioan. *Out of This World: Otherworld Journeys from Gilgamesh to Albert Einstein.* Boston, MA: Shambhala, 1991.

Cox-Chapman, Mally. *The Case for Heaven: Near-Death Experiences as Evidence of the Afterlife.* New York: Putnam, 1995.

Cressy, Rev. Judith. *The Near-Death Experience: Mysticism or Madness.* Hanover, MA: Christopher, 1994.

Cytowic, Richard E. *The Man Who Tasted Shapes: A Bizarre Medical Mystery Offers Revolutionary Insights into Emotions, Reasoning, and Consciousness.* New York: Putnam, 1993.

Dougherty, Ned. *Fast Lane to Heaven.* Charlottesville, VA: Hampton Roads, 2001.

Eadie, Betty J. *Embraced by the Light.* Placerville, CA: Gold Leaf Press, 1992.

Easterbrook, Gregg. *Beside Still Waters: Searching for Meaning in an Age of Doubt.* New York: Morrow, 1998.

Egyptian Book of the Dead: The Book of Coming Forth by Day, trans. Mnata A. Ashbi. Miami, FL: Cruzian Mystic, 1998.

Elffers, Joost. *Play With Your Food.* New York: Stewart Tabori & Chang, 1997.

Ellwood, Gracia Fay. *The Uttermost Deep: The Challenge of Near-Death Experiences.* New York: Lantern Books, 2001.

Elsaesser-Valarino, Evelyn. *On the Other Side of Life: Exploring the Phenomenon of the Near-Death Experience.* New York: Insight Books, 1997.

———. *Talking with Angel: About Illness, Death and Survial.* Edinburgh, Scotland: Floris Books, 2005 (available in the U. S.).

Enright, Rick. "Silent journey: The discovery of the near-death experience of a nonverbal adolescent." *Journal of Near-Death Studies* 22: 3(Spring 2004):195–208.

Enz, Charles P. *No Time to be Brief: A Scientific Biography of Wolfgang Pauli.* New York: Oxford University Press, 2002.

Evergreen Study—James H. Lindley, Sethryn Bryan, and Bob Conley. "Near-death experiences in a Pacific-Northwest American population: The Evergreen Study." *Anabiosis—The Journal for Near-Death Studies* 1:2(December 1981):104–124.

Feather, Sally Rhine, with Michael Schmicker. *The Gift: ESP, the Extraordinary Experiences of Ordinary People.* New York: St. Martin's Press, 2005.

Fenwick, Peter, and Elizabeth Fenwick. *The Truth in the Light.* New York: Berkley Books, 1995.

———. "Science and Spirituality: A Challenge for the 21st Century [The Bruce Greyson Lecture from the International Association for Near-Death Studies 2004 Annual Conference]. *Journal of Near-Death Studies* 23:3(Spring 2005):131–157.

Fenwick, Peter, and Sam Parnia. "Near-death experiences in cardiac arrest and the mystery of consciousness." *Resuscitation: The Official Journal of the European Resuscitation Council* 52:1 (January 2002):5–11.

Flynn, Charles. *After the Beyond.* Englewood Cliffs, NJ: Prentice-Hall, 1986.

Fontana, David. *Is There an Afterlife? A Comprehensive Overview of the Evidence.* Berkeley, CA: O Books, 2005.

Forti, Kathy. *The Door to the Secret City.* (1984) Now available from Kathy Forti, 12401 Wilshire Blvd., Suite 306, Los Angeles, CA 90025; e-mail kjforti@aol.com.

Gabbard, Glen O., and Stuart Twemlow. "Do near-death experiences occur only near death?" *Journal of Near-Death Studies* 10:1(Fall 1991):41–47.

Gallup, George. *Adventures in Immortality.* New York: McGraw Hill, 1982.

Gardner, Howard. *Creating Minds.* New York: Basic Books, 1993.

Gibson, Arvin S. *Echoes from Eternity: Near-Death Experiences Examined.* Bountiful, UT: Horizon, 1993.

———. *The Fingerprints of God: Evidences from Near-Death Studies, Scientific Research on Creation and Mormon Theology.* Bountiful, UT: Horizon, 1999.

———. *Glimpses of Eternity: New Near-Death Experiences Examined.* Bountiful, UT: Horizon, 1992.

———. *Journeys Beyond Life: True Accounts of Next World Experiences.* Bountiful, UT: Horizon, 1994.

———. "Near-death experience patterns from research in the Salt Lake City region." *Journal of Near-Death Studies* 13:2(Winter 1994):125.

Greene, F. Gordon. "A projective geometry for separation experiences." *Journal of NearDeath Studies* 17:3 (Spring 1999):151–191.

Grey, Margot. *Return from Death: An Exploration of the Near-Death Experience.* Boston, MA: Arkana, 1985.

Greyson, Bruce. "Biological aspects of near-death experiences." *Perspective in Biology and Medicine* 42:1 (Autumn 1998):14–32.

———. Section, pages 46–55, in *Encyclopaedia Britannica: 1992 Medical & Health Annual,* ed. E. Bernstein. Chicago: Encyclopaedia Britannica, 1991.

Greyson, Bruce, Emily Williams Cook, and Ian Stevenson. "Do any near-death experiences provide evidence for the survival of human personality after death?: Relevant features and illustrative case reports." *Journal of Scientific Exploration* 12:3(1998):377–406.

Greyson, Bruce, and Charles P. Flynn (eds). *The Near-Death Experience: Problems, Prospects, Perspectives.* Springfield, IL: Charles C. Thomas, 1984.

Grof, Stanislav. "The Transpersonal Vision: The Healing Potential of Nonordinary States of Consciousness." Audiotape and booklet available from Sounds True, P.O. Box 8010, Boulder, CO 80306; 1-800-333-9185; fax (303) 665-5292; e-mail SoundsTrue@aol.com.

Grosso, Michael. *The Final Choice: Playing the Survival Game.* Walpole, NH: Stillpoint, 1985.

Guggenheim, Bill, and Judy Guggenheim. *Hello from Heaven: A New Field of Research Confirms that Life and Love Are Eternal.* New York: Bantam Books, 2005.

Hall, Manly P. *The Secret Teachings of All Ages.* Los Angeles, CA: Philosophical Research Society, 1977.

Hallenbeck, James L. *Palliative Care Perspectives.* New York: Oxford University Press, 2003.

Hallett, Elisabeth Brutto. *Soul Trek: Meeting Our Children on the Way to Birth.* Hamilton, MT: Light Hearts Publishing, 1995.

Hamilton, Edith and Cairns Hamilton (eds). *The Collected Dialogues of Plato.* Princeton, NJ: Princeton University Press, 1978.

Harner, Michael J. *The Way of the Shaman: A Guide to Power and Healing.* San Francisco: Harper and Row, 1980.

The HarperCollins Study Bible: New Revised Standard Version. Ed. Wayne A. Meeks. New York: HarperCollins, 1993.

Harpur, Tom. *Life After Death.* Toronto: McClelland & Stewart, 1992.

Hart, Tobin. *The Secret Spiritual World of Children: The Breakthrough Discovery that Profoundly Alters Our Conventional View of Children's Mystical Experiences.* Makawao, HI: Inner Ocean Publishing, 2003.

Heath, Pamela Rae, and Jon Klimo. *Suicide: What Really Happens in the Afterlife?* Berkeley, CA: North Atlantic Books, 2006.

Heim, Albert von st. Gallen. "The experiences of dying from falls." (Translated by Roy Kletti and Russell Noyes Jr.) *Omega Journal* 1972:45–52. Original journal article in 1892 was entitled "Remarks on Fatal Falls." And appeared in the "Yearbook of the Swiss Alpine Club" (authored by Heim).

Heinberg, Richard. *Memories and Visions of Paradise: Exploring the Universal Myth of a Lost Golden Age.* Los Angeles, CA: JP Tarcher, 1989.

Hinze, Sarah. *Coming from the Light: Spiritual Accounts of Life Before Birth.* New York: Pocket Books, 1997.

Hoffman, Edward. *The Hebrew Alphabet.* San Francisco: Chronicle Books, 1998.

Holm-Oosterhof, Aafke H. *A Journey with the Angel of Light.* Self-published, 1999, in the Netherlands. No English translation as yet. Contact: aafke@holm.myweb.nl; website http://home.hccnet.nl/p.g.holm.

Houston "Friends of IANDS" Chapter. *When Ego Dies: A Compilation of Near-Death & Mystical Conversion Experiences.* Houston, TX: Emerald Ink Publishing, 1996.

Jung, Carl G. *Man and His Symbols.* London: Aldus Books, 1964 (paperback through Dell Publishing, New York, continuous printings).

Kason, Yvonne, and Teri Degler. *A Farther Shore: How Near-Death and Other Extraordinary Experiences Can Change Ordinary Lives.* Toronto: HarperCollins Canada, 1996.

Kellehear, Allan. *Experiences Near Death.* New York: Oxford University Press, 1995.

Kelleher, Colm. "Retrotransposons as engines of human bodily transformation." *Journal of Scientific Exploration* 123:1(Spring 1999): 9–24.

Kelly, Henry Ansgar. *Satan: A Biography.* New York: Cambridge University Press, 2006.

"Ketamine Model." *Journal of Near-Death Studies* 16:1(Fall 1997), entire issue.

Kircher, Pamela M. *Love Is the Link: A Hospice Doctor Shares Her Experiences of Near-Death and Dying.* Burdett, NY: Larson Publications, 1995.

Kotler, Steven. "Extreme states" (about Willoughby Britton's work). *Discover* (July 2005).

Kübler-Ross, Elisabeth. "Beyond the 'Light at the End of the Tunnel.'" Double CD Package. Contact: Sounds True, P.O. Box 8010, Boulder, CO 80306-8010; website www.soundstrue.com.

———. *On Death and Dying.* Berkeley, CA: Celestial Arts, 1991.

Langone, John. *Vital Signs—The Way We Die in America.* Boston, MA: Little, Brown, 1974.

Laszlo, Ervin. *Science and the Akashic Field: An Integral Theory of Everything.* Rochester, VT: Inner Traditions, 2004; revised second edition, 2007.

Long, Jeffrey, and Jody A. Long. "A comparison of near-death experiences occurring before and after 1975: Results from an Internet survey." *Journal of Near-Death Studies* Fall 2003, 22: No. 1 pages 21–32.

Lorimer, David. *Whole in One: The Near-Death Experience and the Ethic of Interconnectedness.* New York: Penguin, 1992.

Lundahl, Craig R., and Harold A. Widdison. *The Eternal Journey: How Near-Death Experiences Illuminate Our Earthly Lives.* New York: Warner Books, 1997.

Macy, Mark. *Spirit Faces: Truth About the Afterlife.* San Francisco: Red Wheel/Weiser Books, 2006.

Mandell, Arnold J. "Toward a Psychobiology of Transcendence: God in the Brain." In *The Psychobiology of Consciousness,* ed. Julian M. Davidson and Richard J. Davidson. New York: Plenum Press, 1980.

Martin, Michael (consultant is Linda A. Jacquin). *Near-Death Experiences* (part of a series of books called *The Unexplained,* for third- to sixth-grade readers). Mankato, MN: Capstone Press, 2005. (Capstone Press, P.O. Box 669, Mankato, MN 56002.)

Ma'sumian, Farnaz. *Life After Death: A Study of the Aterlife in World Religions.* Los Angeles, CA: Kalimat Press, 2002.

Matthews, Dale A., with Connie Clark. *Faith Factor: Proof of the Healing Power of Prayer.* New York: Viking, 1998.

McCarty, Marietta. *Little Big Minds: Sharing Philosophy with Kids.* New York: Penguin Group, 2006.

McClenon, James. "Content analysis of a predominantly African-American near-death experience collection: Evaluating the ritual healing theory." *Journal of Near-Death Studies* 23:3(Spring 2005):159–181.

McCormick, Carol. *A Bridge for Grandma.* Beavers Pond Press, 2006; website www.BeaversPondPress.com; 7104 Ohms Lane, Suite 216, Edina, MN 55439.

McMoneagle, Joseph. *Mind Trek: Exploring Consciousness, Time, and Space Through Remote Viewing.* Norfolk, VA: Hampton Roads, 1993.

Meek, George W. *After We Die, What Then?* Franklin, NC: MetaScience Corporation, 1980. Reissued in 1987 by Ariel Press, 4255 Trotters Way, #13A, Alpharetta, GA 30004.

Mendenhall, Denise, and her father, Doug Mendenhall. *In His Arms.* Self-published, 2006. Available from Publishing Hope, P.O. Box 282, Mount Pleasant, UT, 84647.

Miller, Sukie. *After Death: Mapping the Journey.* New York: Simon & Schuster, 1997.

Montgomery, Ruth Schick. *Threshold to Tomorrow.* New York: Putnam, 1982.

Moody, Raymond A., Jr. *The Last Laugh: A New Philosophy of Near-Death Experiences, Apparitions, and the Paranormal.* Charlottesville, VA: Hampton Roads, 1999.

———. *Life After Life.* New York: Bantam Books, 1975.

———. *Reflections on Life After Life.* New York: Bantam Books, 1977.

Moody, Raymond A., Jr., and Paul Perry. *The Light Beyond.* New York: Bantam Books, 1988.

———. *Reunions: Visionary Encounters with Departed Loved Ones.* New York: Villard Books, 1993.

Morrissey, Dianne. *Anyone Can See the Light: The Seven Keys to a Guided Out-Of-Body Experience.* Walpole, NH: Stillpoint, 1996.

Morse, Melvin, with Paul Perry. *Closer to the Light: Learning from Children's Near-Death Experiences.* New York: Villard Books, 1990.

———. *Parting Visions: Uses and Meanings of Pre-Death, Psychic, and Spiritual Experiences.* New York: Villard Books, 1994.

———. *Transformed by the Light: The Powerful Effect of Near-Death Experiences on People's Lives.* New York: Villard Books, 1992.

———. *Where God Lives: The Science of the Paranormal and How Our Brains are Linked to the Universe.* San Francisco, CA: HarperSanFrancisco, 2001.

Murphy, Michael, and Rhea A. White. *In the Zone: Transcendent Experience in Sports.* New York: Penguin/Arkana, 1995.

Murphy, Todd. "Near-death experiences in Thailand." *Journal of Near-Death Studies* 19:3(Spring 2001):161–178.

The Nag Hammadi Library in English, ed. J. M. Robinson. New York: Harper and Row, 1988.

Osis, Karlis, and Erlendur Haraldsson. *At the Hour of Death: A New Look at Evidence for Life After Death.* New York City: Avon Books, 1977. Current: Winter Park, FL: Hastings House, 1997.

Pagels, Elaine. *The Gnostic Gospels.* New York: Vintage Books, 1981.

———. *The Origin of Satan.* New York: Random House, 1995.

Parnia, Sam. *What Happens When We Die: A Groundbreaking Study into the Nature of Life and Death.* Carlsbad, CA: Hay House, 2006.

Parrish-Harra, Carol E. *Messengers of Hope: The Walk-in Phenomenon.* Black Mountain, NC: New Age Press, 1983. Available now from Sparrow Hawk Village, 11 Summit Ridge Drive, Tahlequah, OK 74464-9215.

Pearsall, Paul. *The Heart's Code: Tapping the Wisdom and Power of Our Heart Energy.* New York: Broadway Books, 1998.

Penfield, Wilder. *The Mystery of the Mind: A Critical Study of Consciousness and the Brain.* Princeton, NJ: Princeton University Press, 1977.

Persinger, Michael A. *Neuropsychological Bases of God Beliefs.* Westport, CT Praeger, 1987.

Radin, Dean I. *Entangled Minds: Extrasensory Experiences in a Quantum Reality.* New York: Paraview Pocket Books, 2006.

Randle, Kevin D. *To Touch the Light.* New York: Pinnacle Books, 1994.

Rawlings, Maurice. *Beyond Death's Door.* Nashville, TN: Thomas Nelson Publishers, 1978.

———. *To Hell and Back.* Nashville, TN: Thomas Nelson Publishers, 1993.

Reed, Henry, and Brenda English. *The Intuitive Heart.* Virginia Beach, VA: A.R.E. Press, 2000.

Reynolds, Pam, and Rob Robinson. Music CD, "The Side Effects of Dying." 2005 Label: *Southern Tracks,* Reynolds/Robsinson. Available through CD Universe or Amazon.com.

Rhodes, Leon S. *Tunnel to Eternity: Swedenborgians Look Beyond the Near-Death Experience.* Available from Swedenborg Foundation, 320 North Church Street, West Chester, PA 19380; e-mail customerservice.swedenborg.com.

Ring, Kenneth. Book Review—"Dying to live: Science and near-death experience." *Journal of Near-Death Studies* 14:2(Winter 1995):117–132.

———. *Heading Toward Omega: In Search of the Meaning of the Near-Death Experience.* New York: William Morrow, 1984.

———. *Life at Death: A Scientific Investigation of the Near-Death Experience.* New York: Quill, 1980.

———. "A note on anesthetically induced frightening near-death experiences." *Journal of Near-Death Studies* 15:1(Fall 1996):17–23.

———. *The Omega Project: Near-Death Experiences, UFO Encounters, and Mind at Large.* New York: William Morrow, 1992.

———. "Religious wars in the NDE movement: Some personal reflections on Michael Sabom's *Light & Death.*" *Journal of Near-Death Studies* 18:4(Summer 2000):215–244.

Ring, Kenneth, and Sharon Cooper. *Mindsight: Near-Death and Out-of-Body Experiences in the Blind.* Palo Alto, CA: Institute of Transpersonal Psychology, 1999.

Ring, Kenneth, and Evelyn Elsaesser-Valarino. *Lessons from the Light: What We Can Learn from the Near-Death Experience.* New York: Insight Books, 1998.

Ring, Kenneth, and Christopher J. Rosing. "The Omega Project: An empirical study of the NDE-prone personality" *Journal of Near-Death Studies* 8:4(Summer 1990):211–239.

Ritchie, George G. *My Life After Dying: Becoming Alive to Universal Love.* Norfolk, VA: Hampton Roads, 1991.

———. *Return from Tomorrow.* Grand Rapids, MI: Chosen Books, 1978.

Roberts, Glenn, and John Owen. Review article, "The near-death experience." *British Journal of Psychiatry* 153(1998):607–617.

Rogo, D. Scott. *The Return from Silence: A Study of Near-Death Experiences.* New York: Harper and Row, 1990.

Rommer, Barbara R. *Blessings in Disguise: Another Side of the Near-Death Experience.* St. Paul, MN: Llewellyn, 2000.

Roszell, Calvert. *The Near-Death Experience: In the Light of Scientific Research and the Spiritual Science of Rudolf Steiner.* Hudson, NY: Anthroposophic Press, 1992.

Roth, Gabrielle. *Sweat Your Prayers: Movement as Spiritual Practice.* New York: Tarcher/Putnam, 1997.

Roth, Ron, with Peter Occhiogrosso. *Prayer and the Five Stages of Healing.* Carlsbad, CA: Hay House, 1999.

Sabom, Michael B. *Light & Death: One Doctor's Fascinating Account of Near-Death Experiences.* Grand Rapids, MI: Zondervan, 1998.

———. *Recollections of Death: A Medical Investigation.* New York: Harper & Row, 1982.

Sanders, Mary Anne. *Nearing Death Awareness: A Guide to the Language, Visions, and Dreams of the Dying.* London: Jessica Kingsley Publishers, 2007.

Saylor, Sidney. *What Tom Sawyer Learned from Dying.* Norfolk, VA: Hampton Roads, 1993.

———. *Tom Sawyer and the Spiritual Whirlwind.* Berea, KY: OmChamois Publishing, 2000.

Schoenbeck, Sue. *The Final Entrance: Journeys Beyond Life.* Madison, WI: Prairie Oak Press, 1997.

Schroter-Kunhardt, Michael. "A review of near-death experiences." *Journal of Scientific Exploration* 1993:219–239. Stanford University, Stanford, CA 94305-4055 (ISSN 0892-3310).

Schwartz, Gary E. *The G.O.D. Experiments: How Science is Discovering God in Everything, Including Us.* New York: Atria Books, 2006.

Schwartz, Gary E., and Linda G. Russek. *The Living Energy Universe: A Fundamental Discovery that Transforms Science and Medicine.* Charlottesville, VA: Hampton Roads, 1999.

Sharp, Kimberly Clark. *After the Light: What I Discovered on the Other Side of Life That Can Change Your World.* New York: William Morrow, 1995.

Sheldrake, Rupert. *A New Science of Life: The Hypothesis of Formative Causation.* Los Angeles, CA: J.P. Tarcher, 1981.

———. *The Presence of the Past: Morphic Resonance and the Habits of Nature.* New York: Times Books, 1988.

———. *The Sense of Being Stared At: And Other Aspects of the Extended Mind* New York: Three Rivers Press, 2004.

Sheridan, Kim. *Animals and the Afterlife: True Stories of Our Best Friends' Journey Beyond Death.* Carlsbad, CA: Hay House, 2006.

Silverman, Linda Kreger. *Upside-Down Brilliance: The Visual-Spatial Learner.* Denver, CO: DeLeon, 2002.

Southern California Study—J. Timothy Green and Penelope Friedman.

"Near-death experiences in a southern California population." *Anabiosis—The Journal for Near-Death Studies* 3:1 (June 1983):77–95.

Steiger, Brad. *One with the Light: Authentic Near-Death Experiences.* New York: Penguin Group, 1994.

Steiger, Brad, and Sherry Hansen Steiger. *Children of the Light: The Startling and Inspiring Truth About Children's Near-Death Experiences and How They Illumine the Beyond.* New York: Signet, 1995.

Steiner, Rudolf. *Staying Connected: How to Continue Your Relationships with Those Who Have Died.* Hudson, NY: Anthroposophic Press, 1999.

Stevenson, Ian. *Twenty Cases Suggestive of Reincarnation.* New York: American Society for Psychical Research, 1966.

———. *Where Reincarnation and Biology Intersect.* Glenview, IL: Praeger, 1997.

Stillman, William. *Autism and the God Connection.* Naperville, IL: Sourcebooks, Inc., 2006.

Storm, Howard. *My Descent into Death: A Second Chance at Life.* New York: Doubleday, 2005.

Strauss, William, and Neil Howe. *Generations: The History of America's Future, 1584 to 2069.* New York: Quill/William Morrow, 1991.

Sutherland, Cherie. *Beloved Visitors: Parents Tell of After Death Visits from Their Children.* Sydney, Australia: Bantan Books, 1997.

———. *Children of the Light: The Near-Death Experiences of Children.* London: Souvenir Press, 1996.

———. *In the Company of Angels.* Dublin, Ireland: Gill & Macmillan/Gateway, 2001.

———. *Reborn in the Light: Life After Near-Death Experiences.* New York: Bantam Books, 1995. (A reissue of *Transformed by the Light: Life After Near-Death Experiences,* available only in Australia and New Zealand, 1992.)

Swedenborg, Emanuel; Anthony Miltenberger (printed and distributed the first American translation from the Latin version). *Heaven and Hell aka Heaven and Its Wonders,* and *Hell, from Things Heard and Seen.* Baltimore, MD: Franklin Printing Office, 1812. Now available from Swedenborg Foundation, 320 North Church Street, West Chester, PA 19380; website www.swedenborg.com; e-mail customerservice.swedenborg.com.

Thurston, Joanie, and Wally Johnston. *Possible Fatal: The Story of Joanie Thurston's NDE.* Available as a book, DVD, and CD. Contact: Acorn Endeavors, P.O. Box 301056, Portland, OR 97294; website www.possiblefatal.com; e-mail Wally@possiblefatal.com.

Tibetan Book of the Dead: The Great Liberation Through Hearing in the Bardo. Trans. Francesca Fremantle and Chogyam Trungpa. Boston, MA: Shambhala, 1992.

Tiller, W. A. "Towards a predictive model of subtle domain connections to the physical domain aspect of reality: The origins of wave-particle duality, electro-magnetic monopoles and the mirror principle." *Journal of Scientific Exploration* 13(1999):41–67.

Tomlinson, John. "Letter to the Editor." *Journal of Near-Death Studies* 19:3(Spring 2001):195–203.

Tucker, Jim. *Life Before Life: A Scientific Investigation of Children's Memories.* New York: St. Martin's Press, 2005.

Unno, Taitetsu. *River of Fire, River of Water: An Introduction to the Pure Land Tradition of Shin Buddhism.* New York: Doubleday, 1998.

VandenBush, Bill. *If Morning Never Comes.* North Platte, NE: Old Hundred and One Press, 2003. (A combat near-death experience.)

Van Dusen, Wilson. *The Presence of Other Worlds: The Psychological/Spiritual Findings of Emanuel Swedenborg.* West Chester, PA: Chrysalis Books, 2004. Available at www.swedenborg.com; customerservice@swedenborg.com.

van Lommel, Pim. "About the Continuity of Our Consciousness." In *Brain Death and Disorders of Consciousness.* Ed. C. Machado and D. A. Shewmon. New York: Kluwer Academic/Plenum, 2004.

———. "Near-death experience, consciousness, and the brain: A new concept about the continuity of our consciousness based on recent scientific research on near-death experience in survivors of cardiac arrest." *World Futures* 2006, 62:134–151, Taylor & Francis Group, Philadelphia, PA. Website at www.tandf.co.uk/journals/titles/02604027.dsp.

van Lommel, Pim, MD, Ruud van Wees, Vincent Meyers, and Ingrid Elfferich. "Near-death experience in survivors of cardiac arrest: A prospective study in the Netherlands." *Lancet* 358:2039–2045.

Vaughan, Alan. *Doorways to Higher Consciousness.* Williamsburg, VA: Celest Press, 1998.

White, John. *The Meeting of Science and Spirit.* New York: Paragon House, 1990 (specifically pages 218-219).

White, Rhea A. *Exceptional Human Experience: Background Papers.* New Bern, NC: Exceptional Human Experience Network, 1994.

Wilber, Ken. *The Spectrum of Consciousness.* Wheaton, IL: Theosophical Publishing House, 1993. Originally printed twenty years ago, this edition marks the book's twentieth anniversary.

Willis, Diane, and John Fish. Music CD, "Improvisations from the Other Side: Healing Music for Meditation and Relaxation." Label: Heartsong Recording Studios. Contact: website www.dianewillis.com; e-mail docflute@aol.com.

Wilson, Colin. *After Life: Survival of the Soul.* St. Paul, MN: Llewellyn, 2000.

Wright, Sylvia Hart. *When Spirits Come Calling: The Open-Minded Skeptic's Guide to After-Death Communications.* Nevada City, CA; Blue Dolphin Publishing, 2002.

Yensen, Arthur E. *I Saw Heaven.* Self-published, available from his son, Eric Yensen, 3407 Fairoaks Circle, Caldwell, ID 83605; or c/o Department of Biology, Albertson College, Caldwell, ID 83605.

Zaleski, Carol. *Otherworld Journeys: Accounts of Near-Death Experience in Medieval and Modern Times.* New York: Oxford University Press, 1987.

Zhi-ying, Feng, and Liu Jian-xun. "Near-death experiences among survivors of the 1976 Tangshan earthquake." *Journal of Near-Death Studies* 11:1(Fall 1992):39–48.

Zweig, Connie, and Steve Wolf. *Romancing the Shadow: Illuminating the Dark Side of the Soul.* New York: Ballantine Books, 1997.

Appendix D

Websites Concerning the Near-Death Experience, Plus Related Materials in This Book

Peg Abernathy's Near-Death Experience
www.self-full-life.com

After-Death Communication—*Hello from Heaven*—(ADC)
www.after-death.com

Afterlife Bookstore (variety)
www.bookdimension.com/bizarre/neardeath/index.htm

Archives of Scientists' Transcendent Experiences (TASTE)
http://psychology.ucdavis.edu/tart/taste/

Association for Research and Enlightenment—Edgar Cayce (various)
www.are-cayce.com

P.M.H. Atwater, LHD (researcher/experiencer)
www.pmhatwater.com
http://pmhatwater.blogspot.com
www.indra.com/iands/pmh.html
www.youtube.com/view_play_list?p=5670A8CDE40DAD2B (two half-hour shows on NDEs)

Keith Augustine—skeptic; critical analysis of NDE research
www.infidel.org/library/modern/keith_augustine/HNDEs.html

Belief Watch—Changing Beliefs in the U.S. (provided by *Newsweek*)
www.Beliefnet.com

Mellen-Thomas Benedict's Near-Death Experience
http://mellen-thomas.com

Dave Bennett and Cindy Griffith-Bennett—Radio Show on NDEs, Chat (inspired by his NDE)
www.PsychicSupport.com
www.Dharma-Talks.com
www.7thWaveNetwork.com

Bibliography on Near-Death Experiences (variety)
http://iands.org/bib.html

Susan Blackmore—*Dying to Live* (book excerpts)
www.susanblackmore.co.uk

Allan L. Botkin, PsyD—Induced After-Death Communication (IADC)
www.induced-adc.com

Dannion Brinkley's Near-Death Experiences (variety)
www.mindspring.com/-scottr/nde/dannionbrinkley.html
www.dannion.com
www.thetwilightbrigade.com

Michael Brown—Creative Inner Space Explorations (service)
www.michaelbrown.org

Chicago IANDS—Large NDE Group with DVD Library of Speakers
www.chicagoiands.org

Compassion In Action (CIA)—created by Dannion Brinkley (hospice service)
www.thetwilightbrigade.com

Bob Coppes, PhD—Touched by the Wonderful Things about NDE
www.bobcoppes.com

Diane Corcoran—Educational Brief for Nurses on NDEs
https://nursing.advanceweb.com/common/ce/

Lynnclaire Dennis—Mereon Social Architecture (inspired by her NDE)
www.sync-q.com
www.indexaward.dk/2007/
default.asp?id=706&show=
nomination&nominationid=291
www.mereon.org

Alfred A. Dolezal—Shangri La Studios (art; insights/transcendence)
www.shangrilastudios.com

Betty J. Eadie—*Embraced by the Light* (near-death experiencer)
www.embracedbythelight.com

Pastor Daniel Ekechukwu—Brief List of Coverage on His Near-Death Experience
www.cfan.org/uk/testimonies/resurrection/page4.htm
www.adivasto.it/testimonianze/morto_torna_in_vita.html

Encyclopedia of Death and Dying
www.deathreference.com

Rocco Errico, ThD, PhD—Biblical Translations from Aramaic (Noohra Foundation)
www.noohra.com

Exceptional Human Experiences (EHEs)
www.ehe.org

Global Mind Project
http://noosphere.princeton.edu/terror.html
http://noosphere.princeton.edu

Diane Goble—*Beyond the Veil* (near-death experiencer)
www.BeyondtheVeil.net

Bill Guggenheim—After-Death Communication (ADC)
www.after.death.com

The Holographic Universe
www.earthportals.com/hologram.html#zine

Mark Horton's Near-Death Experience
www.mindspring.com/~scottr/nde/markh.html

Institute of HeartMath (various)
www.heartmath.org

Institute of Noetic Sciences
www.noetic.org

International Association for Near-Death Studies (variety)
www.iands.org

Greg Kasarik—The Near-Death Experiment (a managed suicide project to cause NDEs)
www.ndexp.com/links.html

Elisabeth Kübler-Ross, MD—Ongoing website about her work
www.elisabethkublerross.com

Cynthia Sue Larson—*Reality Shifters* (e-zine inspired by her NDE)
http://realityshifters.com

Mark Macy—Instrumental Trans-Communication
www.spiritfaces.com
www.worlditc.org

Laurelynn Martin—*Searching for Home* (near-death experiencer)
www.laurelynnmartin.com

Nadia McCaffrey—Variety of Services, Veterans, Hospice (inspired by her NDE)
www.veteransvillage.org
www.north-ca-iands.org

Raymond A. Moody Jr., MD (researcher—initiator of term "near-death experience")
www.lifeafterlife.com

Melvin Morse, MD (researcher)
www.melvinmorse.com

Joseph Murphy—*Memoirs of Joseph* (near-death experiencer)
www.authorhouse.com/

Todd Murphy—NDEs in Thailand and about the Brain
www.spiritualbrain.com

Near-Death and Out-of-Body Experiences (another culture)
www.arts.uwaterloo.ca/ANTHRO/rwpark/WNB/NearDeath

Near-Death Experience Research Foundation (variety—Jeffrey Long, MD, and Jody Long)
www.nderf.org

Near-Death Experiences and the Afterlife—(variety; operated by Kevin Williams)www.near-death.com

Near-Death Information (variety)
www.iands.org/web.html

Juliet Nightingale—Radio Show on NDEs, Chats, Services (inspired by her NDE)
www.TowardTheLight.org

Ode—The Magazine for Intelligent Optimists
www.ode.nl

Omega—Institute for Holistic Studies (school-retreat)
www.eomega.org

Open Directory—Near-Death Experiences (variety)
www.dmoz.org/Society/Death/Near_Death_Experience

Penny Price Media—Exploring Other Dimensions (videos, films)
www.pennypricemedia.com

Perceptual Studies Dept., University of Virginia—Bruce Greyson, MD, and Associates
www.healthsystem.virginia.edu/internet/personalitystudies

Diane K. Pike/Arleen Lorrance—Teleos Institute (service)
www.consciousnesswork.com

Ken Prather—Outreach Programs/Message Boards (inspired by his NDE)
www.reachingforjoy.org

Jan Price's Near-Death Experience
www.near-death.com/experiences/animals01.html

Quebec IANDS for French Speakers—also "Music from the Dawn of Light Programs"
www.inerson.com

Linda Redford—*The Adawee Teachings* (school/service—inspired by her NDE)
www.honorkids.com

Dan Rhema—*Visionary Art* (art inspired by his NDE)
www.danrhema.com

George Ritchie, MD (his NDE)
www.near-death.com/ritch.html

Walter Russell—University of Science & Philosophy (school; inspired by his NDEs)
www.philosophy.org

Sancta Sophia Seminary—Rev. Carol Parrish-Harra (seminary; inspired by her NDE)
www.sanctasophia.org

Sav-Baby of Texas—Donna DeSoto (service; inspired by her NDE)
www.SavBaby.org

Seattle IANDS—Newsletter of NDE Accounts (large experiencer group)
www.seattleiands.org

Seventeen Near-Death Experience Accounts (book excerpts)
www.iands.org/pmh17.html
www.pmhatwater.com

Gary Simmons—Peacemaking (inspired by his NDE; Unity Church International)
www.unityworldhq.org

Skeptic's Dictionary—Near-Death Experiences (variety)
www.skepdic.com/nde.html

Jayne Smith's Near-Death Experience
www.near-death.com/smith.html

Natalie Smith-Blakeslee—Website for the Bereaved (inspired by her NDE)
www.healingheartshaven.com

Spirit Painter (created the Sacred Cow cartoons in this book)
www.sacredcowsonline.com

Swedenborg Foundation (library and service)
www.swedenborg.com

Tell Us Your Near-Death Experience (chat)
www.beyondindigo.com/channels/topic.php/topic/33

Thoughtful Living (on the meaning of NDEs)
www.aleroy.com

Toronto-Ontario IANDS—multi-language
http://webhome.idirect.com/~pelll/IANDS-Ontario.htm

Veriditas—Worldwide Labyrinth Project (labyrinths)
www.veriditas.net

Videos of Near-Death Experiences
www.newcenturytv.com/nde

G. W. Woerlee, MBBS, FRCA—Critique of Pam Reynold's NDE
www.mortalminds.org

Shelley Yates's Near-Death Experience
www.firethegrid.com/eng/eng-home-fr.htm

Appendix E

Getting in Touch

The following people and organizations are mentioned in this book. Additional data and contact specifics are included for your convenience.

Artress, Lauren, Rev. Dr.

Labyrinths: The Rev. Dr. Lauren Artress is active internationally in reviving the sacred use of labyrinths for healing and spiritual development. Her book *Walking a Sacred Path: Rediscovering the Labyrinth as a Spiritual Tool* (Riverhead Books, 1995) is a classic in the field. At Grace Cathedral where she serves, she facilitated the creation of their two labyrinths. Lauren founded Veriditas (an organization and a magazine) to encourage people to use labyrinths, build their own, or put them in churches and hospitals. Contact: Veriditas, PO Box 29204, The Presidio, San Francisco, CA 94129-0204; (415) 561-2921;

website www.veriditas.net;

e-mail contact@veriditas.net.

Association for Research and Enlightenment (ARE)

Institute for Intuitive Studies: Thanks to the work of Carol Ann Liaros (author of *Practical ESP: A Step by Step Guide for Developing Your Intuitive Potential,* available from ARE), and Henry Reed, PhD (a well-known researcher as per intuitive potential), the ARE is now able to offer classes in the healthy development of psychic abilities. This course curriculum is part of the Edgar Cayce Institute for Intuitive Studies. Contact: ARE, P.O. Box 595, Virginia Beach, VA 23451; ask for Registrar at (757) 428-3588, ext. 7192. The ARE is a large membership organization with chapters throughout the world, as well as a university, library, and various schools, services, and publications. Their phone number for general information is (800) 333-4499;

website www.are-cayce.com.

Inquire about their newsletters: *Personal Spirituality* and *Ancient Mysteries.*

Atwater, P.M.H., LHD

Near-Death Research (Experiencer): P.M.H. Atwater is one of the original researchers of the near-death phenomenon. Her website is a "cyber-library" of her articles, and features "The Marketplace," a public service listing of products and services available from near-death experiencers and those like them. Her eleven published books are noted, as well as additional e-books and materials available for free download or purchase over her website. Regular announcements keep her guests up to date with the "latest." Her blog is changed monthly, sometimes more often. She is available for talks, seminars, workshops, private consultations, rune-casting playshops, and prayer service. Two of her half-hour cable TV shows can be accessed over YouTube. Contact: P.M.H. Atwater, P.O. Box 7691, Charlottesville, VA 22906-7691;

website www.pmhatwater.com; e-mail atwater@cinemind.com;
blog http://pmhatwater.blogspot.com;
YouTube cable TV shows:
www.youtube.com/view_play_list?p=5670A8CDE40DAD2B.

Bedard, Gilles

List of "The Music in the Light": During his near-death episode, Gilles Bedard heard music, or more precisely a sound, that made him feel as if he was part of the Sound Current of the Universe. In his quest to later record this sound, he discovered through music a way to unlock memories and information received during his near-death experience. He has since gone on to investigate musical offerings for the purpose of comprising a list of exceptional music for near-death experiencers and anyone else so interested. Gilles also publishes a newsletter on the subject. He gives workshops as well as uses special music and candlelight to help the dying make the transition into spirit, those who are grieving to find comfort, and caregivers and hospice workers to better handle their charge. For more information, contact Gilles at Inerson, 9182 Perinault, St.-Leonard, Quebec, Canada H1P 2L8; (514) 625-4634,

e-mail info@inerson.com.

His main website is www.inerson.com (has a section for French speakers); also www.korprod.com. Gilles is often in France for extended periods, but he always checks and answers his e-mail promptly.

Gilles Bedard's list of "The Music in the Light":

David Darling: *Eight-string religion*

Constance Demby: *Aetema; Novus magnificat; Set free*

Robert Haig Coxon: *The inner voyage; The silent path*

Jon Mark: *The land of Merlin; The standing stones of Callanish*

Vidna Obmana: *The spiritual bonding; The Trilogy '90-'92*

Steve Roach: *Dreamtime return; The magnificent void; Quiet music; Structures from silence*

Steve Roach and Vidna Obmana: *Well of souls*
Therese Schroeder-Sheker: *Rosa Mystica*
Michael Stearns: *Encounter*

Brandt, Raymond W., PhD

Twins and Twinless Twins: Raymond W. Brandt published both *Twins World* magazine and *Twinless Twins* newsletter until his death in 2001. His Board of Directors are now continuing his work. To obtain either or both of these publications plus information about annual conferences, and regional gatherings, contact: Twinless Twins Support Group, PO Box 980481, Ypsilanti, MI 48198-0481; 1-800-205-8962;

e-mail contact@twinlesstwins,org;
website www.twinlesstwins,org.

Brinkley, Dannion

Compassion In Action, "The Twilight Brigade": With the motto, "No one need ever die alone," this volunteer brigade has offices in many locations. Not only do volunteers work in hospice settings, they are available to serve in private homes and in support of the families of the dying. Contact them to volunteer, or to avail yourself of their services: The Twilight Brigade, PO Box 84013, Los Angeles, CA 90073; (310) 473-1941; fax (310) 473-8249;

website www.thetwilightbrigade.com/dannion-info.htm.

Also contact them at West Los Angeles VA Medical Center, 11301 Wilshire Blvd., Bldg. 258, Room 113, Los Angeles, CA 90073.

Brown, Michael, EdS

Creative Inner Space Explorations: Michael Brown has developed an eleven-step process for individuals or groups to explore "the inner self" in a safe and creative manner. His skill with leading vision quests in the wilds and helping people express themselves through mandala art and music is exceptional. He is also available for talks and private sessions. Contact: Michael Brown, 4889 A Finlay Street, Richmond, VA 23231; (804) 222-0483; fax (804) 222-8823;

website www.MichaelBrown.org;
e-mail mbrownlpc@ compuServe.com.

Chicago IANDS

Near-Death Support Group: Unusually large and active, the monthly meetings of the Chicago group are open to the general public as well as near-death experiencers. Speakers are usually filmed; thus they have a growing collection of DVDs available for purchase. Current president is Diane Willis. Contact: Chicago IANDS, P.O. Box 732, Wilmette, IL, 60091; (847) 251-5758;

website www.chicago iands.org;
e-mail docflute@aol.com.

Diane Willis is a flautist, and, because of her near-death episode, she now plays and records special music with Native American flutes.

Corcoran, Diane, BSN, Diploma, MA, PhD, Col

Medically Speaking—Veterans NDE Research: An Army nurse and educator, Diane Corcoran gives lectures, seminars, and classes for health-care givers and other interested groups about the various aspects of the near-death experience and its aftereffects. Involved in researching veterans' NDEs and in educating veterans' hospital units. Contact: Dr. Diane Corcoran, 2705 Montcastle Court, Durham, NC 27705; (919) 624-0547;

e-mail diane.corcoran@kapa.net.

Dennis, Lynnclaire

Social Architecture and TeamPlay: Lynnclaire Dennis works out of her home in Switzerland to design programs utilizing Mereon Principles (ethical guides that are an outgrowth of her near-death experience and witnessing the energy patterns that undergird life). One of her programs, "TeamPlay," is used in schools in Mirano, Italy. International in outreach, her programs, like "Sync-Q TeamPlay for Families." teach the fundamentals of work and ethics in fun and transformational ways that enlighten entire families. Her whole-system dynamics is used in businesses, corporations, and the health-care industry. She travels broadly and was nominated for a special award in Denmark for her programs.

Contact: e-mails lynnclairedennis@mereon.org or
lynnclaire@reweavingharmony.com;
websites www.reweavingharmony.org and www.sync-q.com.

DeSoto, Donna

Sav-Baby, An Alternative to Baby Abandonment: Donna DeSoto is the founder of Sav-Baby, headquartered in Texas. Her idea of how to save unwanted babies is spreading to other states. At present, it's best to make contact through the Texas office. Contact: Sav-Baby, PO Box 100875, San Antonio, TX 78201; (800) SAV-BABY

website www.savbaby.org;
e-mail savbaby@aol.com.

Anyone wishing to set up a Sav-Baby chapter in his or her state is especially urged to call.

Dolezal, Alfred A.

Shangri La Studios: Headquarters of the insightful, metaphysical/mystical paintings of Alfred A. Dolezal. His wife Patti, as a side project, produces the Shangri La Studio newsletter. Filled with poetry, health tips, and gems of wisdom, it is well worth having. For information about either the paintings or the newsletter, contact: Patti Dolezal, Shangri La Studios, 4394 Garth Road, Charlottesville, VA 22901;

website www.shangrilastudios.com; (434) 823-6410;
e-mail shangrilastudios@msn.com.

Errico, Rocco, ThD, PhD

English Translations of Biblical Aramaic: Dr. Errico is the president and founder of the Noohra Foundation, and is the author of over a dozen books, including seven commentaries on the Aramaic New Testament of the Christian Bible. Understanding Eastern "idioms" is the key to unlocking the fuller meaning of biblical scripture. His various taped sets explaining these idioms are exceptional. Contact him through The Noohra Foundation, 4480 South Cobb Drive, Ste H PMB 343, Smyrna, GA 30080-6989; (678) 945-4006.

Guggenheim, Bill

The ADC Project: After finishing *Hello From Heaven!* (with Judy Guggenheim), Bill went on to search out more cases of after-death communication (ADC). He travels the world giving talks on the subject and working with various types of grief groups, hospice, and service organizations. He is available for continuing engagements. Contact: The ADC Project, P.O. Box 916070, Longwood, FL 32791;
website www.after-death.com;
e-mail BillG@after-death.com; (407) 774-1260.

HeartMath

Institute of HeartMath: HeartMath is now quite large and consists of many departments, including research, health, education, classes, and teacher training. Among their goals is to explore and document the value and power of heart energy, and the changes we can make in society when we "come from the heart." Some of the finest scientists in the world are part of the Institute; their clinical work is top-rate. Ask for a free introductory packet of their many services should you query them. Their book, *The HeartMath Solution,* features a ten-step program for "following our hearts." Contact: Institute of HeartMath, P.O. Box 1463, Boulder Creek, CA 95006; (408) 338-8700; (800) 450-9111; fax (408) 338-9861;
website www.heartmath.org.

Herrick, Karen E., LCSE, LMSW, CADC, PhD

Dr. Herrick has been the Founder and Executive Director of the center for Children of Alcoholics in Red Bank, New Jersey, for over twenty years. The power of a spiritually transforming experience to change people's lives not only affected her, but alerted her to the large numbers of professional healthcare givers and their clients who were also undergoing similar experiences, including near-death states, yet were uninformed about what to do next. She found that through specially designed sessions, people could be taught how to recognize spiritual expereiences and what could result from them. She is now convinced that therapists should be trained in spirituality and in how to identify and work with spiritually-transforming experiences. She is also actively engaged in developing a consensus among therapists that these experiences do happen. She is proposing a rewrite to DSM-IV-TR, V-Code 62-89, "Religious or Spiritual Problem," in the diagnostic book therapists use, to embrace and better identify spiritual experiences and any problems that could result from them. Her paper about this is well worth reading. Should you be interested in a copy, request "Proposed Diagnosis Criteria for Extended V-Code 62.89 for Future DSM "Spiritual Problem." Her book *You're Not Finished Yet,* can be obtained directly from her. She is available for lectures and teaching sessions. Contact: Dr. Karen E. Herrick, PO Box 8640, Red Bank MJ 07701; office (532) 530-8513

e-mail keherrick@aol.com;

website www.adult-child.com

Hinze, Sarah

Prebirth Awareness: Sarah Hinze and her husband Brent are actively seeking more accounts of a prebirth experience (PBE), where the child can remember happenings that occurred in the outside environment while he or she was still inside the womb. Contact her through: Royal Child Studies, P.O. Box 31086, Mesa, AZ 85275-1086; (602) 898-3009;

e-mail sarah@royalchild.com;

website www.royalchild.com/prebirth/index.html.

Institute of Noetic Sciences

Magazine on Intuition: *Shift* magazine is an outreach of the Institute of Noetic Sciences, founded by the former astronaut, Edgar Mitchell. Noetic Sciences has chapters throughout the world and actively explores human potential, consciousness studies, leading-edge science, and spirituality. To learn more about this magazine, the events and research they sponsor, or to pursue membership, contact: Institute of Noetic Sciences, 101 San Antonio Rd., Petaluma, CA 94952-9524; (707) 775-3500 or (800) 383-1394;

website: www.noetic.org.

Intuition Network (formerly Global Intuition Network)

Recognizing the Value of Intuition: Weston Agor, PhD, founded the Global Intuition Network in 1991 as a way not only to recognize the value of intuitive insight, but also to enable people to explore its practical application in professional environments. Today, the renamed organization is guided by Jeffrey Mishlover, PhD of consciousness explorations fame and a Board of Directors. As Intuition Network, it exists to help interested individuals contact each other, dialogue, have small group meetings, and participate in conferences and retreats of various kinds. Most of the networking between people is via "cyberspace." Newcomers are welcome. Contact:

e-mail friend@intuition.org;
website www.intuition.org.

Kean, Margaret Fields

Results System Healing Techniques: Margaret Fields Kean, who developed the "Results System" method of hands-on healing, has retired. There are many teachers trained by her who continue to use her methods in their own separate practices. Phil and Verna Seckman are the main contacts. If they cannot help you themselves, they can put you in touch with a trained healer closer to your area. Contact: Verna Seckman, A Healing Knead, 130 Legrande Avenue, Charlotte Court; House, VA 23923-3747; (434) 542-5493. Also active in this network of healers is Sherry Dmtrewycz of "Healing Gateway."

Contact her through her website at
www.healinggateway.com/energyalignment.php.

Larson, Cynthia Sue

Reality Shifters: Cynthia Sue Larson is a bioenergetic field researcher and the author of several books, among them *Aura Advantage: How the Colors in Your Aura Can Help You Attain What You Desire and Attract Success.* A near-death experiencer herself, her e-zine (online newsletter) called "Reality Shifters" is packed full of narratives, the latest science, and tips on how to handle energy "differences" in your life. What she explores is exactly what the majority of near-death experiencers come to face after their episode. Contact: Cynthia Sue Larson, Reality Shifters, P.O. Box 7393, Berkeley, CA 94707-7393;

website http://reality shifters.com;
e-mail cynthia@realityshifters.com.

Lovelidge, Chris

Ghost Photographs and Subtle Energy Systems: To inquire about the two ghost pictures featured in chapter 4, contact: Chris Lovelidge, 9073 Redrooffs Road, Halfmoon Bay, BC, V0N 1Y2, Canada; (604) 740-3883. Remember, Chris is an amateur photographer. He had expected to photograph "something" that evening, but he had no idea what nor did he actually see anything at the time. The ghost images emerged on the film during processing. He has since become involved in "Subtle-Energy Systems."

McMoneagle, Joe

Remote Viewing Projects: Joe McMoneagle is considered by most of those involved in government "psychic spying" as the best of the remote viewers who were on staff. (He did not have this ability before his near-death experience.) Joe now operates his own company and tackles a wide range of projects for his clients. To inquire further of his services, contact: Intuitive Intelligence Applications, P.O. Box 100, Nellysford, VA 22958.

Meek, George W., and Mark Macy

Instrumental Communication with the Dead: Mark Macy continues the work of the late George W. Meek, with the goal of obtaining evidential transcommunication with the dead via instruments such as tape recorders, telephones, television transmissions, and special camera setups. Originally called the "Electronic Voice Phenomenon," this type of endeavor is now referred to as Instrumental Trans-Communication. Contact: Mark Macy, Continuing Life Research, P.O. Box 11036, Boulder, CO 80301; (303) 673-0660;

markmacy@worlditc.org.

websites www.spiritfaces.com and www.worlditc.org.

Along this same line, also contact Electronic Voice Phenomena (founded in 1982 by Sarah Estep), and now under the leadership of Tom and Lisa Butler. The Butler's have written several books about contacting the dead and have the same goal as Macy of obtaining evidential transcommunication between worlds. Contact: Tom and Lisa Butler, American Association of Electronic Voice Phenomena, PO Box 1311, Reno, NV 89507;

website http://aaevp.com; e-mail aaevp@aol.com.

Morse, Melvin, MD

Near-Death Research: Dr. Melvin Morse is the author of numerous books (see appendix C), among them a study of children's near-death experiences entitled *Closer to the Light: Learning from Children's Near-Death Experiences* (with Paul Perry). He publishes a newsletter on his work, *Into the Light,* that anyone can subscribe to, and has a website that explores various aspects of near-death research. To subscribe to his newsletter or purchase copies of his books, contact: Intothelight.com, P.O. Box 59356, Renton, WA 98058-2356; fax (425) 656-5402;

website www.melvinmorse.com.

***Ode* Magazine**

The Magazine for Intelligent Optimists: Headquartered in the Netherlands, the publication is in English and available worldwide. They highlight issues that concern near-death experiencers: what people are actually doing to change the world in real ways, and the return to a sense of authenticity and wholeness in societies everywhere. Their format is colorful and artistic, while being newsy and informative. In the U.S., contact: Ode USA, Puneet Ahluwalia, Mgr., 8230 Boone Blvd., 2nd Floor, Vienna, VA 22182; 1-866-218-0400 (for U. S. and Canada); (212) 741-2365 (for other countries). Headquarters: Ode, The Netherlands, Hanneke Hogerheijde, Mgr., P.O. Box 2402, 3000 CK, Rotterdam, The Netherlands.

Website www.odemagazine.com.

Omega

Omega Institute for Holistic Studies: A leader in holistic (body-mind-spirit) learning for more than twenty years, Omega is a unique blend of education and vacation. Located in the Hudson River Valley, north of New York City, the lakeside campus is set on eighty acres of rolling hills and woodlands and has a veritable village of classrooms, cottages, a cafe, gardens, and the Wellness Center. More than 250 workshops, professional training, conferences, and retreats in a wide variety of subject areas are offered in any given year. A catalogue of selections is available without charge. Contact: Omega Institute, 150 Lake Drive, Rhinebeck, NY 12572-3212; (800) 944-1001 or (914) 266-3769;

website www.eomega.org.

Parrish-Harra, Carol E., Rev.

Sancta Sophia Seminary: To help restore religion to its mystical and spiritual roots, Rev. Carol E. Parrish-Harra founded the Sancta Sophia Seminary. Here pastors, minister-scholars, minister-priests, theologians, and prophet-seers are trained through a full, university-degree program. Intuitive skills are the equal of intellectual prowess at this most unusual school. Contact: Sancta Sophia Seminary, 11 Summit Ridge Drive, Tahlequah, OK 74464-9215; (800) 386-7161;

registrar@sanctasophia.org;
website www.sancta sophia.org.

Perceptual Studies/Department of Personality Studies

Near-Death Studies, Reincarnational Memories, Ghosts/ Apparitions/After-Death and Deathbed Communications: The Personality Studies Department of University of Virginia was formerly headed by Ian Stevenson, MD, the world's most meticulous researcher in the field of past-life memories. His books and his accomplishments are legendary. Dr. Stevenson retired, and then passed away in 2007. Jim Tucker, MD, continues with his work; Bruce Greyson, MD, heads the near-death research; and Emily Kelly, PhD, tackles the rest. Contact: Department of Personality Studies, University of Virginia, Box 800152, Medical Center, UVA, Charlottesville, VA 22908-0152; (434) 924-2281;

website www.healthsystem.virginia.edu/internet/personalitystudies/. The separate e-mail addresses for each Director:

Greyson, cbg4d@virginia.edu;
Tucker, jbt8n@virginia.edu; and
Kelly, ewc2r@virginia.edu.

Pike, Diane Kennedy, and Arleen Lorrance

Consciousness Coaching: Diane Kennedy Pike and Arleen Lorrance have been active in helping people develop higher states of consciousness for many years. Both are authors; the latest from Diane is *Life as a*

Waking Dream. They operate Teleos Institute, and within that school they facilitate courses on "The Theatre of Life" (designed to help you connect with your own life patterns and life purpose). They are available for individual coaching sessions; they also travel to present classes and workshops. Contact: Teleos Institute, 7119 East Shea Blvd., Suite 109, PMB 418, Scottsdale, AZ 85254-6107; (480) 948-1800; fax (480) 948-1870;
website www.consciousnesswork.com; e-mail Teleosinst@ao1.com.

Prather, Ken

Reaching for Joy Outreach and Services: Ken Prather's loss of life, near-death experience, and recovery against all odds are dramatic enough, yet his outreach programs through "Reaching for Joy" are the stuff of "miracles for the many." He is a hospice and near-death counselor, regularly visits the elderly, disabled, and shut-ins, holds group therapy sessions, zoo visits for children, touch therapy with animals, is an alcohol and drug abuse counselor—plus he teaches and lectures whenever invited. He works at the Salvation Army Rehabilitation Center, with Native Americans, and puts spirituality first. Contact: Reaching for Joy, 11322 Rickey Lane, Fort Wayne, IN, 46845;
website www.reachingforjoy.org;
e-mail pratherken@yahoo.com; (260) 637-1705.

Redford, Linda

The Adawee Teachings: For children everywhere, especially in school settings, the Adawee Teachings are a direct outgrowth of Linda Redford's near-death experience, in which she was told to find a way to return honor to the world. The course has been successfully tested at numerous schools and is designed to show children how to overcome anger and violence in favor of respect and honor (parents and teachers take note). I highly recommend this curriculum—so does any teacher who has used it.

Contact: Linda Redford, The Honor Series of Entertainment/Educational Tools, 3231 Ocean Park Blvd., Suite #122, Santa Monica, CA 90405; (310) 392-1200;
website www.honorkids.com;
e-mail honorkids7@aol.com.

Rhema, Dan

Visionary "Found" Art: Dan Rhema's striking and unusual art (see chapter 6) is finding a wide audience, judging by the demand for his creations. His video, "Altered Visions: The Dan Rhema Story," is quite exceptional—a touching reminder of how deeply experiencers can be affected by their near-death episodes. For more information about his art, the video, or his many showings, contact: Dan Rhema, PO Box 17513, Louisville, KY 40207; (502) 635-2457;

website www.danrhema.com;
e-mail rhema@aye.net.

Rousseau, Ruth

The Keys of Sound: Ruth Rousseau is a near-death experiencer. During her episode, she was enraptured by swirling movements of sound that unified her with all Creation. Angelic presences were there, showing her the keys of sound. Just before she returned to life, she asked the angels how she could share what she had learned with the world. "The Keys of Sound" is the result. It's available as a four audiocassette set or as a seventy-two-minute CD. She was also inspired to create "The Keys of Internal Wisdom," a self-teaching, home-study course in spiritual awakening. Contact her through Angel Touch Productions, HC 81, Box 6010, Questa, NM 87556; (505) 586-2196;
e-mail dkclothier@yahoo.com.

Russell, Walter

Visionary Teachings: The writings and teachings of the late Walter and Lao Russell (a husband and wife team) are still available today. Their mail-order courses addressing the greater reality behind creation and the power of consciousness are well worth considering. The best introduction to Walter Russell is the small book *The Man Who Tapped the Secrets of the Universe,* by Glenn Clark. Ask for it when contacting the university if you're interested. Contact: University of Science and Philosophy, P.O. Box 520, Waynesboro, VA 22980; (800) 882-LOVE or (540) 887-5030; fax (540) 887-5030;
website www.philosophy.org;
e-mail usp@cosmiclight.org.

Seattle IANDS

Near-Death Support Group: The very first and the largest of IANDS' near-death support groups, Seattle set the standard for others to follow. Always open to the public, they produced the video, "The Near-Death Experience: Transcending the Limits," which remains today one of the best videos yet made on the subject. Their bimonthly newsletter is devoted to experiencer accounts, and is available to anyone—donations welcome. Current president is Kimberly Clark Sharp. Contact: Seattle IANDS, P.O. Box 84333, Seattle, WA 98124;
website www.seattleiands.org; (206) 525-5489;
e-mail Kimnde@aol.com.

Silverman, Linda Kreger, PhD

Giftedness/Education: Dr. Silverman and her assistant, Betty Maxwell, are actively engaged in clinical and creative work with today's children and with those who test out as genius/gifted. Dr. Silverman's book *Upside-Down Giftedness: The Visual-Spatial Learner* focuses clearly on one of

the biggest problems in our schools: today's children are 80 percent visual-spatial while school curriculums are set up for learners who are 80 percent verbal. Child experiencers of near-death states often become visual-spatial after their episodes (if they weren't already). To contact Dr. Silverman or Maxwell: Institute for the Study of Advanced Development, 1452 Marion Street, Denver, CO 80218; (303) 837-8378;
website www.gifteddevelopment.com.

Simmons, Gary

Peacemaking: Director of Peacemaking for the Association of Unity Churches International, Simmons regularly holds talks and workshops on both integral leadership and peacemaking for any interested group. He authored the book *I of the Storm: Embracing Conflict, Creating Peace.* Contact: Director of Peacemaking, Unity, 1901 N.W. Blue Parkway, Unity Village, MO 64065-0001; (816) 524-3550;
website www.unityworldhq.org.

Sparrow, G. Scott, PhD

Inner Life Mentoring: Dr. G. Scott Sparrow has developed a technique in which he incorporates sound psychological counseling with various spiritual traditions, to offer the individual "the best of all worlds" in his or her desire to grow in consciousness and spirituality. Private sessions are offered. Also, other professionals who want to incorporate his methods into their own practice are invited to query about certification. Contact: G. Scott Sparrow, Ed.D., LPC, 36901 Marshall Hutts Road, Rio Hondo, TX 78583-3467; (956) 748-4350;
e-mail kingfisher@lagunamadre.net;
website www.spiritualmentoring.com.

Also contact him at The University Pen American Ed. Bldg., #1.652,1201 W. University Drive, Edinburg, TX 78539; (956) 316-7953; fax (956) 381-2395.

Stefani, Robert, MA

Special Counseling Technique for Near-Death Experiencers: Robert Stefani came up with a simple but effective way for near-death experiencers to gather in a group with a trained facilitator and explore their near-death episode, what it means to them, and how best to handle the aftereffects. The basic outline can be found in chapter 24 of this book. For more information, write: Robert Stefani, 2808 Forist Lane, Merced, CA 95348.

Strege, Mark

Visionary Art: After his death, Mark Strege left behind a collection of incredible paintings, several of which his parents have now made available to the public via prints and note cards. The most endearing is "Waking Angel" (shown in chapter 9), painted a few months before the auto accident that killed him. To obtain any of his work, or to inquire about the book Mark's mother wrote about his death, contact: Glenda Lee Strege, 8808-36th St. North, Lake Elmo, MN 55042.

Sutherland, Caroline, PhD

My Little Angel Teaching/Comfort Dolls: Dr. Sutherland has become a popular and successful spiritual/energy healer with a special devotion to children after her near-death experience. In a busy schedule of talks, workshops, and healing sessions, she developed a line of cuddly and colorful angel dolls—each one with an audiocassette and booklet that helps children handle the rough spots in life. Four sets currently exist: "My Little Angel Tells Me I'm Special," "My Little Angel Helps Me and My Family," "My Little Angel Helps Me in the Hospital," and "My Little Angel Loves Me." To query about her services or purchase angel-doll sets, contact: Caroline Sutherland, 1 Lake Louise Drive, #34, Bellingham, WA 98229; 1-800-575-6185;

e-mail csutherlandadmin@shaw.ca.

Swedenborg, Emanuel

Library and Headquarters: A key place in the United States for information about the astonishing work and writings of Emanuel Swedenborg is located in Pennsylvania. To visit, check first for the hours and days they are open. Contact: Swedenborg Foundation, 320 North Church Street, West Chester, PA 19380; (800) 355-3222;

website www.swedenborg.com;

e-mail customerservice.swedenborg.com.

Videos on Life and Death Transitions

"Mandalas, Vision of Heaven and Earth" and "The Human Journey:" Both videos feature the powerful, transformational sculpture of artist Mirtala, set to music. Especially helpful in hospice and counseling situations, or for anyone seeking a deeper meaning to life. These videos, along with "From Atom to Cosmos" (about the work of her husband Itzhak Bentov on the evolution of consciousness), are available from Mirtala.

E-mail at mirtala@earthlink.net, or call (928) 649-3908. (Inquire about her gifts brochure on miniatures of her sculptures.)

Virginia Beach IANDS

Near-Death Support Group: Smaller than either Chicago or Seattle, but just as active, the Virginia Beach group is also open to the general public and films their speakers. Their growing collection of DVDs are available for purchase. Contact: Rev. Richard A. Dinges, 1285 Paramore Drive, Virginia Beach, VA 23454; (757) 481-0061 or (757) 575-2779.

White, Rhea A.

Exceptional Human Experiences: Rhea A. White founded the Exceptional Human Experience Network for the purpose of research and to give each person who wishes to an opportunity to register his or her own unusual "peak" experience. Rhea has authored a number of research papers, and coauthored, with Michael Murphy, *In the Zone: Transcendent Experience in Sports* (see appendix C). Rhea died not long ago. The Parapsychology Foundation inherited the EHE publications and the EHE website. Her extensive library and computer files will eventually be integrated into the Eileen J. Garrett Library.

Her website can still be accessed for a limited period at www.ehe.org, and it is well worth visiting. Her publications can be purchased through the Parapsychology Foundation electronic store at www.psi-mart.com. Contact: Parapsychology Foundation, Inc., PO Box 1562, New York, NY 10021-0043; (212) 628-1550; fax (212) 628-1559.

Wickstrom, Jeffrey Spender

Visionary Art and Films/Videos: Jeffrey Spender Wickstrom has turned his childhood near-death experience into an interactive CD-ROM, "Child in the Man," so that viewers can experiment with different endings and different "heavens." He makes documentaries as well, is a scriptwriter, and a ceremonial artist who invokes "the sacredness of spirit" in all his work. He calls his art "Earth Sculpture." To inquire about his many projects and art pieces, contact: Jeffrey Spender Wickstrom, Electric Northern Light Films, Santa Fe Apts., 7060 Palo Verde Way, Apt. 21, Salt Lake City, UT 84121-6601; (801)733-1251.

Index

About the Author

P.M.H. Atwater began her research of the near-death phenomenon in 1978. She has appeared on *Larry King Live, Regis and Kathy Lee,* and *Geraldo* and is a workshop leader at major spiritual/holistic gatherings. She has addressed audiences at International Association for Near-Death Studies conferences, as well as the United Nations.

Hampton Roads Publishing Company

. . . for the evolving human spirit

Hampton Roads Publishing Company publishes books on a variety of subjects, including spirituality, health, and other related topics.

For a copy of our latest trade catalog, call toll-free, 800-766-8009, or send your name and address to:

Hampton Roads Publishing Company, Inc.
1125 Stoney Ridge Road • Charlottesville, VA 22902
e-mail: hrpc@hrpub.com • www.hrpub.com